Contents

GW00546958

Question index

The headings in this checklist/index indicate the main topics of questions, but questions often cover several different topics.

Preparation questions, listed in italics, provide you with a firm foundation for attempts at exam-standard questions.

Mock exam 1

Questions 65 to 70

Mock exam 2

Questions 71 to 76

Mock exam 2 (December 2006)

Questions 77 to 82

Planning your question practice

Our guidance from page 37 shows you how to organise your question practice, either by attempting questions from each syllabus area or **by building your own exams** – tackling questions as a series of practice exams.

BPP LEARNING MEDIA

Topic index

Listed below are the key Paper 3.4 syllabus topics and the numbers of the questions in this Kit covering those topics.

If you need to concentrate your practice and revision on certain topics or if you want to attempt all available questions that refer to a particular subject, you will find this index useful.

Syllabus topic	Question numbers
Automation	28, 42, 55
BCG matrix	14
Bespoke software	31
Business case	59, 64
Business process engineering	28, 43, 55
Business strategy	15, 55, 56, 58, 61, 64, Mock 3 Q2
CATWOE	22, 23, 27, 52
Centralised	4, 5, Mock 1 Q5
Code of practice	47
Commitment, coordination and communication	58
Competitive advantage	18, 54
Cost leadership	53
Critical success factors	45, 52, 54, 60 Mock 3 Q5
Customer focus	53, 60
Data and knowledge work	3
Database management	34
Data mining	32, 34
Data warehouse	32, 34, Mock 1 Q2
Decentralisation	4, 5, 29, 53
Decision making	7
Decision Support Systems (DSS)	9
Differentiation	53, 54
Distributed systems	4, 5, 53 Mock 1 Q5
Earl's grid	12
Earl's three leg analysis	11, 57
E-commerce	38, 41, 55, 64
Employees	Mock 3 Q3
Enterprise analysis	52
Ethical issues	47, 48, 61, Mock 2 Q6, Mock 3 Q4
Evaluation of strategy	17
Executive Information Systems (EIS)	9
Executive Support Systems (ESS)	9
Expert systems	8
Extranet	6, 55
Financial evaluation	24
Five forces	16, Mock 3 Q1
Gap analysis	19, 21, 56, 58
Globalisation	36, Mock 2 Q2, Mock 3 Q2
Global systems	53, Mock 2 Q2
Groupware	35
Hard systems approach	22
Impact of IT/IS	44, 51
Infomate	42, 54
Information Age	47
Information characteristics	51
Information management	17, 30, 32, 39, 44

Syllabus topic	Question numbers
Information overload	Mock 1 Q4
Information sharing	6, 50
Information systems strategy	7, 17, 56, 58, 61, Mock 3 Q2
Insourcing	57
Integration	53
Internet	36, 38, 52, 55
Intranet	6, 55, Mock 2 Q1
Key performance indicators	45, 54
Knowledge management	3, 9, 30, 33, 50, 63
Legacy systems	62
Lewins' three stage model of change	40
Management Information Systems (MIS)	9
McFarlan's grid	14, Mock 1 Q6
Nolan's stage hypothesis	2, Mock 2 Q3
Office Automation Systems (OAS)	9
Off-the-shelf software	31
Open systems	Mock 1 Q5
Outsourcing	57
Parson's generic strategies	2, 13
Peppard's strategic grid	20, Mock 1 Q6
PEST analysis	62, Mock 2 Q6, Mock 3 Q2
Porter's strategies	16, 53, Mock 3 Q1
Porter's value chain	10, 18, 56, 63, Mock 1 Q1
Project risk	55
Providing IT services	51
Rationalisation	28, 42, 55
Rich picture	25, 52
Risk assessment	59
Root definition	27, 52, Mock 2 Q4
Scoring models	21
Security	50, 51
Social issues	47, 48, 49, Mock 3 Q4
Soft Systems Methodology	22, 23, 25, 26, 27, 52, Mock 2 Q4
Strategic decision making	7
Strategic issues	31, 54, 56 Mock 1 Q6
Strategic level systems	1, 55
Strategic plan for IT	7, 17, 38, 54, 55, 58, 61
Structured methodologies	58
Supply chain	43
SWOT analysis	56, 57, 59, 61, 64
System design	53
System evaluation	53, 55, Mock 2 Q5, Mock 1 Q2
Transaction Processing Systems (TPS)	9
Transformate	42, 55
User resistance	Mock 2 Q5
Value Chain	10, 18, 56, Mock 1 Q1
Viability	59
Virtual companies	41
Website (also see Internet, E-commerce)	38, 41, 44, 60, 64
Zuboff (automate, informate, transformate)	42, 55

Using your BPP Practice and Revision Kit

Tackling revision and the exam

You can significantly improve your chances of passing by tackling revision and the exam in the right ways. Our advice is based on recent feedback from ACCA examiners.

- We look at the dos and don'ts of revising for, and taking, ACCA exams
- We focus on Paper 3.4; we discuss revising the syllabus, what to do (and what not to do) in the exam, how to approach different types of question and ways of obtaining easy marks

Selecting questions

We provide signposts to help you plan your revision.

- A full **question index**
- A **topic index** listing all the questions that cover key topics, so that you can locate the questions that provide practice on these topics, and see the different ways in which they might be examined
- **BPP's question plan** highlighting the most important questions and explaining why you should attempt them
- **Build your own exams**, showing how you can practise questions in a series of exams

Making the most of question practice

At BPP we realise that you need more than just questions and model answers to get the most from your question practice.

- Our **Top tips** provide essential advice on tackling questions, presenting answers and the key points that answers need to include
- We show you how you can pick up **Easy marks** on questions, as we know that picking up all readily available marks often can make the difference between passing and failing
- We summarise **Examiner's comments** to show you how students who sat the exam coped with the questions
- We include ACCA's **marking guides** to show you what the examiner rewards
- We refer to the **BPP 2006 Study Text** for detailed coverage of the topics covered in each question
- A number of questions include **Analysis** and **Helping hands** attached to show you how to approach them if you are struggling

Attempting mock exams

There are three mock exams that provide practice at coping with the pressures of the exam day. We strongly recommend that you attempt them under exam conditions. **Mock exams 1 and 2** reflect the question styles and syllabus coverage of the exam; **Mock exam 3** is the actual December 2006 exam. To help you get the most out of doing these exams, we not only provide help with each answer, but also guidance on how you should have approached the whole exam.

Passing ACCA exams

Revising and taking ACCA exams

To maximise your chances of passing your ACCA exams, you must make best use of your time, both before the exam during your revision, and when you are actually doing the exam.

- Making the most of your revision time can make a big, big difference to how well-prepared you are for the exam

- Time management is a core skill in the exam hall; all the work you've done can be wasted if you don't make the most of the three hours you have to attempt the exam

In this section we simply show you what to do and what not to do during your revision, and how to increase and decrease your prospects of passing your exams when you take them. Our advice is grounded in feedback we've had from ACCA examiners. You may be surprised to know that much examiner advice is the same whatever the exam, and the reasons why many students fail don't vary much between subjects and exam levels. So if you follow the advice we give you over the next few pages, you will **significantly** enhance your chances of passing **all** your ACCA exams.

How to revise

☑ Plan your revision

At the start of your revision period, you should draw up a **timetable** to plan how long you will spend on each subject and how you will revise each area. You need to consider the total time you have available and also the time that will be required to revise for other exams you're taking.

☑ Practise Practise Practise

The **more exam-standard questions** you do, the **more likely you are to pass** the exam. Practising full questions will mean that you'll get used to the time pressure of the exam. When the time is up, you should note where you've got to and then try to complete the question, giving yourself practice at everything the question tests.

☑ Revise enough

Make sure that your revision covers the breadth of the syllabus, as in most papers most topics could be examined in a compulsory question. However it is true that some topics are **key** – they often appear in compulsory questions or are a particular interest of the examiner – and you need to spend sufficient time revising these. Make sure you also know the **basics** – the fundamental theories, models and concepts that underpin the subject.

☑ Deal with your difficulties

Difficult areas are topics you find dull and pointless, or subjects that you found problematic when you were studying them. You mustn't become negative about these topics; instead you should build up your knowledge by reading the **Passcards** and using the **Quick quiz** questions in the Study Text to test yourself. When practising questions in the Kit, go back to the Text if you're struggling.

☑ Learn from your mistakes

Having completed a question you must try to look at your answer critically. Always read the **Top tips guidance** in the answers; it's there to help you. Look at **Easy marks** to see how you could have quickly gained credit on the questions that you've done. As you go through the Kit, it's worth noting any traps you've fallen into, and key points in the **Top tips** or **Examiner's comments** sections, and referring to these notes in the days before the exam. Aim to learn at least one new point from each question you attempt, a technical point perhaps or a point on style or approach.

☑ Read the examiners' guidance

We refer throughout this Kit to **Examiner's comments**; these are available on ACCA's website. As well as highlighting weaknesses, examiners' reports as often provide clues to future questions, as many examiners will quickly test again areas where problems have arisen. ACCA's website also contains articles by examiners which you **must** read, as they may form the basis of questions on any paper after they've been published.

☑ Complete all three mock exams

You should attempt the **Mock exams** at the end of the Kit under **strict exam conditions**, to gain experience of selecting questions, managing your time and producing answers.

BPP
LEARNING MEDIA

How NOT to revise

☒ Revise selectively

Examiners are well aware that some students try to forecast the contents of exams, and only revise those areas that they think will be examined. Examiners try to prevent this by doing the unexpected, for example setting the same topic in successive sittings or setting topics in compulsory questions that have previously only been examined in optional questions.

☒ Spend all the revision period reading

You cannot pass the exam just by learning the contents of Passcards, Course Notes or Study Texts. You have to develop your **application skills** by practising questions.

☒ Audit the answers

This means reading the answers and guidance without having attempted the questions. Auditing the answers gives you **false reassurance** that you would have tackled the questions in the best way and made the points that our answers do. The feedback we give in our answers will mean more to you if you've attempted the questions and thought through the issues.

☒ Practise some types of question, but not others

Although you may find the numerical parts of certain papers challenging, you shouldn't just practise calculations. These papers will also contain written elements, and you therefore need to spend time practising written question parts.

☒ Get bogged down

Don't spend a lot of time worrying about all the minute detail of certain topic areas, and leave yourself insufficient time to cover the rest of the syllabus. Remember that a key skill in the exam is the ability to **concentrate on what's important** and this applies to your revision as well.

☒ Overdo studying

Studying for too long without interruption will mean your studying becomes less effective. A five minute break each hour will help. You should also make sure that you are leading a **healthy lifestyle** (proper meals, good sleep and some times when you're not studying).

How to PASS your exams

☑ Prepare for the day

Make sure you set at least one alarm (or get an alarm call), and allow plenty of time to get to the exam hall. You should have your route planned in advance and should listen on the radio for potential travel problems. You should check the night before to see that you have pens, pencils, erasers, watch, calculator with spare batteries, also exam documentation and evidence of identity.

☑ Select the right questions

You should select the optional questions you feel you can answer **best**, basing your selection on the topics covered, the requirements of the question, how easy it will be to apply the requirements and the availability of easy marks.

☑ Plan your three hours

You need to make sure that you will be answering the correct number of questions, and that you spend the right length of time on each question – this will be determined by the number of marks available. Each mark carries with it a **time allocation** of **1.8 minutes**. A 20 mark question therefore should be selected, completed and checked in 36 minutes. With some papers, it's better to do certain types of question first or last.

☑ Read the questions carefully

To score well, you must follow the requirements of the question, understanding what aspects of the subject area are being covered, and the tasks you will have to carry out. The requirements will also determine what information and examples you should provide. Reading the question scenarios carefully will help you decide what **issues** to discuss, **techniques** to use, **information** and **examples** to include and how to **organise** your answer.

☑ Plan your answers

Five minutes of planning plus twenty-five minutes of writing is certain to earn you more marks than thirty minutes of writing. Consider when you're planning how your answer should be **structured,** what the **format** should be and **how long** each part should take.

Confirm before you start writing that your plan makes **sense,** covers **all relevant points** and does not include **irrelevant material.**

☑ Show evidence of judgement

Remember that examiners aren't just looking for a display of knowledge; they want to see how well you can **apply** the knowledge you have. Evidence of application and judgement will include writing answers that only contain **relevant** material, using the material in scenarios to **support** what you say, **criticising** the **limitations** and **assumptions** of the techniques you use and making **reasonable recommendations** that follow from your discussion.

☑ Stay until the end of the exam

Use any spare time to **check and recheck** your script. This includes checking you have filled out the candidate details correctly, you have labelled question parts and workings clearly, you have used headers and underlining effectively and spelling, grammar and arithmetic are correct.

BPP
LEARNING MEDIA

How to FAIL your exams

☒ Don't do enough questions

If you don't attempt sufficient questions on the paper, you are making it harder for yourself to pass the questions that you do attempt. If for example you don't do a 20 mark question, then you will have to score 50 marks out of 80 marks on the rest of the paper, and therefore have to obtain 63% of the marks on the questions you do attempt. Failing to attempt all of the paper is symptomatic of poor time management or poor question selection.

☒ Include irrelevant material

Markers are given detailed mark guides and will not give credit for irrelevant content. Therefore you should **NOT** braindump all you know about a broad subject area; the markers will only give credit for what is **relevant**, and you will also be showing that you lack the ability to **judge what's important.** Similarly forcing irrelevant theory into every answer won't gain you marks, nor will providing uncalled for features such as situation analyses, executive summaries and background information.

☒ Fail to use the details in the scenario

General answers or reproductions of old answers that don't refer to what is in the scenario in **this** question won't score enough marks to pass.

☒ Copy out the scenario details

Examiners see **selective** use of the right information as a key skill. If you copy out chunks of the scenario which aren't relevant to the question, or don't use the information to support your own judgements, you won't achieve good marks.

☒ Don't do what the question asks

Failing to provide all the examiner asks for will limit the marks you score. You will also decrease your chances by not providing an answer with enough **depth** – producing a single line bullet point list when the examiner asks for a discussion.

☒ Present your work poorly

Markers will only be able to give you credit if they can read your writing. There are also plenty of other things that will make it more difficult for markers to reward you. Examples include:

- Not using black or blue ink
- Not showing clearly which question you're attempting
- Scattering question parts from the same question throughout your answer booklet
- Not showing clearly workings or the results of your calculations

Paragraphs that are too long or which lack headers also won't help markers and hence won't help you.

Using your BPP products

This Kit gives you the question practice and guidance you need in the exam. Our other products can also help you pass:

- **Learning to Learn Accountancy** gives further valuable advice on revision

- **Passcards** provide you with clear topic summaries and exam tips

- **Success CDs** help you revise on the move

- **i-Pass CDs** offer tests of knowledge against the clock

- **Learn Online** is an e-learning resource delivered via the Internet, offering comprehensive tutor support and featuring areas such as study, practice, email service, revision and useful resources

You can purchase these products by visiting www.bpp.com/mybpp.

Visit our website www.bpp.com/acca/learnonline to sample aspects of Learn Online free of charge.

BPP LEARNING MEDIA

Passing 3.4

Revising 3.4

3.4 is grounded in academic theory. However, repeating theory will not be enough to pass the exam – you must learn to apply the knowledge you have learnt. In this regard you may find it useful to think about how the theories you have studied could be applied in an organisation that you know.

You must remember that 3.4 is not just an 'IT' paper – it is more about business strategy and how technology can support it.

The examiner, George Bakehouse, often sets exam questions using material he has written for the 'Student Accountant' magazine. You should make sure you keep up to date with such articles.

Topics to revise

Exams over the years have shown that the following areas of the syllabus are very important, and your revision therefore needs to cover them particularly well.

- Strategic planning – the use of SWOT and PEST analysis to audit an organisation's current position and to plan future strategy.

- Systems development – the use of soft systems methodology is regularly examined. The hard approach is also an important model.

- Knowledge management – how IS/IT can be used to develop, share and use the knowledge held by an organisation.

- E-commerce and the Internet – how organisations can use this technology to their advantage.

- Implementing systems – how systems should be implemented and the methods of managing change.

- Ethics and society – the impact of IS/IT on society and handling ethical dilemmas.

- Academic theories – theories may be tested directly in questions, the main theories are those written by Porter, Earl, McFarlan, Peppard, Lewin and the Business Case Development Framework by Bakehouse, Doyle and Waters. However there are others – make sure you cover them all.

Question practice

Question practice under timed conditions is essential, so that you can get used to the pressures of answering exam questions in **limited time** and practise not only the key techniques but allocating your time between different requirements in each question. Our list of recommended questions includes 60 mark Section A and 20 mark Section B questions; it's particularly important to do a number of Section A questions in full to experience the time pressure you will encounter in the exam.

Passing the 3.4 exam

Displaying the right qualities

George Bakehouse has indicated clearly what skills and qualities he expects students to display.

Qualities required	
Understanding and application of academic theory	Questions may test academic knowledge directly or may require you to apply models where appropriate.
Strategic analysis	You must fully appreciate the situation the organisation in the scenario faces. Suggestions and ideas generated to answer the scenario must be realistic given the circumstances.
Evaluation and conclusion	Questions may require you to evaluate alternative solutions and to generate a sensible conclusion for the best course of action.
Depth of discussion	Your answer should not be limited to pros and cons or bullet points. It should be well explained, refer to theories and/or the scenario and be justified.

Avoiding weaknesses

We give details of George Bakehouse's comments and criticisms throughout this Kit. These have hardly varied over the last few years. His reports always emphasise the need for thorough preparation for the exam, but there are various things you can do on the day of the exam to enhance your chances. Although these all sound basic, George Bakehouse has commented that many candidates fail to:

- Apply theory when answering questions
- Answer the required number of questions
- Answer all parts of questions
- Refer to the scenario in the answer
- Gauge how much to write by the marks available
- Read recent articles in Student Accountant
- Manage their time properly
- Appreciate that this is a Business Information Management paper, designed to align IT and business strategy

You will enhance your chances significantly if you avoid there mistakes.

Choosing which questions to answer first

The paper's format is slightly unusual, with three compulsory questions, and two from three optional questions. Because of this imbalance, you need to consider carefully your strategy for tackling the paper.

- You should normally tackle the compulsory questions **first** before moving on to the optional section of the paper. Generally you will have to gain the majority of marks you need to pass the paper on the compulsory questions, so it is best to get them out of the way. However if you think one of the compulsory questions looks particularly difficult, perhaps you might leave that till last.

- Whatever the order, make sure you leave yourself **sufficient time** to tackle all the questions. Don't get so bogged down in the first question that you have to rush the rest of the paper.

The examiner has highlighted in a number of reports, failures to attempt question parts or leaving the compulsory questions till last and having inadequate time to do them.

Tackling questions

You'll improve your chances by following a step-by-step approach along the following lines.

Step 1   Read the requirement

Identify the knowledge areas being tested and see precisely what the examiner wants you to do. This will help you focus on what's important in the scenario.

Step 2   Check the mark allocation

This shows the depth of answer anticipated and helps you allocate time.

Step 3   Read the scenario/preamble

Identify which information is relevant to which question part. Do not get bogged down in detail as some of it may not be relevant.

Step 4   Plan your answer

Consider the formats you'll use and discussion points you'll make. Write down where you will use information from the scenario/preamble

Step 5   Write your answer

Stick carefully to the time allocation for each question, and for each part of each question.

Gaining the easy marks

There are few easy marks in 3.4 as marks are often awarded for theoretical knowledge and application. However, there are a number of areas that you can pick up marks relatively easily.

- Where **specific models** are tested you can earn marks by discussing how they are **used** and **problems** and **advantages** of using them.

- **Diagrams** – marks are often available for drawing the model being examined.

- Much **technical knowledge** of IT systems is at a fairly high level and is therefore likely to already be familiar to you. This is especially true of the Internet and e-commerce.

- **Sensible comments**. 3.4 is a very open paper and this is reflected in the marking schemes. Providing your points are relevant, realistic, well developed and justified, you should earn enough marks to pass.

  This means that you **must** have a thorough understanding of the models to be able to make sensible comments.

Recent exams

Format of the paper

		Number of marks
Section A:	3 compulsory questions	60
Section B:	Choice of 2 from 3 questions (20 marks each)	40
		100

Time allowed: 3 hours

Section A is based on a business scenario. This section will have three compulsory questions from across the syllabus which relate to the scenario. Each question will be worth 20 marks giving a total of 60 marks for this section.

Section B contains three independent questions drawn from across the syllabus, which are not related to the Section A scenario. Each question is worth 20 marks. The candidate must answer two questions giving a total of 40 marks for this section.

Candidates should refer to the Syllabus and Study Guide for details of models and topics likely to be examined.

Additional information

The Study Guide provides more detailed guidance on the syllabus.

Analysis of recent papers

The analysis below shows the topics which have been examined in the current syllabus and includes the Pilot Paper.

December 2006

Section A – Internet based music retailer

1   Porter's five forces
2   Aligning business strategies and information system strategies
3   Employing teleworkers

Section B

4   Ethical/political/legal issues/ethical analysis
5   Critical success factors and performance indicators
6   Portfolio analysis; CAD systems, data warehouses and extranets

Examiner's comments were not available at the time of going to print.

This paper is Mock exam 3 in this Kit.

June 2006

		Question in this Kit
Section A scenario – Retail clothing store chain		
1	SWOT analysis	64
2	Business case report	64
3	Using internal IT professionals; Boehm's spiral model	64

Examiner's comments. The pass rate for this sitting was similar to that achieved in previous sittings. The overall results suggest that many candidates were well prepared for this examination. A general theme identified by the marking team was that many candidates demonstrated a good understating of theories, techniques, and models, but failed to capitalise on the application of these in both sections of the examination. The application of theories, techniques and models is a core requirement of this paper. The marks awarded covered a wide range with many candidates demonstrating an exceptional knowledge of the syllabus material in terms of both breadth and depth.

December 2005

Question in this Kit

Examiner's comments. The pass rate for this sitting is lower than the pass rates achieved in previous sittings. A general theme was that many candidates demonstrated a good understanding of theories, techniques and models but failed to capitalise on the application of these in both sections of the examination. Many candidates did not answer all of the sub-sections in the questions and this practice was more prevalent than usual. Adopting such an examination strategy does limit the marks available.

June 2005

Question in this Kit

Examiner's comments. Overall, results suggest that many candidates were well-prepared for this examination. The general response from the marking team was that many candidates demonstrated a good understanding of theories, techniques and models, but failed to capitalise on the application of these in both sections of the examination paper.

The markers comments were complimentary concerning technique, style and presentation. The majority of candidates answered all the required questions from both sections. The answers were generally well-structured and presented. As in the June 2004 sitting there was a general criticism that some candidates did not read the questions correctly.

December 2004

Examiner's comments. The overall results suggest that many candidates were well prepared for this examination. There was an increase in the number of candidates who did not answer the required number of questions from both sections. A minority of candidates only answered four questions. This makes it very difficult to achieve the required pass mark. An increasing number of candidates only attempted specific parts of some questions, limiting marks available. Overall the answers were generally well structured and presented.

The pass rate for this sitting was similar to the pass rates achieved in previous sittings.

June 2004

Examiner's comments. The overall results for this sitting suggest that many candidates were well-prepared, demonstrating a good understanding of theories, techniques and models. Unfortunately in some cases they failed to capitalise on the application of these to the case study. The application of theories, techniques and models is a core requirement of this paper. Many candidates demonstrated an exceptional knowledge of the module material in terms of both breadth and depth.

The markers comments were complimentary concerning technique, style and presentation. The majority of candidates answered all the required questions from both sections. The answers were generally well-structured and presented. However, there was a general criticism that some candidates did not read the questions correctly.

December 2003

Question in this Kit

Section A scenario – Catalogue retailer (answer all questions in section A)

1	SWOT analysis for a proposed on-line purchasing system	59
2	Business case justification	59
3	Project risk assessment	59

Section B (answer two questions from section B)

4	Database management	34
5	User resistance and system evaluation	ME2 Q5
6	Peppard's strategic grid	20

Examiner's comments. The pass rate for the fifth sitting of this Part 3 option paper was similar to the pass rate achieved at the previous sittings. The results suggested that many candidates were well-prepared for this examination.

June 2003

Question in this Kit

Section A scenario – Department store chain (answer all questions in section A)

1	Aligning information systems strategy with business strategy	58
2	Commitment, co-ordination and communication in systems development	58
3	Gap analysis, applications portfolio and structured methodologies	58

Section B (answer two questions from section B)

4	Global business strategy and IT strategy	15
5	Business process re-engineering; virtual supply chain	43
6	Appraising information systems projects	24

Examiner's comments. Several markers suggested there was a minority of candidates who never really attempted to apply appropriate theories, techniques and models sufficiently to the case study. In comparison with previous sittings, however, there was a higher proportion of marks in the 60 and 70 per cent range.

The majority of candidates answered all the required questions from both sections. This was a marked improvement on previous sittings. In terms of presentation there was also an improvement, although a minority of candidates still present answers to a specific question spread throughout the answer booklet(s). In the worst examples, candidates stop answering a question in the middle of a page, start a fresh page and a new question and then complete the half-answered question somewhere else in the answer booklet, often several pages from the original part of the answer.

December 2002

Question in this Kit

Section A scenario – Life assurance corporation (answer all questions in section A)

1	SWOT analysis and business strategy	57
2	Sourcing of a new system	57
3	Three legs of IS strategy – business led, top-down and infrastructure led	57

Section B (answer two questions from section B)

4	Soft Systems Methodology	23
5	Minimising system failure risks; technical infrastructure; social and ethical issues	48
6	Automate, informate and transformate (automation, rationalisation and re-engineering).	42

Examiner's comments. Unfortunately there is a suggestion that a minority of candidates 'suffered' from poor examination technique. A prime example of this was demonstrated in Section A where a number of candidates failed to apply the theories, techniques and models sufficiently to the case study. Weaker candidates produced answers that were more appropriate to Part 2 papers.

The majority of candidates answered all the required questions from both sections, although the number of candidates failing to answer the required number of questions is steadily increasing. Generally Questions 3 and 4 produced the most variable answers. Answers to Question 3 lacked application to the scenario, and it was surprising that candidates could not construct a conceptual model.

June 2002

Question in this Kit

Section A scenario – Business and IS strategy review for an importer (answer all questions in section A)

1	Intranet characteristics, benefits and impact	ME2 Q1
2	Technology and globalisation; PEST and e-commerce	ME2 Q2
3	Nolan's Six Stage Growth Model	ME2 Q3

Section B (answer two questions from section B)

4	Information systems and knowledge management	33
5	Hard and soft methodologies	22
6	Generic strategies for information systems	13

Examiner's comments. The pass rate for the second sitting of Paper 3.4 was similar to the pass rate achieved in the initial sitting. There was evidence that candidates were well prepared for this examination. Candidates generally performed better on Section A than section B.

Generally Questions 3 and 4 produced the most variable answers. This is rather surprising as both topics are viewed as straightforward and fairly standard.

December 2001

Question in this Kit

Section A scenario – Mail order book company (answer all questions in section A)

1	SWOT analysis and development of an IS strategy	56
2	Porter's value chain and e-commerce	56
3	Business strategy and information strategy development and changes	56

Section B (answer two questions from section B)

4	Data warehousing; DBMS; datamining	32
5	Moral dimensions of the information age	47
6	Virtual companies; web-based v paper-based information	41

> **Examiner's comments.** The pass rate for this new optional Part 3 paper was very encouraging. There was evidence that candidates were well prepared for this examination. The marks awarded covered a wide range with many candidates demonstrating an exceptional knowledge of the syllabus in terms of both breadth and depth.
>
> Markers comments were generally very complimentary concerning examination technique, style and presentation. This was supported by the fact that over 95% of candidates answered all the required questions from both sections. The overall view from all participants in the examination assessment process is very positive.

Pilot paper

Question in this Kit

Section A scenario – Electrical goods retail chain (answer all questions in section A)

1	Use of web-based technologies (Internet, intranet, extranet)	55
2	Integrating IT/IS development with business strategy; business process terms – automation, rationalisation and re-engineering	55
3	Reasons for information systems failure	55

Section B (answer two questions from section B)

4	Checkland's Soft System Methodology	ME2 Q4
5	Porter's value chain and IS/IT strategy	18
6	Purpose-written application software versus a ready-written package (strategic issues)	31

Current issues

Recent articles

Examiners often base exam questions on articles which have appeared in *Student Accountant*. Students should study the following articles. Students should check issues published later than October 2005 for other relevant articles. These articles are also available on the ACCA website www.accaglobal.com. Enter the student section of the site, then select the paper-by-paper listing of resources.

'Defining managers' information requirements', Jim Stone, Student Accountant, August 2006

'Three models of systems development', George Bakehouse, Tony Wakefield, Kevin Doyle, Tom Barnes and Mark Clinton Jones, Student Accountant, May 2006

'Strategic choices and change management', Diarmaid O'Corrbuí and Mark Corboy, Student Accountant, November/December 2005

'Performance measures to support competitive advantage', Graham Morgan, August 2005

'The adaptability of strategic models,' George Bakehouse, Student Accountant, June 2005

'E-commerce' George Bakehouse, Student Accountant, May 2005

'Legacy information systems,' George Bakehouse, Student Accountant, March 2005

'Big Brother,' George Bakehouse, Student Accountant, July 2004

'Soft systems methodology,' Malcolm Eva, Student Accountant, January 2004

'Commitment, coordination and communication,' George Bakehouse and Kevin Doyle, Student Accountant, March 2003

'A generic framework for developing an IS strategy', George Bakehouse and Kevin Doyle, Student Accountant, December 2002

'How to Pass Paper 3.4', Gareth Owen, Student Accountant, November 2002

'Business Information Management', George Bakehouse, Student Accountant, February 2002

'Strategic planning models', Martin Corby, Student Accountant, January 2002

'Outstanding IS/IT services, Jim Stone, Student Accountant, November 2001

'A primer on knowledge management', Peter C Barnes, Student Accountant, July 2001

Useful websites

The websites below provide additional sources of information of relevance to your studies for *Business Information Management*.

- www.bpp.com

  The website of the BPP group.

- www.accountingweb.co.uk

  A UK site with articles on current accounting related issues. The site is searchable by accounting topic.

- www.accaglobal.com

  The ACCA's own website. Includes Student section.

- www.wsj.com

  This website of *The Wall Street Journal*.

- www.computerwire.com

  Aims to provide unbiased information regarding the computer industry.

- www.pcwebopaedia.com

  An online dictionary and search engine for computer and Internet terminology.

- www.ft.com

  The site of *The Financial Times*. Excellent business search facility.

- www.economist.com

  The site of *The Economist*. Another good business search facility.

- www.hbsp.harvard.edu

  The website of Harvard Business School Publishing.

Syllabus mindmap

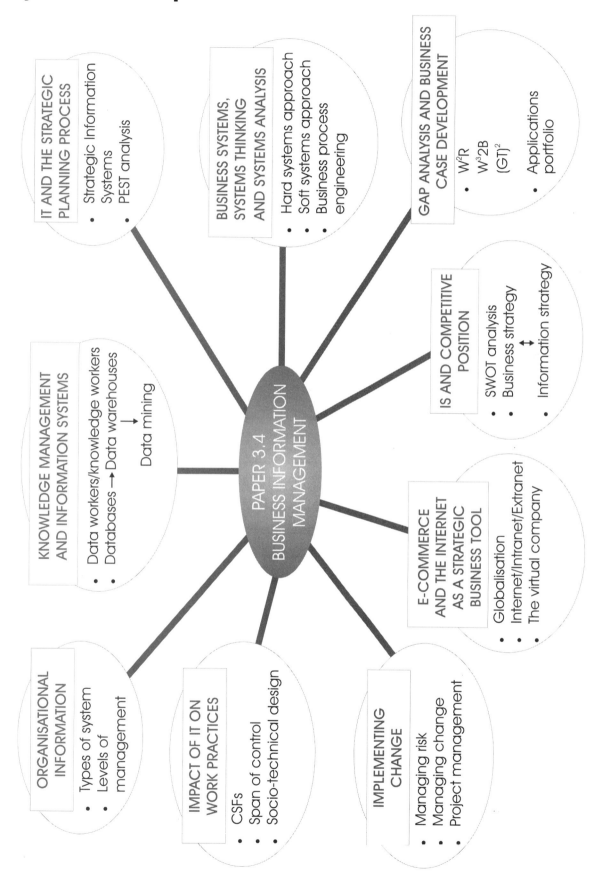

Planning your question practice

Planning your question practice

We have already stressed that question practice should be right at the centre of your revision. Whilst you will spend some time looking at your notes and Paper 3.4 Passcards, you should spend the majority of your revision time practising questions.

We recommend two ways in which you can practise questions.

- Use **BPP's question plan** to work systematically through the syllabus and attempt key and other questions on a section-by-section basis

- **Build your own exams** – attempt questions as a series of practice exams

These ways are suggestions and simply following them is no guarantee of success. You or your college may prefer an alternative but equally valid approach.

BPP's question plan

The BPP plan below requires you to devote a **minimum of 42 hours** to revision of Paper 3.4. Any time you can spend over and above this should only increase your chances of success.

Step 1   **Review your notes** and the chapter summaries in the Paper 3.4 **Passcards** for each section of the syllabus.

Step 2   **Answer the key questions** for that section. These questions have boxes round the question number in the table below and you should answer them in full. Even if you are short of time you must attempt these questions if you want to pass the exam. You should complete your answers without referring to our solutions.

Step 3   **Attempt the other questions** in that section. For some questions we have suggested that you prepare **answer plans or do the calculations** rather than full solutions. Planning an answer means that you should spend about 40% of the time allowance for the questions brainstorming the question and drawing up a list of points to be included in the answer.

Step 4   Attempt **Mock exams 1, 2 and 3** under strict exam conditions.

Syllabus section	2007 Passcards chapters	Questions in this Kit	Comments	Done ☑
Revision period 1 Information systems and the organisation	1 – 3	19	Requires you to think about how information systems should be evaluated.	☐
		2	This question (from the December 2004 exam) requires you to discuss and apply the theories of Parsons and Nolan.	☐
		4	Explores the important issue of ensuring systems/processing methods compliment operations. Prepare an answer plan only.	☐
		5	This question (with an answer plan provided by BPP), covers the relationship between organisation structure and information systems.	☐
		6	Covers a wide-range of issues including how technology (an intranet and an extranet) may be used to share information, and the 'people issues' that may hinder information sharing.	☐
Revision period 2 Business systems, systems analysis and business case development (1)	4 – 5	7	Tests your understanding of information flows and sources at strategic level.	☐
		8	Taken from the June 2004 exam, this question (with analysis from BPP) covers expert systems.	☐
		10	Porter's Value Chain crops up regularly in the Paper 3.4 exam. Ensure you understand the relevance of this theory to IS/IT.	☐
		11	This question cover's Earl's three leg analysis of IS strategy development. Prepare an answer plan only.	☐
		13	Taken from the June 2002 exam, this question covers Parsons' generic IS strategies.	☐
		15	A test of your knowledge of international strategy and applicable IT strategies – from the June 2003 exam	☐
		16	A test of Porter's five forces and its applicability to information systems theory from the June 2004 exam.	☐
Revision period 3 Business systems, systems analysis and business case development (2)	4 – 5	20	Peppard's grid from the December 2003 exam is covered in detail.	☐
		21	This question requires you to think about how the risks and benefits of systems under consideration may be analysed.	☐

Syllabus section	2007 Passcards chapters	Questions in this Kit	Comments	Done ☑
		22	This question appeared in the June 2002 paper. It provides a good test of knowledge relating to hard and soft approaches to systems development.	☐
		24	A question that requires you to think about how investment in information systems may be appraised. Taken from the June 2003 exam.	☐
		25	This question appeared in the June 2004 paper. It provides a good test of knowledge relating to the soft systems approach.	☐
		26	Another excellent test of soft systems methodology – taken from the December 2004 exam.	☐
		27	An excellent test of soft systems focussing of root definitions – from the December 2005 exam.	☐
Revision period 4 Using information competitively	6 – 7	31	You must be able to discuss the strategic implications of developing bespoke software as opposed to purchasing a ready-made package. This question provides a good test in this area.	☐
		32	This question, taken from the December 2001 paper, covers data warehousing and data mining. These topics were examined again in 2005.	☐
		34	Taken from the December 2003 exam, this question covers database management in detail.	☐
		35	This question covering groupware and collaboration appeared in the December 2004 paper.	☐
		36	Covers globalisation, an increasingly topical area.	☐
		37	This question requires you to consider e-commerce from two different perspectives.	☐
Revision period 5 The impact of information technology (1)	8 – 9	41	Virtual companies are as topical today as they were back in 2001 when this question appeared in the December exam.	☐
		42	This question, taken from the December 2002 paper, covers Zuboff's theory of automate, informate and transformate.	☐
		43	A question relating to the supply chain. Taken from the June 2003 exam.	☐
		44	A good test of your ability to select key indicators relevant to a specific situation.	☐

Syllabus section	2007 Passcards chapters	Questions in this Kit	Comments	Done ☑
Revision period 6 The impact of information technology (2)	8 – 9	46	Taken from the June 2005 exam, this question examines how technology affects working relationships.	☐
		47	This question includes a theoretical element (the dimensions of information) and a practical aspect (employee code of conduct).	☐
		48	Another question from December 2002 – this one relates to systems development and social/ethical issues.	☐
		49	Taken from the December 2005 paper, this question requires you to apply the five moral dimensions of the information age.	☐
Revision period 7 Scenario questions covering a range of syllabus areas	1 – 9	50	This scenario provides a good test of your ability to apply what you know about knowledge management. Security, another popular examination topic, also features. Prepare answer plans only.	☐
		52	A short scenario, but the questions all cover highly examinable areas. It's vital you are able to draw and interpret rich pictures, and can apply CATWOE.	☐
		55	This scenario appeared in the Pilot Paper, and therefore provides an indication of the preferred style of the examiner.	☐
Revision period 8 Scenario questions covering a range of syllabus areas	1 – 9	56	Taken from the December 2001 paper, this scenario includes questions covering SWOT analysis and the value chain.	☐
		57	The December 2002 scenario featuring Earl's three legs, sourcing options and SWOT.	☐
		58	The June 2003 scenario covering strategy; commitment, co-ordination and communication; gap analysis.	☐
Revision period 9 Scenario questions covering a range of syllabus areas	1 – 9	59	The December 2003 scenario involving the application of SWOT and IS/IT strategies, cost benefit analysis and the important hot topic of risk assessment.	☐
		60	The June 2004 scenario covering PEST and critical success factors. Prepare answer plan only.	☐
		61	The December 2004 scenario concerning a multi-national clothing retailer and the hot topic of ethical issues.	☐

Build your own exams

Having revised your notes and the BPP Passcards, you can attempt the questions in the Kit as a series of practice exams. You can organise the questions in the following ways:

- Either you can attempt complete old papers; recent papers are listed below.

	3.4									
	Dec'01	Jun'02	Dec'02	Jun'03	Dec'03	Jun'04	Dec'04	Jun'05	Dec'05	June 06
Section A										
1	56	ME2 Q1	57	58	59	60	61	62	63	64
2	56	ME2 Q2	57	58	59	60	61	62	63	64
3	56	ME2 Q3	57	58	59	60	61	62	63	64
Section B										
4	32	13	23	15	20	8	2	19	12	28
5	41	22	42	24	34	16	26	29	27	37
6	47	33	48	43	ME2 Q	25	35	46	49	39

- Or you can make up practice exams, either yourself or using the mock exams that we have listed below.

	Practice exams					
	1	2	3	4	5	6
Section A						
1	59	60	61	62	63	64
2	59	60	61	62	63	64
3	59	60	61	62	63	64
Section B						
4	2	25	4	16	26	17
5	27	33	24	23	32	22
6	45	48	42	41	45	44

- Whichever practice exams you use, you must attempt **Mock exams 1, 2 and 3** at the end of your revision.

Questions

1 Preparation question: strategic level systems   27 mins

It has been said that efficient information systems at the strategic level in organisations reduce risk but stifle entrepreneurial activity.

Required

Explain how information systems can be designed and used effectively at strategic level.   **(15 marks)**

Helping hand. Information systems at strategic level should provide an **overview** of the organisation so that its future as a unit can be planned and controlled. The uses of information systems that might be expected at this level would include the following.

(a)   Financial models for budgeting and planning.
(b)   Systems relating to current performance analysis.
(c)   Systems relating to market research etc.

2 Parsons and Nolan (12/04)   36 mins

Required

(a)   Discuss the principles underpinning Parsons' six generic information system strategies model and Nolan's six-stage growth model. Your discussion should include a brief description of the models and the appropriateness of using the models for the development of information systems and business strategies in a modern business organisation.   **(12 marks)**

(b)   Apply Nolan's six-stage growth model to the development of a specific information system in an organisation of your choice. Your answer should evaluate the appropriateness of applying each of the stages to the information system selected.   **(8 marks)**

   (Total = 20 marks)

3 Data and knowledge work   36 mins

In traditional industrial economies a large proportion of businesses produced or assembled goods and most employees worked in factories.

Many countries now have an information economy – where most wealth originates in information and knowledge production and the majority of workers process or create information. Information work is divided into two groups: data and knowledge work.

Required

(a)   Distinguish between data workers and knowledge workers.   **(5 marks)**

(b)   Outline the role of a professional accountant as both a data worker and a knowledge worker and briefly describe the support systems they require to work effectively.   **(15 marks)**

   (Total = 20 marks)

4 Centralised or distributed?

36 mins

Pound-Go-Far Department Stores Ltd is an established, cut-price department store, located in the centre of a major city. Mr Tom Lee, the owner and general manager, is now considering opening two additional shops in the same city.

Basic operations within the company are computerised and Mr Lee would like this extended to the two new shops using some sort of computer network.

Required

(a)   Explain what you understand by the following terms and their relevance to the networking requirements of Pound-Go-Far Stores:

* LANs
* WANs
* VANs   **(9 marks)**

(b)   Mr Lee could adopt either a centralised Information Systems approach or alternatively a distributed processing strategy.

Explain what you understand by each of these terms and the advantages associated with each type of processing.   **(11 marks)**

(Total = 20 marks)

5 Question with answer plan: organisation and system structure

36 mins

AB plc is a national freight distribution company with a head office, five regional offices and a hundred local depots spread throughout the country. It is planning a major computerisation project. The options which are being considered are as follows.

* A central mainframe system with terminals at each depot.
* Distributed minicomputers at each regional office.

Required

Draft a report to the board of AB plc describing the ways in which each of the options would suit the company's structure and explaining the advantages and disadvantages of each.   **(20 marks)**

6 Information sharing; intranet; extranet

36 mins

CC plc is a company employing 2,560 staff in 20 different offices within one country. The company offers a wide range of specialist consultancy advice to the building and construction industry. This includes advice on materials to be used, relevant legislation (including planning applications) and appropriate sources of finance.

The information to meet client requirements is held within each office of the company. Although most clients are serviced by a single office, a lot of the information used is duplicated between the different offices. This is not surprising given that legislation and other standard information such as details of materials used are the same for the whole country.

In the past there has been no attempt to share data because of the cost of transferring information and the lack of trust on the part of staff in other offices. Some senior managers tend to keep part of client data confidential to themselves.

The company has recently provided all employees with e-mail for communication within CC plc and to clients. Software with internet access is also available so that staff can obtain undated planning information from appropriate websites. The hardware in the company is quite old and only just meets the minimum specification for these purposes.

BPP
LEARNING MEDIA

The Marketing Director has suggested that an Intranet should be established in the company so that common information can be shared rather than each office maintaining its own data. This suggestion is meeting with some resistance from all grades of staff.

Required

(a) Explain the objectives of an intranet and suggest how the provision of an intranet within CC plc should result in better provision of information. **(9 marks)**

(b) Discuss the organisational and human reasons why information may not become more widely available in CC plc, and suggest methods for overcoming these barriers. **(7 marks)**

(c) Briefly explain how an extranet differs from an intranet, and how CC plc could utilise an extranet. **(4 marks)**

(Total = 20 marks)

7 Strategic decision making   36 mins

Decision making at the strategic level in organisations needs to be supported by information systems that are flexible and responsive.

Required

(a) Describe the characteristics of information flows at the strategic level. **(10 marks)**

(b) Describe the sources of information required for strategic decision making and the characteristics of an information system used to provide strategic information. **(10 marks)**

(Total = 20 marks)

8 Question with analysis: expert systems (6/04)   36 mins

Teac Investment Co provides financial services to several thousand clients. Many clients with large financial investment portfolios run and controlled by Teac Investment often make enquiries concerning new investments and changes to their overall portfolio. All the information is currently maintained on a relational database supported by a management information system (MIS), permitting financial consultants to access the clients' current financial status. Following an enquiry from a client, the financial consultant studies the portfolio using the information received from the MIS and his knowledge of successful portfolios, including the spread of investments, the length of the proposed investment and several other financial indicators. The financial consultant then contacts the client and gives his recommendation. This process can often take days and has led to complaints from several clients who are threatening to take their business elsewhere. The CEO of the company is concerned about the current processes and the difficulty in maintaining the current level of competent financial consultants. Following an initial consultation with an information systems consultant he is contemplating investing in the development of an expert system (ES).

Required

(a) For the information provided by management information systems and expert systems to be useful to the organisation, it should possess particular qualitative characteristics.

Explain, in the context of management information systems and expert systems, the terms timeliness, relevance/volume, accuracy/completeness and user confidence. Your answer should emphasise any differences between the two contexts. **(8 marks)**

(b) With reference to Teac Investment Co assess the advantages and disadvantages of implementing an expert system. **(12 marks)**

(Total = 20 marks)

8 Question with analysis: expert systems (6/04)

36 mins

Annotations (left margin)
Capacity of MIS?
Flexibility?
Up to date system needed
Meaning?
Confidentiality issues?
Why this long?
How would this help?

Teac Investment Co provides financial services to **several thousand clients**. Many clients with large financial investment portfolios run and controlled by Teac Investment **often make enquiries** concerning **new investments and changes** to their overall portfolio. All the information is currently maintained on a **relational database** supported by a management information system (MIS), permitting financial consultants to **access the clients' current financial status**. Following an enquiry from a client, the financial consultant studies the portfolio using the information received from the MIS and **his knowledge** of successful portfolios, including the spread of investments, the length of the proposed investment and several other financial indicators. The financial consultant then contacts the client and gives his recommendation. This **process can often take days** and has led to complaints from several clients who are threatening to take their business elsewhere. The CEO of the company is concerned about the current processes and the difficulty in maintaining the current level of competent financial consultants. Following an initial consultation with an information systems consultant he is contemplating investing in the development of an **expert system** (ES).

Depends upon consultant technical skill

Required

As identified in the question requirement

(a) For the information provided by management information systems and expert systems to be useful to the organisation, it should possess particular **qualitative characteristics**.

Keep your answer focused

Explain, **in the context of management information systems and expert systems**, the terms **timeliness, relevance/volume, accuracy/completeness and user confidence**. Your answer should emphasise any differences between the two contexts.

(8 marks)

Define and apply to the context

(b) With reference to Teac Investment Co assess **the advantages and disadvantages** of implementing an expert system.

(12 marks)

Identify at least three of each

(Total = 20 marks)

9 Information systems functions

36 mins

Information systems used to collect, generate and manipulate information can be classified as follows:

- Transaction Processing Systems (TPS)
- Office Automation Systems (OAS)
- Knowledge Work Systems (KWS)
- Management Information Systems (MIS)
- Decision Support Systems (DSS)
- Executive Information Systems (EIS) [also known as Executive Support Systems (ESS)]

Required

Describe each of the categories identified above in terms of the functions information systems perform, and the level they serve in the organisation.

(20 marks)

10 Porter's value chain

36 mins

The SFA Company manufactures clothing and operates from one location in a major city. It purchases cotton and other raw materials and manufactures these into garments of clothing, such as sweatshirts, T-shirts and similar articles in its factory. There are approximately 20 administration staff, 30 sales staff and 300 production workers. Although the company is profitable, three major concerns were raised at a recent Board meeting about the operations of the company:

1 The company does not always appear to obtain the best prices for raw materials, which has decreased gross profit in the last few years of trading.

2 Many garments are made to order for large retail shops, but the company has spare capacity and so it maintains an active salesforce to try and increase its total sales. However, the salesforce does not seem to be making many sales because of lack of information about the garments in production and stocks of finished garments.

3 Some production is carried out using Computer Assisted Design and manufacture although the company has found limited use for this application to date. The system was purchased in a hurry two years ago with the objective of keeping up with competitors who had purchased similar systems. The Board believes that greater use could be made of this technology.

The Value Chain model produced by Porter provides a good summary of the primary and support activities of the company. An adaptation of Porter's general model follows:

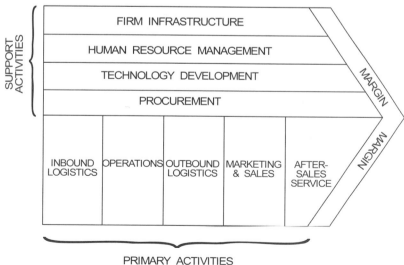

The Board of SFA is currently considering implementing some form of information system or systems, such as a MIS, into the company for all staff to use. Because of the perceived weaknesses in the current systems already mentioned, the directors are particularly interested in the areas of:

1   Inbound logistics.
2   Marketing and sales.
3   Technology development.

Required

(a)   Explain what inputs will be needed for the information systems designed to support the operations of the business in the three areas mentioned above.   **(14 marks)**

(b)   Explain what outputs will be required from those information systems.   **(6 marks)**

Note. Do **not** describe Porter's general model.   **(Total = 20 marks)**

11 Strategic plan for IS/IT (Earl)   36 mins

A strategy is a course of action, including the specification of resources required, to achieve a specific objective. A strategy for IS may be described as: Business led (top down emphasis), Infrastructure led (bottom up emphasis) or Mixed (inside out emphasis).

Required

Explain why many large organisations now produce strategic plans for the introduction of IS/IT. Your answer should include a brief description of the three approaches named above.   **(20 marks)**

12 Earl's audit grid (12/05)   36 mins

The results obtained from conducting a current situation analysis are often depicted in Earl's audit grid format.

Required

(a)   Evaluate the use of current situation analysis and the resulting audit grid within the context of developing an information systems strategy.   **(10 marks)**

(b)   Examine a key information system in an organisation of your choice using Earl's audit grid as a framework. In your answer you should discuss which of the four quadrants is more applicable to your chosen information system and why.   **(10 marks)**

(Total = 20 marks)

13 Parsons' generic IS/IT strategies (6/02)   36 mins

Parsons identified six possible generic Information System (IS) strategies.

Centrally planned
Leading edge
Free market
Monopoly
Scarce resource
Necessary evil

Required

(a)   Briefly describe the six generic information strategies, linking the strategy with the role of the IS function and the user.   **(12 marks)**

(b)   Discuss which IS strategy best applies to an organisation of your choice. You should explain clearly why your chosen organisation is suited more by that strategy than by any of the other five.   **(8 marks)**

(Total = 20 marks)

14 McFarlan's strategic grid and the BCG matrix

36 mins

The Strategic Grid, developed by McFarlan, shows the level of dependence on IS/IT within an organisation.

The BCG matrix, developed by the Boston Consulting Group, plots a company's products in terms of potential cash generation and cash expenditure requirements.

Required

(a) Briefly explain each of the quadrants of McFarlan's Strategic Grid. **(6 marks)**

(b) Explain each of the quadrants of the BCG matrix and the types of decisions the matrix may be useful for. Also explain how each quadrant of the matrix could be related to a section of McFarlan's Strategic Grid.

(14 marks)

(Total = 20 marks)

15 International business strategies (6/03)

36 mins

When an organisation adopts a global business strategy it is imperative that it adopts a suitable information technology strategy to complement it. The four main business strategies that can be used in a global setting are: Domestic exporter, Multinational, Franchiser and Transnational.

Required

(a) Briefly describe each of the four business strategies: Domestic exporter, Multinational, Franchiser and Transnational. **(8 marks)**

(b) Briefly describe **four** main Information Technology strategies that are applicable on an international basis.

(4 marks)

(c) For each of the business strategies in (a) describe which type of information technology strategy in (b) best complements it, giving reasons for your choice. **(8 marks)**

(Total = 20 marks)

16 Porter's five forces (6/04)

36 mins

Michael Porter identified five competitive forces that determine the extent of competition in an industry: Potential entrants, Competitive rivalry, Threats from substitutes, Buyers' bargaining power and Suppliers' bargaining power.

Required

(a) Discuss in general terms how the five forces model can enable an organisation to develop an information systems strategy that will enable the organisation to trade competitively in the market. **(8 marks)**

(b) Discuss any **three** of the five forces giving specific examples of information systems that are appropriate in each force to provide competitive advantage. **(12 marks)**

(Total = 20 marks)

17 Evaluation of strategy

36 mins

(a) Explain what Information Systems strategy, Information Technology strategy and Information Management strategy are and the link between them. **(9 marks)**

(b) The Information Systems strategy within the MG organisation has been developed over a number of years. However, the basic approach has always remained unchanged. An IT budget is agreed by the Board each year. This budget is normally 5% to 10% higher than the previous year's to allow for increases in prices and upgrades to computer systems.

Systems are upgraded in accordance with user requirements. Most users accept that the IT systems are there to perform tasks such as recording day-to-day transactions and providing access to accounting and other information as necessary. There is no Executive Information System (EIS). Benchmarking and similar comparisons with other companies are not performed.

The Board tends to rely on reports from junior managers to control the business. While these reports generally provide the information requested by the Board, they are focused at a tactical level and tend to contain some annoying errors and occasional omissions

Required

Evaluate the Information Systems strategy of the MG organisation, recommending any changes that you consider appropriate. **(11 marks)**

(Total = 20 marks)

18 The value chain (Pilot paper)

36 mins

Porter contends that competitive advantage cannot be understood by looking at a firm as a whole. It does, however, stem from the many discrete activities a firm performs in designing, producing, marketing, delivering and supporting its products. A generic value chain is shown below.

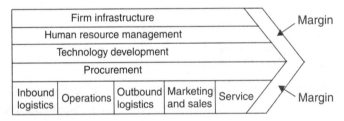

Figure 1: The Value Chain (from Porter, M. Competitive Advantage)

Required

(a) Define what is meant by a 'value activity'. **(2 marks)**

(b) Briefly explain the difference between primary and support activities. **(3 marks)**

(c) Briefly describe each of the activities named in the value chain. **(5 marks)**

(d) Explain why the value chain technique is important when developing an information system and an information technology strategy. **(10 marks)**

(Total = 20 marks)

BPP
LEARNING MEDIA

BUSINESS SYSTEMS, SYSTEMS ANALYSIS AND BUSINESS CASE DEVELOPMENT

Questions 19 to 28 cover 'Business systems, systems analysis and business case development', the subject of Part B of the BPP Study Text for Paper 3.4.

Further questions on these subject areas are included in the Scenario Questions and the Mock Exams in this Kit – refer to page 6.

19 Evaluating information systems (06/05) 36 mins

Required

(a) Explain why it is important for management to assess the viability of investing in a business information system and to identify the key factors which should be taken into account before making such an investment decision. **(6 marks)**

(b) Senior managers have to decide on the value of specific information systems when they are evaluating information system proposals. Some of the general factors used to assess the value of an information system are:

  (i) What information is provided?
  (ii) What is it used for?
  (iii) What is achieved by using it?

  Identify further general factors that might be relevant in the evaluation process. **(4 marks)**

(c) Using the three factors given above plus the additional factors you have identified in (b), discuss how the factors can be used to evaluate an information system within an organisation of your choice. **(10 marks)**

(Total = 20 marks)

20 Peppard's grid (12/03) 36 mins

Required

(a) McFarlan suggested that information systems could function strategically in four different ways within an organisation. There are several adaptations of this grid including one by Peppard.

  Describe Peppard's information systems strategic grid. **(8 marks)**

(b) Briefly discuss the appropriateness of classifying organisations using Peppard's information systems strategic grid. **(4 marks)**

(c) Examine key information systems in an organisation of your choice according to the principles behind Peppard's grid. In your answer you should discuss which of Peppard's four functions is more applicable to your chosen organisation and why. **(8 marks)**

(Total = 20 marks)

21 Question with answer plan: application selection: risks and benefits

36 mins

Required

Describe the non-financial techniques available for analysing the risks and benefits of potential IT applications an organisation could utilise.

(20 marks)

22 Hard and soft approaches (6/02)

36 mins

Required

(a) There has been much debate amongst both practitioners and academics concerning the differences between hard and soft methodologies for developing information systems (IS).

Discuss the differences between hard and soft approaches to IS in terms of their handling of:

(i)   Problem definition
(ii)   The organisation
(iii) The reasons for modelling
(iv) The outcome

(8 marks)

(b) Checkland's soft systems methodology (SSM) encourages organisations to investigate system requirements and take into account the differing views of the human participants within the system. The system in the following example is a state run college. Given below are three CATWOEs from three different actors within the system; the actors are a student, a lecturer and a college administrator.

The Student

Client	Me
Actor	The lecturer
Transformation	Education
Weltanschauung	We all pay taxes therefore I am entitled to it
Owner	The government or taxpayer
Environment	The College

The Lecturer

Client	The students
Actor	Me
Transformation	Providing education using specialised equipment, services and student support/care
Weltanschauung	It is important to educate as many people as possible
Owner	College administrators
Environment	State owned college versus working for a private college. My work versus my private life

The College Administrator

Client	Lecturers
Actor	Me
Transformation	To enable lecturers to teach as many students as possible
Weltanschauung	Create efficient departments within strict cash budgets
Owner	The college governors
Environment	Politics

Required

(i) For **two** of the three CATWOEs above produce a root definition   **(6 marks)**

(ii) Construct a CATWOE and a root definition for either a taxpayer or a politician within the state run college education system.   **(6 marks)**

(Total = 20 marks)

23 Soft systems methodology (12/02)   36 mins

In the context of Peter Checkland's Soft Systems Methodology, the following Root Definition describes a system.

'A student owned and operated system which turns trainee systems analysts, with no professional qualifications, into professionally qualified systems analysts, through the acquisition, by whatever means are necessary, of full membership of the Systems Analyst Guild (SAG) from a highly rated academic institution, in order to enhance the trainee system analysts' CV and thus their career prospects.'

Required

(a) List an appropriate set of CATWOE criteria for the Root Definition.   **(3 marks)**

(b) Having created root definitions and CATWOE criteria for a system, why do we then continue to draw conceptual models?   **(4 marks)**

(c) Draw a conceptual model for the above organisation based on the root definition and the CATWOE criteria.   **(10 marks)**

(d) Determine suitable measures of efficacy, efficiency and effectiveness for the SAG qualification scheme.   **(3 marks)**

(Total = 20 marks)

24 Appraisal of information systems projects (6/03)   36 mins

Management have traditionally focused on financial techniques for evaluating whether to invest in information systems.

Required

Discuss whether reliance on purely financial techniques is wholly appropriate for the appraisal of information projects.   **(20 marks)**

25 Soft systems methodology; rich pictures (6/04)   36 mins

Required

(a)   In the context of Peter Checkland's Soft Systems Methodology, discuss the purpose and role of developing rich pictures.   **(6 marks)**

(b)   The Systems Analyst Guild (SAG) is a professional association for Systems Analysts. SAG enrols approximately one thousand new student members per year and this figure has dramatically increased during the past three years. Before this period the number of new student members was consistently around two hundred per year. SAG's popularity has risen because many employers have realised the benefits of encouraging their systems analysts to gain membership of a professional association. The membership committee is keen to maintain this rise in membership applications.

To become a full professional member of SAG students have to pass a series of examinations that are examined at 10 test centres throughout the country. Many of these centres offer the relevant courses that students may attend prior to taking the examinations. SAG currently employs two education assistants who have to deal with applications and the progress of the student members. They often complain of overwork and the need for new computerised systems to help them in tracking student records and progress. Currently much of the record keeping is still processed manually, with student records physically kept in filing cabinets. An education secretary has overall responsibility for the student system and liaises with the test centres and manages the education assistants. She is not sympathetic to their concerns. She has ambitions of replacing the association's membership manager who is retiring shortly. The membership manager has a personal assistant (PA) who, amongst other tasks, supplies all members with updates and quarterly magazines concerned with their profession. The PA has concerns over his workload and has made his manager aware of this.

When the students pass their examinations they can become professional members of SAG. Professional members vote representatives to the council of SAG. The council provide all the usual services to members of professional associations. Membership fees vary according to the status of the members ie student membership or professional membership. The accountant responsible for maintaining the membership accounts is also finding difficulty in processing his records. Although he has an accounting package on his personal computer, the majority of his transactions are manually input.

Construct a rich picture of the current situation in SAG.   **(14 marks)**

(Total = 20 marks)

26 Soft systems methodology; root definition (12/04)   36 mins

Required

(a)   Explain the use of Checkland's Soft Systems Methodology (SSM) for the development of information systems.   **(8 marks)**

(b)   In the context of Checkland's Soft Systems Methodology, the following Root Definition describes a system.

Root Definition:

'A system owned and operated by GJKD Bank to accurately transform details of client company employee payment entitlement into electronic funds transfer, at the duly appointed date and time, in accordance with the requirements of the client company, national accounting practice and national commercial law. This is one of several services the bank offers its clients. The bank's overriding business strategy is concerned with maintaining client confidence and trust in all services provided.'

List an appropriate set of CATWOE elements for the Root Definition.   **(6 marks)**

(c)   Using the Root Definition given in part (b) define suitable measures of performance in terms of Efficiency, Effectiveness and Efficacy.   **(6 marks)**

(Total = 20 marks)

27 Soft systems and root definitions (12/05)   36 mins

The human resources (HR) department at the GB University is developing a system that will enable junior lecturers to apply for promotion to the senior lecturer grade. Currently promotions are given on an individual basis within faculties. This procedure has been strongly criticised by many of the stakeholders including: the lecturers' union, junior lecturers and the heads of faculties who all complain about the lack of fairness of the system. The university executive is planning to develop a university wide promotion strategy that it hopes will alleviate the criticisms of the current system. The executive managers are developing general criteria based on teaching ability, management responsibility and academic achievements. When the criteria are established, prospective applicants will be requested to complete a standard application form informing the HR department of their relevant details. Applicants will be shortlisted based on their ability to match the criteria. A panel selected from faculty professors within the university will interview shortlisted applicants. Successful applicants will be offered promotion while unsuccessful applicants will be given feedback on their applications. A predetermined number of promotions will be offered.

Required

(a)   Produce a root definition for the GB University's promotion system.   **(3 marks)**

(b)   Using the root definition produced in part (a) draw a conceptual model of the GB University's promotion system.   **(9 marks)**

(c)   Discuss the reasons why a soft systems approach is appropriate to the development of the university's promotion system.   **(8 marks)**

(Total = 20 marks)

28 Automation, rationalisation and re-engineering (6/06)

36 mins

Explain the following terms and discuss how they could be applied in the context of a national supermarket chain.

(a)   Business automation   **(4 marks)**
(b)   Business rationalisation   **(6 marks)**
(c)   Business process re-engineering   **(10 marks)**

(Total = 20 marks)

29 Database systems (06/05)
36 mins

GBAW Investment Co is a national company providing financial services to over ten thousand clients. The services provided include life assurance, a variety of insurance services, investment portfolios and mortgage brokering. The company is organised into several departments, each one dealing with a specific area within the finance sector. Many clients have dealings with more than one department. Several departments have dealings with the same outside organisations that support the services offered by GBAW. Currently all of the information relating to clients, products and suppliers is held on a single relational database.

Albert Thompson, a manager in the investment department, recently read an article in one of the financial journals that analysed the use of data warehousing and the successful results obtained from implementing data mining techniques within organisations in the finance sector. The following day he asked the IT services manager, Nigella Smythe, if GBAW was considering the introduction of such applications. In her reply Nigella stated, 'It is not a simple matter of acquiring a piece of software and attaching it to an existing database. It is a complex and expensive exercise to implement a data warehouse system supported by data mining techniques.

Required

(a) How are integrity, independence and integration within a database management system maintained, with reference to GBAW where appropriate. **(12 marks)**

(b) Nigella Smythe's statement at the end of the scenario highlights potential issues regarding the implementation of a data warehouse system supported by data mining techniques.

Explain the terms data warehouse and data mining and identify the potential problems of integrating a data warehouse system into the existing platform. **(4 marks)**

(c) Describe, in general terms, how the introduction of a data warehouse system with data mining facilities may help GBAW to improve its position in the marketplace. **(4 marks)**

(Total = 20 marks)

30 Information and knowledge management
36 mins

Increasingly the management of information sharing and group working ventures is a fundamental part of business management.

Required

(a) Discuss how the management of information might differ from the management of knowledge. **(12 marks)**

(b) How can an organisation develop a knowledge strategy? **(8 marks)**

(Total = 20 marks)

31 Question with answer plan: purpose written or ready made? (Pilot paper)

36 mins

The choice to develop a purpose-written application software system or to purchase a ready-written package is one that faces all company executives with responsibility for IS/IT strategy.

Required

Discuss the strategic issues involved.

(20 marks)

32 Data warehousing and data mining (12/01)

36 mins

'Users and information system specialists need to spend inordinate amounts of time locating and gathering data' (Watson and Hale, 1998).

Recent developments in the area of Data Warehousing and its associated technologies claim to be able to improve information management in organisations.

Required

(a) Discuss how the Data Warehousing approach to information management improves on the Data Base Management Systems (DBMS) approach.

(10 marks)

(b) In the UK, car retailing is becoming increasingly competitive and profit margins on new car sales to the general public are being squeezed. Most new cars are sold by main dealers committed to one car manufacturer and selling new and used cars, servicing cars and hiring out cars. The main dealer will also provide service for fleet cars, which will have been bought in bulk by large companies direct from the manufacturer at a discount.

Explain how the concept of Data Mining could be exploited by a large Main Dealer who has a string of garages associated with a number of different car manufacturers. All the individual garages have computerised systems for their major functions – and the IS systems have been in existence for more then 10 years.

(10 marks)

(Total = 20 marks)

33 Question with helping hand: Knowledge management (6/02)

36 mins

Knowledge management is generally described as comprising four major functions:

(a) Create knowledge.
(b) Capture and codify knowledge.
(c) Distribute knowledge.
(d) Share knowledge.

Required

For each function discuss the types of information system which support that function. Give examples where appropriate.

(20 marks)

Helping hand. To score good marks in all four categories, discuss the types of information system with particular reference to the given knowledge management functions.

- For the first function, create knowledge, CAD/CAM, virtual reality systems and investment workstations could be cited

- 'Capture and codify knowledge' can include the family of artificial intelligence systems including expert systems and robotics

- 'Distribute knowledge' should include office automation systems

- 'Share knowledge' should include groupware systems

---

34 Database management (12/03)   36 mins

Required

(a)   In the context of Database Management Systems (DBMS) briefly discuss the concepts of physical and logical design.   **(4 marks)**

(b)   Describe how data is logically stored and accessed when using a Relational Database.   **(6 marks)**

(c)   CETA owns a chain of twenty-five car accessory stores. Each store supplies a range of non-specialist spare parts for the majority of popular manufacturers' models. They also supply car accessories ranging from key rings to specialised car seats. CETA's core business is cash and carry to the general public, although they do supply local garages with parts. Normally these small businesses are given discounts depending on their annual spend. Two years ago CETA introduced a reward card scheme to their public customers. To receive a reward card the customers register in a store – the reward card is valid in any of CETA's stores. The reward card entitles the holder to a 5% discount on all goods purchased. The date of registration signifies the start of a year for each customer. If a customer spends more than five hundred pounds during any year for the remaining period of that year the customer receives an extra 2% discount.

All of the stores have computerised inventory systems that are linked to CETA's head office. CETA has recently implemented a data warehousing system with data-mining facilities.

Discuss how CETA can use each of **five** different types of results normally associated with data mining to advance its business.   **(10 marks)**

                                                                              (Total = 20 marks)

---

35 Groupware and email (12/04)   36 mins

Required

(a)   Beko Co is an independent motor car manufacturer. It is currently developing a new two-seater sports car. The development program is expected to take two years to complete. A new project team has been established to perform the task. 32 members of the 38 strong design team are located throughout the country in six locations. The remaining six members are located in two locations in neighbouring countries. The design project has very stringent deadlines. Mike Beko, the Chief Executive Officer, has some reservations concerning the coordination of the design team and of the project as a whole. An independent information systems consultant has suggested that the use of groupware systems would aid the design process.

Define the term groupware and describe the main facilities of groupware systems with reference to Beko Co.   **(15 marks)**

(b)   Describe the possible disadvantages for a company of using email for communication and business information management within organisations.   **(5 marks)**

                                                                              (Total = 20 marks)

36 The Internet and globalisation

36 mins

The term 'the global village' has never been more appropriate.

Required

Explain the role of the Internet and communications technology in globalisation.

(20 marks)

37 E-commerce (6/06)

36 mins

The development of e-commerce, particularly e-trading, has changed society in many ways.

Required

(a) Discuss the impact of e-trading from a consumer perspective.   **(10 marks)**
(b) Discuss the impact of e-trading from a business perspective   **(10 marks)**

(Total = 20 marks)

38 Internet strategy

36 mins

The SDW Company has been trading for one year. It provides an airline service between three major cities in the country in which it operates.

Mr M, the majority shareholder and Managing Director, is keen to expand its operations and, in particular, to use the Internet as the major selling medium. He has discovered, for example, that doubling sales on the Internet usually results in no additional costs. However, doubling sales using a call centre normally results in a doubling of staff and an increase in costs.

All tickets are currently sold via the company's call centre. The company has an Internet site although this is used for publicity only, not for sales or marketing. Competitors currently use a mixture of selling media, although detailed information on the success of each medium is not available to the SDW Company.

Mr M has asked you, as a qualified accountant, to assist him in upgrading the company's Internet site and, in particular, showing how this will help to reduce operating costs.

Required

(a) Advise Mr M on how to establish and implement an appropriate Internet strategy for the SDW Company.

(10 marks)

(b) Discuss the key customer-orientated features of an Internet site, showing how these can be used to meet the objective of cost reduction required by Mr M.   **(10 marks)**

(Total = 20 marks)

THE IMPACT OF INFORMATION TECHNOLOGY

Questions 39 to 49 cover 'The impact of information technology', the subject of Part D of the BPP Study Text for Paper 3.4.

Further questions on these subject areas are included in the Scenario Questions and the Mock Exams in this Kit – refer to pages 6.

39 Lewin – an evaluation (6/06)

36 mins

(a)   Describe and evaluate Lewin's 3-step model of change   **(12 marks)**

(b)   Briefly discus why an implemented version of an information system so often differs for the initial requirements specification   **(8 marks)**

(Total = 20 marks)

40 Preparation question: Lewin's three stage model of change 18 mins

The CLS Company provides pharmaceutical testing services involving the testing of drugs produced by third parties to ensure the drug meets specification. The tests are highly sensitive due to the minute amount of drugs being tested and the potential for adverse litigation if errors are made. The computer systems supporting research assistants involved in the testing process are fairly old – although they are easy-to-use and provide appropriate analysis of drugs.

However, new government legislation on drug testing means that computer systems need to be upgraded in the next six months. Unless new systems are implemented, CLS's customers will move to other companies. Research assistants in CLS see little point in change. CLS has yet to sign purchase orders for the hardware and software that will form the new system and have not yet discussed implementation and training plans with staff.

Required

Explain, using the three stage model outlined by *Lewin* and *Schein*, how the research assistants can be encouraged to accept the new system.   **(10 marks)**

41 Virtual companies and web technologies (12/01)   36 mins

'In today's dynamic global business environment, forming a virtual company can be one of the most important strategic uses of information technology'.   (O'Brien, 2000)

Required

(a)   Discuss O'Brien's statement (above). In your answer you should include an analysis of how recent technological advances have enabled the widespread formation of virtual companies.   **(12 marks)**

(b)   Web based technologies are becoming a 'standard' tool for many traditional companies. Explain the advantages and disadvantages of advertising and providing information on a website compared to paper-based catalogues.   **(8 marks)**

(Total = 20 marks)

42 Automate, informate and transformate (12/02)

36 mins

The implementation and development of information systems can have an impact on an organisation in several different ways. The terms Automate, Informate and Transformate are often used for describing such an impact.

Required

(a) Briefly explain, with examples, the three generic terms Automate, Informate and Transformate. **(12 marks)**

(b) Discuss which of these purposes for development best applies to an organisation of your choice. You should explain clearly why the impact of information systems on your chosen organisation is better described by your chosen term than either of the other two. **(8 marks)**

(Total = 20 marks)

43 Question with answer plan: BPR and supply chain (6/03)

36 mins

ABC has a chain of twenty supermarkets. When stock items reach their re-order level in a supermarket the in-store computerised inventory system informs the stock clerk. The clerk then raises a request daily to the ABC central warehouse for replenishment of stocks via fax or e-mail. If the local warehouse has available stock, it is forwarded to the supermarket within twenty-four hours of receiving the request. If the local warehouse cannot replenish the stock from its inventory holding, it raises a purchase order to one of its suppliers. The supplier delivers the stock to the warehouse and the warehouse then delivers the required stock to the supermarkets within the area. The ABC area warehouse staff conduct all business communication with suppliers.

ABC recently contracted an IT consultant to analyse and make recommendations concerning their current supply chain briefly described above. Following the initial investigation the consultant reported.

'To enable an established traditional company like ABC to develop a Virtual Supply Chain system it may be necessary to employ a Business Process Re-engineering (BPR) approach.'

Required

(a) With reference to the above scenario, describe what is meant by a Business Process Re-engineering approach. **(8 marks)**

(b) Discuss the notion of a supply chain, identifying the major activities and supporting information systems that are required to develop a virtual supply chain. **(12 marks)**

(Total = 20 marks)

44 Electronic trading room

36 mins

DLN manufactures a range of standard parts for domestic products such as washing machines, refrigerators and freezers. The parts manufactured include motors, gears, cooling elements and standard doors for different manufacturers. The company has 12 main customers who assemble the products prior to selling them to shops and consumers.

The company has been in existence for 75 years and has remained profitable during this time. The directors pride themselves in keeping up-to-date with recent technological change. They have implemented a range of systems within the company including computerised stock control, sophisticated accounting systems and on-line ordering systems for customers via Electronic Data Interchange (EDI). DLN does not maintain a website because no sales are made to the general public.

However, DLN's main customer, GKR, has now decided to start using an electronic trading room to order parts. Rather than place orders direct with manufacturers, GKR will now offer the contract to any supplier via a restricted website. Any manufacturer can bid for the order, and, after a specified period of time, the contract will be awarded to the lowest bidder. Bidders such as DLN will have no knowledge of other bids, which will significantly reduce the likelihood of DLN obtaining contracts.

Trade journals suggest that other companies will also start using a similar system within the next six months.

Required

(a) Discuss the effects that the electronic trading room is likely to have upon DLN. **(11 marks)**

(b) Identify and explain the information that will be required and where this will be obtained, in order for managers in DLN to ensure that bids are placed into the trading room on an appropriate timescale.

(9 marks)

(Total = 20 marks)

45 Question with helping hand: Key indicators   36 mins

EF Ltd is a long-established company which manufactures a large range of computers, from mainframe to portable, on a single site. Its turnover is about £500 million per annum. The company has recently undergone a major information systems change involving the following.

(a) Capital expenditure of £50 million over three years (the NPV will be £7 million).

(b) Workforce change from 10,000 to 7,000 employees.

(c) Radical changes to work practices, both in the manufacturing systems (use of CAD/CAM) and reorganisation of managerial and administrative functions.

The new Managing Director needs to identify and understand some indicators which can be used to evaluate the success or otherwise of this change.

Required

Recommend to the Managing Director up to five key indicators that he can use and explain why each is relevant to his requirements. **(20 marks)**

Helping hand. As with many questions in high level papers, a wide range of possible answers could be provided to answer this question. Don't worry if the indicators you specify differ from those provided in the model answer. If you provide a valid explanation for the indicators in your answer you will score well.

---

46 Working relationships and communication (6/05)   36 mins

Required

Identify and discuss five examples of how, in your opinion, the introduction of business information management systems can significantly affect working relationships and the communication of management information between employees and employers within an organisation.

(20 marks)

47 Information age and employee conduct (12/01)   36 mins

'Rapid changes fuelled by information technology are creating new situations where existing laws or rules of conduct may not be relevant. New 'grey areas' are emerging in which ethical standards have not yet been codified in law. A new system of ethics for the information ages is required to guide individual and organisational choices and actions.' (Laudon 2000)

A model often used as a framework to encourage debate and policy-making decisions concerning ethical issues is the Five Moral Dimensions of the Information Age. This model identifies five major dimensions:

(a)   Information rights and obligations.
(b)   Property rights.
(c)   Accountability and control.
(d)   System quality.
(e)   Quality of life.

Required

Describe each of the five moral dimensions of the information age. For each of the five moral dimensions, outline the contents of a possible general code of practice that could be incorporated into an organisation to serve as guidelines to staff.

(20 marks)

48 Social and ethical issues (12/02)   36 mins

Teac Household Exteriors Ltd specialises in supplying customers with exterior home products. Teac has been in operation for five years; its business is expanding by an average of 20% per year. Teac's business strategy is primarily based around telephone sales. It currently employs 15 telephone sales personnel in it offices situated in the centre of the city. There is a high rate of turnover amongst the telephone sales personnel.

The telephone sales personnel contact potential customers and explain the services provided by the company. If the customer is interested they arrange an appointment with a sales representative who makes a home visit. They then confirm the details of the visit by post. The home visit is where the sale is normally completed.

Office space is currently at a premium, as the office houses the senior management and central administrative staff. It also houses the Local Area Network computer system. The computer system maintains all the relevant data required by the telephone sales personnel. Normally a new telephone sales person can be trained in a week. Following training, targets are set for the number of calls and number of appointments made during a week long period. Meeting these targets determines salary received.

The company accountant recently reported to the Chief Executive Officer (CEO) that an analysis of the cost structure of supporting the current business suggested that increasing the office space in their current prime position was not economically viable or physically possible. The CEO decided that a change in business strategy is required; she is currently contemplating designing and implementing a system that will involve a dramatic change in working practices. This system will enable the telephone sales personnel to work from home. She is aware that most of the telephone sales personnel appear to be happy with the current system of working; during their breaks they discuss sales strategies, successes and failures and generally socialise. Rumours concerning a possible re-organisation of working practices have already spread amongst the workforce; the general opinion of the management is that there will be resistance to change and many of the staff are concerned about re-organisation.

Required

(a)   Briefly describe two of the three methods listed below, which may minimise the risks of failure involved in designing and implementing the proposed system.

(i)   Organisational impact analysis
(ii)   User involvement
(iii)   Sociotechnical design

(6 marks)

(b)   Outline the technical infrastructure required for implementing the proposed system, in general rather than specific terms.

(6 marks)

(c)   Identify the social and ethical issues arising from implementing the home-based telesales system. **(8 marks)**

(Total = 20 marks)

49 The moral dimension (12/05)

36 mins

A model often used as a framework to encourage debate and policy-making decisions concerning ethical issues is the Five Moral Dimensions of the Information Age. This model identifies five major dimensions: (1) Information rights and obligations (2) Property rights (3) Accountability and control (4) System quality (5) Quality of life.

Required

(a)   Briefly describe each of the five moral dimensions within the context of an organisation.   **(5 marks)**

(b)   (i)   For each of the five moral dimensions, identify an example where an infringement on the principle of the moral dimension may have occurred in the context of any organisation.   **(10 marks)**

(ii)   Identify what steps the organisation could have taken to minimise the risk of each infringement, identified in part b(i).   **(5 marks)**

(Total = 20 marks)

SCENARIO QUESTIONS

Questions 50 to 64 cover a range of syllabus areas.

---

50 TBS – Accounting partnership

90 mins

TBS is a London-based accounting and audit partnership with 65 offices situated throughout Europe, the U.S., Asia and Southern Africa.

Knowledge Management (KM) Launch Presentation

The partner responsible for global IT, based in London, has been pressing for some time to install a Knowledge Management system throughout the firm. At the initial launch presentation, held during the annual partnership gathering that took place 18 months previously, the system was described thus:

'The purpose of the system is that all staff can access all knowledge in this firm. By indexing documents and through the extensive use of hypertext referencing any staff member can quickly find documentation on similar issues that have been faced and how solutions were found.'

'As soon as new legislation or GAAP emerges it can be shared over the KM system. For example if one of our tax practitioners discovers a new tax loophole the information will become available to every other tax practitioner. Ideas can be shared across offices and across teams – a good idea in the oil industry team in Texas could be just as useful to the oil team in Aberdeen, Abu Dhabi or Angola or to the chemical process team in New Delhi. With KM, the idea will travel automatically.'

KM system – development programme

There are a number of elements to the KM system and these have evolved over time (and are continuing to do so) starting in the week after the launch presentation. The programme has currently been implemented up to Stage 3 with the remaining stages due to come on stream over the next 18 months.

Stage 1 – E-mail subscriptions. TBS's research department produced research in the following headings 'Accounting/GAAP', 'Audit', 'Financial Services', 'Tax' and 'Market News'. Staff could subscribe to one of these services and would then receive e-mails on the subject that interested them. The number of e-mails depended on the activity of that research section. Most research sections provided output only when there was a change in legislation or regulation (eg new accounting standards that required analysis or comment). The market news e-mail was produced weekly, as was a tax e-mail that provided reminders of tax rates and allowances and other standard information in the absence of new rules or interpretations.

Stage 2 – Internet Site development. Through the TBS Internet site the company published internal information such as global directories of staff by area of expertise, partnership rules and so on.

Stage 3 – Links to external Internet sites. The TBS Internet site established a series of 'hot links' to external sites that provide information on accounting standards, tax legislation, professional practices etc. Many of these sites are subscription-based and only very limited information is available without substantial subscription payments.

Stage 4 – Client database. A searchable database of each client within the global firm is to be set up. There will be a number of searchable indexes within the database – accounting standards that apply, country of tax domicile, audit reports issued, fee details etc. By combing these indexes staff should be able to see the results of previous decisions.

Stage 5 – Document database. Through similar referencing structures as stage 4 a document database is to be set up showing engagement letters, tax correspondence, quality control checklists and all other documentation. These will be searchable and accessible by all staff within the global firm.

Management and staff reaction

Reaction by the senior partners was enthusiastic. They believed that the sharing of ideas from small local 'silos' to the entire firm would give a massive boost to the firm's skill level that would translate to improved client service and fee income. As one partner said 'When we were a partnership of 50 we could open our office door and shout for help or show off a great idea. This system will let us open the door and start shouting and sharing again.'

Other partners and staff have not been so enthusiastic. From the outset partners in the smaller offices were complaining that they were going to be forced to subsidise a new system that would only be used by the London office. Other partners have expressed concern that if the system can be hacked into, all of the firm's expertise and confidential client data could be lost to outsiders.

Scepticism has been rife. Many staff have said that the task – documenting, indexing and making accessible all knowledge within TBS – is impossible. Many, especially older, staff believe that the level of skill and depth of detailed knowledge that the best professionals have cannot be replicated by a computer.

As implementation of stages 4 and 5 near, this criticism is becoming more vocal. Senior partners in local firms are refusing to give access to client details, claiming that they have a professional duty of confidentiality to their clients. Most partners have expressed the opinion that they are not seeing major benefits from the system and so will not require that staff spend time referencing documents or creating hypertext links in work that they have done in order to make it searchable on the KM system.

Required

(a) Evaluate the actions taken so far by the partner responsible for IT in the development of the Knowledge Management system, and describe how buy-in to the rest of the implementation could be improved.

(20 marks)

(b) For the system to be of optimum benefit all offices must share all knowledge. Suggest how partners in smaller firms might be motivated to encourage staff in their control to contribute their knowledge to the KM system. **(8 marks)**

(c) Suggest security controls that can be used to prevent unauthorised access to TBS's global bank of electronically-held knowledge. Your answer should deal specifically with the issue of staff accessing the system from clients' premises. **(14 marks)**

(d) Describe what you understand by 'Knowledge Management' and suggest other applications for this type of technology. **(8 marks)**

(Total = 50 marks)

51 ARG International Airlines

90 mins

Background

ARG is an international airline operator, based in a central European country. It maintains a fleet of approximately 350 aircraft, and its core activity is to provide passenger and freight services to over 200 destinations worldwide.

ARG maintains offices in each country to which its aircraft fly. Each office provides the following services:

(a)   Information provision on the airline services offered by ARG, including flight times and destinations serviced by ARG.

(b)   Access to ARG's passenger and freight booking system for customers who wish to book either passenger or freight carriage services with ARG.

Each office also has access to ARG's confidential internal data systems which provide information on aircraft location, servicing history and the company's personnel. The latter includes salary details as well as staff locations.

Systems specification

To support its core business activity, ARG recently invested in a high-speed international WAN. This system enabled ARG to transfer large volumes of data relating to its operations between its 200 offices worldwide with a minimum of delay. The systems specification for the new ARG system was quite rigorous. The specification included the following requirements:

(a)   The basic infrastructure of the WAN, including such items as the cabling and communication hardware, had to have an expected life of 10 years.

(b)   Computer chips and other similar system elements had to be upgradable as technology improved.

(c)   The entire system had to be easily upgradable with a fixed capital amount being allocated for this upgrade each year. System upgrades were not to exceed this capital amount under any circumstances.

ARG also assumed that its WAN infrastructure and its core business as an international airline operator would remain unchanged for the next 10 years.

Very few equipment suppliers were willing to provide this level of commitment to the system. Finally, a small but financially stable company called AP Ltd successfully tendered for the contract, even though some of AP Ltd's systems were not industry standard.

Systems implementation

The actual systems changeover and implementation were performed with few problems. The staff at ARG were using the new system efficiently within one week of implementation.

It should be noted that the Board of ARG made the decision to invest in the WAN on the basis that the company must be at the forefront of the use of technology to support its core business activities. This strategy is seen as being essential to produce a sustainable competitive advantage in the airline industry.

Post-implementation review

In the three months since the system was installed, ARG has seen significant increases in productivity and levels of customer service. The investment has therefore been judged to be a success.

During the post-implementation review of the system, it was found that the WAN had considerable excess capacity to take additional network traffic. ARG's initial forecast showed that it would use only one third of the capacity of the network in its first two years of operation. Even optimistic forecasts of network traffic growth indicate that this excess capacity would not be used by ARG for at least another 7 years. The Board of ARG therefore asked the IT Director to consider ways of providing additional revenue to the company from this excess capacity.

After detailed consideration of the problem, the IT Director reported back to the Board. The main proposal was to make this excess capacity available to other companies which required a WAN but either did not have the money, or the strategy to build a WAN for themselves. Should the proposal be accepted, then it is expected that these other companies would require:

(a) A guarantee of the level of service that they can expect from ARG, including access rights to the WAN and delivery times of information across the network.

(b) Internet access to transfer data to customers and receive information back from customers.

(c) A guarantee of security of data from both non-ARG WAN users and from the staff of ARG itself.

The IT Director considers that ARG could provide this service whilst at the same time giving a positive contribution to profits. The Board has therefore decided to accept the IT Director's proposal and make the required additional investment to provide the additional services noted above. This decision was made against the advice of a minority of Board members who saw potential conflicts between the core business strategy and the IT strategy of ARG.

Required

(a) (i) Explain why large companies should have an IT strategy. You should make reference to ARG's situation in your explanation. **(8 marks)**

(ii) Comment on the decision of ARG to diversify away from its core business by making the WAN services available to other users. Explain the potential advantages and disadvantages this will provide for the company. **(9 marks)**

(b) Explain the characteristics that information provided across the ARG WAN, to ARG offices, must have. Show why these characteristics are relevant to ARG. **(10 marks)**

(c) Comment on any problems that will arise in ARG's IT systems from the decision not to upgrade ARG's basic IT infrastructure for the next ten years. Explain any impacts this will have on the core business of ARG. **(7 marks)**

(d) (i) Evaluate the potential dangers and benefits, both to ARG and to its potential WAN users, of providing Internet access. **(10 marks)**

(ii) Explain how ARG can provide adequate data security to the companies which are paying to use its WAN. **(6 marks)**

(You should consider the potential security problems posed by other WAN customers, by ARG's airline customers and by the employees of ARG itself.) **(Total = 50 marks)**

52 Orion Insurance

108 mins

- **The Company** – for many years, the business focus of Orion has been selling computers to medium-sized companies. With the recent decline in business from these organisations, the Chief Executive Officer (CEO) of Orion, David Gray, decided to shift the business focus from the commercial to the personal market.

- **Sales Department** – since all the Orion customers are business users, the current sales channel relies solely on the sales team. Sales generated are put into the sales database. These are called the 'hard' orders. To ensure the immediate product availability for anticipated contracts, the sales department also put estimated orders into the sales database. The sales department's database makes no distinction between hard and estimated orders.

- **Planning Department** – the planning department checks into the sales database to find out the different configurations and the quantity required for different types of configurations. Since all the customers are business customers, the configurations are standard. The planning team estimates the number of RAMs, video cards, sound cards, CPUs, motherboards, monitors, hard disks, mouse and operating systems needed for the next two months. Purchase orders are placed to buy the parts to build the required computers as reflected by the sales department's database. The planner orders 2 to 3% spare parts, as some parts may be dead on arrival. However, the planning department must strive to minimise the parts stock kept by Orion to avoid the tie-up of capital and to protect the company from having obsolete parts.

- **Assembly Department** – the assembly department builds the required number of computers per planners' order.

- **Engineering Department** – before the computers are shipped to the customers, the engineering team tests the computers and keeps track of the defective parts in the engineering database.

- **Shipping Department** – to lower the cost of shipping, the shipping department ships the computers to each customer in batches.

Problem – the CEO recognises that the business process for the company is not ready to handle the consumer market and is asking your company to re-engineer the processes and to develop software to go with the processes. The new process should be able to handle the sales generated through the Internet and telephone sales through a free number.

He is also keen to establish the information requirements for the re-engineered company.

Required

(a)   (i)   Express the real-world problem situation using a Soft System Methodology rich picture.   **(6 marks)**

(ii)   The root definition of this problem domain is given as following:

'Orion will acquire 30% of the West Midland's consumer market by focusing on catering to elite/sophisticated computer buyers and by providing superior high-end products and service.'

Support the above root definition with CATWOE, and identify the CATWOE elements in Orion.

(6 marks)

(iii)   Build a conceptual model for Orion and explain the major benefits of conceptual models.   **(8 marks)**

(b)   David Gray realises that to develop the information systems plan, the management team must have a clear understanding of the long and short-term information requirements for Orion.

In a report to the CEO, describe how both the enterprise analysis approach and the critical success factors approach are used to establish the organisational information required for the new market. Compare and contrast the strengths and weaknesses of two approaches from Orion's point of view.   **(20 marks)**

(c)   Identify how the Internet can be used for e-commerce and put forward reasons why Orion should not abandon its traditional business model to rely on e-commerce totally.   **(20 marks)**

(Total = 60 marks)

53 Question with helping hand: The SI Organisation   108 mins

The SI Organisation builds and sells computers in 35 different countries. A customer can order a computer by telephone, mail order or the Internet. The computer is then built to the customer's specification using parts manufactured by SI or supplied from one of 86 different suppliers. The completed computer is then shipped to the customer and installed by SI technicians. The whole process takes between 5 and 7 days.

Following installation, the customer is given access to the country-specific support system of SI. This comprises a country-specific Internet site containing detailed information on installation, errors with SI computers and answers to Frequently Asked Questions. The errors database is the same as that used by SI staff, so customers are effectively being given access to SI's own systems. Technical staff are also available to provide human assistance if customers cannot find the answer to a query within the other support systems.

Databases are maintained in each country and contain information on the different customers, types of computer sold, queries raised and solutions to those queries, along with standard accounting and financial data.

No other computer manufacturer provides this type of service. Most other manufacturers prefer to sell computers via retail stores on the assumption that customers wish to 'try out' the computers prior to purchase. This strategy of differentiation from competitors has provided SI with a substantial market share, along with significant profits.

Customers are prepared to pay for the enhanced service. SI's distribution costs are slightly less than those of its competitors although selling prices are the same, providing additional contribution for SI.

SI organisation structure

Within each country, the SI organisation is run as a separate company. Each company has its own unique information system, resulting in a range of hardware, software and database formats being used. Although this is unusual, the philosophy of SI has been to allow each country to establish systems to meet its own individual requirements. This has resulted in an extremely successful SI company in each country, at the expense of worldwide compatibility.

Similarly, local suppliers supply parts for SI computers, so the SI company in that country can form good working relationships with the suppliers. Again, this has worked to the benefit of SI, as the quality of parts supplied has consistently exceeded expectations and resulted in fewer hardware failures in SI computers compared to other brands.

Each SI company is therefore run as a separate business unit. The head office of SI is located on a small island close to Western Europe. Budgets for each SI company are set after discussions with head office. Apart from this, as long as each company meets budget, no other intervention by SI's head office is considered necessary.

There is a centralised R&D unit, which provides model specifications for new SI computers to all locations. This unit employs 75 research and development specialists. Their main activities include:

* Research into existing SI products in order to make them more reliable and economical to run
* Amending existing SI products incorporating minor design changes such as larger hard disks or additional RAM
* Reviewing current developments in computing
* Building and testing new products
* Providing specifications for new SI computers to the individual SI companies in each country

Information is provided by the R&D unit on a regular basis to sales and other departments in SI. However, the information flow is one way. The R&D unit does not have access to the sales staff or databases within each SI company.

Recent developments

In the last few years, the sales pattern of SI has shifted significantly away from individual customers purchasing one or two computers, to larger organisations purchasing up to 1,000 computers at a time. These requirements cannot always be met by the production capacity in one SI company, so orders are transferred to other SI companies in other countries.

Many customers also request additional support, including 24-hour telephone hotlines and access to worldwide databases of errors and information, which SI currently cannot provide.

The Chief Executive of SI recently made a decision to provide this support, effectively authorising a worldwide network to be put in place to link all SI companies. All accounting, customer, financial, support and similar databases are to be linked within one year. Failure to meet this target may result in significant loss of sales if the larger corporate customers move to other suppliers.

Required

(a) Evaluate the current use of IT within the SI organisation, clearly identifying:

   (i)   The strengths and weaknesses of the decentralised systems.   **(12 marks)**
   (ii) The problems of integrating the systems into one worldwide system.   **(8 marks)**

Helping hand. You should review the scenario information and from this, and syllabus knowledge, identify relevant points to evaluate. Your answers should reflect the issues within the SI organisation.

(i)   *Strengths*

Customer requirements
Direct contact with local suppliers
Budgets
System breakdown
Local configurations
High staff morale each country
More creativity allowed
Other relevant points

Weaknesses

Duplication
Sharing information
Cost
Staff support
Duplication of information
Customer service
Stock holding
Other relevant points

(ii)   *Issues with integrating decentralised systems*

Different standards of data and database formats
Resistance from and de-motivation of staff
System set-up
Cultural issues
Customer service
Possible lost business if supplies delayed from another country
Delay in obtaining information
Timeframe
Cost
Be careful however not to spend more time answering the parts of the question than justified by the marks on offer.

(b)   Evaluate the current information system for the R&D unit in SI. Include in your answer an outline of an appropriate information support system to enable R&D and sales staff to communicate with each other, justifying your choice of system.   **(20 marks)**

(c)   (i)   Explain Porter's concepts of differentiation and cost leadership.   **(4 marks)**

        (ii)   Using Porter's differentiation and cost leadership concepts as a framework for your answer, discuss whether the recent decision of the Chief Executive of SI will detract from the overall customer-focus strategy of SI.   **(16 marks)**

(Total = 60 marks)

54 Gravy Train

108 mins

Gravy Train is a specialist training company offering traditional tuition to banking and accountancy students. The company was formed nine years ago when Jo Stafford became disillusioned with the training company that she worked for and decided to form her own company.

Jo has three full-time lecturers working for her, together with a number of freelancers and also employs two administrative assistants to handle inquiries, take course bookings, issue joining instructions, photocopy lecture notes, and book freelancers. Basic accounting transactions are automated using a stand-alone PC.

Students attend day-release classes, weekend courses, and some evening classes although recently there has been a decline in all of them. The courses provided are of a high quality and pass rates are well above average, although she does have occasional problems finding freelancers to cover some of the specialist subjects. Teaching and staffing pressures mean that the marking and return of student's work is often late, and there is difficulty in providing support to students experiencing difficulty outside of the classroom.

Up to now, Jo has been happy with a steady income rather than aiming for rapid growth. However, the decline in traditional business in terms of evening classes and day release students is causing concern, and the news that another finance and accounting training company is to open an office nearby is seen as a major threat.

A major strategic planning review has recently been completed, which identified not only that the existing market is likely to decline, but also that to maintain their position in this market, Gravy Train will need to differentiate its service.

From articles that she has read and advice that she has been given Jo realises that there is also great potential for distance learning in both the UK and overseas using on-line technologies.

The business strategy has identified some objectives – they include the following:

- The company should have 600 on-line distance learners by 2007.
- All students registered for traditional classes should have on-line support by 2005.
- The quality of service must show an improvement.

Required

(a)   Explain why Gravy Train should develop an IS/IT strategy and the problems that are likely to arise if the organisation does not develop an IS/IT strategy.   **(20 marks)**

(b)   (i)   Explain how the use of critical success factors (CSFs) can help to determine the information requirements of an organisation.   **(12 marks)**

        (ii)   Describe how critical success factors and performance indicators can be used to measure whether the objective to improve the quality of service is being met.   **(8 marks)**

(c)   Describe how Gravy Train can use on-line technology strategically to differentiate its service and gain a competitive advantage.   **(20 marks)**

(Total = 60 marks)

55 Pattersons Electrical Suppliers (Pilot paper)

108 mins

Pattersons Electrical Suppliers own a chain of retail outlets throughout the city and surrounding area. In recent years they have expanded these outlets from their one original store to the current seven stores. The head office is based on the original site. The business originated as a cash and carry company supplying the public with all types of electrical appliances, varying from light bulbs to fridge freezers. Electrical goods supply is a very competitive business; Pattersons have to compete with all the national suppliers that tend to dominate the market. In order to compete successfully they have adopted a business strategy of fast turnover and low profit margins coupled with a high customer service level.

Each store holds approximately nine thousand item lines; the majority of the smaller items are on display in the sales area, a selection of the larger appliances are also on display, this is complemented by a variety of brochures that carry information about the whole range of products. Experienced sales personnel are available to assist customers in their selection of appropriate goods. Following selection and payment of goods, customers tend to 'carry' the smaller items from the store; larger items are delivered within forty-eight hours. Each store has its own warehouse that is replenished when necessary from the company's main storage depot; the main storage depot's inventory control system is managed by head office.

Every store has its own computer system to control the day-to-day business; all of these are linked to the head office system. Information technology and information systems (IT/IS) development strategy has gone hand-in-hand with the business strategy that has enabled the dramatic expansion of the business. The IT centre is based in the head office and offers support to all of the satellite stores.

The Chairman and the Board of Directors recently employed the services of a business management consultant; the major aim of the exercise was to aid the development of a business strategy for the medium-to-long term. At a recent meeting of the board, the directors discussed the consultant's report. One of the recommendations stated 'Pattersons have previously been successful in automation and rationalisation of its business processes, maybe it's time for the business to consider reengineering in its future long-term business strategy'. This statement resulted in a heated discussion and disagreement, so much so that it was eventually decided to commission an internal study that would report back to the board at a later date.

A further recommendation involved the development of an integrated inventory distribution system. Currently when goods reach their re-order level in the individual stores and the main storage depot cannot supply the goods, they are purchased from suppliers even though other stores have more than adequate levels of the goods. It was decided to conduct a feasibility study, including a cost-benefit analysis before the proposed project would be given support.

Overall the consultant's report was encouraging, generally indicating a healthy business position from a management perspective. One point of concern was the recent implementation of a company-wide computerised shift scheduling system, for the shop workers, warehouse personnel and support staff. This system basically involves the scheduling of shift patterns and hours worked by the individuals. Previously individuals negotiated their working shifts with middle management within the bounds of certain parameters, number of shifts per week, maximum number of hours etc. There is resistance to the imposition of the system, thus the system is not fully utilised. To work successfully the system requires a great deal of manual intervention and updating. Generally the system is viewed as a failure by both middle management and the staff affected.

Required

(a)   Currently Patterson's computer-based systems applications portfolio predominantly consists of in-house business systems. They are considering expanding this portfolio to include the 'new' web-based technologies and systems.

'There is one major change in information technology on whose importance business executives, academics and technologists all agree. It is the explosive growth of the Internet and related technologies and applications and their impact on business, society and information technology. The Internet is changing the way businesses are operated and people work and how information technology supports business operation and end-user work activities' O'Brien (1999).

Describe and discuss the impact of the above quote with reference to the case study where appropriate in terms of:

(i)   Business-to-Consumer commerce (Internet).   **(10 marks)**

(ii)   Business-to-Business applications (extranet).   **(8 marks)**

(iii)   Internal business processes (intranet).   **(7 marks)**

(b)   A statement in the scenario states: 'Information technology and information systems (IT/IS) development strategy has gone hand-in-hand with the business strategy, this has enabled the dramatic expansion of the business.'

(i) Discuss the implications and importance of this statement in respect of Pattersons and other businesses, if they wish to survive and succeed in the twenty-first century market place. **(10 marks)**

Mr Smith, the business consultant, claimed, 'Pattersons have previously been successful in automation and rationalisation of its business processes, maybe it's time for the business to consider re-engineering in its future long term business strategy'.

(ii) Explain in terms of business processes what he meant by the terms: automation, rationalisation and reengineering, sometimes referred to as 'automate, informate and transformate'. (Give examples where appropriate in relation to the case study.) **(10 marks)**

(c) In the scenario it was stated that the implementation of the computerised shift scheduling system had 'failed'. Recent research suggests that IT investment has emerged as a high-risk, hidden-cost process. At least 20% of such spend is wasted, and between 30-40% of IS projects realise no benefits whatsoever, however measured, failures and rejections are commonplace.

Discuss the reasons for the apparent high levels of failure in the implementation of information systems. Make reference to the computerised shift scheduling system recently installed into Pattersons. **(15 marks)**

(Total = 60 marks)

56 Ancient World (12/01)   108 mins

(The 'current date' for this scenario is December 2001)

'Ancient World' (AW) is a mail order book company that specialises in books on archaeology, particularly related to pre-history. The company is organised on two sites. The company is based in a rural area; the distribution centre is situated near enough to a main road to enable delivery and distribution of stock, and the administrative centre is in a similar situation just one and a half miles away on the same road. Both sites are a long way from any urban centre.

AW employs 84 staff to perform all the administrative and packing tasks. It has a catalogue of 2300 titles, of which 75% are usually in stock. The operations director has set a target of 1800 titles on their list, of which 95% would be always in stock or available for dispatch within twenty-four hours. This target has been set because of the increasing problems with regards to the 'guaranteed' dispatch within 48 hours of receipt of an order. This strategy has caused concern with the board of directors who previously had encouraged growth in the number of titles available. Details of titles, stockholding and orders are held on a specialist database called 'Book Manager'.

Business has grown from a turnover of £2,800,000 in 1992 to £11,000,000 in 2000. Much of the business is repeat business and consists of major retailers. Regular customers of AW are placed on a permanent mailing list, and are sent every updated catalogue. Some customers, such as retailers, schools and colleges, are 'Account Customers', who have a discount awarded to them. Because of the overheads, AW keeps the number of Account Customers low.

Orders, received via post or fax, are normally packed and dispatched within 24 hours, unless the titles are out of stock.

In 1998, AW experimented with taking on-line orders over the Internet. The experiment has been quite successful, with 5% of their business being carried out electronically. The only difference in the operation is that the orders are printed off each day at 15.00 hours and packed later the same afternoon. The packers do not notice any difference between orders from the different modes.

Currently the site receives 200 – 220 hits per day; AW would like to see 1000+ hits per day. They have bought a good domain name, which increases the hit rate. They have recently installed software which manages 'cookies', so that they can monitor customers who order on-line.

There has been an unexpected side effect of this development: AW have become aware that prospective customers are studying their catalogue to identify titles, and then buying from companies such as Amazon and BOL, who are selling the same titles at greatly reduced prices. The prices from Amazon and BOL are lower than AW themselves have to pay for the books. The directors are contemplating their response to this.

The directors have produced three options:

(i)   Withdraw their presence from the Internet and revert to the traditional mail order practice they have built up.

(ii)   Attempt to compete with the rival companies on price.

(iii)   Buying the rights to as many titles as they can and branch out into publishing, so that the competition must buy from AW rather than undercut them.

At a recent board meeting the directors briefly discussed the three options. Following this discussion the managing director suggested that, before making any final decisions concerning long-term business plans or strategies, a full analysis of the current situation should be conducted. The newly appointed information technology manager supported this motion, stating, 'The company has expended during the last five years due to customer demand for our products. The market is changing, now is an appropriate time to take stock of the company's current position. Following an analysis the board will be better informed to make business plans and identify technology requirements to support the plans.' The IT manager was given the task of performing the analysis and reporting back to the next board meeting with his results. The board has particularly asked him to concentrate on positioning the business to be able to develop opportunities for e-commerce.

At the same board meeting the sales director commented on a major perceived problem. He stated that it was becoming very difficult, if not impossible, for traditional companies such as AW to compete with the new trend of Virtual companies.

Brief historic review of the development of Ancient World's technological infrastructure

1980 Company founded. Limited number of titles aimed at a niche market. Fifteen staff supported by paper based systems, electronic typewriters, orders received by post and telephone.

1985 Due to the success of the business more staff employed, introduction of twenty stand-alone personal computers. Functions include, basic office software, desktop publishing, spreadsheets and accounting software.

1987 Due to the increase in business and limitations of the building space on the original site. AW purchased another site in the same locality. The second site housed the management and administrative personnel.

1988 Implementation of a stock recording system, this was purely a system that recorded the inventory levels of stock and produced periodic lists of stock levels. All inputs to the system were manual.

1993 10 more PC's were purchased, each site purchased a local area network.

1994 A new IT department was created bringing the existing IT/IS staff formally together. A business analyst headed this department supported by two analyst programmers and two operations personnel. The original IT staff were recruited from within the company.

1995 An integrated stock recording software package was purchased and implemented. The package used an Oracle database as its platform. This package included modules that performed the basic stock control function, produced purchase orders, produced various management reports and integrated with the existing accounts package.

1997 The PC's and LAN's were updated working in a Windows NT environment.

1998 The company experimented with the internet, establishing its own site and receiving orders via the net. The electronic ordering system is not integrated with the inventory management system. No further development has taken place.

1995 Present (which is December 2001). The company has encountered problems with maintaining permanent IT staff. The target of ten specialists has rarely been met. Currently the department has eight personnel; five permanent and three contract staff.

2001 The current date is December 2001. The company has recently appointed an IT director.

Summary: During the last twenty years the IS/IT infrastructure has been developed to support the business growth and the demands that this has created.

Required

(a) (i)   Construct a strengths, weaknesses, opportunities, threats (SWOT) analysis for Ancient World using the information given in the scenario. **(8 marks)**

     (ii) Select the elements from the SWOT analysis produced in (a) above, which will make most contribution towards the development of an information systems strategy, particularly supporting the early introduction of e-commerce, within Ancient World. For each element chosen, explain its significance in the formulation of the IS strategy. **(12 marks)**

(b)

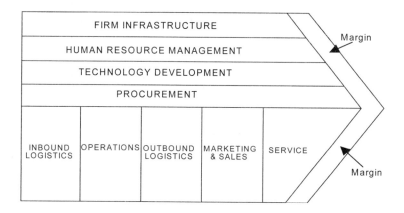

Figure 1: The Value Chain (From Porter, M. Competitive Advantage)

     (i)   For each primary activity in Porter's Value Chain (Inbound logistics; Operations; Outbound logistics; Marketing and Sales; Service) briefly describe the activity and suggest an appropriate information system that could support the activity within Ancient World. **(10 marks)**

     (ii) From the point of view of the Board of Directors, discuss the impact of the need to develop a range of new IS systems to support e-commerce on the four support activities in Porter's Value Chain (Infrastructure; HR management; technology development; procurement). **(10 marks)**

(c) A general framework for combining the development of business strategy and information systems strategy can be shown as a three-stage process:

1   Where we are   First stage
2   Where we want to be   Second stage
3   Going to get there   Third stage

The first stage, 'Where we are', is a detailed analysis of the current position in terms of both business position and information technology position, possibly a SWOT analysis output.

The second stage is concerned with the development of a business strategy/plan, 'Where we want to be', and leads to the development/design of the target system. The business objectives and constraints will drive the information systems strategy, which should be developed simultaneously.

The third stage, 'Going to get there', is the practical development and application of the two strategies.

Required

     (i)   Discuss the relationship between the business strategy and the information systems strategy in the second stage, 'Where we want to be'. Your answer should include the major components of an information systems plan or strategy. With reference to Ancient World where appropriate. **(15 marks)**

(ii)   During the development stage, 'Going to get there', there may be a requirement to review and make changes to the overall business and information system strategies. Briefly discuss the reasons why these changes may be required.

(5 marks)

(Total = 60 marks)

57 Moonshine Corporation (12/02)   108 mins

In order to understand the emergence of Moonshine Corporation's current IT strategy as well as the environment in which new systems are under development, it is necessary to look at Moonshine Corporation and its market-place to establish some cogent terms of reference.

The company was formed in 1930 as a City life assurance office. Throughout the years Moonshine Corporation established itself as an innovative provider of life assurance, pensions and investment products, primarily through independent financial advice to customers. By the 1980s, the market had been opened up to increased competition as the government of the day sought to increase the private sector provision of financial services and decrease the reliance on state benefits. Product innovation saw Moonshine Corporation dominate the small self-administered pensions market-place in the 1980s and gain huge successes in the investment market with the establishment of the first distribution fund – a medium to low risk, balanced, investment bond.

A number of challenges arose in the late 1980s, which saw new business growth levels difficult to maintain and business profitability steadily declining. As well as unstable stock market conditions in the 1990s, compared to huge growth throughout the 1980s, the industry was also beset with massive regulation. Moonshine Corporation was therefore in a position where it had to fight harder for a share of a shrinking marketplace, just to stand still. This could be achieved in terms of product innovation, but market research indicated that areas of contention within the industry were those concerned with servicing the customer (policy holder or independent financial adviser) accurately and with greater speed. The customer had become 'king' and was more assertive and selective.

Moonshine Corporation can therefore be seen to have been product focussed and, while this encouraged innovative product design, the mechanisms were not in place to provide adequate customer supporting a way that could be seen as competitive. It was apparent that Moonshine Corporation would have to adapt its organisational structure (re-engineer) if it were to remain competitive within challenging market conditions.

The Customer Review Requirement study (CRR) conducted in 2001 identified a requirement to move from line processing departments into customer servicing teams. Currently Moonshine Corporation's organisational processes and its IT infrastructure are product focussed, rather than customer focussed; this results in a very bureaucratic process when providing customer service. The conclusions of the CRR study recommend the following objectives: to develop a flatter organisation structure, whilst providing speedy, accurate customer support. Teams will be made up of case managers, each of whom would be responsible for processing a case through to its conclusion. Customers would have one point of contact with the organisation with which to develop a customer/insurer relationship. Staff will become multi-faceted or cross– functional. The cross-functional nature of CRR work-roles, as well as the resulting flatter organisation structure should encourage a move away from some of the current very bureaucratic processes and structures within the organisation.

CRR is seen as a radical development within the industry and is viewed as a vital part of a successful vision of customer oriented change. This move to a customer centred focus is widely viewed within the financial sector as imperative in terms of future requirements, thus all of Moonshine Corporation's major competitors are considering ways to meet this requirement.

This change in business requirement cannot be supported by Moonshine Corporation's existing information systems and the technical infrastructure. Moonshine Corporation's product focussed mainframe information systems environment originated in the early 1970s. It was updated throughout the late '80s and early '90s with the purchase of several IBM mainframes. During this period Moonshine Corporation was viewed as one of the leaders within the financial sector with regard to technological innovation and support systems. Currently the mainframe environment is robust. Many of its original legacy systems are still in place. The system serves the product but is unable to serve the customer support centres. Several product databases exist with separate architectures and are updated by independent overnight batch runs. A product database may support several million customers. An outline feasibility study concluded that a move to a successful CRR solution would require the design and development of a Common Interfacing System (CIS). Such a system would allow case mangers to interrogate the product databases using customer identifiers, which would enable the managers to receive full information on customer details. The existing IT personnel could not undertake a project of this proportion.

The historic development reflected an environment where management was hardware oriented (move to an IBM mainframe) and the software development was facilitated fortuitously as the result of a new hardware platform. The development environment was not always in tune with the business that deployed it, and can therefore be seen to display a technological determinist character. All the current hardware and communications infrastructure maintenance is outsourced to a local vendor. Two engineers are permanently on site.

One consequence of the purchase of the IBM mainframe in the mid 1980s was the introduction of the IBM PCs into the user environment. Many within the 'user community' began to see benefits of using the stand-alone capacity of desktop PCs. Word processing and basic graphics packages enabled reports, memos and customer service letters to be presented in a more effective format. The use of stand-alone PCs in user departments had a twofold impact.

(1)   A considerable amount of data redundancy within the Moonshine Corporation. This situation emerged as departments were encouraged to be profit centres, responsible for their own budgets and in competition over output, turnover and bonus rates.

(2)   In terms of the delivery of these applications to the user, ie the hardware and communications environment. As user locations' data requirements were expressed and expanded, access to localised databases and applications became an issue. A number of locations were equipped with LANs on IBM Token Ring networks, which led to an expansion in the number of PCs as servicing areas went towards a workstation environment. This enables users to access the mainframe and use graphics/spreadsheet/word-processing applications whilst interrogating shared local data, such as policy tracking systems and other MIS applications. These requirements meant that desktop machines required more memory, more disk space and better processing speed. Moonshine Corporation was therefore committed to reacting to these localised business requirements, as well as trying to achieve a corporate hardware and software policy.

This corporate reaction to the business channels in the provision of hardware and software can be seen as adopting an organisational choice perspective. This is because technology was being seen as a useful tool that could be manipulated to carry out business requirements. What was required was a vision of where the business was headed and what distributed systems and hardware could support this. In hindsight, senior management believe that the systems infrastructure should have been considered along with business applications requirements so that technology could have been future-proofed to some degree, instead of continually reacting to business requirements, thus incurring costs.

An IT Strategy Study began in 2000 with the aims of providing sufficient data to support large scale technology developments, as well as setting up corporate criteria of requirements for any systems development for approval by General Management. This would therefore link strategic business objectives with strategic IT objectives. One important offshoot of the strategy study was the way in which the business and systems elements were to be united. In order to understand the way in which strategic systems were to fulfil business requirements, technologists were required to understand, at the highest level, cost benefit analysis and the markets that Moonshine Corporation were in or were moving towards. At the same time, General Management needed to understand the important transaction processes and data requirements in order to direct the annual budgeting of expenditure. This had been reflected in the corporate trend in system development being controlled at top-level management, whilst IS managers take a more prominent role within the business.

In terms of overall requirements for systems development, it was agreed that systems development must fulfil the following requirements. Firstly that systems must be flexible in order to support a changing business environment. The second requirement identified that there be an annual budgeting basis of expenditure. The study concluded that IT projects would therefore need to be kept small, with a maximum duration of two years, and hitting specific business targets.

QUESTIONS

The IT Division is currently looking at devolving its roles and responsibilities into the business areas in order to provide closer service to the customer. One possibility is that the division is divided into business system centres within customer services and distribution areas. Within its remit is the possible development of customer call centres and the expansion of electronic data interchange. An important aspect is ensuring that the business process provides the best customer service in the most profitable way. The technology must therefore be flexible enough to support these objectives.

Currently a self-employed sales force services ninety percent of customers. There is a current business plan that will enable the sales force to purchase, rent or hire a laptop computer from Moonshine Corporation. These laptops will enable the sales force to provide the customer with instant information concerning policy, investments etc when they are considering purchasing any of the company's products. The initial project suggests that the latest product information will be downloaded periodically onto these laptops. On a daily basis new customer information, details, and amendments will be uploaded on to the company's mainframe from the sales personnel.

Required

(a) (i) Construct a Strengths, Weaknesses, Opportunities and Threats (SWOT) analysis of Moonshine Corporation's position with regard to the Customer Review Requirement (CRR) study. **(8 marks)**

(ii) With reference to the CRR study, why is a SWOT analysis useful in developing an IS strategy in conjunction with a business strategy. **(12 marks)**

(b) The IT manager has to determine how to source the development of the Common Interfacing Systems (CIS); she has requested that you, as her deputy, produce a report. The report should include a general overview, an outline of the possible alternatives available (eg total outsourcing, multiple/selective sourcing, and insourcing) with reference to the project, and conclude with your recommendation as to the most viable alternative.

Write the report to the IT manager. **(20 marks)**

(c) A method for the development of IS strategies can be described as having three legs. These are: Business led – top down emphasis, Infrastructure led – bottom up emphasis, Mixed – where the emphasis is inside out.

(i) Briefly describe each of the three legs: business led, infrastructure led and mixed. **(6 marks)**

(ii) With reference to the Moonshine Corporation, identify where each of the three legs has been used in the development of their information systems. **(9 marks)**

(ii) 'One of these legs may be dominant at any one time but all may/should be employed, since the three IS strategy planning approaches are not mutually exclusive.'

Discuss the above statement with reference to the Moonshine Corporation. **(5 marks)**

(Total = 60 marks)

58 TEAC (6/03)   **108 mins**

TEAC Plc has 74 department stores located around the UK. Some of these are situated in high streets or in town centre shopping precincts and others are located in out-of-town retail parks. TEAC Plc is a holding company trading under its own name. It also currently owns four subsidiaries, which consist of several retail outlets. During the past twelve years TEAC has acquired seven independent retail outlets, three of which have been sold. This practice of buying and selling retail outlets has been integral to TEAC's business plans for the past twenty years. The subsidiaries tend to specialise in specific areas of the retail trade eg Menswear, Ladieswear.

At the hub of TEAC's Information Technology (IT) infrastructure is a group of three IBM AS/400 minicomputers. These are located in the Headquarters (HQ) and are connected to the stores via a packet switched Wide Area Network (WAN). Each store has a number of NCR point-of-sales (POS) units connected to an NCR Tower UNIX system in the back office. This collects sales data from the POS terminals and uploads it to the central system overnight. Other operations in the store are undertaken on terminals connected through to the central system. Some of the larger stores have expanded back-office computer facilities that allow them to process sales data and update a local stock file. This gives local managers the opportunity to generate information locally and request overrides to the ordering system. This approach encourages the duplication of data but gives the large retail outlets some local management autonomy.

The table below is a summary of the historic development of IT within TEAC.

1960s	Use of an IBM mainframe computer for basic management accounting tasks.
Late 1960s –1970s	Implemented computerised warehousing system designed by a newly formed IT department. Introduction of basic management information systems.
1980s	Introduction of Electronic Point-Of-Sale (EPOS) systems into the retail outlets, supporting accurate sales reporting and stock control. Accompanied by the gradual, un-coordinated, introduction of Personal Computers into HQ.
1990s	Increasing exploitation of information made available by EPOS in marketing and management decision making. The introduction of Local Area Networks (LANS) and Wide Area Networks (WANS). Increasing the development of large corporate relational databases accompanied by downsizing from mainframe to networked minicomputers. The introduction of Electronic Data Interchange (EDI) and Electronic Funds Transfer (EFT) systems.
Mid 1990s–	The introduction of web based technologies. The implementation of a data warehousing system.

The buying and merchandising departments based at HQ work on Personal Computers (PCs), accessing the AS/400s by use of a bridge from a token ring Local Area Network (LAN). HQ provides information to TEAC's four main regional distribution centres geographically dispersed across the country. Major applications at HQ are spread between the three AS/400s.

Historically all the major software developments have been in-house projects. The in-store side of the business relies heavily on custom-written code. Some general packages have been purchased but all applications relating to stock and sales management remain very much internally developed and maintained. There are over one hundred full time employees in the IT department. Specification, development and acceptance of new systems follow a methodology that has evolved in-house, a form of structured systems analysis and design methodology. IS projects are normally initiated by the IS steering committee, formed some fifteen years ago and consisting of senior managers drawn from the operational divisions and chaired by the IS director. This committee appears to be comfortable with the structured methodology approach. Many have the view, 'if it's not broken don't mend it'. This committee reports to the board, where approval must be given for projects that exceed a predetermined amount of financial investment. Smaller projects can be authorised by the IS steering committee.

When TEAC acquired its subsidiaries during the last twelve years, they also acquired different IS systems. The company strategy has been to gradually install the same management systems across all the subsidiaries. Currently all of the outlets have similar systems, although each subsidiary can develop systems to meet its specific requirements. All subsidiaries are maintained as separate entities. TEAC maintains five systems simultaneously, one corporate system plus one for each subsidiary.

In the past, the TEAC company culture has been to control its IT operation entirely in-house. This has been justified partly by the internally perceived uniqueness of its warehouse and showroom operations, partly by concerns over confidentiality of information and competitive edge and partly by the belief that an internal IT department will have a better understanding of the needs of the business.

The Board of Directors is committed to the exploitation of IT and indeed the group was among the first to bring electronic point-of-sale technology into the retail outlets. The newly appointed IT director believes that the business management need to become more involved in and take responsibility for, the IT infrastructure. She often refers to the term of 'system ownership' where senior management in the operational business division most affected by the system will take the responsibility for the commissioning of an information system. Currently, authority for the development of information systems is delegated to the IT department via the IS steering committee and there is a shortage of user input and commitment to new projects. Coordination of information system projects are generally controlled by the IT department based around a promised delivery date and the actual implementation of a system.

The IT department has recently been criticised for the size of its budget, its overall effectiveness and value for the business. During the past few years several IS projects have been over budget, delivered late and perceived as not meeting the original business requirements. One project was completely abandoned after one year of development, resulting in a substantial financial loss. These criticisms have come at board level from several of the directors responsible for specific functional areas. The IT director initially reacted to the criticism by explaining the strategic importance of information systems and its central role in the effective running of the business. She then commented on the growing demand for new or enhanced information systems throughout the corporation. These demands were outstripping the resources of her department, which has recently encountered problems with maintaining its staffing levels.

The IT department recently conducted a gap analysis study. The findings of the study supported the IT director's fears concerning supply and demand of information systems throughout the corporation. Currently the results of the study are not widely available as the study was commissioned by and within the IT department.

These explanations did not alleviate the criticisms. Currently the IT department is an independent cost centre financially supported by each of the functional areas. The amount of financial support paid by each functional area to the central IT department was historically calculated on the number of personnel, the number of transactions processed per area, the number of terminals and the number of outlets etc. The IT director has volunteered to produce a report for the next board meeting outlining alternative methods of financially supporting the IT department. The report will outline how the IT department's costs can be allocated fairly across the functional areas and the different roles the IT department can take within the company.

A further area of concern expressed at the last board meeting, directed towards the IT director, was the lack of knowledge of recent systems developments in certain parts of the company. For example websites have recently been updated for all of the subsidiaries, although it is believed that one subsidiary may start to trade electronically on the internet. The IT director immediately responded by stating she had recently commissioned a pilot study into internet trading. The study was currently being undertaken in two outlets specialising in teenage products and services and she believed everyone was aware of this study.

Required

(a) (i) Discuss the importance of formulating an information systems strategy that aligns with a business strategy. **(10 marks)**

(ii) Discuss how effective TEAC have been in aligning their business and information systems strategies over the past 40 years. **(10 marks)**

(b) Commitment, coordination and communication are vital ingredients to the success of information systems development.

Describe how each of commitment, coordination and communication play an important role in the context of developing information systems with reference to TEAC where appropriate. **(20 marks)**

(c) (i) Describe the use of gap analysis and its use of an applications portfolio approach in the context of developing an information systems strategy. **(10 marks)**

(ii) The IT director is very concerned with the findings of the TEAC gap analysis. The findings suggest there is an ever-increasing gap between supply and demand of information systems throughout the corporation. She believes some of the problems are caused by the company's continued use of a structured methodology. She intends to submit a report to the next meeting of the IS steering committee that briefly explains and critiques the use of structured methodologies. She has asked you to write her a draft report.

Prepare a draft report for submission to the IS steering committee. **(10 marks)**

(Total = 60 marks)

59 CAET Co (12/03)

108 mins

Introduction

Caet Co is a catalogue store chain with an annual turnover in excess of £500 million. Caet has just over 150 stores throughout the UK. Each store sells a variety of products including household furniture, electrical goods, jewellery, sports and leisure items etc. Each store supplies several thousand item lines; the item lines are standard throughout all stores. A company wide catalogue is produced twice a year containing pictures, descriptions and prices for all products. These catalogues are available in each store where customers can obtain free copies. Stores have a selection of items on display. There is a standard procedure for customers purchasing items. The customer chooses which item(s) they wish to purchase. They complete a simple order form, stating the item number and quantity required. The customer then takes the completed order form to one of the many payment points within the store, where a sales assistant enters the item number into the point of sales terminal; the item(s) are then displayed. A validation check is conducted with the customer. The sales assistant confirms if the item is in stock and checks with the customer, using the description to ensure that the order is correct. The customer then pays for the item(s) using cash, cheque or credit card. Upon receipt of payment the customer is given a till receipt and informed of the appropriate pick-up point within the store. After a few minutes the item(s) are brought to the pick-up point where the till receipt is stamped and the customer receives the goods. Caet offer a free delivery service for large items.

Problems with the current system

Several store managers have produced a joint report to the operations director, requesting a change in the current store systems. The report recognises that customers often take their order forms to the payment points and discover that an item may not be in stock. Upon making this discovery they decline to make any other purchases on the order form. This also leads to complaints from the customers. This happens frequently and is becoming a problem, affecting sales. The proposal is to develop an in-store system that will permit customers to access information concerning stock availability. If this is feasible the system could inform customers when an item is out of stock and suggest viable alternatives available within the store. The operations director has had preliminary talks with the information technology (IT) director, who initially supports the idea. He even suggested that there might be a case for expanding the proposal and permitting the customers to complete their orders, including payment via credit card, automatically within the store. This would give customers a choice between methods of placing an order. The operations director believes such a system would be unique amongst Caet's major competitors. They have initially called the proposed system, Public Inventory Preview System (PIPS). The operations director and the IT director are planning to put a formal PIPS project proposal to the full board of directors at the next board meeting. The initial proposal will confine itself to allowing the public access to the inventory system; it will not include purchasing facilities.

Company structure and strategy

Head office functions are centralised at a site in a large regional city. The IT centre operates from within this site. Currently the centre houses two IBM mainframes, plus three AS/400 minicomputers. The minicomputers provide the personnel, payroll, finance and distribution functions. One of the mainframes supports the day-to-day business of the entire operation, while the second mainframe runs smaller business functions and acts as a backup for the first mainframe, running many of the major functions in parallel. Also, many networked PCs are used within head office. The retail stores have recently been equipped with new NCR point of sale equipment, linked to the back-office server running an application written in C++ on UNIX. The stores have their own local stock recording systems linked to the head office mainframe. Therefore each store can process its own data locally and the head office has sight of the stores' information. Replenishment of stock is normally controlled by head office systems. When item lines have fallen below re-order level the head office inventory system automatically informs the appropriate distribution warehouse to deliver the required items to the store. The four geographically dispersed distribution warehouses have their own inventory systems, linked to the head office main inventory system. The head office system automatically organises the replenishment of stock from the suppliers.

Caet has recently updated its overall business strategy. The new strategy document is nearing completion. High priority is being given to the exploitation of information technology with regard to improving customer service, customer satisfaction and meeting customer requirements. New proposals for improvements in any of these areas are being encouraged throughout all functions and levels within the organisation. This new initiative requires potential user groups or managers to prepare a business case, to be considered by senior management. The strategy document is reinforcing the board's long-term commitment to developing both business and information strategies that complement each other rather than compete with each other.

During the last five years Caet has successfully implemented an intranet, which has enhanced communication within the company. They have also implemented an extranet; this has been initially successful and developments in this business-to-business system are constantly being undertaken. Many of Caet's key suppliers now share access to the main inventory system and have the ability to automatically supply goods as and when appropriate.

The in-store side of the business relies heavily on custom-written programs. The bulk of the head office mainframe applications were also written in-house. Some generic packages have been bought in for the mini-computer based functions, but all applications relating to stock and sales management remain internally developed and maintained. There are over eighty IT staff permanently employed in the IT centre, with just over half of them working on mainframe products while the remainder are supporting in-store systems. When the new point of sales systems were being installed, Caet used external sourcing for the first time; this was due to the size of the project. The outsourcing company installed the new hardware and developed the required bridging software within the stores. Caet's IT department developed the corresponding new back office in-house. It was considered that Caet's store operations are unique to the extent that no package was suitable for their purpose.

The website

Throughout the 1980s and most of the 1990s Caet's business was flourishing and allowed them to expand throughout the country. During the late 1990s Caet developed a basic website on the Internet. This site advertises the company's products and services; the site does not permit on-line purchasing or allow for two-way interaction. During the last three years Caet's market share, and thus their profits, have been steadily falling. They are in a very competitive market place. It is believed within the company that their recent fall in profitability is due mainly to the emergence of competitors offering customers on-line purchasing facilities. This is exacerbated by the dramatic increase in dot com companies in the same business sector. Caet is now considering developing its existing website system to include on-line home purchasing facilities for its customers. A proposal for this enhancement, named Public On-line Purchasing System (POPS), will be placed on the agenda for the next board of director's meeting. The proposal states that POPS will supplement their existing operation. Currently there are no plans to downsize the existing stores.

The board of directors generally agree that Caet's major business strategy will continue to involve the support and promotion of their high street stores. If the development of the on-line shopping system, POPS, is given approval by the board of directors, the financial director, a strong supporter of POPS, has already stated that adequate funds and resources will be available.

Required

(a) (i) Construct a Strengths, Weaknesses, Opportunities and Threats (SWOT) analysis with reference to Caet's proposal to develop the Public On-line Purchasing System (POPS). **(8 marks)**

(ii) The figure below represents four possible IS/IT strategies that can result from a SWOT analysis.

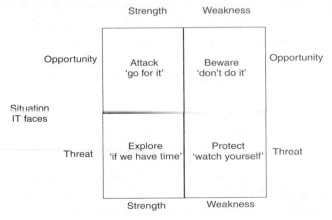

Evaluation of IS capability

Briefly explain in general terms how the above grid can help a company determine the most appropriate IS strategy to follow. **(6 marks)**

(iii) Discuss the four strategies given in (b) above and how they might apply to the case study. Of the four, identify which strategy in your opinion best applies to CAET's current position with reference to the Public On-line Purchasing System (POPS) and why. **(6 marks)**

(b) (i) Those store managers who wish to join the Public Inventory Preview System (PIPS) program have been asked to prepare a business case justification. However, none of them has any experience of producing a business case.

The IT manager has asked you as his deputy to prepare some guidelines for store managers on how to produce a business case report.

Your brief includes:

- An explanation of the structure of the report, including a high-level explanation of cost-benefit analysis

- Outline suggestions for the content of the report

- A high-level outline of at least one possible technical solution for the proposal (NB without including a cost benefit analysis)

Write the guidelines. **(15 marks)**

(ii) With close reference to the PIPS application, discuss briefly possible approaches to evaluating the intangible benefits that may be identified in a cost-benefit analysis. **(5 marks)**

(c) (i) The history of IS development shows a large number of failed projects as well as successful ones. One way to try and avoid failure is to perform risk analysis.

Discuss three key factors that a project risk assessment should consider. **(12 marks)**

(ii) Using the three factors discussed in Part (a) above, prepare a risk assessment for the Public Inventory Preview System (PIPS). **(8 marks)**

(Total = 60 marks)

60 Seemore Co (6/04)   108 mins

Introduction

Seemore Co is a family owned and managed video and DVD rental business. Currently the business has 35 stores located throughout the region. The company was established in 1982 when Michael Seymour opened a video rental shop on the outskirts of the city. Originally, many of the information systems were paper based, although Michael was quick to implement computer based systems as and when required. He viewed himself as a pioneer in the adoption of the latest technology. During the last twenty years the business has expanded from the original single outlet to its current 35 stores. In line with this expansion the company moved to a central office, which incorporates an adjacent warehouse.

Stock control and product range

The central office is the hub of the business where all the business operations are managed. Each store is automated in so much as membership details, video/DVD rental details and local stock recording systems are held locally on personal computers. Each store's computer system is networked to the central office computer system. This network permits details of business operations to be transmitted automatically to the central office. As well as the financial information collected, the central office maintains a company wide stock recording system. Seemore currently holds more than nine thousand titles in stock. Stock levels have always been viewed as a major problem for Seemore; they realise effective and efficient stock management is a key factor for the company's continued success. Questions of under-stocking and over-stocking are raised regularly within the company with regard to both the central warehouse and the individual stores. The titles are classified into ten subdivisions including: Thriller, Action, Romantic and Classical. All classifications are then further categorised into suitable viewing age ranges. The central office analyses data concerning rental patterns, volumes and classifications etc per store. Following this analysis the central office determines the stores' predicted requirements and normally despatches replacement stock to the stores from the warehouse once a fortnight.

Membership and reservations

Each store maintains a membership database. To become members customers must register with a local store. Following identity checks, members are issued with a membership card. These cards are valid in any of Seemore's outlets. Membership is free. Members may visit a store and pick a video/DVD of their choice. The transaction is recorded and the member pays the rental fee if the film is available. Members can reserve a film for a specific date either by visiting a store or making a reservation by telephone or fax. There is an increasing trend by members to use this reservation facility, as it avoids the disappointment of films not being available when required. Reserved stock is automatically allocated within the local store on its stock system. If this allocation is not possible due to lack of stock, then a request is sent to central office via email and the required stock is despatched immediately from the warehouse. Seemore Co has always adopted the policy that the customer comes first. Maintaining high levels of personal service and customer satisfaction has always been a high priority within the business. Michael views this approach as a cornerstone to the company's success.

Extranet

The central office conducts all business transactions with its suppliers via an extranet. The extranet, implemented three years ago, is widely viewed as successful. Speedy stock replenishment and acquisition of new titles are essential to the running of this highly competitive business. Special offers and promotional deals are determined centrally and conveyed to the stores via the network. There are three permanent IT professionals based in the central office. Between them they maintain and enhance the business information systems. One of the IT personnel specialises in network management. The majority of the existing business systems are 'off-the-shelf' packaged based software that in some cases have been adapted to meet Seemore Co's specific requirements. During the past fifteen years if the permanent IT staff could not develop or enhance the business information systems to meet Seemore's requirements then external staff were contracted in to supply the service. The initial implementation of the network was outsourced to a local vendor and the same vendor has implemented all the corresponding upgrades. All of the technical changes and developments have been welcomed by the majority of staff, whether in the local stores or in central office.

The postal membership system

In the early 1990's Seemore Co developed a postal membership system (PMS). To become a postal member, customers pay a monthly premium. Each month they are sent brochures of the latest releases and classic titles available. The members complete an order form and return it to central office. They are permitted to receive a certain number of videos/DVD's per month, depending on the classification of membership and hence the amount of their monthly premium. Within two days of receipt of an order the rental packages are despatched from the warehouse together with a pre-paid package label for the return of rentals. Details of members and their transactions are maintained in a customer database. Although PMS was initially successful, attracting over ten thousand members, during the late 1990's membership fell to less than a thousand. Currently the system is still running but is becoming increasingly less profitable. Reluctantly Seemore Co is considering suspending the service altogether.

The current business position

Although generally business has been steady, fierce competition has been negatively affecting profit margins. Senior management is concerned about the current position and is attempting to develop ideas that will reverse the downward trend. One suggestion proposed by Michael's brother Edward is to open more outlets. This would increase Seemore's profile and make their services available to more potential customers. Edward believes that the business strategy of opening more outlets that has served the business well in the past is the best way forward. In Edward's own words 'this is a tried and tested approach with little or no risk involved. The more stores we have the more likely we are to attract new customers'.

The way forward

Michael's son Irvine, the company's sales and distribution director, has recently been developing an idea that Seemore Co should expand its business to incorporate video ordering via the Internet. He believes the power of the web can strengthen the company's business position and help to increase its share of the rental market. Irvine is not a technical expert, but in recent weeks he has been consulting with one of the internal IT professionals. He discussed some of his ideas with the rest of the board of directors informally at the end of last month's board meeting. He believes that ordering via the Internet will not only attract web surfers but may well attract individuals seeking the convenience of ordering films from their own homes, especially those living in rural areas. The business objective is to encourage people to become members of the company.

Irvine stated, 'There are many advantages of using the web as the vehicle for extending the business potential and increasing the company's market share. Before we make any decisions concerning the best business strategy and corresponding information systems strategy to adopt, we require a full investigation. In the past we have adopted technology to support our business objectives. If we pursue my proposed route we may need to change our business strategy to support our information systems strategy.'

In reply to Irvine's comments Edward warned of the dangers of embracing new technology. He continued, 'I am not against any proposals that will enhance business prospects. However before we make any final decisions we need to take into account our current position, how we got to this position and where we see ourselves in the future.'

Michael suggested the best way forward would be to appoint an independent IT consultant to conduct the study and report back to the board at the next bi-monthly meeting.

Required

(a)   (i)   Analyse Seemore's current position with regard to developing the proposed Internet video ordering system using a Political, Economic, Social and Technological (PEST) analysis.   **(8 marks)**

(ii)   Irvine Seymour has requested that you, as an internal IT specialist, produce a briefing report concerning the viability of the development and implementation of the Internet video ordering system. He wants to use this report to begin a discussion at the next meeting of the board of directors. The briefing report should take into consideration the results obtained in part (a) of this question. You are not required to produce a cost-benefit analysis.

Write the report to Irvine Seymour.   **(12 marks)**

(b)   Critical Success Factors (CSFs) can be identified at different levels of management; strategic, tactical and operational.

Required

(i)   Discuss how the use of CSFs can help determine the information requirements of an organisation.   **(8 marks)**

(ii)   Identify two specific CSFs at each level of management (strategic, tactical and operational) that could be used to determine the success of implementing the Internet video ordering system at Seemore Co.   **(6 marks)**

(iii)   For each level of management (strategic, tactical and operational) choose one of the CSFs identified in part (b) of this question and explain how the CSF could be measured and specify what type of information might be required in each case.   **(6 marks)**

(c)   Seemore Co decides to proceed with the development and implementation of the Internet video ordering system.

Required

(i)   Discuss the characteristics of an effectively designed website with reference to Seemore Co.   **(10 marks)**

(ii)   Discuss the advantages and disadvantages of Seemore's decision to proceed with the Internet video ordering system from the perspective of a customer.   **(10 marks)**

(Total = 60 marks)

61 Question with helping hand: ACET Co (12/04)   108 mins

Introduction

ACET Co, a leading multinational clothing company, has divisions that include offices, manufacturing facilities and distribution centres located throughout the world. ACET's information systems strategy has been predominantly decentralised. Divisions have been permitted to develop their own IT systems, although in the majority of cases divisions are normally required to submit proposals for major developments to their appropriate national head office. During the last ten years company guidelines have been introduced that require all developments to follow certain standards with regard to software and hardware implementation.

Throughout the company, ACET have encouraged the introduction of new technologies. Many divisions have developed electronic links with their suppliers and distributors eg Electronic Data Interchange (EDI) and Electronic Funds Transfer (EFT) applications. For many divisions this has resulted in an improvement in their supply chain operations.

ACET are experienced in web technology. For six years they have had an internet website with the address http://www.acet.com, which has served as a shop window, advertising their lines and giving the public a controlled insight into the scale and scope of their operations. The website currently receives approximately 10,000 hits per day. The number of hits per day has been declining for several years, from an early high point of 35,000 per day.

The intranet project

ACET have made a decision to expand their web capability by establishing a company-wide intranet. The intranet is intended to improve internal communications across the whole company; more significantly, it is intended to help them gain a competitive advantage over their rivals. Major competitors in recent years have been attracting ACET's customers by copying many of ACET's lines and retailing them at lower prices. Economic recession has also adversely affected sales.

Employees at ACET are full of good ideas, but it is not always easy to share them with 20,000 worldwide colleagues. An innovative idea developed at a company office in Europe might take weeks or months to reach corporate headquarters in Chicago, and by then it might be too late to use it. Similarly, those outside the company's financial community might never see or hear about the Chief Financial Officer's recent speech. What is needed is a way to quickly and effectively capture and share corporate knowledge across the globe. The 'NetWorkShare' (NEWS) initiative was therefore devised by the communications executives and involves using an internal system to share information about best practice. 'The goal of the intranet is to empower the organisation by cutting down barriers created by different time zones and disparate computing platforms' says Joan Brown, Corporate Communications Manager at ACET. The idea of this system is that employees can post their experiences and insights on NEWS for anybody searching for information, instead of trying to synchronise time zones between distantly separated colleagues, or having to battle through unknown email gateways. There have been some reservations concerning the development of the NEWS system. Several managers throughout the organisation have queried the necessity for developing yet another communications system. A common view amongst opponents is that the existing internet system and other media for communications are sufficient to meet the Company's requirements.

Improving communication

ACET's North American and European organisations recently completed a long business process re-engineering exercise focused on improving customer service to retailers. The company's Asia-Pacific region is undergoing a similar process and will benefit from the experiences of the other two regions. The NEWS initiative is expected to help this process and therefore become the cornerstone of continuous improvement. Along with dissemination of best practice information, NEWS may also be used to help ACET's employees learn more about the business they are in.

Global marketing and purchasing project

Due to the decrease in sales during recent years, ACET are planning to introduce a global marketing and purchasing project (GMPP). This project should enable ACET to support one of its main business objectives, to be one of the leading fashion retailers in the world. It is hoped this project will be able to collect and publish brand information ranging from consumer research to information from the external world wide web, to data from a company sales kiosk, to video clips from ACET's TV commercials around the world. Users will be able to take a tour of the products, seeing all the information presented to customers. In the past ACET have predominantly relied on their brand names to secure sales worldwide. For many years it was accepted they were market leaders in certain areas of the fashion industry.

Fashion trends are continually changing. New market entrants appear almost on a daily basis. Global markets are no longer restricted to large corporations like ACET. This trend was highlighted at a recent board meeting by Harry Fowler, a senior member of the European based marketing team. He added, 'We are in danger of falling behind in our quest to maintain and secure a leading position in the worldwide fashion arena. We must put ourselves in a position where we can achieve a substantial and sustainable global market presence'. Nicola Wheatley, a member of the newly formed technology for the future team, commented, 'In the past we have developed and utilised technology to support our current business requirements. It has been difficult to forecast where the business was heading. I believe we as an organisation have been complacent and we need to exploit our position in the market place through the use of technology. Failure to take action may threaten our overall position'. There was overwhelming support and enthusiasm for the statements being made within the board meeting until Arnold Sigmund, a member of the corporation's financial executive group, said, 'Before we try to solve all our problems by implementing yet another information system, we must consider the cost in terms of both possible success and failure of the GMPP project. Although I support the concept of the project, I suggest we progress the idea with some caution. Many of our previous technology projects have not been as successful as originally envisaged.'

Damon Defollie, European Director for Purchasing, stated, 'As a company we are missing opportunities to enhance our purchasing capability. Recent analysis of our purchasing systems has identified that some divisions are competing with other divisions for the supply of goods. Often suppliers are supplying the same goods to different divisions for different prices. This situation does not make economic sense and cannot be permitted to continue. We need to take control of the situation.'

Dilemma

An accountant in one of ACET's European divisions has developed her own system, using a conventional spreadsheet application package. This system permits the accountant to interface with several company in-house systems and analyse information pertinent to her job. The development and use of this system has enabled her to analyse information faster than her colleagues, and thus makes her performance more efficient and her job easier. This has upset her colleagues, who have subsequently made a formal complaint to their section manager; they want to use the system to enhance their jobs. The accountant claims that she developed the system in her own time and predominantly on her own computer at home and is therefore refusing to share the system with others.

Required

(a) A general framework for combining the development of business strategy and information systems strategy can be shown as a four-stage process:

First stage	Where We Were
Second stage	Where We Are
Third stage	Where We Want To Be
Fourth stage	Going To Get There

Use the general framework given above to evaluate the development of ACET's business strategy in general and the Global Marketing and Purchasing Project (GMPP), in particular. **(20 marks)**

(b) (i) Construct a Strengths, Weaknesses, Opportunities and Threats (SWOT) analysis of ACET Co.

(8 marks)

(ii) With reference to the proposed introduction of the NEWS initiative, why is a SWOT analysis useful in the development of an information system? **(12 marks)**

(c) (i) Discuss how the introduction of information systems can raise ethical questions for individuals and organisations. **(5 marks)**

(ii) Dilemma

An accountant in one of ACET's European divisions has developed her own system, using a conventional spreadsheet application package. This system permits the accountant to interface with several company in-house systems and analyse information pertinent to her job.

The development and use of this system has enabled her to analyse information faster than her colleagues, and thus makes her performance more efficient and her job easier. This has upset her colleagues, who have subsequently made a formal complaint to their section manager; they want to use the system to enhance their jobs. The accountant claims that she developed the system in her own time and predominantly on her own computer at home and is therefore refusing to share the system with others.

Required

Produce an ethical analysis for the dilemma referred to in the last paragraph of the case study.

(15 marks)

(Total = 60 marks)

Helping hand. Suggested approach to ethical dilemmas:

(i)   Identify and separate facts from judgements
(ii)   Define the conflict or dilemma and identify the issues requiring judgement
(iii)   Identify all the stakeholders
(iv)   Identify the options that are available
(v)   Evaluate the consequences of the options identified
(vi)   Is a compromise available?
(vii)   Decide, communicate and implement the most appropriate course of action

---

62 Mercord Co (6/05)   108 mins

Introduction

Mercord Co is an engineering manufacturing company specialising in the production of mobile machinery for use within the construction industry. Its products include welding plants, lighting plants, pumping units, cement mixers and other made to order products. The company was founded in the mid 1950s. It currently employs approximately five hundred people. Seventy-five per cent of its workforce is engaged with manufacturing and assembling its products. Mercord maintains a well-deserved reputation within its sector, particularly in the home market, and has supplied many of its existing customers for decades. It has long-term contracts with several national construction companies for the supply of machinery. Mercord's business has remained fairly static for the last decade, not matching its growth during the nineteen seventies and eighties. On several occasions Mercord has with little success attempted to break into the lucrative export market.

Mercord has historically developed its information systems to support its business strategy. The company has an IT department responsible for developing new systems and maintaining existing systems. The majority of the information systems have been developed in-house. Many of the applications use a hierarchical database as their data source. Some packages have been purchased and modified where necessary to meet the company's specific requirements. The production design team use a standard CAD/CAM package. At the centre of the computing infrastructure is a minicomputer.

Personal computers (PCs) are used throughout the organisation. Most of the PCs are linked to the minicomputer via a local area network. The information systems strategy has been generally one of centralisation. Most of the existing IT resources are spent maintaining and modifying current systems. During the past decade or so the IT department has rarely been able to develop new systems due mainly to its workload. One innovation that was attempted some five years ago was the development of a website as part of a business strategy to increase its overseas sales. Some clients found the website useful, but it failed to attract many new customers.

The take over

Three months ago Mercord successfully bought one of its biggest rivals Rendi Co. The CEO and all of Mercord's directors were delighted with the acquisition. Rendi Co began trading in similar products to Mercord ten years ago. Rendi was not viewed as a serious threat to Mercord in the home market but it aggressively developed a significant export market. The company has a smaller manufacturing base than Mercord, which is located sixty miles to the north.

Rendi Co

Rendi has sales personnel located throughout the continent. Rendi had a different business approach to Mercord. It adopted a lean and mean business strategy, eg it bought in most of its components from suppliers and assembled them rather than manufacturing the components. Rendi developed an efficient electronic supply chain to support this strategy.

Rendi developed its information systems in unison with its business strategy. The majority of information systems development was outsourced. Rendi permanently employed a small team of IS professionals whose main function was to specify IS requirements, assist the outsourcers during the development process and generally support the systems and users after implementation. The information systems are supported by a relational database management system running on a client-server network. Several years ago Rendi developed an effective website. This site enabled customers to view Rendi's products. Within the site customers could view videos of the products in action. Customers could also order items online. In some cases customers were permitted to specify required components, eg types and sizes of engines, power output from lighting units, colour of units. Thus many of Rendi's products were made to order within certain parameters.

The current position

The euphoria of the take-over of Rendi has settled down. The board of directors is now considering how to internally merge the two companies. From a business strategic view the take-over will permit Mercord to pursue its overall strategy of entering the export market. Mercord intends to develop and expand in this crucial area. There are some concerns over the future information systems strategy. Prior to the take-over and during the last three months the IT director has constantly warned of the problems that would emerge when Mercord realises that it must eventually integrate all of the existing systems. The alternative is to support two entirely different information system strategies. During a recent departmental meeting involving the IT director, the IT departmental manager and all of the current IT staff the IT director stated, 'We are fighting an uphill battle at board level, many of the directors believe it's a fairly simple task to integrate the Mercord and Rendi information systems. They do not understand that the Mercord information systems are years behind the Rendi information systems in terms of technology and infrastructure.' The departing Rendi IS manager often refers to the Mercord systems as 'legacy systems or dinosaurs from a bygone age.' During the next couple of months the board of directors is going to develop a new information systems strategy that in their view will align with the business strategy. The IT director continued, 'I believe we need to participate in the development of the strategy. We need to be in a position to put forward suggestions as to the best way forward in terms of the impending integration project'.

The business perspective

The business strategy has changed since the take-over of Rendi. The company wants to be seen as a single unit, maintaining its home market and developing the export market. Changes in production are inevitable, as the Mercord manufacturing facilities will expand in order to supply the Rendi operations. The procurement director has gone on record stating 'It makes no sense to purchase all parts from outside suppliers when the company has the facilities to manufacture and supply parts internally.' The design teams have merged and are situated in a single location. Many support departments are in various stages of merging, eg marketing, human resources, payroll and advertising. The merging of these departments is fairly straightforward as they were using similar information systems in several areas. Different versions of standard software packages were being used eg word processing, spreadsheet and desktop publishing packages. In these circumstances the latest version has been adopted. There has been a general downsizing in terms of personnel from many of the departments. Much of this has been achieved by natural wastage although there have been some compulsory redundancies.

The way forward

The board of directors believes the next stage is to integrate the major core business information systems. The general opinion within the board is to commission a study that will investigate the current systems and make proposals as to the best way to pursue the integration project. The long-term strategy is to integrate all existing Mercord and Rendi systems.

This will establish the basis for developing a company wide information systems strategy. The proposed study is known as the Total Integration Project (TIP). The study should identify alternative approaches to the problem of integrating or not integrating existing information systems. The finance director has already suggested that the IT department may need to be reorganised and rationalised. For many years she has been a firm advocate of outsourcing; she has outsourced buildings maintenance, general office and factory cleaning and more recently all catering services.

Required

(a) (i) With specific reference to Mercord's recent acquisition of Rendi, assess the internal impact of sociological and technological factors. **(8 marks)**

(ii) Discuss the importance of formulating an information systems strategy that aligns with a business strategy with reference to Mercord/Rendi where appropriate. **(12 marks)**

(b) (i) Evaluate the current position within Mercord with regard to the Total Integration Project. **(8 marks)**

(ii) Discuss the term legacy systems and the problems of migrating legacy systems to new target systems with reference to Mercord where appropriate. **(12 marks)**

(c) The Mercord board of directors is meeting next month. One of the items on the agenda is a discussion of the way forward with regard to the Total Integration Project (TIP). Prior to this meeting a group of senior managers is meeting to brainstorm the possibility of outsourcing the development and implementation of the TIP.

(i) The finance director, who will be attending the brainstorming meeting has requested that you prepare some briefing notes for her highlighting the benefits of outsourcing information systems development at Mercord.

Prepare the briefing notes for the finance director. **(6 marks)**

(ii) The Mercord IT manager, who will be attending the brainstorming meeting has requested that you prepare some briefing notes for him highlighting the problems of outsourcing information systems development at Mercord.

Prepare the briefing notes for the IT manager. **(6 marks)**

(iii) If Mercord decides to outsource its information systems function, there are various types (levels, degrees, approaches) of outsourcing that Mercord could adopt.

Briefly describe two types of outsourcing that Mercord may consider and evaluate their appropriateness to Mercord's current situation. **(8 marks)**

(Total = 60 marks)

63 Gervil Investment Co (12/05)

108 mins

Introduction

Gervil Investment Co provides financial services nationwide. These services include: life assurance, home insurance, pensions, mortgages, investment products and the management of investment portfolios for individuals and companies. Gervil's head office is located in the financial district of the capital city. Gervil has existed with its current structure for ten years. During the late 1980s and early 1990s George Vilsen, the founder of the successful Vilsen Finance Co, began a business strategy of purchasing small/medium sized independent finance companies, thus expanding his business portfolio and customer base. In 1994 George Vilsen, with the assistance of several financial backers, established Gervil Investment, which is now one of the top ten financial companies in the country.

Where they were

Throughout the 80s and early 90s Gervil adopted a decentralised strategy in terms of information systems development. In each region, Gervil has regional offices normally situated in a major city. These regional offices support smaller branches within the region. The head office developed company systems that were rolled out to the regional offices. The regional offices often enhanced the basic systems locally, some used technical staff employed by Gervil, while others used local consultants. If new developments within the regional offices were reported to be successful then changes were made via head office to all regional office systems.

Changing the infrastructure

Until 1995 there was a senior investment advisor at each of Gervil's 45 branches. The advantage of employing these specialist managers was the ability to make decisions quickly, face-to-face, using local client knowledge. A major disadvantage was that decisions were not always consistent across the company. Some clients had complained to head office, concerned that best advice was dependent on which branch they contacted. The financial director accepted these criticisms. At a board meeting she declared, 'We must adhere to our business strategy of providing the most up-to-date advice, consistently, throughout the company'. George Vilsen, the CEO, was quick to react to this statement. This latest criticism strengthened the CEO's view that the company had been moving away from its core business objective of providing the best service to all its clients throughout the country. For some time the CEO had viewed the acquisition of the independent companies as positive in terms of market growth but negative in terms of inheriting numerous information systems and business practices. He was aware there was a gap between Gervil's business strategy and its information systems strategy. He also knew he would have to take positive action to prevent the gap from widening.

The CEO decided to centralise the investment decision-making process. He commissioned the in-house development of an automated investment advisory system (AIA). The AIA system was based on expert system technology. The system encompassed a variety of investment products and services. The core of the system was designed to use best practice. The knowledge base was created focusing on the knowledge of the top investment managers. A major decision taken at the time of design was whether to make the AIA system stand-alone on unconnected computers in the branches, or to make it a networked system controlled from head office. The stand-alone option would be relatively cheap and easy to install while the network option would be initially more expensive and technically demanding. Gervil chose to develop the AIA system using the network option. Using the same infrastructure, several new front-end applications have been successfully developed. The successful development of the AIA system and its associated infrastructure has proved to be he cornerstone of Gervil's continued success in aligning its business strategy with its information systems strategy.

Gervil always has adopted, and will continue to adopt, a policy of exploiting technology whenever the company can demonstrate a benefit from the introduction or enhancement of information systems. During the last decade Gervil has continually updated its support information systems, eg the company has always upgraded its office automation systems with the latest versions available.

Product database

All client details were stored within a product database. Therefore, if a client purchased several products, their details would be stored several times. Gervil, appreciating the need to become more client based, developed a front-end enquiry system that permitted a user to enter a client's details and retrieve details of all the products that the client had purchased. Gervil was among the first financial companies to develop such an enquiry system. This system has proved invaluable to the telesales personnel, who can now target specific clients based on consumer knowledge.

The sales process

Currently in each of the main branches there is a sales manager who is responsible for meeting sales targets which are set by head office. The branch sales manager leads a team of sales personnel who visit existing and potential clients to sell Gervil products. When a sale has been finalised the details are downloaded into the product database. Administrative staff in the sales department prepare all the relevant documentation and distribute it to the clients. Applications for some products, such as mortgages, can take several weeks to process. In such cases a specific administrator is assigned to the application. The administrator maintains a file locally for each ongoing application. It is the administrator's task to ensure the procedure is completed and to monitor progress. Clients are informed of the administrator's details, ensuring a one-to-one contact.

Most of the sales personnel specialise in particular products although they have a limited knowledge of all other products and services. The sales personnel are all equipped with the latest mobile technology – phones and laptops. Sales are obtained in a variety of ways, eg via telesales where existing clients are contacted periodically and informed of new services and products. If interested, their details are sent by e-mail to a sales person and an appointment is made either in their place of work, their home or at one of Gervil's offices. Another form of attracting new clients is through advertising new products in the press, on radio and on television. When potential clients contact any of Gervil's offices, the same procedure as the telesales process is adopted. If clients want specific advice, the point of contact at the office will pass on their details to an appropriate sales person who will then arrange an appointment. Gervil also has a website that attracts many enquiries. The website, along with providing visitors with an overview of the company, advertises the company's products. Because of the nature of many of the products, the website is normally used to gather basic client information. Once this is collected, the sales process is as stated above. Some of the basic products such as home insurance can be purchased online. The website provides contacts to a central help desk where personal advice can be given. Sales staff have commented on the rather reactive role of the website, where communication is instigated by the client. All enquiries are logged on a client database and the date, type of enquiry and action taken are input into the system. This database is checked frequently to ensure appropriate action has been taken.

A customer service centre is based at head office. Clients can contact this centre if they have specific enquiries concerning details of products. Within the centre there is a team of expert staff, each having expert knowledge of specific products.

Product development

Product innovation has always been the cornerstone of Gervil's success. New products or services are normally developed and designed in the head office in the Product and Services (PS) department. When a new product is ready to be launched, details are placed on the intranet. Frank Maloney, an executive director of Gervil, manages the PS department. Within his remit he has to be constantly aware of new financial products being offered by Gervil's main competitors and, where appropriate, develop new products or services ahead of Gervil's competitors. During the last few years many areas within the financial services have become very competitive. The ease and willingness of clients to move from one provider to another has made it necessary to provide the best quality service at competitive rates. Frank's team in the PS department is consistently gathering information from a variety of sources both internal and external in an effort to keep ahead of competitors. Frank has always believed his work would be made easier if communication throughout the company was better. He is sure that knowledge within the organisation is not always shared and communicated to the appropriate people. He is committed to improving knowledge management throughout Gervil.

In a recent meeting with George Vilsen, Frank stated his concerns about the use of the intranet. He said, 'The implementation of the intranet was fairly successful, especially as the appropriate infrastructure was in place. The intranet could be used more effectively as a forum for two-way information provision. Currently the company uses the intranet as a method of communicating one-way predominantly down through the structure'. Frank continued, 'I believe we need to adopt a knowledge management strategy throughout the company. We have most of the technology in place; now we need a strategy'. George, who has always been a strong supporter of exploiting technology, replied, ' I am not entirely sure what you mean by a knowledge management strategy. But the concept sounds very interesting. Give me your views on the idea and I will discuss it informally with other members of the board'.

Required

(a) (i) Discuss in general terms how Porter's value chain model can assist the development of an information systems strategy that will enable an organisation to trade competitively in the market.

(10 marks)

(ii) For each of the five primary activities suggested in Porter's value chain evaluate the current position within Gervil Investment Co. Your evaluation may include suggestions where new information systems could improve the current activity. **(10 marks)**

Following his recent discussion with George Vilsen, Frank Maloney is eager to pursue his idea of introducing a knowledge management strategy. He has asked you, a business analyst within his department, to write a draft report that should include:

(b) (i) An evaluation, in general terms, of the need for developing a knowledge management strategy. The concept will be new to many of the members of the board. He believes they will require information on the necessity of developing such a strategy.

(ii) An assessment of the four functions normally associated with knowledge management with reference to the existing information systems within the company. This section should include recommendations regarding the development or enhancement of information systems where appropriate.

The four functions normally associated with knowledge management are: distribute knowledge, share knowledge capture and codify knowledge and create knowledge.

Section (i) should be approximately 40% of the report.

Write the draft report. **(20 marks)**

(c) (i) Explain how the application of gap analysis can contribute to the development of an information systems strategy that aligns with a business strategy. **(8 marks)**

(ii) 'The successful development of the AIA system and its associated infrastructure has proved to be the cornerstone of Gervil's continued success in aligning its information systems strategy with its business strategy.'

Discuss the above statement from the scenario in the context of the model referred to in part (i). **(12 marks)**

(Total = 60 marks)

64 KGDB Co (6/06)

108 mins

Introduction

KGDB Co owns a chain of retail clothing stores specialising in ladies' designer fashion and accessories. Katherine Goodison, one of the company's original founders, has been pleasantly surprised by the continuing growth in the fashion industry during the last decade. KGDB was established fifteen years ago, originally with one store in the capital city. Katherine and her close friend David Boswell originally set up the business, and during the first five years the company opened three more stores within the city limits. David's entrepreneurial skills were the driving force behind the expansion. Katherine designs many of the exclusive ranges supplied by the company. She also maintains control over the quality and manufacture from her limited number of suppliers. It is Katherine who decides which new designs are developed, marketed and sold. The company now has twelve stores located in seven cities throughout the country and takes pride in providing exclusive fashion creations to its clients. KGDB's clients demand the highest standard of personal service.

The current position

Currently each store has a shop manager and an appropriate number of staff. Each store has been computerised in so far as stock recording is conducted locally. Monthly reports on sales are sent to the main office via email. If a store requires replenishment of stock it contacts head office by email, telephone or fax. On receipt of a request the purchasing manager at head office either arranges the supply of required goods from the central warehouse or places an order with a supplier to deliver the goods to the central warehouse. Following inspection of the items the goods are despatched to the requesting store. The centrally controlled stock recording system is updated accordingly. The store managers have complete control over the items they stock so long as they are listed and supplied by the head office.

Some stores are continually late in supplying their monthly sales figures. KGDB runs several analysis programmes to enable management information to be collated. This information typically provides statistical data on sales trends within categories of items, between categories of items and between stores. The analysis and preparation of these reports are conducted in the marketing department. In some cases the information provided is out of date in terms of trends and seasonal variations before it is produced. David is aware that the unavailability of relevant management information is a major weakness within the company.

In the early days prior to the expansion of the business the management information systems were adequate. The systems were developed and implemented by a local consultancy company. As the business expanded the systems were rolled out to the new stores. Minor changes have been introduced in line with the expansion but the core systems have remained virtually the same for the last ten years. The hardware and software platforms are predominantly standard configurations. An internationally renowned manufacturer supplies the hardware. The majority of the software systems are standard packages that have in some cases been modified by the external consultancy to suit KGDB's requirements. New versions of software and hardware products have been introduced periodically over the last six years.

David is considering investing in a company wide information system that would coordinate the business activities and sales. He believes the investment would permit the company to expand further. Katherine is of the opinion further expansion would be detrimental to the business but she supports David's idea of the need for better management information.

Information systems development

During the last decade personnel throughout the company have suggested many new ideas. When David and Katherine support a suggestion they consult with their external information systems consultancy. There is no formal outsourcing contract with the external consultancy; they just provide services as and when required. When agreement has been reached the new programmes/systems are developed and implemented. In the last few years several information system projects have been abandoned, mainly due to lack of clear requirements definitions and problems with integration within existing systems. In two specific cases spiralling costs of development were blamed for non-completion.

Concerns with IS development

David was recently discussing these information systems problems with Anne Brown, the senior accountant. She suggested that the company should consider employing a small team of in-house IT professionals. On several occasions she has formally complained about the service provided by the external IT consultancy. Anne wrote to David several months ago highlighting her concerns. In her correspondence she stated that the external consultancy had conducted an extensive review of the company's requirements using a standard systems life cycle approach a couple of years ago. Following this review they attempted to implement some major modifications to the accounting system. The modifications required integration with other inventory related systems. The result of the project implementation was only a moderate success. She also claimed that all the modifications to existing systems are based on the initial review. She firmly believes they are only interested in quick fixes and do not fully understand the business and its information requirements. They do not involve the users in determining the best solutions. She added that the company's information systems are becoming generally out of date when compared to other companies in their sector. David agreed to meet with Anne to discuss the matter further.

Website development

At the last senior management quarterly meeting, attended by various senior managers from head office and all the store managers, Michael Jones (a store manager) raised concerns over the lack of a company website. He stated that many customers, either in the store or by telephone, request details of the company website. His response to the customers was always apologetic as he explained the company does not have a website. He reported that many customers complain about wasting time and experiencing disappointments when arriving at the store to find that there is nothing to match their requirements. On many occasions customers quote KGDB's competitors as having more up-to-date facilities. From the following debate it became apparent that many of the store managers shared his concerns. It was also apparent that a minority of store managers, led by Alexandra Smith, were apprehensive about the development of a website as they feared it may affect sales at their individual stores. KGDB regularly produces league tables of sales between stores, and staff annual bonuses are dependent on sales. David Boswell, a keen supporter of exploiting technology to enhance business opportunities, suggested that Michael write a business case report for the development of a website that would be placed on the agenda for the next meeting. He added that he had some ideas regarding the development of a website and he would convey his ideas to Michael after the meeting.

Katherine Goodison believes that the development of a website may be advantageous from an advertising perspective, but she is positive that such a development should not be designed to sell goods of such a specialist nature and fears such a move would upset many customers who prefer face to face contact. In contrast David would like to see the development of a website that fully integrates with all the back office information systems, permitting customers to purchase goods directly on the web. David suggested to Michael after the meeting that he should include his idea of providing purchasing facilities as an option in his business case report.

(a) Construct a Strengths, Weaknesses, Opportunities and Threats (SWOT) analysis with reference to KGDB's proposal to develop a website facility. **(8 marks)**

(b) The figure below represents four possible IS/IT strategies that can result from a SWOT analysis:

		Strength	Weakness	
Situation IT faces	Opportunity	Attack 'go for it'	Beware 'don't do it'	Opportunity
	Threat	Explore 'if we have time'	Protect 'watch yourself'	Threat
		Strength	Weakness	

Evaluation of IS capability

Required

(i) For each quadrant in the grid, assess the extent to which that quadrant's strategy applies to KGDB's proposed website development. **(8 marks)**

(ii) Briefly explain why David Boswell, Katherine Goodison, Anne Brown and Alexandra Smith may each support a different strategy from within the grid. Justify your choice with information from the case study. **(4 marks)**

Michael Jones has agreed to present the business case report for the development of a website to the next senior management meeting. Following his discussion with David he has agreed to include, in a single report, two options: option one is the development of a website that will permit customers to view goods and option two is the development of a website with online purchasing facilities. Michael has instructed you to prepare the report. Your report should include a brief description of cost benefit analysis. DO NOT attempt to calculate a cost benefit analysis.

(c)   Write the report.   **(20 marks)**

Anne Brown has arranged a meeting with David Boswell to discuss her suggestion of employing internal IT professionals. She has asked you as her assistant head of department to prepare some briefing notes prior to the meeting. Her instructions to you are to identify the current problems with IS provision and the benefits of employing internal IT professionals.

(d)   Write the briefing notes.   **(6 marks)**

(e)   Briefly describe Boehm's spiral model of the systems development lifecycle.   **(6 marks)**

(f)   Evaluate the appropriateness of using Boehm's spiral model approach for the development of the proposed website with online purchasing facilities in KGDB Co.   **(8 marks)**

(Total = 60 marks)

Answers

1 Strategic level systems

The function of management at strategic level or in a strategic role is to **plan organisational objectives**, and to assess whether those objectives are being met in practice. The information required for this function includes information obtained externally and internally.

Environmental influences affecting strategy include the following.

(a)   Domestic government policy and legislation.

(b)   International agreements, developments in international institutions (eg the European Union).

(c)   Policies of foreign governments affecting the organisation's export markets.

(d)   Economic and financial changes (eg interest rates, exchange rates).

(e)   Social changes affecting an organisation's marketing strategy and focus.

(f)   Competitors.

(g)   Developments in technology etc.

Internal matters affecting the long-term future of the organisation, and which are therefore of a strategic nature include the following.

(a)   Industrial relations and the work force.

(b)   Segmental profitability both of particular products and of markets.

(c)   Productivity.

(d)   Product cost-structure.

(e)   Overheads.

(f)   Management style and culture (authoritarian or consultative).

(g)   Information systems.

Because it is providing an overview, the type of data provided internally at strategic level will largely be in the form of summaries, or specially commissioned ad hoc reports, or models. Spreadsheets and modelling packages, which are flexible tools for financial and numerical analysis, will be used at strategic level. A further possibility is the use of database systems at PC level, so that particular types of information can be held for access and use. Public databases now available might also be accessed for in-depth reports, for example, on individual countries.

Management at strategic level might also avail themselves of **Executive Information Systems**. These are systems designed for senior managers, who may not necessarily be systems professionals, to help them access and model information. An EIS typically features:

(a)   A modelling facility (such as a spreadsheet).

(b)   A database facility so that the executive can store information he or she finds especially useful.

(c)   A drill-down facility so that the executive can access the organisation's main systems at any level for information at any level of detail.

(d)   Links to external information sources such as the Internet.

The prime characteristic of information systems at strategic level must be **flexibility**, so that inputs from a variety of sources can be processed together in a coherent manner. The increased awareness of the range of external information and easy availability of that information by means of efficient strategic information systems certainly permits management to reduce risk by gathering more data about the environment. However, far from stifling entrepreneurial activity (presumably suggested because the awareness of risks is heightened) it is probably true to say that existence of such systems encourages entrepreneurial activity by providing good information to management enabling them to identify opportunities to gain competitive advantage.

2 Parsons and Nolan

Text reference. Parsons is covered in Chapter 2 of the text, Nolan in Chapter 6.

Top tips. The first part of this question requires you to discuss the principles underpinning Parsons' six generic information systems strategies model and Nolan's six-stage growth model. The key word here is **discuss**. In the exam the majority of candidates merely described both models, limiting the marks available.

Easy marks. Demonstrate your knowledge of an information system within an organisation and evaluate the application of each stage of Nolan's model with reference to it.

Examiner's comments. In part (a), many candidates appeared to simply describe the models, whereas half of the marks available were for discussion. This approach therefore limited the marks that could be obtained.

In part (b) weaker candidates simply repeated the stages of the model from part (a); stronger candidates applied the model to a situation.

Marking scheme

			Marks
(a)	Nolan: Award 1/2 mark for each stage.	Max	3
	Parsons: Award 1/2 mark for each strategy.	Max	3
	Award up to 1 mark for each valid point in the explanation of their use to integrate business and IS strategies, 3 marks per model.	Max	6
(b)	Award up to one mark per valid point	Max	8
			20

(a)   **Nolan 6 stage growth model**

1   **Initiation**

The company begins involvement with IT with individual clerical applications being automated

2   **Contagion**

The benefits of IS/IT are seen and the use of IS/IT spreads within the company.

3   **Control**

The excesses of the contagion stage – that is too many applications being purchased and not providing value for money) lead to tight management controls on IT.

4   **Integration**

IS/IT begins to be considered as integral to the business. Information systems area linked between different business departments.

5   **Data administration**

The organisation gains confidence in managing IS/IT. Information is seen as a resource. Information requirements now seen as the focus of management attention rather than the technology.

6   **Maturity**

Information flows now reflect the real life requirements of the organisation. Business strategy and IS strategy are developed together.

Parsons' generic information system strategies model

1   Centrally planned

A manager planning IS developments needs an understanding of the overall strategic direction of the company. Business and IS strategy are closely linked.

2   Leading edge

Belief that the innovative use of technology can create competitive advantage. The company makes speculative investments in IT that may or may not generate large returns.

3   Free market

The IS function is viewed as a business unit which must be prepared to make a return on its resources. Free market implies that the IS function may have to compete with external providers.

4   Monopoly

Information is viewed as a corporate asset and so it should be controlled by a single service provider. The directly opposite strategy to free market.

5   Scarce resource

Belief that information systems use limited resources and so all IS development requires a clear justification. There are strict budgetary controls with new projects being subject to Cost Benefit Analysis.

6   Necessary evil

IS/IT is seen as a necessary evil of modern business. Therefore IS/IT is only allocated enough resources to meet basic needs.

Appropriateness of models

Nolan's model was developed in 1974, before the use of PCs, Windows, the Internet and WANs etc. The theory assumed that the use of IT would follow a specific linear path through an organisation with one stage following on from the last. In the 1970's, IT was also relatively expensive, and so the use of information systems was severely limited by the cost of those systems.

The model was therefore fairly well suited to the initial introduction of IT into an organisation. The principles of the model are not necessarily relevant to the modern businesses for the following reasons:

- Most organisations already have some element of IT usage – there is no initiation stage

- One stage of development does not necessary follow on from the last. The use of IT is now closely linked to business strategy – very little IT expenditure is speculative

- There are few business applications where automation is required – IT is used to enhance information so most companies are in the maturity stage of the model

- High costs of IT are no longer valid. IT usage is therefore much more pervasive that Nolan imaged

Nolan's model may be useful in identifying where a specific application is within the model, but not necessarily the overall business.

Parsons' model was also developed during the early stages of computerisation. The model assumed that an organisation's strategy regarding the development of information systems could be clearly defined and explained. There was also the assumption that only one strategy was being followed.

In reality, the principles of the model can be queried for the following reasons:

- Businesses tend to follow more than one strategy at a time, particularly where they have many autonomous business units

- The trend towards globalisation implies a need for information systems, making some of Parson's strategies, such as necessary evil, effectively redundant

- The strategies of free market and scarce resource can also be queried as relevant; organisations do control their IT expenditure but not to the extent that information provision is deliberately limited

Parsons' model can still be used to identify IS usage, although recognising that strategy is unlikely to fall clearly into one section of the model.

(b) A new online bookseller needs to develop an appropriate information system to manage stocks of books in their warehouse.

Initiation

The initiation phase will effectively be the production of a requirements specification. The requirements of the IT system will need to be clearly stated and the software developed and implemented, prior to the bookshop trading. Links to the Internet ordering system will also have to be specified and established.

Initiation is not therefore so much automating an existing system, as actually specifying information usage within the company.

Contagion

The benefits of IT have already been identified. Contagion appears to be more relevant to seeing additional uses of IT post implementation. For example, customers may want to order a book in advance of it being in stock. The software will need to be amended to take account of this request.

Control

Control will be exercised at all times during IT development and implementation, not at a specific time. IT expenditure is unlikely to go 'out of control' because budgets will need to be set. In a new business particularly, systems will not be developed unless an adequate return can be seen.

Integration

Again, systems will tend to be specified for the whole organisation, rather than disparate systems being integrated at a later date. Linking of the customer facing internet site and the ordering system is an example of this planned linking.

Data administration

Information will become more of a resource as customer history files are built up showing purchase patterns. This information can be mined to promote more effective advertising eg sending customers details of similar books they have purchased in the past to encourage new purchases.

Maturity

While systems will still be amended, the maturity stage is almost relevant from initiation. The organisation knows what it requires from its IT systems and will plan to ensure that those objectives are met.

3 Data and knowledge work

(a) **Knowledge work** is defined as creating/generating new kinds of information or knowledge. It involves the development of ideas or of expert opinions.

Knowledge workers are professional people, such as engineers, financial and marketing analysts, production planners, lawyers, and accountants, to mention just a few. They are responsible for finding, developing and maintaining knowledge for the organisation and integrating it with existing knowledge.

Knowledge workers are experts in their particular functional area and therefore must keep informed of all developments and events related to their profession. They also act as advisors and consultants to the members of the organisation, and as change agents by introducing new procedures, technologies, or processes.

Knowledge work is supported by a **body of knowledge** such as a collection of books, articles, standards and research, which is widely accepted as valid. In other words, knowledge is **codified**. This body of knowledge must be capable of being taught at educational establishments rather than merely passed on as experience. There must be principles, procedures, and methods, independent of pure experience, for work to be considered knowledge work.

Data work is defined as using, manipulating, or distributing symbolic information. Typical data workers include bookkeepers, clerical workers and sales personnel. Both data workers and knowledge workers deal with **information**. The difference is in how they deal with this information. Data workers **keep track of and disseminate** information; knowledge workers **generate new** kinds of information.

(b) As a data worker, the accountant may add value to an organisation by supporting management planning, decision-making and control. This work is based on data and information processing and reporting. To work effectively as data workers, accountants use operational level information systems (transaction processing systems) and management level systems, such as MIS and DSS.

Operational level systems support managers and accountants by keeping track of the elementary activities and transactions of the organisation eg, sales, payroll and credit decisions. **Management level** systems support the monitoring, controlling, decision-making and administrative activities of accountants. They provide periodic reports rather than one-off type information on operations and may provide facilities for 'what-if?' analysis.

As well as wanting to know what happened in the past, accountants should provide information that helps senior management decide what action should be taken in the **future**. As knowledge workers, accountants add value to the organisation in several ways.

Accountants are required to interpret ever-expanding **external knowledge bases**, they may perform internal system/workflow reviews – requiring them to recognise problems and possible solutions within a complex and changing business environment. Accountants may be called upon to act as organisational change agents.

The information required by the decision-makers of the future, is likely to come increasingly from **environmental scanning** and **intelligence gathering**. Information must be readily available, of reasonable quality, in the right form, and not too costly. And the knowledge worker must have the skills and knowledge to use it effectively.

For **accountants** to work effectively **as knowledge workers** they need easy access to electronically stored knowledge bases. They also need powerful software that facilitates communication and analysis, and they must be able to manipulate data and graphics for modelling and presentation purposes.

The **IT tools** the accountant will use should be powerful, but **user-friendly**. A user-friendly interface is particularly important, designed to maximise the use of knowledge workers' most limited resource – time.

Knowledge level systems include office automation systems and knowledge work systems; they support accountants in their roles as both knowledge and data workers in organisations. Office automation systems increase productivity through co-ordination and communication. These systems include document managers, schedulers and communication tools.

The **purpose of knowledge level systems** is to discover, organise and integrate new knowledge into the organisation. One way that IT can integrate the expertise of knowledge workers into an organisation and assist in improving worker performance is through the use of intelligent systems. These systems contain the knowledge of super-experts and can disseminate that knowledge to all employees who need it.

The main **support systems for knowledge workers** range from Internet search engines that help them find information, to expert systems that support information interpretation and even to hyperlinks that help them increase their productivity and the quality of their work.

Within most organisations, knowledge workers are the major users of the Internet because it is an effective way of accessing up-to-date information on a wide range of topics. Accountants need to keep abreast of developments in accounting, business and information technology, to communicate with managers and colleagues, and to **collaborate** with knowledge workers in other organisations ('knowledge networking') to solve problems.

4 Centralised or distributed?

Text reference. Much of this question is brought forward knowledge from Paper 2.1. Chapter 9 of the text includes material on decentralised processing.

Top tips. This question focuses on the number of different ways that exist to organise telecommunications components to form networks. They can be classified by their shape, their geographic scope and the type of service provided.

(a)   There are two major types of network: the local area network **(LAN)** and wide area network **(WAN)**.

    (i)   The **local area network** is a small network to allow efficient connection between users within a limited geographical area, usually one building or several buildings in close proximity. LANs are often used to connect PCs in an office to shared printers and other resources or to link computers and computer-controlled machines in shops or factories. Most LANs connect devices within a relatively small radius and so would not be the total solution for the Pound-Go-Far Stores. Mr Lee would need to incorporate a network gateway so that the LAN can exchange information with networks external to it.

    (ii)   **Wide area networks** span broad geographical distances outside the LAN boundaries, ranging from several miles to the whole world. They link organisational units on a national or international basis, usually connecting individual LANs. WANs may use dedicated communication lines linking different sites. Dedicated lines are continuously available for high-speed transmission and the lessee pays a flat rate for total access to the line. These are suitable for high volume applications so might not be the solution for Mr Lee. Switched lines are shared telephone lines that a person can access from a terminal to transmit data to another computer (modems required); the call is routed through paths to the designated destination.

BPP
LEARNING MEDIA

(iii) Individual firms may maintain their own private WAN but they are expensive. **Value added networks** (VANs) are an alternative to organisations designing and managing their own networks. They are data communication networks, usually administered and maintained by external communications companies, that providing data transmission services and access to commercial databases. The name 'value added network' is derived from the additional value a user of this system gains by having access to the databases and being free from the administration of the network. If Mr Lee decided on a VAN, he would not have to invest in network equipment and software to perform his own routing and protocol conversion, and might achieve savings in line charges and transmission costs because the costs of using the network are shared among many users.

(b) **Centralised processing** involves all data/information being processed in a central place, such as a computer centre at head office. The hub of the system would be a reasonably powerful central computer (server) holding all the program and data files used by the system. The terminals at the shops would not require any great processing or data storage facilities.

Many users are able to access the central computer at the same time and process data simultaneously. The terminals may be geographically dispersed, for example they could be located in individual shops and connected by an external data link. The benefits to be derived from a centralised service may be summarised as follows:

(i) Economy of capital expenditure due to having only one large computer for use by the organisation instead of several located in various units.

(ii) If one powerful computer is installed, the resultant advantages are increased speed of operation, storage capacity and processing capability.

(iii) Economy in computer operating costs due to centralisation of support staff.

(iv) Centralisation would also facilitate the standardisation of applications.

Distributed processing is where the system includes multiple computers linked by a communications network, allowing the processing to be 'distributed' around the system. For example, Mr Lee could have computing facilities at each local shop, which are linked together to form a Local Area Network. Each network of computers could be linked to the head office forming a wide area network ie, enabling each shop to communicate with the head office, and with each other. Distributed processing is characterised by:

- Computers distributed or spread over a wide geographical area.
- Processing of data at more than one location.
- Shared data files.
- Ability for each computer within the system to process data 'jointly' or 'interactively'.

The **advantages** of distributed processing are:

- End-users of facilities control and are responsible for their own data.
- Less effort is expended on data transmission.
- The end user has greater freedom to determine processing requirements.
- The data-processing systems that make up the total system can cooperate on common problems or function independently.
- Results may be obtained more quickly as data is processed locally.

5 Question with answer plan: organisation and system structure

Answer plan

Standard report heading (addressees, date, subject)

A　　*Terms of reference and executive summary*

　　　Further to your letter of instruction.....

B　　*The options*

　　　Outline of the two options being considered

B 1　*Centralised system*

　　　Explain how it would work, what would be needed

　　　List advantages and disadvantages (three or four of each)

B 2　*Distributed system*

　　　Explain how it would work, what would be needed

　　　List advantages and disadvantages (three or four of each)

C　　*Recommendation*

　　　Make one, and justify

REPORT

To:　　　　The Directors, AB plc
From:　　　A Consultancy
Date:　　　30 March 20X1
Subject:　 Configuration options for the new computer systems

A　　*Terms of reference and executive summary*

　　　Further to your letter of instruction of 28 January 20X1, we were asked to produce a report for the half-year board meeting specifying the reasons for and against using different computer systems. The current manual system was documented, and a number of options discussed with management. This report summarises the results.

B　　*The options*

　　　The two options being actively considered are the following.

　　　(a)　　A central mainframe with terminals at each depot (the 'centralised system').

　　　(b)　　Minicomputers such as IBM AS/400s at each regional depot connected together over a network (the 'distributed system').

B 1 *Centralised system*

A centralised system would involve setting up a room at head office or a central location in which to run the mainframe-based system. This room will have to have good environmental control, together with security. In addition you should consider establishing a back-up computer facility which could be used in the advent of a breakdown or catastrophe on the main machine.

The centralised system will be linked to the depots by leased telephone links. These will be expensive to run, but in the case of the larger depots will provide voice facilities, allowing you to save on the current voice phone charges.

The system will require specialised staff to run it. This will impose a new department on the organisation, and will result in an additional headcount of approximately fifteen. There will be a small loss of jobs at the regional level.

The centralised system will facilitate the keeping of all the figures up-to-date, and will allow for economic production, in batches, of the printouts which will come off the system. Data would be entered at the depots and reports produced either at the depots or at the head office computer.

Advantages of the centralised system include:

(a) Having a central up-to-date set of data which will be accessible by all depots.

(b) Maintaining a single set of data, which will eliminate inconsistencies in data used for different purposes.

(c) Providing the head office with the centralised control which the current system lacks, as freight can be tracked from one depot to another.

(d) Setting up of a centralised and specialised DP team with expert knowledge focused in one department.

The **disadvantages of a centralised system** include:

(a) Capital costs. The back-up system and the high cost of the main computer are both major factors.

(b) Operating costs, for example, high telecommunications costs.

(c) The problem of being entirely dependent on one machine. Computers do fail, and the impact on the business of the central machine failing would be great.

B 2 *Distributed system*

This would involve installing a minicomputer at each region, and another at the head office. Although space would have to be found for each they can be installed and run in standard office environments. Some staff would have to be trained at each site to work the machines, but staff could back up different regions in the event of others being off on leave or ill, which would largely do away with the need for specialist staff.

Advantages of this approach would include:

(a) Keeping the responsibility for the system with the regions. This would encourage the regions to adopt the computers and would also encourage them to keep the data accurate.

(b) In the event of any single machine failing it would be reasonably easy to acquire another on a short-term basis, and it would be able to be installed with a minimum of work.

(c) Lower communication costs, as most line usage will be within individual regions.

(d) Speed of processing is improved and local priorities can be better satisfied.

The **disadvantages** of this approach would include:

(a) Control would require on-going monitoring and effort. A supervisor at each region would have to be designated as the person responsible for ensuring procedures were adhered to.

(b)   Installation of, and training on, new versions of software would take more time and cost more. In addition, the logistics of installing later releases of software would require careful monitoring.

(c)   Capital costs, involving acquisition of six minicomputers, will be high, although with phased regional implementation this can be spread more easily than a single mainframe purchase.

(d)   Operating costs, particularly staff costs, will be high as it will be necessary to maintain a certain level of expertise at each regional office, resulting in some duplication.

(e)   It is not clear how this solution would embrace the individual depots, and tracking freight could be problematic.

C   *Recommendation*

I believe the advantages described under the second option, using a network of minicomputers, are most relevant to AB plc. Encouraging the regions to take ownership of the data should result in greater accuracy. Together with the flexibility provided by the network, and the improved processing speed the network best suits AB's requirements.

6 Information sharing; intranet; extranet

Text reference. Material in this question is covered in Chapter 3 of the text.

Top tips. This question broken up into manageable parts. Use the mark allocations as a guide as to how much information to provide for each part – and ensure you apply your knowledge to CC plc.

BPP marking scheme

			Marks
(a)	Award 1 mark for each valid objective up to a maximum of 5	5	
	Award 1 mark for each valid suggestion up to a maximum of 4	4	
			9
(b)	Award 1 mark for each valid reason up to a maximum of 4	4	
	Award 1 mark for each valid suggestion up to a maximum of 4	4	
	Maximum available		7
(c)	Award 1 mark for each valid point up to a maximum of 4		4
			20

(a)   An intranet uses software and other technology originally developed for the internet on internal company networks. An intranet comprises an organisation-wide web of internal documents that is familiar, easy to use and comparatively inexpensive. Each employee has a browser enabling him or her to view information held on a server computer and may offer access to the internet.

The main objective of an intranet is to **provide easy access to information** that helps people perform their jobs more efficiently. Many roles require increased access to knowledge and information. An intranet is a way of making this knowledge readily available.

Other objectives are outlined in the following paragraphs.

To encourage the use of reference documents. Documents on-line are more likely to be used than those stored on shelves, especially if the document is bulky (for instance procedure manuals).

To create a sense of organisational unity. An intranet 'pulls together' in a co-ordinated fashion information from disparate parts of an organisation. It may be the only visible way some parts of a large organisation are linked.

The provision of an intranet within CC plc should result in **better provision of information** by:

Ensuring consistency in information held and provided to clients. The intranet will enable one set of data to be held and accessed by all 20 offices.

Providing easy access to a larger pool of data. Information that managers previously 'kept to themselves' will be available to others.

The intranet-Internet link will ensure the most up-to-date planning information is available. It would be useful to develop an intranet page complied from appropriate websites. (This must be kept up to date.)

(b) Even after an intranet and e-mail have been implemented at CC plc, organisational and human reasons will hinder the process of making information more widely available. Steps need to be taken to overcome these barriers to information sharing.

Human reasons that will need to be overcome include the following.

- **Information is only available if people know how to find it**. The people at CC plc who could use the information held on the intranet must be told that the information is available, and trained so that they are confident enough to access it.

- Efficient **communication** (including a company-wide e-mail explaining the intranet) and staff **training programmes** demonstrating intranet use will help overcome this problem.

- **Some staff will not choose to share information or knowledge**. People may protect the information they have to boost their own performance relative to their colleagues. A culture change within CC plc is required before staff will be willing to share knowledge and information so that the organisation as a whole can benefit.

- To tackle this problem, techniques and processes to **encourage the sharing of information** could be included as part of a communication and knowledge management programme.

Organisational reasons that will need to be overcome include the following.

- The **hardware** used by CC plc is too old to support the new communication tools. This is likely to lead to user frustration with slow response times and problems gaining access to various systems. Unless the systems provided are efficient, users will abandon them.

- To overcome this problem CC plc will need to make a **significant investment** in new hardware.

- **Work practices** that do not involve or encourage the sharing of information have become established. A significant number of CC plc staff are likely to have a building and construction background, and not be enthusiastic towards computing developments. These staff may see these new communication tools as an unnecessary waste of resources by IT staff who do not have a feel for the business.

- This problem could be minimised by **involving staff** in the design of systems from the outset. Staff should be asked what information would make them more efficient. A tool that helps them do their job better will be welcomed by even the most sceptical.

- **Staff training programmes** and a **user friendly human-computer interface** should also reduce staff resistance.

(c) An extranet differs from an intranet in that it is able to **be accessed by authorised outsiders**. Those outsiders authorised to access parts of the intranet will usually be provided with a user name and password that will enable them to view **certain information**.

CC plc could provide valued customers with access to relevant information (such as advice and legislation updates) via an extranet. This should **encourage closer relationships** with selected clients.

If valued clients do not have access to computer links (still possible in industries such as building), some alternate method of making this information available may be required – to prevent these customers feeling neglected.

7 Strategic decision making

Text reference. Material in this question is covered in Chapter 1 of the text.

Top tips. Remember that at a strategic management level, sound decision making is critical to the long-term success of the business. Information systems should provide information that helps decision makers.

(a) **Long-term outlook**

Information flows at a strategic level will be geared towards information expected to impact on the long-term future of the business. There is a need for high quality information to enable sound long-term decisions to be made.

Flexible

Organisations are complex systems.

In order to maintain control in a constantly changing organisation the information flows and systems at strategic level need to be flexible and able to respond quickly to new demands.

For example, if a new competitor enters the market place, or environmental legislation is introduced affecting production processes or a trading opportunity arises in an overseas territory, then strategic decisions will be required to formulate the most appropriate response.

Good decisions can only be made when all the implications can be quantified with an acceptable degree of certainty. Management information systems must be flexible enough to provide concise, accurate and timely information relevant to the new environment.

Multi-directional

In a business organisation information flows both vertically and horizontally. The familiar pyramid hierarchy of an organisation sets out three levels of control and information.

Information flows at the strategic level facilitates decision-making that will affect the whole organisation and provide the framework for long term strategic plans. Internal information will flow from middle management up to senior management and vice versa.

Information also flows horizontally between different activities in a business. For instance overtime hours provided by the payroll section may be used by the production department, delivery lead times from warehouses may be used by the sales team and the level of future orders from the sales department will be used to forecast turnover and cash flows by the accounts department. The quality of these information flows will dictate both the efficiency of the business operations and will impact on the type and quality of information received by senior management.

The complex nature of strategic decisions makes information sharing vital.

An external component

Strategic level information flows will include information from external sources (eg government, suppliers, media etc). Strategic decisions are generally non-routine and require a high degree of judgement. The quality of information is critical at the strategic management level.

(b) Information used at a strategic level is often ad hoc – strategic decision making is non-routine and potentially risky.

Strategic information comes from both internal and external sources.

Internal sources

Most management information systems are now computer-based because of processing speed, accuracy and the ability to process large volumes of data. Internal data needs to be captured from day–to-day operations, processed into relevant information and made available in a suitable form at a strategic level.

Senior management information requirements should play a part in the development of information systems to ensure that the information required for strategic decision making is able to be produced.

Centralised systems are relatively powerful and usually controlled at senior level. However, a flexible response to non-routine problems may be lacking.

Decentralised systems may provide more flexibility, however central control and standard formats are often lacking.

Currently, popular solutions revolve around **networked and distributed** processing systems. These can provide information to different levels of management – often from the same database. They combine the advantages of local control, speed and ease of use with flexibility and the potential for standardised presentation of information.

Executive Support Systems (ESS) can be particularly useful in this area, providing summarised high-level information with the ability to view the underlying data if required.

The introduction of an ESS will also encourage senior management to consider which type of information is really relevant to the business.

An **intranet** may also be appropriate to encourage the sharing of knowledge and opinions relevant to strategic decisions (eg bulletin boards).

External sources

External information may be in the form of official reports, tax leaflets, technical updates, press updates and often just word of mouth.

Much of this information is now available via the **Internet**. **Intelligent agents** and **newsclipping services** can also be utilised on the Internet, to find user-defined information and forward it – usually via e-mail.

Some organisations are able to access external information through an **extranet** – allowing them to enter certain parts of another organisation's intranet.

8 Question with analysis: expert systems

Text reference. Chapters 1 and 3 contain material relevant to this question.

Top tips. See the examiner's comments below. As always, the key to scoring well on this type of question is to *apply* your knowledge.

Easy marks. The first part of this question requires you to explain specific terms given in the question, in the context of management information systems and expert systems. Explain the terms quickly first, and then place them in context.

Examiner's comments. Parts (a) and (b) were answered very well where candidates applied knowledge to the specific situation of Teac outlined in the scenario. Weaker answers therefore tended to provide information about the MIS and ES, but without showing how this applied to Teac.

Marks

(a)   Award up to 2 marks for identifying each difference.   8

(b)   Award 1 mark for each advantage up to a max of 3 marks and award up
to 3 marks for relating them to the scenario. Award 1 mark for each
disadvantage up to a max of 3 marks and award up to 3 marks for
relating them to the scenario.   12
                                                                                                                    ——
                                                                                                                    20
                                                                                                                    ══

(a)   **Timeliness**

Timeliness means that information should be available when it is needed – in time to make a difference.

In the case of Teac this means that information is available as soon as possible after the consultant makes a request for that information. The MIS should provide information within a few seconds as only a small amount of processing is required – information is only being processed regarding one client. The ES should also provide information within a few seconds, although this will depend on the speed of the computers used and the size of the knowledge base being searched.

Relevance/volume

Information that is not needed for a decision should be omitted, no matter how 'interesting' it is. Only the necessary information should be supplied.

Both the MIS and the ES will be searched to obtain relevant information for each client. The extent to which the systems return relevant information will depend largely on the accuracy of the search details entered into each system by the consultant. With the MIS, searching the database on specific conditions will help to return relevant information. In the ES, producing output in terms of probability will help to place more relevant results first in the list of outputs.

Accuracy/completeness

Accuracy implies that information should be accurate to an appropriate level of detail. Completeness means that information includes everything that it needs to include.

The accuracy and completeness of information produced by the MIS and the ES will depend to a large extent on the ability of the consultant to enter precise requests into the systems. If input requests are accurate, then information produced by the MIS will be complete and accurate as the appropriate sections of the database will be accessed and results displayed for the consultant. With the ES, there is a risk that information provided will not be complete if the knowledge base is not updated or the inference engine does not contain appropriate links to determine exactly what output is required.

User confidence

The needs of the user need to be considered, particularly users must be able to trust the output as being relevant to their requirements.

The consultants will normally trust information produced by the MIS because this relates mainly to facts on specific investments. Output from the ES may be more difficult to trust because the ES itself will attempt to interpret requirements of the consultants and provide a range of answers based on those requests. Where the inference engine provides potentially irrelevant output, then trust in the ES will fall.

(b) **Advantages of an Expert System**

Interpretation of data

The ES will be able to compare the specific investment requirements of different clients from the client database and investments already provided, compare this to a range of investments available, and provide similar recommendations for clients with similar requirements. The ES will therefore help to provide appropriate recommendations for each client, enabling Teac to provide better client service and retain its clients.

Consistent output

The consultants may not be able to remember some specific client recommendation leading to potential inconsistencies in recommendations being made. The ES will not 'forget' any details, as common input will result in the same output being produced. The ES will assist consultants to provide relevant and consistent recommendations for investments for specific circumstances of each client, therefore providing better client service.

Knowledge retention

The ES will remain in Teac in the form of rules within the knowledge base of the ES. However, consultants can leave taking their knowledge with them, especially as the CEO is concerned about retaining the number of consultants in Teac. The ES therefore provides a way of retaining and increasing knowledge within Teac.

Audit Trail

The ES will, on request, be able to show exactly how a recommendation has been reached by providing a listing of the different rules used to produce an output. This will help the consultants place trust in the ES as the precise logic used can be seen and checked. As trust increases over time there will be less need to check the logic used.

Disadvantages of an Expert System

Update of system

The accuracy of recommendations provided by the ES is limited by the accuracy of the knowledge base in the system. If the ES has not been updated, or new circumstances arise which the ES has not met before, there is a risk that output will be incorrect. In Teac, the consultants will be aware of changes needed to financial advice, eg changes in legislation. This will take time to program into the ES, limiting its use until changes are complete.

Consistency of output

The ES will provide the same recommendation based on the same or very similar inputs. However, humans can use their 'intuition' or feel for a specific set of circumstances to provide different suggestions based on detailed knowledge of a situation. A consultant may therefore suggest specific investments for one client based on that detailed knowledge which the ES will not be able to emulate.

Cost

The time needed and cost to develop and maintain an ES can be high. Information in the financial sector can change frequently, meaning that the ES must be continually updated. The CEO will need to check that the costs of developing and maintaining the ES do not outweigh the benefits derived from it.

Narrow focus

The ES will only be able to make recommendations based on the 'knowledge' it has been programmed with. In this situation, this knowledge will be insufficient because actions required by humans may appear to be illogical. For example, a client may want to amend a financial portfolio, even though the ES would recommend not to do this. The provision of an ES does not therefore remove the need for human interpretation or assistance in specific situations.

9 Information systems functions

Text reference. Chapter 1 covers material examined in this question.

Top tips. There are six major types of information systems to serve the needs of each of the four levels of an organisation. These may be represented on the following diagram, which you may have chosen to incorporate into your answer:

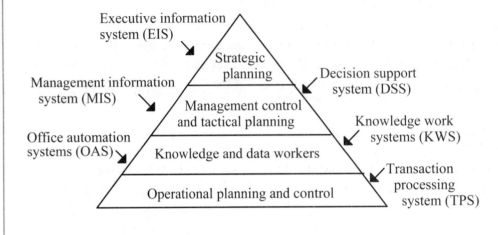

BPP marking scheme

	Marks
Award up to 3.5 marks for each type of system discussed – up to a maximum of 20	<u>20</u>

(a) **Transaction Processing Systems (TPS)** – are operational level systems that perform and record the daily routine transactions necessary to conduct business. They provide information about the efficiency of operations and activities, but are limited in the support they provide to management decision-making.

The TPS routinely captures, processes, stores and outputs the low-level transaction data. It is normally characterised by the use of one of the following methods of processing.

- Batch processing – eg, payroll systems
- On-line processing – sales order entry systems
- Real time processing – stock control systems

(b) **Office Automation Systems (OAS)**. Serve the information needs of the data workers at the knowledge level of the organisation. Typical office automation systems create, handle and manage documents (through word processing, desktop publishing and digital filing), manage workflow and scheduling (through electronic calendars), help financial managers manage client portfolios, manage projects and communication (through electronic mail, electronic bulletin boards, voice mail or teleconferencing). Text and image processing systems evolved from word processors to desktop publishing, enabling the creation of professional documents with graphics and special layout features. Spreadsheets, presentation packages (like PowerPoint), personal database systems and note-taking systems (appointment book and notepad) are all part of OAS and are designed to increase the productivity of data workers in the office.

(c) **Knowledge Work Systems (KWS)**. Support knowledge workers at the knowledge level of the organisation. They are information systems that aid knowledge workers in the creation and integration of new knowledge in the organisation. To do this they need to link the worker to external and internal (organisation) information.

KWS require much more powerful analytic, graphics, document management, and communications abilities than a typical microcomputer. They also need more computing processing power because knowledge workers tend to do more data-intense and computing-intense work than other workers. Examples of KWS include the following:

- Computer Aided Design (CAD) systems

- Virtual Reality systems for simulating the real world eg, flight simulators

- Investment workstations – used in the financial industry

- Group collaboration systems – although the software can be counted among office automation systems, it is used to support knowledge workers also. Groupware is software that supports shared activities: documents, ideas, calendars, e-mail, meeting software, etc

- Intranet environments include Internet technologies used for communication purposes eg, e-mail, chat groups, web tools

- Artificial Intelligence (AI) systems – are based on human expertise, knowledge, and some reasoning patterns. They extend the power of experts, but lack the general reasoning capabilities. These systems are useful to preserve the expertise that can be lost when workers leave a firm.

(d) **Management Information Systems (MIS)**. Information systems at the management level of an organisation that serve the functions of planning, controlling, and decision making by providing routine summary and exception reports. An MIS is defined as 'a system to convert data from internal and external sources into information, and to communicate that information in an appropriate form to managers at all levels and in all areas of the business to enable them to make timely and effective decisions'.

The format of the information supplied is determined by the abilities of the user and by the use that will be made of it.

- Strategic management will require information that is broad, aggregated and summarised

- Tactical management requires information that is more detailed and tailored to the user's needs or area of responsibility

- Operational management require very detailed information specific to their responsibility area

The MIS produces reports that are mainly summarised and inflexible, eg scheduled reports, demand reports, exception reports etc.

(e) **Decision Support Systems (DSS)**. Information systems also at the management level of an organisation that combine data and sophisticated analytical models to support semi-structured and unstructured decision-making. A DSS is defined as 'a computer-based system which enables managers to confront ill-structured problems by direct interaction with data and problem-solving programs'. Their aim is to provide information in a flexible way to aid decision-making.

The DSS does not itself make the decision, it merely assists in going through the phases of decision making. The system sets up various scenarios and the computer predicts the result for each scenario by using a process of 'what if?' analysis.

There are three basic elements to the DSS.

- A language sub-system, which is likely to be non-procedural (called a structured query language or SQL)

- A problem processing sub-system, which includes spreadsheet, graphics, statistical analysis

- A knowledge sub-system, which includes a database function

(f) **Executive Information Systems (EIS)**. Information systems at the strategic level of an organisation designed to address unstructured decision-making through advanced graphics and communication. Information is provided in a very summarised way and is specially designed for the non-IT executive. The EIS has the ability to:

- Call up summary data from an organisation's main systems eg, summary income statement, balance sheet etc

- Analyse the summary data to a more detailed level eg, analysis of the inventory figure shown in the balance sheet

- Manipulate summary data eg, rearrange its format, make comparisons with similar data

- Set up templates so that information from different areas of the business is always summarised in the same format

- Perform complicated 'what if?' analysis

10 Porter's value chain

Text reference. Porter's value chain is explained in Chapter 6 of the text.

Top tips. Using a logical structure and short paragraphs should help ensure you cover all of the points required. Do not repeat the same inputs and outputs in Parts (a) and (b). Ensure you **explain** the importance of the inputs and outputs you mention – if your answer lacks explanation the marks awarded will be limited.

(a)   **Introduction**

As a result of concerns raised at the recent board meeting a new Management Information System (MIS) is currently being considered. Output from the main transaction processing systems will form the input of the MIS.

The MIS manipulates this data into summary level information for control and decision– making purposes to support the monitoring and control of the key functions of the organisation. The MIS will require inputs relating to the three key primary activities of inbound logistics, marketing and sales and technology development.

Inbound logistics

The inbound logistics function aims to ensure the **right materials are available, at the right price and at the right time**. A key element of this involves ensuring the best possible price for raw materials of the required quality is negotiated. Output from the Computer Assisted Design (CAD) and Computer Assisted Manufacture (CAM) systems will become inputs into the MIS. The MIS will manipulate and summarise this data, resulting in information that will enable the purchasing department to **plan** and meet its responsibilities in the most efficient manner. For example, negotiations with suppliers can be faced with **improved knowledge** of the quantities of raw materials required in the medium term which should help win **improved prices**.

Marketing and sales

The MIS can provide information on the activities of customers and salespeople, showing who is buying and selling what. Over time, useful **trends** should become apparent. The links with the CAM system will enable customers to be given accurate information relating to both orders in progress and finished goods. Forecast demand can be made available via the feeder systems to the MIS, and when matched with production scheduling information, instances of **spare capacity** should be able to be established and appropriate action taken.

Technology development

The new MIS should provide information that will allow the increased use of **Computer Assisted Design** (CAD) and **Computer Assisted Manufacture** (CAM). Use of CAD and CAM techniques will **improve**

efficiency, resulting in the **faster** production of garments, and **improved garment quality**. **Prototypes** can be produced rapidly allowing customer feedback to be acted on at the design stage.

The MIS can **monitor sales and production** information and when necessary provide **control information** to ensure orders are delivered on time. One difficult area to predict in the clothing industry is future demand levels for fashion items, as a change in consumer taste can often be rapid and on the surface unpredictable. The MIS will therefore require information feeds from **'outward looking'** sources such as fashion show trends and market research.

(b)   **Outputs required**

Outputs from the CAD/CAM systems should include **performance measures** that show whether the design, development and production activities are **achieving their targets**, and how these functions are contributing to the overall performance of SFA. The performance measures should be available for on-screen viewing, and be included in control reports that highlight areas in need of corrective action.

Reports from the MIS should also show supplier and buyer performance, including information on price, quantity and quality (including service quality). Marginal cost information should feed from the accounting system to the MIS, as this information is vital when negotiating prices relating to 'extra' production runs to utilise any spare capacity.

Conclusion

The proposed MIS will consolidate information from the main transaction processing systems. It will 'pull-together' information from the separate functions of SFA, allowing the **overall picture** to be seen more clearly. This will enable SFA to identify and respond quickly to circumstances that require action. The MIS will enable SFA to operate more **efficiently and effectively** and should be implemented as soon as possible.

11 Strategic plan for IS/IT (Earl)

Text reference. Earl's three leg analysis is covered in Chapter 2 of the text.

Top tips. Strategic planning is a process of deciding the objectives of the organisation, or changes in these objectives, or the resources used to attain these objectives, and the policies that govern the acquisition, use and disposal of these resources. Information is a key resource, as the provision of, and use of information is vital to an organisation's decision making and ultimate success. The role of information technology in information provision and communication should therefore be an integral part of an organisation's overall strategy.

An **IS/IT strategy** is **required for the following reasons**.

(a)   The strategy document is a visible statement of the importance of effective systems in the eyes of senior management. This should ensure an acceptance of new innovations throughout the organisation. It also demonstrates commitment.

(b)   It establishes an agreed view on the role that information technology should play in the organisation.

(c)   The strategy document guides IS/IT investment decisions. It sets a framework for both hardware and software standards and provides for the co-ordinated timing of capital expenditure.

(d)   The sums involved are often significant.

(e)   It discourages the acquisition of incompatible systems by different departments.

(f)   Developing a strategy encourages departments to plan ahead. Short-term decisions are likely to be taken with long-term plans in mind.

A related question is, 'how should the strategy be developed?'. **Earl** has devised a method for the **development of IS strategies**. His method describes three strands or 'legs' – as described below.

(1) **Business led** (top down). The overall objectives of an organisation are identified, then IS/IT systems are implemented to ensure that these objectives are met. Detailed information analysis involving the identification of information needs required to enable the organisation to meet its objectives is required. This is an analytical approach which requires the involvement of senior management and often a team of specialists.

(2) **Infrastructure led** (bottom up). The focus is on transaction processing systems used to provide basic operational information. Information systems are seen primarily as tools for doing business. The trading activities of the organisation are dependant upon IS/IT. The most important people in relation to IS/IT under this approach are users and systems specialists.

(3) **Mixed**. The mixed approach is said to have an 'inside out' emphasis. This involves the organisation exploiting its current IS/IT resources. IS and IT may be used to ensure a new idea or process progresses, but the system or technology itself is not the innovation. This approach relies upon innovation.

The three IS strategy planning approaches described by Earl are not mutually exclusive. Organisations should not therefore restrict themselves to a single approach. Different approaches may be appropriate at different times – depending on the current business environment.

12 Earl's audit grid

Text reference. Earl's audit grid is covered in Chapter 5 of the text.

Top tips. In part (b), select an organisation and system that makes selecting an appropriate quadrant relatively easy. Our answer relates to an on-line ordering system for a web-based retailer. Our answer is just one example of how this question could be approached.

Easy marks. In part (a), two marks are available for explaining the overall purpose/use of Earl's grid. Your answer to (a) should then cover each quadrant in turn – within the context of developing an information systems strategy.

Examiner's comments. The first part of the question was answered well many candidates correctly evaluated the general use of current situational analysis and correctly evaluated the audit grid. Part (b) gave candidates the opportunity to identify an information system in an organisation of their own choice and apply the theory to a practical situation. This style of question has been incorporated in several previous 3.4 examinations. Some excellent answers were provided to this question. Weaker candidates gave examples of systems and organisations that would be appropriate for each quadrant, thus limiting the marks that were available.

Marking scheme

		Marks
(a)	Award up to 2 marks per quadrant (four quadrants) and up to 2 marks for overview	10
(b)	Award up to 2 marks per valid point.	10
		20

(a) **Current situation analysis** (CSA) involves a review of all information systems and information technology used within an organisation. The review includes all aspects of hardware, software, communications devices, network topologies, systems development methodologies, maintenance procedures, contingency plans and IS/IT personnel.

CSA may be used in conjunction with Earl's grid. Earl devised a grid to analyse an organisation's current use of information systems. Current systems are plotted on the following grid – the grid is shown below.

	Low	High
High	Renew	Maintain, enhance
Low	Divest	Reassess

Business Value (vertical axis, High / Low)

Technical Quality

The **four quadrants** in the grid suggest the following.

If a system has little business value and is low on technical quality the system should be disposed of (**divest**). In the context of information systems strategy, these systems will have very little impact on strategic planning.

If a system has a high business value and low technical quality, then the appropriate action is to **renew** the current system by investing in it. The information systems strategy should take the need for investment in these systems into account.

If the system is judged to have high technical quality but low business value, the system should be **reassessed**. An investigation is required before a course of action for these systems can be devised. Relevant questions could include whether the system is meeting an information need – is the system really required?

Finally, if a system has high business value and high technical quality the system should be well **maintained** and if possible **enhanced**. Systems in this quadrant contribute significantly towards the achievement of organisational goals and must be given due consideration in the information systems strategy.

(b)   Considering an '**Internet retailer**' such as Amazon, their **website** represents an information system that has high technical quality and high business value. As such, this system would be placed in the '**maintain/enhance**' quadrant on Earl's grid.

This quadrant is most appropriate for this system for the following reasons.

- The **technical quality** of the system is important in terms of the customer experience it provides and in ensuring reliability (as downtime means lost revenue as potential customers will simply click onto another site).

- As the site is in effect the organisations 'retail outlet', it is the means by which it is able to attract customers and earn revenue. The **business value** of the website as an information system is therefore extremely high.

- The site is also a potential source of **competitive advantage** relative to traditional retailers and other websites. To achieve an advantage requires a user-friendly, reliable site and **order fulfilment** procedures of equally high quality.

- To ensure Amazon remains the 'e-trailer' of choice for many customers requires almost constant improvements (ie maintain and enhance) to make things easier for users and to remain ahead of the competition.

- For these reasons, the website definitely represents an information system of strategic importance in this organisation and belongs in the maintain/enhance quadrant of Earl's grid.

- The fact that **both business value and technical quality are high** discounts all of the other three quadrants of the grid as possibilities.

13 Parsons' generic IS/IT strategies

Text reference. Parson's generic strategies are covered in Chapter 2 of the text.

Top tips. To answer this question you require some knowledge of Parsons' strategies. Refer to your BPP Text if you lack this knowledge.

Examiner's comments. This question listed Parsons' six generic information systems strategies and required candidates to describe the strategy and to link the strategy with the role of the IS function and the user. Many candidates ignored the latter part of the question and only described the strategy.

The last part of the question required candidates to discuss which of the IS strategies best applies to an organisation of their choice. Many answers demonstrated a good understanding of an information systems strategy and why it is applicable to a specific organisation.

Marking scheme

		Marks
(a)	Award up to 2 marks for each generic strategy explained to a maximum of 12 marks	12
(b)	A wide range of answers will be given. Award up to 2 marks for each valid explained point up to a maximum of 8.	8
		20

(a)   Parsons six generic information strategies are described below.

Centrally planned. The logic of this approach is that those planning IS developments should have an understanding of the overall strategic direction. Business and IS strategy are viewed as being closely linked. Users identify opportunities to ensure IS possibilities are fully explored.

Leading edge. There is a belief that innovative technology use can create competitive advantage, and therefore that risky investment in unproven technologies may generate large returns. The organisation must have the motivation and ability to commit large amounts of money and other resources. Users must be enthusiastic and willing to support new initiatives.

Free market. This strategy is based on the belief that the market makes the best decisions. The IS function is a competitive business unit, which must be prepared to achieve a return on its resources. The department may have to compete with outside providers. Users are required to identify and acquire IS services.

Monopoly. The direct opposite to the free market strategy. This strategy is based upon the belief that information is an organisational asset that should be controlled by a single service provider. Users express their needs and negotiate to have them met.

Scarce resource. This strategy is based on the premise that information systems use limited resources, and therefore all IS development requires a clear justification. Budgetary controls are in place and should be adhered to. New projects should be subject to Cost Benefit Analysis (CBA). Users are required to 'bid' for IS resources.

Necessary evil IS/IT is seen as a necessary evil of modern business. IS/IT is allocated enough resource only to meet basic needs. This strategy is usually adopted in organisations that believe that information is not important to the business. Users take no or little active role in the development of information systems.

(b)   Chosen organisation – a private sector provider of professional education tuition and materials (ie a similar organisation to BPP). Of the six generic IS strategies suggested by Parsons, the '**leading edge**' strategy fits this organisation best – for the reasons outlined below.

Senior management believe **innovative technology** (such as lectures delivered using PowerPoint and interactive learning material on CD-ROM and on the web) can be used for competitive advantage. Competitors are yet to produce a significant e-learning product suite.

Although significant investment is required to produce this material, management believes there is the potential to generate significant returns (particularly for e-learning). Therefore, senior management are providing the **commitment**, the funds and the **other resources** required to produce high quality material in these new formats.

Users (in this context 'users' refers to staff involved in the development and use of PowerPoint slides and the development of e-learning material) must be **enthusiastic** and willing to **embrace** the **opportunities** presented by new technology.

This means lecturers/tutors must have a **reasonable level** of IT literacy to teach using PowerPoint, and those involved developing e-leaning materials require both an understanding of the topics they are dealing with and of the strengths and weaknesses of electronic media.

This strategy is relatively **high risk** as significant investment is required – and some observers suggest that the impact of e-learning has been overestimated with many students preferring to study using traditional paper-based materials.

14 McFarlan's strategic grid and the BCG matrix

Text reference. McFarlan's grid and the BCG Matrix are explained in Chapter 5 of the text.

Top tips. The strategic grid developed by *McFarlan* can be related to the BCG matrix. The relationship between the two models is referred to in the syllabus – and is one of the few areas yet to be examined.

Easy marks. Quick marks will be available for drawing each of the diagrams. They will also provide a focus and a reference point for your answer.

(a)   The Strategic grid devised by McFarlan shows the level of dependence on IS/IT within an organisation. The grid classifies four levels of dependence as shown below.

		Strategic importance of current information systems	
		Low	**High**
Strategic importance of planned information systems	**High**	Turnaround	Strategic
	Low	Support	Factory

- Organisations in the **strategic** quadrant currently depend on IS/IT for competitive advantage, and expect to continue to do so.

- Organisations in the **turnaround** quadrant do not currently view IS/IT as having strategic importance, but expect IS/IT will be strategically important in the future.

- Organisations in the **support** quadrant see no strategic value in IS/IT.

- Organisations in the **factory** quadrant see IS/IT as strategically significant at the moment, but predict this will not be the case in the future.

(b)   The **Boston Consulting Group** (BCG) devised a matrix that plots a company's products in terms of potential cash generation and cash expenditure requirements.

Organisations use the BCG matrix when making decisions related to investment priorities between a range of products (or a business units), whether to use a product (business unit) as a source of finance for investment in other products or when to cease production of a product (divest).

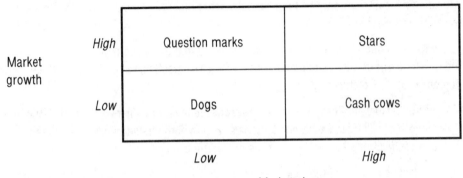

The quadrants or classifications are explained (and related to the strategic grid) in the paragraphs below.

Stars

In the short term, Stars require capital expenditure in excess of the cash they generate, in order to maintain their market position. These products are expected to produce high returns in the future.

The closest equivalent classification in the strategic grid would be 'Strategic', strategically important systems requiring significant investment, a possible source of competitive advantage.

Cash cows

It may be that eventually Stars will become Cash cows. Cash cows need very little capital expenditure and generate high levels of cash income, they in effect finance the Stars.

The closest equivalent classification in the strategic grid would be 'Factory', systems that were originally state of the art, are now slightly dated but are still performing well.

Question marks

How best to deal with Question marks is not obvious. Relevant considerations include whether these products justify considerable capital expenditure in the hope of increasing their market share, or should they be allowed to die quietly as they are squeezed out of the expanding market by rival products?

The closest equivalent classification in the strategic grid would be 'Turnaround', systems that would require significant updating (investment) to remain in use.

Dogs

Dogs may be ex-cash cows that have now fallen on hard times. Although they will show only a modest net cash outflow, or even a modest net cash inflow, they are cash traps which tie up funds and provide a poor return on investment. However, they may have a useful role, either to complete a product range or to keep competitors out.

The closest equivalent classification in the strategic grid would be 'Support', systems that are not strategically important and are therefore unlikely to justify significant investment

15 International business strategies

Text reference. Parts (a) and (b) contain material covered in Chapter 7 of the text, Part (c) covers material in Chapter 9

Top tips. Ensure you provide a justification for each information system that you nominate for the various global strategies. There may be more than one applicable system – don't worry if the systems in your answer differs from ours.

Easy marks. Explain what each strategy entails as a first step: basic descriptions can gain quick marks. You may find that a simple diagram is a good way to answer part (c) and keep your answer clear and focused.

Examiner's comments. The question provided a 'polarisation' of marks, with candidates tending to score either 4 to 8 or 15 to 20 marks. The mark range was indicative of candidates either knowing the theory or guessing at solutions. Weaker answers also tended to focus on individual systems such as intranets and Internet rather than describing strategies.

Marking scheme

			Marks
(a)	Award up to 2 marks for each description. 4 × 2	Max	8
(b)	Award up to 1 mark for each description. 4 × 1	Max	4
(c)	Award up to 2 marks for identifying and justifying each suitable information system. 4 × 2	Max	8
			20

(a) The four headings relate to different global strategies that an organisation can follow.

    (i) **Domestic Exporter**

       In this strategy, most activities are based in the organisation's home country. Offices in other countries are controlled from the central office in the home country. There is therefore little or no autonomy for the other offices as all finance, marketing and human resources are controlled centrally.

    (ii) **Multinational**

       In a multinational, some activities are centralised but others are managed within individual countries. Most multinationals set administrative and control procedures centrally and then allow local offices to decide on individual production and marketing strategies. Many service and manufacturing companies such as accountants and motor vehicle manufacturers operate this type of business strategy.

    (iii) **Franchiser or licensing**

       The product or service is designed to strict specifications at a central location, but individual countries then have their own production and distribution systems. As long as the product meets the specification then this policy is allowed. For example, McDonalds decide on the product range centrally, but this is implemented locally, partly due to the high cost of transporting raw materials for McDonald's products.

(iv) **Transnational**

In a transnational, activities are viewed and managed on a global basis. Activities tend to be managed on a national basis without reference to national boundaries. There may be a 'head office' although its geographical location is irrelevant. Each country may have a local office for convenience purposes, allowing some degree of localisation. There are few examples of this type of company, although Internet portals such as Yahoo and Google are probably the closest to this definition.

(b) Four Information Technology Strategies that are applicable on a global basis are:

(i) **Centralised**

All systems development and operation is performed in one location.

(ii) **Decentralised**

Each country is allowed to develop and operate its own systems. Different systems may be implemented making global data difficult to obtain.

(iii) **Duplicated**

All systems development is carried out in one place. However, each country is then allowed to implement and maintain its own systems, based on the initial systems development.

(iv) **Networked**

Systems development and operation is performed in many locations. Some or all of the different systems may be implemented worldwide.

(c) The best match of business strategy for each type of system configuration is shown below:

System configuration	Business strategy			
	Domestic exporter	Multinational	Franchiser	Transnational
Centralised	X			
Decentralised	x	X	x	
Duplicated			X	
Networked		x		X

X shows the best match with x showing a less important but still viable strategy.

A **domestic exporter** will normally be suited to a **centralised** system as activities are based in the home country. Some minor amendment may be required to local systems to meet local laws eg Data Protection legislation.

Multinational strategy is normally suited to **decentralised** IS approach. The head office maintains overall financial control but individual functions are at a local level. This implies a need for decentralised IT to maintain the local systems but with some networking so that results can be transferred to head office.

A **franchiser** develops systems centrally and then duplicates them in each country. This strategy fits the **duplicated** system configuration best, as IT systems become a duplicate of the main country.

A **transnational** entity has no main head office and maintains a global business. Good communication links are needed implying a **networked** system configuration.

16 Porter's five forces

Text reference. Porter's five forces are covered in Chapter 6 of the text.

Top tips. Your answer should discuss each of the five forces with reference to the development of an information systems strategy. Make sure that your answer to part (b) does not simply repeat the material you have written in part (a).

Easy marks. A brief description of the five forces model will earn marks, but make sure that it is placed in the appropriate context to earn them efficiently.

Examiner's comments. In part (a), many candidates missed the requirement word 'discuss' and described the five forces but not the information systems strategy, limiting the marks that could be awarded.

Part (b) provided some better answers (with a few 'excellent' answers being identified by the Examiner), although a few weaker answers simply repeated the information from part (a).

Marking scheme

		Marks
(a)	Award up to 2 marks for each valid point. Max 8 marks.	8
(b)	Award up to 2 marks for each description of a force and up to 2 marks for identifying appropriate supporting information systems. 4 × 3.	12
		20

(a) The five forces model can help an organisation to develop an information systems strategy that will enable it to trade competitively in the following ways:

How to respond to forces

The model helps an organisation to identify the different forces that are affecting that particular organisation in terms of potential entrants, suppliers, customers etc. Having identified the specific forces, an appropriate response or responses can be developed to overcome that force. Specifically within the information systems strategy, this will mean amending current systems or establishing new systems to overcome information deficiencies in respect to each threat.

IS builds barriers to entry?

Having identified the different forces within a marketplace, an organisation can use IS to build barriers to entry within that market place. For example, provision of better information may limit the ability of new entrants to break into the market. In marketplaces with a high information intensity such as newspapers or provision of financial services, provision of appropriate information is essential. If new entrants cannot match the information provision of existing organisations, they will be excluded from that marketplace.

Threat or opportunity to business

Monitoring the five forces may provide an organisation with indications of threats affecting the business or opportunities within the marketplace. For example, a competitor may develop a new information system, and the organisation will have to respond by updating its own information systems. Similarly, research into IS within an organisation may present opportunities for that company to expand, or provide new products or enhanced features to existing products. Various threats and opportunities can be graded and information systems amended to take account of the 'worst' threats and the 'best' opportunities.

Change in industry structure

One of the main reasons for developing the five forces framework was to monitor changes in the industry structure. Monitoring the industry structure will enable a company to plan effectively for IS usage. For example, the analysis may identify the appearance of substitutes which will adversely affect the organisation. IS systems will then have to be amended to provide additional information on those substitutes and amend existing products to take account of them.

(b)   Examples of information systems that are appropriate to provide competitive advantage.

Competitive rivalry

This force relates to competition between different companies in the same market sector.

Information systems can be used to gain competitive advantage either by reducing the cost or production or by providing some element or uniqueness to a product, essentially focusing on the Porter theory of cost leadership or differentiation.

Cost leadership can be obtained by using IS to decrease the costs of production. For example, in car manufacturing, the use of Computer Assisted Design and Computer Assisted Manufacture not only decreased design time but also enabled production volumes to be increased using cheap robots rather than more expensive humans.

Product differentiation is also relevant to the car industry. IS can be used within the motor vehicle to provide computer diagnostics, limiting servicing time and expense. Similarly, the driver can be provided with additional information including a Global Position System to enable effective navigation and use of the diagnostic system to provide alerts such as low petrol warning.

If competitors cannot match these features, the organisation will have gained some competitive advantage using IS.

Buyer's bargaining power

This force relates to the power of buyers to purchase from another organisation in the same industry. In many situations, this power may be quite high because customers can switch suppliers very easily. IS must therefore be used to attempt to limit the ability of buyers to switch supplier, or provide reasons for the customer retaining their existing supplier.

In many situations, use of IS can be a useful method of retaining customers, particularly with Internet sites. Organisations can ensure that their web sites are quick and efficient to use, encouraging repeat visits. Data obtained from customer purchases can be 'mined' to identify purchasing patterns. Details of new products or offers on existing products can be e-mailed to the customer, encouraging repeat visits to the site.

IS can also be used to monitor customer purchases and provide incentives for re-purchase away from the Internet. For example, supermarkets provide loyalty cards to accumulate 'points' based on purchases made and airlines provide frequent flyer programmes. Customers are provided with information about the points or miles they have collected by the organisation's IS again encouraging repeat purchases to obtain a specific 'reward'.

Suppliers' bargaining power

This force relates to the suppliers of an organisation. Suppliers provide the raw materials and other inputs needed. Their power relates to the ability to increase prices of materials being provided or to move limited supplies of that material to another customer. Organisations need to ensure continuity of supply at a reasonable price.

Where there are a large number of suppliers for a particular product, IS can be used to limit their power by providing price comparisons between the different suppliers. Monitoring of Internet sites and obtaining price information is one method of obtaining this information.

However, in situations with only one or a limited number of suppliers, price comparison will not be effective. In this situation, IS can be used to lock the supplier into the purchasing company by providing a partnership. The supplier benefits from provision of information about the customer and probably guarantee of price, while the purchasing company benefits from continuity of supply. For example, a book is normally available from one publisher. Resellers can provide the publisher with forecast demand for the book helping the publisher to identify how many copies of the book to manufacture.

Similarly, Electronic Data Interchange systems allow transfer of data between customer and supplier. This will enable the supplier to monitor sales at its customers and provide stock replenishment on a timely basis. The customer benefits from not having to monitor stock levels so closely, allowing more time to focus on selling products.

17 Evaluation of strategy

BPP marking scheme

		Marks
(a)	Three strategies (Systems, Technology, Management)	
	Explanation of strategy (3 marks max)	
	Link between strategies (2 marks max)	
	Maximum marks awarded for part (a)	9
(b)	Up to 2 marks per issue with strategy and up to 2 marks per recommendation for change	
	IT is a cost	
	Internal/external focus	
	Lack of innovative use of IT	
	EIS	
	Benchmarking	
	Strategic planning	
	Errors in reports	
	Other relevant points	
	Maximum marks awarded part (b)	11
		20

Text reference. IS and IT strategy are discussed in Chapter 2. IM is covered in Chapter 1.

Top tips. You should be familiar with these terms from your studies. A pass standard candidate will recognise the need to discuss all three strategies and show the link between them.

(a) **Information Systems strategy**

Information Systems (IS) strategy is concerned with determining the information required within an organisation and the information systems required to deliver it. The IS strategy will state what information is required at all levels of an organisation – strategic, tactical and operational – and the systems at each level that will provide it.

The IS strategy is closely linked to the overall strategy of the organisation, as it provides the information that enables progress towards overall goals to be monitored. For example, information is required to monitor Critical Success Factors and Key Performance Indicators.

Information Technology strategy

The Information Technology (IT) strategy has a narrower focus. It is concerned with the hardware and software is required to deliver the information specified by the IS strategy.

The IT strategy explains what IT systems are required to support the IS strategy. This will involve examining the information needs at all levels of the organisation, and outlining the hardware and software required to meet those needs. For example, senior management may require summarised high level 'Balanced scorecard' style information, with the ability to drill down to view underlying data. In this case, an Executive Information System would form part of the IT strategy.

Information Management strategy

An organisation's Information Management (IM) strategy explains how information processed and held within the organisation will be managed. Issues such as information storage, archiving and back-ups are covered.

The IM strategy should aim to ensure that staff receive of have access to all information they require. IM is also concerned with examining whether all information produced is actually used. If not, some systems or processes may be removed.

(b)

> **Top tips.** A pass candidate will be able to use the scenario to identify where the IS strategy is being implemented – correctly or otherwise. This information should then be used to show how the strategy could be improved.

Evaluation of the Information Systems strategy of the MG organisation

The Information Systems strategy of the MG organisation appears to be inadequate. Four of the main reasons why are outlined below, with suggestions for improvement.

Lack of strategic level information

MG does not have an Executive Information System (EIS). Even the Board relies on tactical level reports, which are highly unlikely to provide the strategic information required to formulate an effective, forward-looking strategy.

An EIS should be implemented that includes relevant external information and provides appropriate planning tools.

IT budget setting process

The main driver of Information Systems development within MG appears to be the IT budget. IT is treated simply as a cost with a 'standard' increase allocated each year. There is no review of what systems are actually required to improve information processing or provision.

This approach is a weakness as it is likely to discourage any attempt to actually determine the information requirements of staff and the organisation as a whole. A more appropriate method of budgeting would be to determine the cost of providing the IT systems required to meet the demands of MG's information systems strategy.

No investigation of potential benefits IT could bring

Information systems development within MG has focussed on basic transaction processing and the provision of operational and tactical information. Information Systems strategy development should include looking outside the organisation, for example at current trends and new IT products that could possibly be utilised to make MG more competitive.

The Board could employ external consultants to identify information systems and recent developments in IT that could be beneficial to MG. It may be possible to re-engineer some processes using IT.

No use of benchmarking

It appears that no effort is made to establish how competitors utilise IS and therefore whether MG is utilising IS as effectively as those recognised as following 'best practice'.

A benchmarking exercise could be attempted. It may prove difficult to obtain all the relevant information from competitors, but a general idea at least should be able to be obtained.

18 The value chain

> **Text reference**. Porter's value chain is covered in Chapter 6 of the text.
>
> **Top tips**. The first three sections of this question rely on knowledge of the value chain. Explaining the nine sections of the value chain in part (c) for 5 marks means you have less than one minute on each point, so be concise. Part (d) requires a little more thought. Think about how the value chain breaks an organisation up into different activities, then go on and explain how IT/IS applies.

Marking scheme

		Marks
(a)	Award up to 2 marks	2
(b)	Award up to 3 marks	3
(c)	Award 0.5 of a mark for each correct description (maximum 5 marks)	5
(d)	Award 1 mark for each valid point up to a maximum of 10 marks	10
		20

(a) A **value activity** is an activity which adds value to the product or service being produced by an organisation. The activity contains two parts:

   (i) A physical component includes all the physical tasks required to complete that activity.

   (ii) The information processing component encompasses all the steps required to capture, manipulate, and channel the data necessary to perform the activity.

(b) A **primary activity** is an activity which involves the making of a product or service, including the distribution, sale and after-care service for that product or service.

A **support activity** is an activity which supports the primary activities or other support activities. Support activities include procurement, product and technology development, human resource management and administration and infrastructure services.

(c) **Activities in the value chain**

   (i) **Inbound logistics**

     Activities to receive, store and distribute the inputs required to produce goods and services, such as stock control and contacts with suppliers.

   (ii) **Operations**

     Activities involved with producing the product or service including manufacture, packaging and testing.

(iii) **Outbound logistics**

Activities to send the product to the consumer including warehousing and distribution.

(iv) **Marketing and sales**

Activities to receive orders from customers to purchase products and services and other activities involved in inducing potential customers to purchase the product or service such as advertising and promotion.

(v) **Service**

Activities to help retain product value including after-sales service, provision of parts and training of installers and repairers.

(vi) **Procurement**

Purchasing any necessary inputs.

(vii) **Technology development**

Development of machines, computers, processes and systems and expertise of staff.

(viii) **Human resource management**

Activities to train, develop and provide remuneration to staff.

(ix) **Infrastructure**

Maintenance of the general infrastructure of the organisation including management, finance and planning.

(d) The value chain is important when developing an IS or IT strategy because it allows the organisation to be split into the distinct activities outlined in the value chain. This model can then be used to assess the effectiveness and efficiency of resource use within each activity in the chain.

Efficiency is a measure of how well resources are being used, with measures including profitability, capacity use and the yield obtained from that capacity. Effectiveness relates to how well resources are allocated to those activities which are most competitively significant within the value chain. The assessment will involve monitoring the activities in terms of people, capital technology use and possibly R&D.

Having identified areas which could be more efficient or effective from the value chain analysis, the IS/IT strategy can be used to try and determine how those activities, and in particular the competitively significant activities, can be improved. Specific areas that may be investigated include:

(i) Can **linkages** between the different activities be improved by the use of IT? For example, information from support activities may be made available to primary activities on a timelier basis.

(ii) Can the **information flow** through primary activities be improved? For example, linking sales and marketing with operations or outbound logistics using a central database to provide sales and marketing with on-line details of products being produced.

(iii) Can more effective links be formed with **external entities**? For example, can inbound logistics be improved by using EDI or allowing suppliers access to Intranet databases concerning stock availability (in other words setting up an Extranet).

(iv) Can using IT **decrease the cost** of any activity? For example, is there room for more automation or transformation of activities, or even re-engineering using currently available IT tools and techniques?

In conclusion, the value chain provides a valuable method of looking at the organisation, helping managers to focus on the linkages between activities, allowing consideration of where IT can improve effectiveness and efficiency of those links or individual activities.

19 Evaluating information systems

Text reference. Chapter 5 and 8 of the text have material relevant to this question.

Top tips. This is a straightforward question requiring the application of theory to an organisation of your choice. This style of question has been used before so you should be prepared to use your knowledge in this way.

Easy marks. In part (a), concentrate on the balance between cost and benefits in relation to the information provided. For part (b), provide an additional two or three factors for the marks available.

Examiner's comments. Part (a) attracted some excellent answers. In part (b), strong candidates provided four relevant factors and obtained full marks. Weaker candidates listed the same factors that were given in the question. For (c), some candidates interpreted the question differently and provided examples of different information systems in a variety of organisations. Many candidates managed to obtain reasonable marks for parts (a) and (b), but only a minority of candidates gained high marks for (c).

Marking scheme

		Marks
(a)	Award up to 2 marks per valid point, max 6 marks.	6
(b)	Award up to 1 mark per factor, max 4 marks.	4
(c)	Award up to 2 marks per factor evaluated, max 10 marks.	10
		20

(a) Management need to assess the viability of investing in business information systems for a number of reasons:

Firstly, to ensure that the system will **meet the aims of the organisation**. The information system should support the business strategy.

Secondly, to ensure that the system is **financially viable**. Some form of cost benefit analysis will be carried out to ensure that the benefits of the system (tangible and intangible) outweigh the costs.

Thirdly, to ensure that the system **meets user requirements**. It is inappropriate to invest in systems if users won't use them.

Key factors to take into account prior to making an investment decision for a particular system include:

- **Acceptability**, in terms of users, and meeting business strategy, as noted above

- **Suitability** in terms of functionality, that is ensuring that the system will provide the necessary information

- **Feasibility**. Any system must meet the tests of political, economic, social and technological feasibility

- **Environmental fit.** Ensuring that the system fits with existing systems and also with any environmental constraints such as linking to suppliers or customer systems where necessary

(b) General factors relevant to evaluation process include those listed below.

- The cost of the system (is it justified, is it best value)?
- Does the system provide competitive advantage (and if so how long will this last)?
- Will the system require changes to current business processes?
- Is implementation of the system crucial to the success of the organisation?

(c) This answer relates to the implementation of a new centralised Customer Relationship Management (CRM) system in a large bank. Previous to this there was no specialised CRM system – customer details were held only on the main banking system.

What information is provided?

The CRM will hold and analyse information relating to customer details, demographics, accounts and transactions. The CRM system will enable use to be made of this data (eg with targeted marketing; help identify high value 'prestige customers'.

What is it used for?

The CRM will be used to manage customer details and for marketing purposes. Evaluation will focus on efficiencies of managing those details. More accurate and effective communication should result.

What is achieved by using it?

In this case, the CRM was necessary partly to keep up with other banks and partly to meet customer expectations. Our bank was falling behind in provision of customer information and customers were becoming annoyed in delays in obtaining relevant information. The system was necessary simply to maintain position in the marketplace.

The cost of the system (is it justified, is it best value)?

The overall cost was in the millions of GBP, although I was not able to determine the exact amount. Estimating the benefits was difficult as many were intangible eg enhanced customer communication.

Does the system provide competitive advantage (and if so how long will this last)?

The system did not so much as provide competitive advantage as enable the bank to keep up with competitors. Implementation was necessary to protect market share.

Will the system require changes to current business processes?

The system did not require changes to how business was done. Staff were able to access the CRM through the same terminals used for the main banking system. However, evaluation did identify some additional benefits of the system such as access to national databases and longer retention of information.

Is implementation of the system crucial to the success of the organisation?

The quick answer was 'yes'. Market research had shown competitors who were using specialist CRM systems were creating a better impression with their customers. CRM systems were enabling competitors to provide better quality information to customers – which threatened our market share.

20 Peppard's grid

Marking scheme

		Marks
(a)	Award up to 2 marks for each element. 4 elements, max 8 marks. Give credit if candidates name elements as 'turnaround' and 'factory', instead of 'high potential' and 'key operational' respectively.	8
(b)	Award 1 mark for each valid point. Max 4 marks.	4
(c)	Award up to 2 marks for each valid point. Max 8 marks.	8
		20

(a) Peppard developed the Boston Consulting Groups strategic grid into his applications portfolio. The portfolio was presented as a grid which is then used to analyse the strategic impact of individual applications within an organisation.

The grid considers the strategic importance of applications in the current competitive environment and then the predicted future competitive environment.

The four sections of the grid are:

Support

Support applications are not critical to business success and do not necessarily improve management effectiveness. Systems have a low importance in the current competitive environment and the future predicted competitive environment. The systems therefore have little relevance to the core activities of the company, being more 'support' activities. Examples of these types of systems include wages and accounting. An industry using mainly support activities is cement manufacture. In this example there is little room for automation so information systems have little relevance to the actual manufacture of cement.

Key operational

Key operational applications support the established core business activities. They are of high strategic importance now but may have a less important role in the future as they may be replaced by other systems. The systems do not necessarily add to the competitive advantage of the organisation, but are still essential for the timely production of goods and services. An example is inventory control systems. These are needed to provide efficient manufacture of products, but not necessarily to enhance the value of the actual product itself to customers.

Strategic

Strategic applications are vital to the organisation's future success. They are of a high strategic importance now and in the future. The organisation could not run efficiently or provide its services without these systems. For example, banks and financial services companies rely on information systems to provide customer service staff with information so appropriate advice can be given to clients. Without the systems, the staff and therefore the organisation, could not operate.

High potential

High potential applications may be important to the future success of an organisation. They may have a significant impact in the future, but are less important in the current competitive environment. Systems are likely to be innovative with an element of risk as to whether they will be successfully used in the future. Examples include the use of information technology in supermarkets, where stock control and EPOS help maintain a real-time record of stock balances, but also monitor customer spending patterns for data mining. Following implementation those systems are likely to become more important, or strategic, in terms of the grid.

(b) The Peppard grid is useful as it provides **an analysis of the current use of information systems** within an organisation. Placing applications onto the grid can show the importance of information systems and therefore whether those systems are needed to support the core strategies of an organisation. The fact that some organisations may not have any strategic applications, eg cement manufacture, is not necessarily bad, it simply shows that the organisation relies less on IS.

The grid also allows the use of IS to be **tracked over time**. The importance of information systems may change, and this can be identified by producing the grid every few years. For example, the use of IS in supermarkets has changed from being basically support or back office, to strategic with EPOS and data mining being used to provide competitive advantage. The grid underlines the importance for investment in these areas.

(c) The **banking system** is used as an example in this section.

In many banks, the customer sees only a **limited number** of information systems. For example, if a customer applies for a mortgage, the IS is shown to be supporting the mortgage analyst by providing details of different mortgages, rates of repayment etc which the mortgage analyst could not obtain for themselves. These systems are strategic because they are **essential** in the current competitive environment and likely to remain so in the future.

However, other systems may be **under development**. For example, 'smart cards', that is credit cards with computer chips embedded in them which are used as a form of money, have been trialled in many locations. A traveller's cheque card with money on the card itself has also recently become available. These applications may become important in the future, although at present their use is limited, so they have **high potential** in terms of the Peppard grid.

Banks also have to pay their employees and keep track of their training requirements, promotion details etc. In other words there are some systems that the customer never sees, but are still being used. These systems **support** the business in terms of Peppard, failure would not stop the bank operating in the short term.

Finally, the bank must keep track of the numerous **individual transactions** being carried out each day. Customers pay for goods and services using debit cards, withdraw cash from ATMs, receive payments from their employer for salaries and expenses etc. These systems are **important** now because customers expect them to be there and to have access to real time information about their account. Without the systems the bank would not be in business. However, the systems themselves are common to all banks and so do not provide any competitive advantage. In terms of Peppard they are **key operational**.

21 Question with answer plan: application selection; risks and benefits

> **Text reference.** Chapter 5 of the text contains material in this answer.
>
> **Top tips.** When an organisation has alternative investments to choose from, there are several non-financial techniques for determining the risks and benefits, and selecting and evaluating information systems. Risks are not necessarily a problem, they can be tolerated if they are justified by potential benefits.

Answer plan

Outline some possible risks and benefit – use a table

List of techniques to use (explain and apply):

- Scenario models
- Decision trees
- Gap analysis
- Synergy analysis
- Opportunity matrix analysis
- Portfolio analysis
- Scoring models

Potential benefits to the organisation

	High	Low
High (Project risk)	Cautiously examine	Avoid
Low (Project risk)	Identify and develop	Routine applications

Each application carries risks and benefits – explain the action to take to minimise with reference to the grid. Make the point that there is no right answer as all organisations are different.

Some possible risks and benefits are outlined in the table below.

Benefits	Risks
- Increased productivity	- Benefits may not be obtained
- Cost savings	- Costs of implementation may exceed budgets
- Reduced workforce	- Proposed implementation time exceeded
- Improved asset use	- Technical performance less than expected
- More information	- System is incompatible with existing software and/or hardware
- Improved decision-making	
- Higher customer satisfaction	
- Improved operations	

The selection methods include the following:

- **The use of scenario models** – attempts to match specific options with a range of possible future situations (or scenarios). This approach is essentially qualitative and used as a means of addressing some of the less well-structured or uncertain aspects of evaluation. Scenarios will produce information regarding the relevance or otherwise of different courses of action.

- **The use of decision trees** – in which probabilities can be assigned to different outcomes. The greatest limitation of decision tree analysis is that the choice at each branch on the tree can tend to be simplistic. Nevertheless, as a starting point for evaluation, decision trees can often provide a useful framework.

- **Gap analysis** – which is used to identify the extent to which different options will fail to meet the needs/requirements of the organisation in the future. A variety of gaps can be analysed. These include a profit gap, a performance-risk gap, a sales revenue gap, a manpower gap and so on. In each case, there must be a target for achievement and a projection or forecast based on an extrapolation of existing conditions.

- **Synergy analysis** measures the extra benefit which could accrue from providing some sort of linkage between two or more activities.

- **Opportunity matrix analysis** – which can assess different options against potential opportunities identified within the strategic analysis.

- **Portfolio analysis** – this grid (shown below) focuses on the project risk versus the potential benefit of several applications to select among the alternatives.

Potential benefits to the organisation

	High	Low
High	Cautiously examine	Avoid
Low	Identify and develop	Routine applications

(Left axis label: **Project risk** — High / Low)

Each application carries risks and benefits, and the overall portfolio will have a profile of risk and benefit to the organisation.

In general, applications with a low benefit and high risk should be avoided; high benefit and low risk should be developed, and those with low benefit and low risk should be re-examined with the possibility of rebuilding them and replacing them with alternative systems having higher benefits.

However, there is no single ideal mix that would suit all organisations. For example, an organisation involved in an information-intensive industry may benefit from some high risk, high benefit applications to help them remain at the cutting edge of technology. Other organisations may prefer high benefit, low risk applications.

- **Scoring models** – alternative selections are scored relative to each other in various areas of weighted criteria. The sum of the weighted scores produces an overall value for each selection. This value is then used to determine or rationalise a final selection. Scoring models rely heavily on qualitative assessment of the suitability or fit of the system with the overall evaluative criteria.

The example below shows a scoring model used to choose between three alternative systems.

Criteria	Weight	System 1		System 2		System 3	
User needs met	0.40	2	0.8	3	1.2	4	1.6
Purchase cost	0.20	1	0.2	3	0.6	4	0.8
Financing	0.10	1	0.1	3	0.3	4	0.4
Ease of maintenance	0.10	2	0.2	3	0.3	4	0.4
Chance of success	0.20	3	0.6	4	0.8	4	0.8
Final score			**1.9**		**3.2**		**4.0**

The weight is given on the importance the decision makers attach to the criterion. The relative merit of each system is judged on a scale of 1-5 (lowest to highest). The model above ranks system three higher than the other two.

It is usual to cycle through the scoring model several times, changing the criteria and the weights to see how sensitive the outcome is to reasonable changes.

Scoring methods are used mainly to confirm, rationalise and support decisions rather than as the final arbiters of the system selection.

22 Hard and soft approaches

Text reference. Hard and soft approaches are covered in Chapter 4 of the text.

Top tips. Soft systems methodology crops up regularly in the exam. Ensure you're able to produce appropriate root definitions for a range of situations. Question practice is key in this area. Remember also that a range of answers are likely to score well on these type of questions. Don't assume that if your root definition differs to the answer we provide that you are wrong.

Examiner's comments. This question was extremely popular and well answered by the majority of candidates. This was particularly true of the first part of the question covering the differences between the hard and soft approaches.

The second part of the question required candidates to choose two from three CATWOE's cited and produce an appropriate root definition. Unfortunately a minority of candidates drew conceptual models or rich pictures to answer to this part of the question, others wrote paragraphs for each root definition. The overall majority of candidates however produced very good root definitions and were awarded high marks.

The final part of the question required candidates to construct a CATWOE and a corresponding root definition for either a taxpayer or a politician with reference to the state run college education system. The answers produced by the majority of candidates were of a high standard.

Marking scheme

		Marks
(a)	For (i) to (iv), award up to 2 marks for each valid, explained point. Max of 2 marks for each of (i) to (iv).	8
(b)	For (i), award up to 3 marks for each Root Definition. Max of 6 marks for part (i).	
	For (ii), award up to 3 marks for the CATWOE and up to three for the root definition. Max of 6 marks for part (ii).	12
		20

ANSWERS

(a) The differences between the hard and soft approaches to the development of information systems include the approach taken to the following aspects.

(i) **Problem definition**. A hard approach views the problem the system is addressing in a narrow, logical way. The soft approach takes a wider view, considering a wider range of issues rather than focussing solely on the nuts and bolts of the system.

(ii) **The organisation**. Under the hard approach the identity and workings of the organisation are taken for granted. The soft approach on the other hand sees what makes up the organisation in the context of the system being developed as something to be decided upon following thought and negotiation. The organisation is seen as a Human Activity system rather than simply as a legal entity.

(iii) **The reasons for modelling**. The hard approach sees modelling as a relatively simple way of representing the real world situation. The soft approach develops a model to generate debate and insight about the real world rather than aiming to represent a single 'correct' way of modelling the situation.

(iv) **The outcome.** The hard approach aims to produce a system recommendation or specification to address the needs of the situation. The soft approach aims to produce a better understanding of the problem that will be useful when considering potential system designs.

(b) (i) *(Any two of the following)*

The student' root definition. A college is an institution that offers education and teaching by qualified staff. The college offers students the opportunity to receive a good quality education in their chosen field funded from taxes.

The lecturer's root definition. A college provides an educational environment funded by taxpayers that enables teaching staff to educate/teach students. The environment should include specialised equipment and support services that enable high quality teaching to be delivered to students.

The administrator's root definition. A college is an institution that brings together students and lecturers to allow teaching to take place. This requires a number of other administrative and support activities to be performed by other staff.

(ii) *(One of the following)*

(1) CATWOE and root definition from the point of view of a **tax payer**.

Client or customer: Students

Actor: The government (particularly the inland revenue)

Transformation: Tax paid from wages/salaries into educational services

Weltanschauung: The need to obtain maximum value for taxpayer funds spent on education

Owner: The government

Environment: The needs of society and limited taxpayer funds

A taxpayer funded system which transforms tax revenue into provision of educational services. Students receive an education that enables them to contribute to society in the future, although students themselves benefit directly from improved employment/salary prospects.

(2) CATWOE and root definition from the point of view of a **politician**.

Client or customer: Taxpayers (who are also the voting public)

Actor: Government policy makers

Transformation: Tax revenue into education provision

Weltanschauung: Need to supply high quality state education cost-effectively – and to receive voter support for doing so

Owner: The government and voters

Environment: Political balance between the need to provide high quality public services while keeping taxation levels as low as practicable.

A government funded system of education provision that equips students with the tools required to contribute to society. There is a need to balance the service offered against the expenditure required and to provide the best service possible for the taxpayers (voters) funds spent.

23 Soft systems methodology

Text reference. Soft systems methodology is discussed in Chapter 4 of the text.

Top tips. Ensure you understand the basics of drawing conceptual models as this is a popular area for examination. Remember though that your diagram doesn't have to be 'perfect' to earn a good mark. Some candidates spend too long on this type of question trying to achieve perfection – resulting in insufficient time to pick up easier marks available on other questions. Sometimes it pays to be satisfied with what you've already got – remember your main objective is to pass which 'only' requires you to score 50% or more.

Examiner's comments. Part (a), requiring candidates to list an appropriate set of CATWOE was answered very well. The discussion of the need to construct conceptual model was also generally answered well. However, only a few candidates actually drew a conceptual model. Those who did were awarded excellent marks. Too many candidates did not attempt this part, others produced models that ranged from rich pictures to data flow diagrams. As 10 marks were allocated to the model candidates limited their possible attainable marks severely by not being able to draw a conceptual model or anything that resembled one. Part (d) was answered satisfactorily.

Marking scheme

		Marks
(a)	Award ½ a mark for each acceptable entry to a maximum of 3	3
(b)	Award up to 4 marks for an appropriate explanation. To obtain 3 or 4 marks candidates should include notions of logical activities, achieving transformation, logical dependencies.	4
(c)	Eleven activities have been defined in the suggested solution; many students will not identify all. Award 1 mark for each correctly defined (or equivalent) activity up to a maximum of 7 marks. Award 1 mark for monitor (max 1). Award 1 mark for each boundary correctly identified (max 2).	10
(d)	Award up to 1 mark each to a maximum of 3	3
		20

(a)   An appropriate CATWOE for this root definition would be:

Client or customer: Students and potential students

Actor: Trainee analysts/teachers

Transformation: Education and training transforming unqualified students into members of the Systems Analysts Guild (SAG)

Weltanschauung: Full membership of the SAG gained from a highly rated academic institution will enhance career prospects.

Owner: Students

Environment: Education and career opportunities. Other available SAG programmes. Programme regulations and support.

(b) Checkland states that a conceptual model is '… an account of the activities which the system must do in order to be the system named in the definition'. Therefore, conceptual models add to the information provided by the root definition and CATWOE.

These models identify the activities undertaken within the system to achieve the named transformation – and also show the logical dependencies between these activities.

(c)

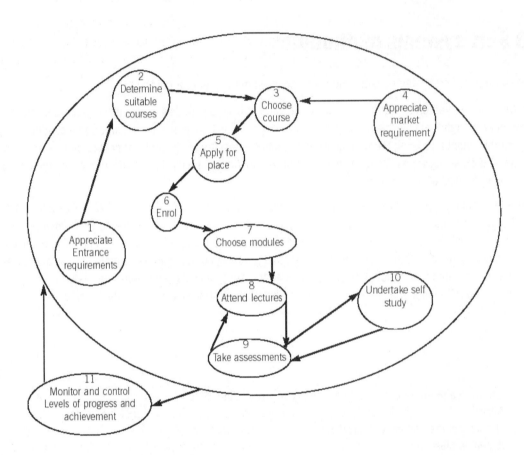

(d) A measure of **efficiency**: The cost of training a student to obtain full membership of SAG.

A measure of **efficacy**: A measure of pass-rates at each stage combined with some measure of the on-going standing/status of the qualification.

A measure of **effectiveness**: Employment rates of graduates.

24 Appraisal of information systems projects

Text reference. Project appraisal is covered in Chapter 5 of the text.

Top tips. Don't' be afraid to 'state the obvious'. It may not seem worth mentioning that assigning values to the intangible benefits information systems bring is difficult – but if you don't mention it you won't earn a mark for it!

Easy marks. A good answer will include, as a first step, a brief discussion of financial techniques with a short discussion of their strengths and weaknesses, followed by a discussion of non-financial techniques that alleviate these weaknesses. Twenty marks are available for the discussion – include ten explained points.

Examiner's comments. The examiner indicated that good answers to this question discussed financial techniques, indicated their weaknesses and then discussed some appropriate non-financial techniques that attempted to overcome those weaknesses. However, many answers were too short, limiting the marks that could be awarded.

Marking scheme

	Marks
Award up to 2 marks for each valid point. Lengthy descriptions of accounting techniques should not attract high marks.	20

Introduction

Financial techniques can be used to appraise information projects, although difficulties establishing realistic values for costs and particularly for benefits mean the calculations are highly subjective.

Use of financial techniques

Typical financial techniques used to appraise information projects include:

- Payback – the length of time a project will take to recoup in initial investment

- Accounting rate of return – also called the return on investment, calculates the profits from a project and expresses these as a percentage of the capital invested. The higher the percentage, the higher a project is ranked

- Internal rate of return – compares the expected rate of return with costs of capital of the organisation

These techniques enable projects to be ranked in terms of financial return.

Criticism of financial techniques

Financial techniques focus on financial information. They rely on predictions of cash flows and the use of discount factors.

The techniques can also be criticised because they require a value to be assigned to intangible costs and more significantly benefits.

Inclusion of intangibles – how to quantify?

Intangibles are by definition costs and benefits that are not easily quantifiable. This means a value needs to be assigned (for example) to improved decision making that a new information system may facilitate.

Examples of intangible costs

Examples of intangible costs include:

- Learning curve – staff taking time to learn new systems
- Staff morale decline due to imposed changes

- Investment opportunities not undertaken (opportunity cost of the current project)
- Incompatibility resulting in changes required to other systems

Examples of intangible benefits

Intangible benefits of systems projects include:

- Greater customer satisfaction and loyalty arising from better customer service
- Improved staff morale from working with more efficient and up-to-date systems
- More informed decision makers as more information of a higher quality is available
- Time savings resulting from staff working more efficiently
- Potential benefits from competitive advantage from use of new systems.

Including intangibles in system appraisal

The fact that there are so many intangible costs and benefits means that financially based appraisal techniques are too subjective to be completely reliable.

Alternative methods of appraising system projects taking into account intangibles include:

- **Estimating the value of intangibles**. While this is possible, in some situations this is little more than guesswork.

- **Ignore the 'too intangible' benefits**. Values can be placed on some intangibles, but the 'very' intangible ones are ignored. As benefits are likely to be more difficult to quantify than costs, the overall benefit of a project will still be understated.

- **Adopt a qualitative approach**. In other words find a reasonable method of measuring the intangibles. For example, customer satisfaction ratings can be used to determine customer satisfaction or increase in market share as an indication of increased competitive advantage. This approach also has weaknesses as much of the information will only be available after implementation and appropriate measures may be hard to determine.

Sensitivity analysis

One method of incorporating financial and non-financial factors is to use sensitivity analysis. This approach involves using financial and non-financial factors and then asking 'what if' questions (eg what if customers are 50% less keen on the system than expected?). Changing the values provides a number of different scenarios. Factors providing higher risk scenarios can then be identified and a scenario with lower risk chosen as a basis for the information project.

Conclusion

Financial techniques have a part to play in the appraisal of information projects, but the need to include values for intangible costs and benefits means the calculations do have a relatively high level of uncertainty.

25 Soft systems methodology; rich pictures

Text reference. Soft systems methodology is discussed in Chapter 4 of the text.

Top tips. Refer to the marking scheme for part (b) as this demonstrates that you do not need to produce a perfect model to score well on this type of question.

Easy marks. Part (a) has six marks available for simply explaining the purpose and role of rich pictures.

Examiner's comments. Answers to part (a) were generally good with the role of rich pictures being explained. Weaker answers tended to describe rich pictures in some detail rather than focusing on their role and purpose, as required by the question.

In part (b), most candidates provided good rich pictures. A minority of answers were in the form of a conceptual model, which was inappropriate. The Examiner also noted that relatively few candidates attempted this question, indicating that SSM is not a popular area – but it is examined regularly.

Marking scheme

		Marks
(a)	Award up to 2 marks for each valid point. Max 6 marks.	6
(b)	Award 1/2 mark for each element correctly identified: actor max 4 marks, concern max 4 marks and relationship max 4 marks. Award up to 2 marks for general layout/construction of a rich picture. Max 14 marks.	14
		20

(a)   A **rich picture** is a diagrammatic representation of a situation compiled through examining elements of structure, process and the situation climate. It is produced as part of the investigation stage of Soft Systems Methodology (SSM). The aim is to provide a pictorial representation of a problem situation which can then be used later in the process of SSM to provide solutions to the problems.

A rich picture will include:

- **Structured elements** such as departmental boundaries to show who or what is involved in the problem situation

- **Process elements** showing what actually takes place in the system. Many of the different elements are difficult to describe using words; use of a picture helps to clarify exactly what is happening

- **Relationships and interactions** between people in the system. Again, these may be difficult to describe using words, or more clearly expressed using a picture. For example, a conflict situation can be shown using crossed swords which immediately identifies the problem. Use of icons in this way helps to show the 'soft' elements of the system which traditional hard system approaches cannot do.

When drawn, the picture can be discussed with stakeholders to ensure completeness and to attempt to identify why problems are occurring. The picture will then assist management and the analyst to move forward from thinking about the problem situation itself into identifying what can be done about the situation and provide suitable solutions.

The 'solutions' may mean changes to processes or changes to human elements in the system. Again, use of the rich picture helps to show both these elements ensuring the 'soft' elements of system design are fully considered.

(b)

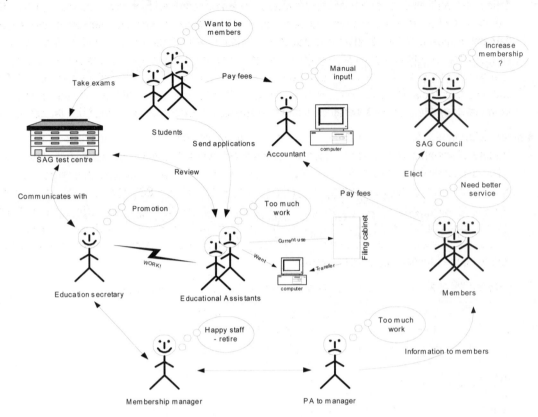

26 Soft systems methodology; root definition

Text reference. Soft systems methodology is discussed in Chapter 4 of the text.

Top tips. When answering part (c), remember that efficiency refers to the use of resources, effectiveness tests whether the long-term objectives are being met and efficacy checks whether the means chosen produces the required output.

Easy marks. Part (a) has eight marks available for simply explaining the use of SSM.

Examiner's comments. Weaker answers tended to list the stages of SSM without any explanation.

Marking scheme

		Marks
(a)	Award up to 1 mark for each valid point up to a max 8 marks.	8
(b)	Award 1/2 mark each for C, A and O. Award up to 1 1/2 marks for T, E and W. Max 6 marks.	6
(c)	Award up to 2 marks per term. 3 × 2.	6
		20

(a)   The **Soft Systems** approach to systems development aims to take into account the soft properties implementation. Specifically, Checkland's Soft System Methodology (SSM) can be used to tackle unstructured and poorly defined problems. This may be particularly true of information systems where the human aspects of change are not sufficiently well addressed by hard systems approaches such as SSADM.

Within SSM, the world is seen to contain many complex relationships which means that situations cannot be defined scientifically. For example, implementation of a new computer system affects staff, such as their morale and attitudes to work. These attitudes will also differ between different members of staff meaning that any proposed actions to change attitudes, for example, will not be relevant for all staff members. Furthermore, as attitudes change over time, the actions to be taken will also need to change to reflect changes in attitudes. This issue is particularly relevant to information systems, where staff have different attitudes to computers based on experience, age and other factors. Those attitudes change over time, for example, computers are now accepted within the workplace whereas 20 years ago this was not necessarily the case.

Traditional systems design also focuses on completion of tasks. The task itself is therefore defined and training focused on being able to carry out that task. However, in many situations, managers will not know what the problem is, let alone the tasks required to solve the problem. SSM allows investigation of the whole problem situation before defining what actions are needed to remedy the problem. This approach may be appropriate for information systems as 'problems' may involve human issues such as staff not being willing to use e-mail as a communication medium. Training must therefore be focused on changing attitudes, not simply on the functionality of the systems.

SSM therefore allows analysis of what may be termed unstructured problems.

- Takes into account human experience of the real world
- Looks at how humans interpret situations based on that experience
- Produces purposeful actions based on that experience

(b) **Client or customer**   Client company and its employees

     Actors   The payroll division/department in the GJKD bank

     Transition   Employee payment entitlement into electronic funds transfer

     Worldview   The degree to which a payroll service can be relied on by its employees. The GJKD bank overall strategy is selling and maintaining client confidence and trust, not providing a payroll service.

     Owner   GJKD Bank

     Environment   National accounting practice and commercial law

(c) **Efficiency** ensures that a process uses the minimum amount of resources possible to produce the desired results. In this situation, there is a need to determine how efficient the system is in transferring employee payment details into the EFT system. An appropriate measure is cost per transaction.

Effectiveness tests whether long term objectives are being met. The banks long term objectives are to maintain customer confidence and trust, which can also be applied to the EFT system. If confidence and trust are not maintained, employees will complain. An appropriate measure is therefore number of complaints per 100,000 payments made (or a different figure if this is more suitable).

Efficacy checks whether the means chosen produces the required output. Given this is a payroll system, payment must be made accurately on a specific date. An appropriate measure is therefore checking the accuracy of the payment and whether the date of payment is correct.

27 Soft system and root definitions

Marking scheme

		Marks
(a)	Award up to 3 marks for complete root definition. To obtain max marks all CATWOE criteria should be included.	3
(b)	Eleven activities have been defined in the suggested solution; many students will not identify all. Award 1 mark for each correctly defined (or equivalent) activity up to a maximum of 7 marks, plus 1 mark for monitor. Award 1 mark for boundaries. Max 9 marks.	9
(c)	Award up to 2 marks per each valid point. Max 8 marks	8
		20

(a) **Root definition** for the GB university's promotion system:

'A system operated by the human resources department of the GB University to facilitate the promotion of the most suitable junior lecturers to a senior lecturer grade. The system operates across the whole university in accordance with established criteria. It aims to provide a fair and impartial system of promotion.'

(b) See next page.

(b)   A **conceptual model** of the GB University's promotion system is shown below.

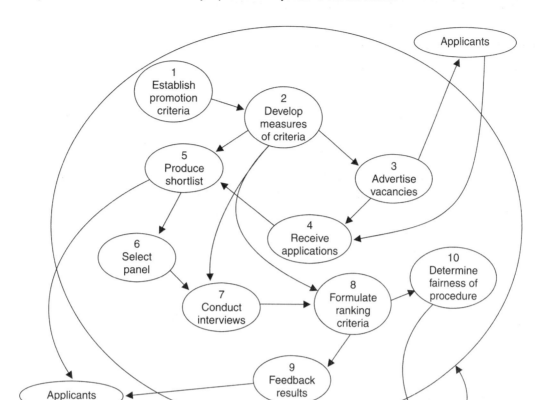

(c)   A **soft systems approach** is appropriate to the development of the university's promotion system for the following reasons.

The soft systems approach is suited to **unstructured**, **complex** problems that involve a number of relatively **unpredictable** variables and different groups of **stakeholders**. The university wide promotion system is a good example of this type of system.

The promotion system is part of a larger **human activity system**. Changes to the promotion system will affect many other systems – a soft approach is able to take this into account.

Also, many of the decisions made within the promotion system are not **clearly defined** – they require the exercise of judgement eg what should promotion criteria be ; how can meeting the criteria be measured; is the system fair etc?

The soft approach will allow many **perspectives** to be considered eg management wish to provide a career path within the constraints of limited resources whereas junior lecturers as a group are likely to favour a system that provides a career path achievable to as many of them as possible. This approach means the investigation will encompass the differing perspectives arising from different attitudes or world-views.

The proposed system also requires a change in the culture of the organisation moving from a decentralised system to a centrally based system. This has implications for the **'power'** and **feelings** of local managers. Taking these into account would be impossible using a hard systems approach.

A soft systems approach recognises that many problems in organisations are affected by **culture**, **informal interactions** and **attitudes**.

The soft approach will allow the new promotion system to be developed after suitable consideration and investigation of a variety of problems that underpin the problem identified.

28 Automation, rationalisation and re-engineering

Text reference. Business automation, rationalisation and business process re-engineering are all explained in Chapter 4 in the text.

Top tips. Pay close attention to the mark allocation as it is easy to assume each part is worth the same number of marks. The allocation should guide the length of your answer to each part and the length of time you spend on it.

Easy marks. Begin each part with a definition of the term concerned and then use separate paragraphs to explain it. You should be able to pick up a good chunk of the marks very quickly by doing this.

Examiner's comments. Strong candidates noted the allocation of marks and provided answers accordingly. Weaker candidates provided a short paragraph answer for each of the parts, thus limiting the number of marks available. Overall this question was answered well.

Marking scheme

		Marks

In many questions suggested model answers were given to open-ended questions. Credit will be given for any valid alternative responses within the limits of the marking scheme.

(a)	Award up to 2 marks for explanation, award up to 2 marks for application.	4
(b)	Award up to 3 marks for explanation, award up to 3 marks for application.	6
(c)	Award up to 5 marks for explanation, award up to 5 marks for application.	10
Total marks		20

(a) **Business automation** is the use of computerised work methods to **improve the efficiency** (and therefore speed), that business tasks are performed.

Automation is often used where the task itself **cannot be changed** (there may be no other way of performing it), but **elements of the task** are suitable for **computerisation**. By removing **human input** from a task, the **process** is **sped up** and often the **quality** of the output improves.

A recent application of business automation within supermarket chains was the introduction of **bar code scanning**. Beforehand, checkout operators had to **manually** enter the price of the goods into the cash register. This manual entry, slowed the process down, and often caused **input errors** and **customers** either being **charged too much** or **too little** for their goods. Bar code scanning improved the process as **prices** are held centrally and matched against a particular **bar code**. When the cash register recognises the bar code at the check out, the price is automatically added to the customer's bill, therefore speeding up check out time and reducing errors.

(b) **Business rationalisation** seeks not only to improve **individual processes** by making them more **efficient**, but by also considering the **links between processes** that often cause problems such as bottlenecks. It seeks to exploit not only the advantages of technological automation, but takes matters a stage further by seeking ways of **embedding** technology further into the business.

To achieve rationalisation, a business must consider **what it does** and then **question** the current **processes** used to perform it. Technological improvements are often integrated into the design process so best use can be made of new advances.

Many supermarkets have recently implemented **stock control systems**. These systems form a link between many processes within the business. For example, when a customer takes product A to the checkout it is **scanned**. This tells the stock control system that a **replacement** product is needed on the supermarket shelf and instructs the warehouse controller. At the same time, the **purchasing system** is updated with the number of products required to restock the shop and accurate orders can be made to the **central warehouse**. The process of ordering between the central warehouse and suppliers are often now made using **electronic data interchange** (EDI) that represents further rationalisation of the ordering process.

(c) **Business process re-engineering** (BPR) involves a **fundamental re-evaluation and radical redesign** of business systems to achieve **dramatic improvements** of **measures of performance** such as cost, quality, service and speed.

BPR goes further than automation and rationalisation by questioning **why** the business does what it does. It **considers alternative ways** of carrying out the business, involving technology to dramatically improve the processes.

Very often, BPR requires **structural changes** of how work is **organised** and **performed**. For example, several old tasks may be combined into one new task, the order of tasks may be changed if they can be performed more **logically** in a **different order**, **quality** is often built into the process and **workers** may be **empowered** to make decisions themselves. Such change is often made at **high risk**, but the potential benefits are such that they generally outweigh it.

There are several ways in which BPR has been applied in supermarkets.

Virtual supply chains. Many supermarkets have revolutionised the **ordering process** by having their orders driven by suppliers. Suppliers have **embedded links** into the supermarket's own stock system so they are able to **despatch goods** when current stocks fall below an agreed level.

Internet shopping. The introduction of Internet home shopping by chains such as Sainsbury's and Tescos in recent years has changed they way goods are sold. Shoppers no longer have to **visit their local store**; instead orders are sent electronically to the store and are picked by staff. The orders are bagged and sent by road to the customer.

Marketing. The development of **loyalty cards** over recent years has enabled supermarkets to change the way they **gather data** about their customers. Beforehand, customers had to be persuaded to fill in questionnaires about their shopping habits, but now, all the information is gathered electronically. Data such as **products purchased**, the **date of purchase**, **quantities bought** and **method of payment** are collected at the checkout. Data mining and warehousing have an important role to play regarding the storing and analysing of data that is of vital importance when planning an expensive marketing campaign.

29 Database systems

Text reference. Databases are covered in Chapter 3 of the text.

Top tips. This question uses a mini-case study, your answers must relate to GBAW. Note the mark allocation – don't spend more time on parts(b) and (c) than justified by the marks available.

Easy marks. An explanation of integrity, independence and integration will earn some easy marks in (a) – but ensure your answer explains how each of these are maintained.

Examiner's comments. In part (a), many candidates clearly did not understand the three principles, details of which appear in all study texts related to this paper. Strong candidates were awarded high marks for an appropriate understanding of the principles, supported by reference to the mini-case study. Marks awarded for this part of the question varied from zero to twelve, with too many at the very low end of the scale.

For (b), the majority of candidates provided excellent explanations of the terms, although some answers were very long in relation to the number of marks available. Surprisingly, weaker candidates were unable to discuss the ways in which data warehouses and data mining can assist a business in (c), despite the fact that they demonstrated a clear understanding of the terms in (b).

Marking scheme

		Marks
(a)	Award up to 4 marks per category. To obtain full marks, each category should include reference to the case study. 3 × 4 marks.	12
(b)	Award up to 2 marks for explanations and up to 2 marks for identifying a potential problem. Max 4 marks.	4
(c)	Award 1 mark per point, max 4 marks.	4
		20

(a) **Independence**. Data independence refers to the maintenance of data independent from the application programs that access that data. This means that individual programs do not maintain their own data, but access and amend data in a central database. This also allows applications to written and amended independent of the data being used.

In GBAW, there is a single relational database. The various departments in GBAW (eg insurance services, investments and mortgages) will use their own application programmes to provide client advice. However, actual client data will be maintained on the database. When one client record is updated, by say the mortgage department, then there is no need to update that data in the investment department as the latter uses the same record in the central database.

Integration. Integration refers to the storing of data in a single location (rather than each individual program storing its own data). If each program stored its own data, there would be a danger of data inconsistencies. For example, if a client changed job and income this data could be updated in the mortgage department data, but not in the investment department data. This could potentially lead to incorrect advice being given by the investment department. However, because GBAW maintains data on one central database this problem is avoided as updated data is available to all departments.

Similarly, the mortgage department may find that additional client information is required which is held by the investment department. If all departments had access to the same data, obtaining this information would be a simpler task. Maintaining one single database also saves staff time and is therefore cheaper than maintaining separate databases.

Integrity. Database integrity means keeping data correct and secure, and that only authorised amendments are made. The database management system must allow different applications to access and update data but still maintain integrity.

For example, in GBAW, it's possible that two departments may request data on the same client at the same time. The database management system will have to ensure that changes being made by say the mortgage department are not overwritten by concurrent changes in the investment department. This may be achieved by temporarily 'locking' data files in use to other departments until the first department has completed changes.

Data in the central database must also be kept secure and backed up to maintain integrity. The central database in GBAW allows a central back-up to be taken, making controls easier to enforce and reducing the risk of data corruption or loss.

(b)   A **data warehouse** consists of a database, containing data from various operational and legacy systems. It may also include external data from different sources. The warehouse maintains copies of operational data as it is not an operational system in its own right.

Data mining refers to the process of looking for hidden patterns and relationships in large stores of data. Any hidden patterns and relationships identified can be used to assist decision making and predict future behaviour.

Potential problems of integrating a data warehouse into an existing platform include:

- The warehouse needs to be **a separate system** to allow data analysis and ensure that the original data is protected from corruption. Decisions will need to be taken regarding the data to transfer into the warehouse.

- **Data formats will need to be checked**. Whilst data formats in the central database will already have been determined, any additional data from legacy systems or external data may need to be amended in order to provide a common format.

- The **method of transferring data** from the central database to the warehouse must be determined, set up and tested.

(c)   The introduction of a data warehouse system with data mining facilities may help GBAW to improve its position in the marketplace by:

Improved access to data. Storing data in a separate warehouse will allow access on demand and running of reports as necessary. At present, if one department has accessed data in the database, then other departments will be barred from access and amendment of data by the database management system.

Improved customer service. Customer service will be improved as the 'live' system will not be slowed down by additional requests – this should improve response times meaning relevant data is found more quickly.

Uncovering hidden relationships. The use of data mining software may help uncover hidden relationships in the data. For example, customers taking out a mortgage may normally be identified as needing investment advice 6 months later. This information can be used to proactively contact customers offering the appropriate service. This may be a service feature that GBAW's competitors may not be able to provide.

Measuring the effect of marketing initiatives. The warehouse may be useful in determining which type of marketing initiatives work best. For example, following different marketing campaigns, the warehouse can be interrogated to find how many new customers were obtained or new mortgages taken out etc. GBAW's position in the marketplace will be improved by focusing marketing activities on the most effective methods.

30 Information and knowledge management

(a)   **Information management** entails identifying the current and future information needs, identifying information sources, collecting and storing the information and facilitating existing methods of using information and identifying new ways of using it. It should also ensure that the information is communicated to those who need it and not to those who are not entitled to see it.

Mayo defines **knowledge management** (KM) as 'the management of the information, knowledge and experience available to an organisation – its creation, capture, storage, availability and utilisation – in order that organisational activities build on what is already known and extend it further'.

More specifically, **knowledge** is interpreted in terms of **potential for action** and distinguished from **information** in terms of its more immediate link with performance. This interpretation is consistent with what the information systems philosopher and professor Charles West Churchman observed three decades ago in his pioneering work *The Design of Inquiring Systems*: 'knowledge resides in the user and not in the collection of information… it is how the user reacts to a collection of information that matters'.

Databases, or more correctly **knowledge bases**, need to be designed and developed to store the organisation's knowledge. This will be particularly difficult because of the **tacit** nature of much of the knowledge and also because it is largely inside the heads of individuals. Recording this knowledge will be very different to recording the fields and records of a traditional database. An **expert system** seems one way forward as this has a knowledge base made up of facts, rules and conditions. But much of this knowledge may have to be represented pictorially as images and 'knowledge maps'. An intranet that lends itself to full multimedia representation and intelligent searching may therefore be the way forward.

Knowledge-based companies will vary from industry to industry but there are some broad common principles about where knowledge resides and how to capture its value. The intellectual capital can be divided between human capital (the bodies that go home at night), and structural capital. Structural capital includes innovation capital (intellectual property), customer capital (address lists and client records), and organisational capital (systems for processing policies and claims). A number of organisations are creating knowledge management programmes for **protecting and distributing knowledge** resources that they have identified and for discovering new sources of knowledge.

- One such programme is the identification and development of informal networks and communities of practice within organisations. These self-organising groups share common work interests, usually cutting across a company's functions and processes.

- Another means of establishing the occurrence of knowledge is to look at knowledge-related business outcomes eg, product development and service innovation. While the knowledge embedded within these innovations is invisible, the products themselves are tangible.

- Every day companies make substantial investments in improving their employees' knowledge and enabling them to use it more effectively. Analysis of these investments is a third way of making KM activities visible. For example how much technical and non-technical training are individuals consuming? How much is invested in competitive and environmental scanning, and in other forms of strategic research?

The process by which an organisation develops its store of knowledge is sometimes called **organisational learning**. A **learning organisation** is centred on the people that make up the organisation and the knowledge they hold. The organisation and employees feed off and into the central pool of knowledge. The organisation uses the knowledge pool as a tool to teach itself and its employees.

There are dozens of different approaches to KM, including document management, information management, business intelligence, competence management, information systems management, intellectual asset management, innovation, business process design, and so on. Many KM projects have a significant element of information management. After all, people need information about where knowledge resides, and to share knowledge they need to transform it into more or less transient forms of information.

(b) A **knowledge management strategy** might take the form shown in the diagram below:

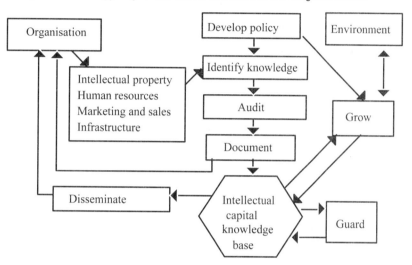

The stages may include the following:

(i) Develop and determine a policy for owning, growing and sharing knowledge within the organisation.
(ii) Identify critical knowledge functions within each department.
(iii) Audit knowledge to determine its type, location, longevity and whether it is explicit or tacit.
(iv) Document knowledge in a medium that best suits the purpose for which it will be used.
(v) Store it in a repository where it can be easily updated and retrieved.
(vi) Determine ways in which it can be grown and tracked.
(vii) Decide how the knowledge will be disseminated inside the organisation and possibly outside.
(viii) Ensure this valuable organisational asset is kept secure.

31 Question with answer plan: purpose written or ready made?

Text reference. The issues in this question are discussed Chapter 6 of the text.

Top tips. This is a very 'open' question as a wide range of points could be made. For 20 marks, try and identify about six or seven strategic issues that would be affected by, or would affect, the chosen information system.

Answer plan

Pick out relevant strategic issues, such as:

- Company IT strategy
- Business requirements
- Business risk
- Competitive advantage
- Timescale
- Skills available
- Software licensing agreements
- Availability of software language

Explain all, and discuss whether each would be more suited to a purpose-written or a ready-written package.

Marking scheme

	Marks
Award up to 4 marks for each issue raised up to a maximum of 20	<u>20</u>

The strategic issues regarding choice of software development are explained below.

(a) **Company IT strategy**

The strategy concerning previous application development can be considered. If applications have been written in-house or always purchased externally, then the organisation is more likely to continue. Changing strategy will need a careful review, especially as integration of software may be more difficult.

(b) **Business requirements**

The choice of software must match the requirements specification for the particular application. Commercially available software may not meet all the specific requirements of the organisation because the software is written for general use. A strategic decision must be made whether to accept the limitations of the commercially available product or write the application in-house. Taking the latter option may involve higher risk of software failure because module and program testing will also be required; commercially available software will already have passed these tests.

(c) **Business risk**

Purchasing ready written packages means placing reliance on the third-party supplier to maintain and upgrade the software. If the software is business critical then this reliance may be unacceptable so in-house development is necessary.

(d) **Competitive advantage**

The organisation may have seen an area of competitive advantage in the use of software. In house writing may be required because commercially available software does not support this requirement or because the idea needs to be kept secret as long as possible. Involving third parties in user acceptance testing of ready-written software may mean that the competitive advantage from using the software becomes public knowledge sooner than expected.

(e) **Timescale**

The amount of time before the software has to be implemented may affect choice of development. Ready-written software is available straightaway but in-house development will take months, and in some cases years. If the software is required immediately, then purchase is likely to be the only alternative.

(f) **Skills available**

If the organisation has an experienced in-house software development team, then in-house writing is feasible. The lack of in-house experience raises the strategic decision of whether or not to establish this team, or purchase ready-written software. Establishing a new development team also involves risk because the team will not have worked together before and they will have to understand the interfaces with other software in the organisation to ensure that the new software is compatible.

(g) **Software licensing agreements**

One alternative to simply purchasing ready-written software is to amend that software to meet the specific business requirements of the organisation. This may provide a relatively cost-effective method of meeting specific requirements without full software development in-house.

However, the licensing implications of this decision must also be investigated. The option may become too expensive where significant licensing costs have to be paid. The issue of whether the software writer will release the source code of the software, or whether amendments have to be made by the writer must also be considered. Amending the software at a third party involves strategic risks of loss of control of development and placing reliance on the third party for software maintenance. These risks may not be acceptable so in-house development will be required.

(h) **Availability of software language**

Some ready-written software is developed in specific software languages that are not generally available for purchase. If that language cannot be purchased, then this limits the development decision to purchasing the ready-written software or possibly writing the software in a different, and possibly less effective, language.

32 Data warehousing and data mining

Text reference. DBMS, data warehousing and data mining are covered in Chapter 3 of the text.

Top tips. Remember that data warehousing involves the use of a separate system to live systems used in day-to-day operations. This division means the data can be manipulated and analysed without disrupting operations. This is a popular area for examination – ensure you understanding the principles and are able to apply your knowledge.

Examiner's comments. The examiner noted that this question produced a wide range of answers. Part (a) asked candidates to discuss how the Data Warehousing approach to information management improves on the Data Base Management Systems (DBMS) approach. Many candidates described DBMS and stated 'data warehousing is bigger and better'. This is not a good answer. The required answer should discuss the differences – it should focus on the facilities available in a data warehouse system. Some answers were excellent demonstrating a distinction between the two systems and discussing the advantages of using data warehousing.

A short scenario was used as the focus for the second part of this question. The question asked candidates how data mining could be exploited in the scenario. Generally this part of the question attracted higher marks than part (a). Many candidates citing different types of results including associations, sequences, classification, clustering and forecasting giving examples of each from the scenario. However a few candidates made no reference to the scenario limiting the marks earned.

Marks

(a) Guidelines for mark allocation

0-4 marks. Answers that fail to demonstrate an understanding of the advantages between an operational database and a data warehouse.

5-10 marks. Answers that demonstrate a clear understanding of the differences. Better answers will include the warehouse's ability to model and remodel data without affecting operational data, and to support on-line queries.

10

(b) A key feature is identification of patterns in the data.

0-4 marks. Answers that just define/describe the concept of data mining.

5-10 marks. Answers that demonstrate a clear understanding of the concept of data mining. Application: use in strategic decisions, competitive advantage, marketing etc. Better answers will illustrate these points with close reference to the car dealer case study.

$\frac{10}{20}$

(a) A **database** is a collection of data that is able to be utilised by many applications. A database management system (DBMS) is the software used to create, maintain and manage a database. The DBMS enables users and programs to access and use the data they require from the central pool.

A **data warehouse** is a large data store that holds historical data extracted from a wide range of sources. It Is a central source of standardised data that may be utilised for a wide range of purposes. A data warehouse could. This information is available to be analysed and reported upon from a single location.

Data warehousing improves the process of information management, including data storage and retrieval, in the following ways.

- They allow a wider range of data to be stored in a single pool than using a DBMS
- Data warehouses may be significantly larger than traditional operational databases
- The warehouses are often a combination of operational databases
- Data warehouses include internal operational data and data from external sources
- Data warehouses may contain data that is collected over long periods of time
- Although the amount of data held is vast, data warehouses often include user-friendly query features
- Data warehouses include the ability to model and remodel the data, without disrupting systems used in day-to-day operations
- They enable decision makers to access and manipulate data without affecting operational systems

(b) The amount of data that organisations are able to capture and store has increased dramatically over the past 20 years. In order to utilise this data, **datamining software** has been developed. Datamining software looks for hidden patterns and relationships in large pools of data. True datamining software discovers previously unknown relationships.

The **hidden patterns** and **relationships** the software identifies can be used to guide decision making and to predict future behaviour. This can be used to help managers make decisions about strategic changes in business operations to gain competitive advantage. For example, a Skoda car dealer may find a shift in the type of customer purchasing Skoda cars, and on the basis of this change, decide to move to a different location – to be closer to the new target market.

A large main car dealership could also use data mining software to more accurately target its **marketing campaigns**. For example, datamining software could discover that a high proportion people of a certain age, that live in a specific post-code are more likely to purchase a certain type of vehicle eg a 'people-mover'. A direct mail campaign related to the launch of a new people-mover could then be targeted at these people.

Datamining software could also discover patterns related to customer characteristics and likely time between vehicle purchases, enabling customers to be targeted with marketing material when most likely to be considering a purchase.

Other possible patterns that may be exploited could relate to financing options, purchasing patterns throughout the year and loyalty to particular manufacturers or models. Another practical application could involve targeting potential customers that are viewed as likely to value innovation and being among the first to purchase a particularly distinctive design.

33 Question with helping hand: Knowledge management

Text reference. Material relevant to this question is covered in Chapters 1 and 3 of the text.

Top tips. Cover each of the four functions separately and provide sufficient explanation to earn five marks for each.

Examiner's comments. Candidates were required to discuss the types of information system that support the listed four functions of knowledge management: create knowledge, capture and codify knowledge, distribute knowledge and share knowledge.

Weaker candidates ignored the requirement to discuss information systems and merely described in very general terms the knowledge management functions. Some answers suggested that all four functions were supported by a database system or a management information system. A discussion of Anthony's hierarchy was certainly inappropriate for this question.

Better prepared candidates scored some very high marks in all four categories. Specific examples of the use of data warehousing, data-mining and other information systems not listed in the model answers were awarded marks where the application was appropriate.

Marking scheme

		Marks
(a)	Award up to 2 marks for discussion of the function and up to three marks for discussion of supporting information systems – to a maximum of 5	5
(b)	Award up to 2 marks for discussion of the function and up to three marks for discussion of supporting information systems – to a maximum of 5	5
(c)	Award up to 2 marks for discussion of the function and up to three marks for discussion of supporting information systems – to a maximum of 5	5
(d)	Award up to 2 marks for discussion of the function and up to three marks for discussion of supporting information systems – to a maximum of 5	5
		20

(a)   Information systems which support knowledge **creation** are referred to as Knowledge Work Systems (KWS). A KWS typically includes access to external information sources and knowledge bases. They usually include sophisticated graphics, the ability to build models, and powerful data analysis tools.

Examples of KWS include the following:

- Investment workstations. These are used for analysing and manipulating vast quantities of financial data – applied to trading situations and portfolio management.

- Computer Aided Design (CAD). CAD systems automate the design process (usually) in industrial design and manufacturing. Sophisticated graphic software is key to CAD systems.

- Virtual reality systems. These systems emulate real world (reality) activities, situations and sometimes sensations. The feature interactive computer generated simulations that provide realistic simulations of objects. Medical workers and engineers may use these systems to help gauge the effect of different actions in an environment as close to the real world as possible.

(b)   Information systems which **capture** and **codify knowledge** include many systems that utilise Artificial Intelligence (AI). AI systems are distinguished by an ability to 'learn' – they analyse the knowledge captured and make sense or draw conclusions from it. This knowledge can then be codified and used to make future decisions.

Examples of AI systems include the following:

- Expert systems. AN expert system uses knowledge held in a knowledge base as a means of devising rules used in decision making. The expert system takes data entered that requires a decision and uses the rules based on historic data to make a decision. Expert systems have been applied to credit decision management, diagnostic/troubleshooting situations and process monitoring and control.

- Robotics refers to the technology of building machines with some physical capability, sometimes coupled with an ability to learn. An object that can perform tasks without being subject to human feelings such as boredom, fatigue and worry are particularly useful performing routine and unsatisfying jobs. Robotics may also be suitable when tasks involve exposure to physical or mental danger.

(c)   The information systems used to **distribute knowledge** are the same as the systems used to send or communicate information ion a business environment. Examples include word processing software, spreadsheets, schedulers/calendars, desktop publishing, e-mail, voice mail, and other 'office type' software.

These systems are sometimes collectively referred to as Office Automation Systems. Word processing, spreadsheet and e-mail software are probably the most widely used applications in a business setting. Together they enable knowledge to be presented and distributed efficiently in a manner that enables efficient and effective communication of knowledge and information.

(d)   Information systems used to **share knowledge** are those systems used to hold knowledge in a way that makes it available those who may wish to access it.

Examples include Group collaboration systems or Groupware. These systems provide functions and services that support and encourage collaboration activities between group members.

Groupware enables individuals who may be located in different locations and time-zones to act as a team. Examples include internal networks (intranets) and databases accessible via the Internet, group scheduling and e-mail software (eg Lotus Notes, Microsoft Exchange), teleconferencing and videoconferencing.

Groupware therefore facilitates communication, collaboration and coordination. It allows groups to work together on documents, schedule meetings, route electronic forms, access shared folders and develop shared databases.

34 Database management

Marking scheme

		Marks
(a)	Award up to 2 marks for each discussion. 2 discussions.	4
(b)	Award 1 mark for each valid point. Max 6 marks.	6
(c)	Award up to 2 marks for each category up to a max 10 marks.	10
		20

(a) The **logical data design** of a database refers to the way in which information within the database needs to be linked. Initially, the design is produced by agreement with users to confirm how they need to access data in the database. The design is then completed on paper prior to programming to show database designers exactly how the database needs to be designed.

The **physical data design** of a database refers to the way data is actually organised and stored in the database. The database management system keeps a record of where data is stored, allowing individual programmes to access and share the same data in the database.

(b) In a **relational database**, data is stored in two-dimensional tables consisting of rows and columns. A row represents a record (or entity) while each column shows the fields or attributes relating to each entity. For example, a customer entity will have attributes such as name, address and customer number.

One column or attribute will be used as a key field; data in that column will be unique to each entity. For example in a customer table, the customer reference number field will contain a different reference number for each customer.

Using key fields, tables can be linked to each other. For example, an invoice table will contain fields such as quantity, part number and customer number. Because the customer number is in the invoice table, all details of that customer can be obtained from the customer table. Details of the customer do not have to be stored in the invoice table. This feature of a relational database means that data redundancy, or duplication, is minimised within the database.

Using the key fields, data can be extracted from different tables. For example, the invoice table can be searched to find all invoices relating to one customer. The report will then show customer details from the customer table and a list of invoices from the invoice table. As long as there are appropriate links between the tables in the database, reports can be produced on an ad hoc basis, as required by users.

(c)   Data mining relates to using software to find hidden patterns and relationships in large pools of data. Five main types of relationships are normally identified in data mining.

(i)   Classification

Classification refers to the situation where a group has been identified (or classified) as being associated with a certain behaviour. This group can then be targeted with marketing material to try and persuade other members of that group to follow the behaviour.

For example, in CETA, loyalty card information can be used to identify purchase trends by demographic analysis; CETA may find that males between 20 and 30 purchase specific types of car accessories. Marketing information can be sent to other members of this group who have not purchased those accessories in an attempt to increase sales.

(ii)   Clustering

Clustering involves finding groups within the database that share some characteristics. The term is therefore similar to classification although no group have yet been identified.

For example, in CETA, the database could be split by geographical region or age group and then analysed to see if there are common trends within that group. CETA may find, for example, that customers from specific post code areas have predominately one make or model of car, enabling it to stock more accessories for that model in stores in that area.

(iii)   Sequences

Sequences occur when events are linked over time, that is, one event is found to lead to another later event.

In CETA data mining may identify that purchase of one particular item for vehicles is followed by another purchase later. Eg purchase of new brakes may follow purchase of new tyres by on average six months. Marketing material can be sent an appropriate time to exploit this trend.

(iv)   Association

Association is similar to sequencing in that one event is able to be linked or correlated to another event. However, the order in which the events occur is not consistent or relevant.

In CETA, it is possible that sales of car washing shampoo are linked to purchases of refills for windscreen cleaner. Providing promotional material on one item may help to increase the sales of the other item.

(v)   Forecasting

Trends are identified within the data that can be extrapolated into the future.

In CETA, history of sales of individual items can be maintained. This may enable CETA to identify specific trends such as more de-icer being sold during the autumn and winter. Monitoring when sales of de-icer start and the overall trend in quantity sold each year will enable CETA to plan to purchase appropriate quantities at specific times of the year, rather than keeping large stocks for the whole year.

35 Groupware and email

Text reference. Groupware is discussed in Chapter 3 of the text.

Top tips. The main facilities available in groupware products are covered in your BPP Text. These include: communication and messaging, scheduling of meetings, workflow management, document management, application development, video conferencing and security.

Easy marks. There are 15 marks available in part (a). To earn these your answer should include an appropriate definition of groupware and successfully describe the main facilities of groupware systems – with references to the case study.

Examiner's comments. Many candidates provided good answers to part (a), referring the features of groupware to the case study. Weaker candidates tended to describe other products such as Internet and intranets and made little or no reference to the case. These candidates needed to check their knowledge and their exam technique.

Part (b) was generally well answered with some candidates obtaining full marks. A limited number of candidates misread the question and discussed advantages instead of disadvantages.

Marking scheme

		Marks
(a)	Award up to 3 marks for definition. Award up to 3 marks for each facility, to obtain max marks candidates must apply facility to Beko Co. 4 × 3 = 12 marks. Max 15 marks	15
(b)	Award 1 mark for each disadvantage up to a max 5 marks.	5
		20

(a) **Groupware** is a term used to describe software that provides functions used within collaborative work groups. Typically, the workgroup will be a relatively small team engaged on a specific project with tight deadlines – all features of the group in Beko. Examples of workgroup software include Lotus Notes and Microsoft Exchange.

The main features of groupware are described below (*your answer should only provide four or five features – we provide more for study purposes*).

- **Messaging**. Each member of the team will have e-mail access. The facilities available include standard e-mail features of being able to send and receive messages including sending the same message to a group of people. This is clearly useful where the team is in many different locations, making normal verbal communication difficult. Groupware will also allow the same message to be sent sequentially to a number of people (who may also add or comment on that message before sending it on). Again this will be useful where specific design features may need input from specialists in different locations.

- **Information database**. Access to an information database which can be amended is needed to standardise the way information is viewed in the workgroup. Members of the project team will need access to common information, such as designs of previous cars. The information database will provide this, as well as allowing new information on new design to be added and viewed by all group members.

- **Group scheduling**. This feature keeps track of workgroup members' itineraries. Meetings can also be arranged by the software by accessing diaries and finding free time common to members who are attending a meeting. This feature will be useful where team members may have to travel to attend meetings. Fixing the date and time well in advance will be helpful, particularly as this will be carried out automatically.

- **Public folders**. Documents being used by team members can be maintained within the groupware product. Documents can be viewed and amended by any member. This is particularly useful where design specifications will need to be amended by different members at different times. Groupware will also allow joint-working on documents so two or more members can update lengthy documents, without having to wait for one member to finish updates before another can start.

- **Conferencing**. Where team members are not in the same location, video conferencing can be arranged to simulate face-to-face discussions. This feature has obvious benefits to Beko where project members are in different locations. Video conferencing will also minimise travel time and costs.

- **Assigning tasks/workflow**. Specific tasks can be created within groupware and then assigned to specific individuals. The groupware product will also provide a record of progress on each task, and automatically move the task onto the next worker on completion. This feature will be used in Beko to monitor overall progress on the project, with important milestones being marked as achieved, or reasons for non-achievement noted. Again, given that team members are working in different locations and time zones, traditional task assignment and monitoring, in terms of talking to workers, is difficult.

- **Voting**. Allows a tally to be collected of answers to multiple choice type questions sent out in mail messages. For example, one team member may ask for advice on colour options for part of the car from other workers. Responses will be collected and presented automatically by the groupware product.

(b) **Disadvantages** of using e-mail for communication and information management:

- **Time wasting**. Staff tend to use e-mail to send many small queries when they could probably find the answer quickly themselves.

- **Lack of thought**. E-mail can be sent quickly and without thought as to the words used or the effect on the recipient. The result may be that communication degrades into exchanging insults rather than useful information. There is also the possibility of libel.

- **Junk mail**. E-mail systems can become less efficient as messages are simply not required, but time is still needed to view the message and delete it, again causing time wasting.

- **Filing systems**. Filing systems are generally personal to an individual. This limits access by other people requiring information. E-mail has limited potential for centralised information sharing unless 'group e-mail boxes' are used.

- **Security**. E-mail is not necessarily secure, so confidential information should not be sent using the media. This is particularly relevant where e-mails are sent to outside a company. Confidential client data should not be sent in this way in case the e-mail is intercepted and read by unauthorised people.

36 The Internet and globalisation

Text reference. Internet and globalisation are covered in Chapter 7 of the text.

Top tips. Globalisation is a term that has been fashionable since it began to replace words like 'internationalisation' and 'transnationalisation' as a suitable term to denote the increasing cross-border interaction in many areas of activity: social, political, cultural, financial and economic. The term provides a convenient label for a whole series of trends related to the influence of geography, and how it shapes organisations and their transactions.

Information and communication technologies have created a **global environment** in which communication – by telephone, television, radio or computer network – around the globe is no more difficult and not much more expensive than communication within the same town.

The growth of **global communications** has led to the development of common expectations, shared experiences and social norms among different cultures and people. These general cultural factors and the growth of powerful communications technologies create the conditions for global markets. Responding to this demand, global production and operations have emerged with on-line co-ordination between far-flung production facilities and central headquarters thousands of miles away. This is all possible through the Internet.

The **Internet's** global connectivity, ease of use, low cost and multimedia capabilities can be used to create interactive applications, services and products. By using **Internet technologies** the benefits to the organisation include reduced communication and transactions costs, enhanced co-ordination and collaboration and a speedy distribution of knowledge.

Although the Internet started off as a communal medium for **sharing information** among academics, it is now used by a wide range of users – including transnational corporations to market their information products around the world. The value of the Internet lies in its ability to easily and inexpensively link so many people from so many places all over the globe. The Internet enables one computer to communicate with any other computer on the network, regardless of location, computer type or operating system.

The Internet's **global connectivity** and **ease of use** can provide companies with access to businesses or individuals who normally would be outside their reach. Companies can directly connect to suppliers, business partners or individual customers at the same low cost, even if they are on the other side of the world.

Organisations can find **new outlets** for their products and services abroad because the Internet facilitates cross-border transactions and information flows. The Internet provides a low-cost medium for forming **global alliances** and **virtual organisations**. The web provides a standard interface and inexpensive global access, which can be used to create inter-organisational systems between almost any organisations.

Many within **developing countries** see the Internet as an opportunity to gain access to **knowledge** and **services** from around the world in a way that would have been unimaginable previously. Internet kiosks, mostly facilitating e-mail with overseas relatives, for example, are springing up in many parts of Africa. The Internet may also facilitate opportunities for **economic development** in industries such as tourism.

The Internet and technologies such as mobile telephony allow developing countries to **leapfrog** steps in their development of infrastructure. A poor landline telephone system in the Philippines, for example, is being rapidly bypassed by mobile phones with Internet access.

Globalisation has drastically improved the access technological latecomers have to advanced technologies and, to the extent that technological upgrading is important for development, it provides a unique opportunity for low-income countries to raise per capita income. Research shows that improved access to technology imports is improving the demand for skilled labour in many low-income countries.

In today's **information economy**, rapid access to knowledge is critical to the success of many organisations. Organisations are using e-mail and access to databases to gain immediate access to information resources in key areas eg, business, science and law. As well as accessing **public knowledge** resources on the Internet, organisations can create internal Web sites as repositories of their own organisational knowledge. Multimedia Web pages can organise this knowledge, giving employees easier access to information and expertise.

37 E-commerce

Text reference. The issues surrounding e-commerce are described in Chapter 7 of the text. However, you could equally answer this question using your own knowledge and experience of the subject.

Top tips. This question specifically requires you to discuss the impact of e-trading on the consumer and on businesses. Students who 'knowledge dump' all they know about e-trading will fail this question so this should be avoided.

A good plan will help you organise your thoughts and ensure you make enough points. Brainstorm both sections. You need to think of at least five impacts for each, if you can think of more you will be able to discard any weaker ones.

You may be able to use consumer impacts to generate business impacts or vice versa. In the answer below, the 'improved ability to compare prices' consumer impact was used to generate the 'increased competition' impact on a business.

When considering the impacts, try to include any relevant real-world examples that you can think of to illustrate your points. It is a good idea to demonstrate wider knowledge where possible.

Easy marks. The marking scheme offers up to two marks per valid point. You must ensure your points are all different as the examiner is looking for a broad range of ideas. As always, make each point a separate paragraph to make it easier for the marker to award you marks. Include enough detail to justify your point and then move on.

Examiner's comments. The majority of candidates were awarded high marks for this question. Strong candidates discussed many impacts in both parts. Weaker candidates provided lists without any discussion and thus limited the marks available. Overall this question was very well answered.

Marking scheme

Marks

In many questions suggested model answers were given to open-ended questions. Credit will be given for any valid alternative responses within the limits of the marking scheme.

(a)   Award up to 2 marks per valid point.   10

(b)   Award up to 2 marks per valid point. $\underline{10}$

Total marks $\underline{\underline{20}}$

(a)   E-trading has had many impacts on **consumers**, these include:

Improved ability to compare prices

Consumers can easily **compare prices** between e-traders as all websites are **equally accessible** and they no longer have to spend time visiting shops personally to gather price information. **Price comparison** sites such as Kelkoo will also directly compare prices on a single page so consumers can instantly be directed to the cheapest supplier. **Speed of comparison** has made consumers increasingly **price sensitive** and has helped to reduce the price of many goods such as CDs and DVDs.

Greater convenience of shopping

Consumers now only have to travel as far as their computer to do their shopping and as e-traders can **open all day and night** there are **few restrictions** on when customers can shop. Online supermarkets such as Ocado will even arrange a delivery slot within one hour on a specified delivery day.

Online fraud

By submitting credit or debit card details over the Internet, consumers are now at **greater risk of fraud** by those stealing card numbers and passwords than ever before. E-trading has increased the importance to consumers of internet security packages by companies such as Norton and McAfee to counter the risk.

Greater range of goods available

E-trading has enabled consumers to **purchase a greater variety** of products from all over the world as the internet has created a truly **global market**. For example, a record collector can now easily obtain all the different versions of a record that are available in each country rather than just the one that is available to them locally.

Reduced personal service

Shopping on the Internet **removes** the interaction between the customer and the shop assistant. This can have a negative effect. **Customers often prefer the advice** and service provided by a salesperson, (especially when purchasing expensive electrical goods). Internet consumers are largely on their own when making such choices.

(b)   E-trading has impacted **business** in the following ways:

Increased competition

Opening an Internet shop is **relatively cheap**, especially when compared with a traditional high street shop. This has increased the competition that established brands and high street shops face as they now compete on a **level playing field** with **many small retailers** across the globe. Old loyalties that consumers had with shops are lost as consumers are increasingly buying products where they can obtain them cheaply.

Increased need to consider foreign laws and regulations

Almost every country in the world can access Internet sites and every country has its own rules that govern issues such as advertising or what goods can be imported legally. E-traders must seek advice and **ensure their sites** and activities **comply with any country** that can access them.

Supply chain management

E-traders are able to buy products or materials from one country and sell them to another. This requires a **good supply chain system** between the **business**, its **suppliers** and **customers**. Additional investment may be required from the business to achieve this and the trader should consider it at an early stage. Amazon is an example of an internet business that has invested large sums of money to ensure its back-office can support the amount of trade the website generates.

Staff skills

Internet shops require **different skills from employees** than high street shops. Where as high street shops require staff with good **interpersonal skills** or **product knowledge**, internet shops require staff that possess **web design** and **IT skills**. This is an important consideration, as businesses must ensure they employ staff with the right skills for the job.

Cyber crime

Just as consumers are at risk from crime as criminals attempt to steal their credit card details, businesses are also at **risk** from **cyber crime**. Websites are at risk from **hackers** and **viruses** that may attempt to close down the site or disrupt its activities. Such is the security risk that e-traders must invest in security systems to ensure they can continue to **trade without interruption**.

38 Internet strategy

Marks

Issues available for discussion are highlighted within the scenario, and range
from the strategic to the operational. Your answer should identify a range of
these issues and show why they are relevant to this particular situation.

(a)   *Establish strategy (2 marks maximum for each point)*
        Link to business strategy of company
        Amendment of current Internet site
        Incompatible systems
        E-commerce impact on other sections of business
        Upgrade of website
        Determine services to offer on website
        Budgets

        Implement strategy (2 marks maximum for each point)
        Selling the site to customers – benefits of use
        Advertising other websites
        Obtain resources – test system
        Other similar points
        Maximum marks awarded part (a)   10

(b)   *(2 marks maximum for each point)*
        Limit manual intervention in system
        Ease of use
        Incentives to use site
        New support systems
        Provision of additional information
        Ideas to increase sales using Internet technology
        Decrease other expenditure such as office space, heating and lighting
        Other similar points
        Maximum marks awarded part (b) $\underline{10}$
                                                                               $\underline{20}$

Text reference. The Internet is discussed in Chapter 7 of the text.

Top tips. Issues available for discussion are highlighted within the scenario, and range from the strategic to the
operational. Your answer should identify a range of these issues and show why they are relevant to this particular
situation.

(a)   The following issues should be considered when establishing and implementing an appropriate Internet
        strategy for the SDW company.

   •   **The Internet strategy must support the overall business strategy**

        SDW has devised a business plan to expand operations beyond the three cities it currently flies
        between, and to introduce Internet sales. In the future Mr M wishes Internet sales to be the main
        selling media of SDW tickets.

An Internet strategy should be established that supports these aims. Site capacity and response times must be able to cope with forecast site traffic.

- **The existing website**

  The current website is used for 'publicity'. As SDW has already established a web presence, it needs to consider whether this site address should be kept, and the site content modified/replaced, or whether a new address may also be required.

  As SDW does not have this type of expertise in-house, an external website development consultancy should be employed to explain the various options and recommend an appropriate course of action.

- **Integration and compatibility with other systems**

  To bring efficiency gains and lower the cost of processing a transaction, the on-line purchasing system must be integrated with other systems, such as ticketing, payment and accounting systems. Site security for on-line payments must be addressed by experts in the field.

  Supporting processes and procedures also need to be set up, for example a process that will enable paper tickets be delivered and possibly procedures for paperless 'e-ticketing'.

- **Impact upon other areas of the business**

  The move to e-commerce will impact upon other areas of SDW. The call centre is likely to be scaled down as increasing numbers of customers move to on-line purchase. This could potentially bring significant cost savings to SDW.

  The downsizing of the call centre should be anticipated and planned for. Staff should be kept fully informed, and realistic information provided about possible redundancies.

- **On-going site maintenance**

  Establishing the site is the first stage. SDW must also implement policies and procedures to ensure information (particularly fight schedules and prices) are kept up-to-date. This should be able to be performed in-house, following suitable training from the consultants who implemented the site.

- **Other implementation issues**

  Once built, tested and implemented, the site should be publicised. Thorough testing is essential as potential customers who encounter difficulties are unlikely to return to the site. A large-scale, highly advertised launch may best be avoided, as these often result in site overloading – giving a poor first impression to potential customers.

(b)

Top tips. The focus in this answer should be on cost reduction, so it is not sufficient to explain features of the site – you must show how this will reduce costs.

The following customer orientated features should be incorporated into the SDW site to help reduce costs.

- **Effective integration with back office procedures**

  When a customer books a ticket on the website, this should result in a correct booking being made and a ticket issued and delivered, without further customer contact. Effective integration between the website and back-office functions will mean fewer customer queries to answer. This will help keep staff costs to a minimum.

- **Incentives to book on-line**

  Processing a website order will be cheaper than processing an order through traditional channels. Therefore, to maximise savings, SDW should encourage on-line bookings. Incentives could include slightly discounted fares or 'double air miles'. Increased on-line bookings will allow downsizing of the call centre, bringing savings from reduced property and staff costs.

- **Frequently Asked Questions (FAQs)**

  The site should include a FAQs, section containing questions and answers relating to flying with SDW (eg baggage allowances, check-in times etc). This will enable cost reduction by enabling customers (both those who book on-line and those who just use the site for information) to answer their queries without making a call to SDW staff.

- **User friendly layout and limited graphics**

  User friendly layout (eg logical site structure and screen design) will encourage increased use of the site – and the associated savings obtained from minimising person-to-person contact. Potential customers may be irritated by graphics that take too long to load (eg 'Flash'). This is particularly so for users using a dial up telephone line connection. SDW may be able to attract a greater number of customers to the site by keeping the site simple.

- **On-line partners**

  SDW could develop partnerships with complimentary businesses such as car hire firms. The website could then incorporate either a link to the partner site or (preferably) the ability to book a car at a discounted rate at the same time as booking the flight. A convenient, time saving booking facility such as this may bring in commission revenue from car hire firms – and will also encourage increased use of the site as opposed to phone bookings.

39 Lewin – an evaluation

Text reference. Lewin's model of change is covered in Chapter 8 in the text.

Top tips. This question is a typical example of how the examiner likes to test academic theories. The two words 'describe' and 'evaluate' should have given you the clue that the twelve marks are allocated equally between the two elements. As only two marks are available for the description of each stage of Lewin's theory, only a general outline of them is required. This should generate six marks, enough to pass Part (a).

Easy marks. The easy marks for Part (a) are for the description of the model; this is basic knowledge that you must ensure you are completely familiar with. You should be able to think of at least four common-sense reasons why a final version of a system differs from the initial plan in Part (b). The key to maximising your marks here is to make sure you use separate paragraphs for each point.

Examiner's comments. In order to achieve high marks for part (a), candidates were required to describe and evaluate Lewin's 3-step model of change. The majority of candidates provided an excellent description of the model but did not attempt to evaluate the model, thus limiting the marks available. Weaker candidates described a variety of models, including Earl's three legs, the three Cs, the Ws framework etc.

Part (b) was generally well answered although many candidates weighted their answers around misunderstood user requirements, poor analysis, and parts of the development cycle being inappropriately used. As a result, their answers were more appropriate to Paper 2.1 level questions. Strong candidates identified the possibility of changes in business strategy and the business environment, and technological advances as key factors. Overall this question was answered fairly well.

BPP
LEARNING MEDIA

		Marks

In many questions suggested model answers were given to open-ended questions. Credit will be given for any valid alternative responses within the limits of the marking scheme.

(a)	Award up to 2 marks for each stage.	$3 \times 2 =$	6
	Award up to 2 marks for each valid evaluation point.		6
(b)	Award up to 2 marks per valid point.		8
Total marks			20

(a) **Lewin's 3-step model of change** depicts how behaviour patterns of those involved in a change process can be altered to accept new required behaviours. The key is for **old behaviour** to be 'unlearnt' and for **new behaviour** to be developed and consolidated.

The three stages are:

(i) **Unfreeze**

This is the most **difficult** stage, as it requires **obtaining acceptance** that change is needed. Individuals or groups require **motivation** to change their attitudes. An old, slow, unfriendly computer system could be enough of a trigger to generate acceptance for a new one.

(ii) **Move**

The move stage puts the **necessary changes** needed by stage one into effect and seeks those affected by the change to **adopt it**. This stage could involve the development and introduction of the **new computer system**. It is more likely to succeed if those affected by the new system are involved in the change process, (for example when designing the new system).

(iii) **Refreeze**

Refreeze involves the **reinforcement of the new behaviour** from the 'move' stage until it becomes the 'norm'. Organisations may use **positive reinforcement** (by reward or praise for compliance), **negative reinforcement** (by some form of punishment for non-compliance), or a **combination of both**.

Lewin's model is useful for those **managing a change process** as it offers simple, clear advice of how to change the behaviour of individuals and groups. However, real individuals are **complex**, so changing behaviour may not be as simple has the model makes out. For example, negative reinforcement may be unworkable if all employees decide to fight the change.

There are numerous situations where the model is **ineffective**. For example, where change is required within a very **short timespan**. There would not be enough time to gain acceptance that change is needed and to involve those affected in the move process. Managers would have to adopt a **dictatorial approach** to force change through.

The model **assumes** that the new system will be **implemented successfully**. In reality there are often implementation problems, or it may turn out that the new system is no better than the old system it replaces. Such issues will **undermine the credibility** of the new system and may make the move stage impossible to complete. The model gives **no advice** of how to deal with such eventualities.

A final criticism of the model is that it assumes once the change has been implemented, the **business returns to stability**. This may have been true in the 1950s when Lewin developed his model, but now over fifty years later, **business has changed**. Modern organisations are in an almost **constant dynamic state** with changes happening all the time, partly due to the increased rate of **technological change**. There is often little time after a refreeze stage before that behaviour needs to be unfrozen. Modern businesses may find it easier to keep employees in a 'slushy' state where behaviour is never quite frozen so they can adapt to future change quickly.

(b)   There are many reasons why a final implemented system differs from its initial requirements specification.

The needs of the business may change

During the development of an information system, **business needs may change**. A business may take a strategic decision to email product lists to customers rather than send them by post. Therefore an information system originally designed to hold postal addresses may need to be amended to store email addresses and to automatically send out product lists on request.

Technological changes

During the implementation of a long-term project, **technology is likely to evolve**. Organisations want to take advantage of these technological advances so that the **lifespan** of the system is **extended** and to enable it to utilise the new features that have become available.

Insufficient consultation at the design stage

The system may be designed in a way that is **logical** to the designer but does not actually reflect the way that **users need to work**. Also, during testing, users may suggest **additional features** that would aid their work processes. Such last-minute changes can be avoided if users are involved in the design stage.

Cost reasons.

If development costs come in **over budget**, or if the business experiences **financial difficulties** during implementation, some features may have to be **removed** from the final system in order to complete the project within the financial constraints.

40 Lewin's three stage model of change

> **Text reference**. Lewin and Schein's model is covered in Chapter 8 of the text.
>
> **Top tips.** This is a ten mark preparation question, but still ensure your answer relates to the context faced by CLS as described in the scenario.
>
> **Easy marks.** Use the 'unfreeze – move – refreeze' framework to provide structure and focus to your answer.

Amending the behaviour of the research assistants can be explained using the three stage approach outlined by *Lewin* and *Schein*.

Step 1: Unfreeze. The current behaviour of the research assistants must be unfrozen, that is they must be made willing to change.

This process would be helped by emphasising that this change simply has to go ahead as the government require it. This should provide justification for the change and open the research assistants mind up to the change.

Change can then be 'sold' to the research assistants using both the need for change from CLS' point of view (no change = no work) or the benefits of change in terms of better working conditions, enhancement to CVs, improved employability etc.

Step 2: Move. This stage is concerned with identifying the new behaviour pattern required and then communicating this new 'norm' to the individuals, in this case the research assistants. The reason for communication is to allow individuals to associate with that norm so it can be accepted. To be accepted, the new behaviour or idea must be shown to work.

CLS can help research assistants accept the new culture by providing specific training on the new computer systems and involving staff in changeover talks and preparations. This should encourage a feeling of ownership towards the new system.

Step 3: Refreeze. This is the final stage where the new behaviour is consolidated or reinforced to ensure continued acceptance. Reinforcement can be positive (by praise or reward for example) or negative (sanctions being applied to individuals who do not accept the new behaviour).

In terms of CLS, removing the old computer systems will provide a relatively easy method of ensuring that the old systems are not used. However, some positive reinforcement to encourage use of the new system to its full potential may be beneficial, perhaps by rewarding those employees able to demonstrate a good understanding of the system.

41 Virtual companies and web technologies

Text reference. Chapter 7 of the text contains material relevant to this question.

Top tips. Virtual companies are a topical area likely to be examined regularly. Ensure you read the requirements carefully, provide an answer that meets these requirements and refer to the scenario.

Examiner's comments. The examiner noted that a key notion overlooked by many candidates was 'advances in technology are enabling companies to be held together not through formal structure and physical proximity of people, but by partnership, collaboration and networking.' Many candidates misinterpreted this and gave extended descriptions of companies making themselves available on the 'Internet' claiming having a presence on the Internet defined a virtual company.

A specific application of web based technology was the focus of part (b), namely advertising and providing information on a website compared with paper-based catalogues. Generally this part of the question was answered particularly well, many candidates being awarded maximum marks.

Marking scheme

		Marks
(a)	Guidelines for mark allocation 0-5 marks. Answers that demonstrate some understanding of structure, difference between virtual and physical; should mention some of the technology required; may just name an example without an explanation/description. 6-12 marks. Answers that demonstrate a clear understanding of the concept of virtual companies; mention the technology required to support virtual companies. Award credit for examples given of virtual companies.	12
(b)	Award up to 4 marks in total for advantages and up to 4 marks for disadvantages.	8
		20

(a)   **A virtual company** is a collection of separate entities (eg companies, departments, individuals) each with a specific expertise, who work together, sharing their expertise to compete for bigger contracts/projects than would be possible if they worked alone.

The technologies that support virtual companies tend to be the **Internet** and related systems such as **intranets** and **extranets**.

Many companies, large and small, are setting up virtual companies that enable executives, engineers, scientists, writers, researchers, and other professionals from around the world to **collaborate** on new products and services without ever meeting face to face. Advances in technology, particularly the widespread use of the Internet, has fuelled this growth.

These virtual companies are held together by the **technologies** that allow entities in different locations to operate in **partnership**, collaborating on mutually beneficial projects. By combining in the virtual world, the collaborators are able to present themselves to clients as a single entity.

Successful virtual companies combine ideas and assets that **compliment** each other in relation to the enterprise being undertaken. The virtual company requires extremely close business relationships and a high degree of mutual trust.

A virtual company may be the best way to implement **key business strategies** that promise to ensure success in today's turbulent business climate. For example, an opportunity to move into a new market may be available, but to prevent competitors 'getting there first', it is necessary to move quickly. The opportunity could be seized by quickly forming a virtual company with reputable partners.

In situations such as this, organisations that pursue **traditional methods** of expansion, requiring the establishment of a traditional 'brick and mortar' infrastructure, would be exposed to a greater extent to the likelihood of competitors seizing the opportunity first.

(b)   **Advantages of a website over a paper-based catalogue**

- A website will be cheaper. Paper, printing and postage costs will be avoided
- World-wide coverage is easily possible
- A website can include moving images and sound
- A website offers interactive, two-way communication
- On-line orders may be processed quickly and efficiently, with users inputting their own orders
- Site registration and the use of 'cookies' will allow communication to be personalised

Disadvantages of a website compared to a paper-based catalogue

- Outside expertise may be required to set up the site and this can be expensive

- The site will require constant monitoring and updating. A clear policy should be defined and followed

- An out-of-date site could make the company look unprofessional and discourage prospective customers

- Not all potential customers have access to the Internet

- Many people may be reluctant to purchase on-line for fear of Internet credit card fraud (even though there may be no more real risk than providing the number on a paper order-form)

42 Automate, informate, transformate

Text reference. The framework examined in this question is covered in Chapter 4 of the text.

Top tips. This type of question is popular in that it permits you to apply theory to an organisation or organisations of your own choice. Try to select examples that are simple and clearly demonstrate the point you are making.

Examinor's oommonts. Part (a) required candidates to briefly explain the terms giving examples where appropriate – most candidates provided very good responses to this.

Answers to the second part varied. Many were excellent – demonstrating both a good understanding of the impact and why it is applicable to a specific organisation. Some very high marks were awarded accordingly.

		Marks
(a)	Up to 3 marks for each description of the stage and up to 1 mark for an example. 3 stages.	12
(b)	Award up to 2 marks for each valid explained point up to a maximum of 8.	8
		20

(a) The generic terms automate, informate and transformate are explained below.

Automate corresponds to the **automation** stage in the automation, rationalisation, re-engineering framework.

Automate involves the automation of repetitive manual tasks. Automate type changes typically take place during the initial introduction of information systems and information technology into an organisation.

The new system replaces or speeds up previously manual tasks. The initial introduction of IS into organisations involved the automation of repetitive and costly manual tasks. These processes weren't redesigned – they were just performed using automatic tools such as computers.

Automate changes are therefore relatively low in risk strategy. Examples include word processing, payroll systems and other transaction processing systems. This.

Informate corresponds to the **rationalisation** stage in the automation, rationalisation, re-engineering framework.

Informate describes the situation where some processes are redesigned to exploit the potential of information technology. A change in user attitudes is involved as they demand better quality information.

This realisation of the potential IS/IT may bring leads to the questioning of the way things are currently done. Operating procedures are streamlined and the organisation infrastructure becomes more integrated. These are more significant changes than simple automation, with a corresponding increase in risk.

Integrating previously separate information systems, for example linking the order processing system with the stock control system, is an example of informate type change.

Transformate corresponds to the **re-engineering** stage in the automation, rationalisation, re-engineering framework.

Transformate describes the situation where information systems and information technology are used to change the way the organisation operates and the way business is done. Systems are utilised that allow the organisation to conduct business in a way that was previously not possible. Transformate type changes may bring competitive advantage.

Transformate type changes may involve significant changes in organisation structure. This is a more risky strategy, which goes much further than rationalisation of processes.

A traditional retail business moving completely to web-based e-commerce could be viewed as a transformate type change.

(b) Organisation chosen – a traditional **'High Street' bank** such as the UK bank Nat West.

This organisation's use of IS/IT would fall into the informate categorisation – although a reasonable argument could also be made that the systems have caused 'transformate' type change.

Nat West and other established banks have developed information systems that have **redesigned** the way certain tasks have been done. For example, Internet and website technology is utilised to enable customers to manage their funds and accounts on-line using 'on-line banking'.

In the past, all customers performed their banking business face-to-face in a branch (except for a limited number of transactions available via Automatic Teller Machines). **On-line banking** has massively expanded the range of banking services able to be performed without visiting a branch (eg direct debit maintenance, funds transfers, loan applications etc). To cope with this change, the bank has developed working methods that enable web-originated transactions and information to merge with the on-going traditional forms of banking.

These type of changes are more significant than a simple automate situation. The fact that business may now be done using a completely different **customer contact mechanism** signifies a greater change than solely using IS/IT to make existing processes more efficient (and could be used to argue that the systems have caused transformate rather than informate type change).

Although there may be some debate, I don't believe the changes introduced by banks such as Nat West should be categorised transformate type systems, as the new web-based systems **do not** replace the old way of doing business – they **compliment** them by providing additional choice to customers. Although the overall impact on the organisation is significant, on-line banking still only accounts for a **relatively small** proportion of banking business.

43 Question with answer plan: BPR and supply chain

Text reference. BPR is covered in Chapter 4 of the text, supply chains and virtual supply chains in Chapter 7.

Top tips. Ensure you revise the features of supply chains in general, and virtual supply chains in particular. Remember at all times that the examiner is interested in your ability to apply your knowledge in a practical setting.

Easy marks. The bulk of the marks (part (b)) are available for discussing the 'notion' of a supply chain. As with part (a) on BPR, start off with a definition to focus your thoughts.

Examiner's comments. Part (a) was normally well answered with most answers relating comments made to the case study. In part (b), many candidates provided good examples of the supply chain and the information systems required, as requested by the question. A minority of answers focused on explaining Porter's value chain with little or no reference to virtual supply chains, limiting the marks that could be awarded.

Marking scheme

		Marks
(a)	Award up to 2 marks for each valid point. Max 8 marks.	8
(b)	Award up to 4 marks for describing supply chain, up to 4 marks for identifying major activities and up to 4 marks for identifying information systems to support virtual supply chains.	12
		20

Answer plan

(a)   Business Process Re-engineering (BPR) – definition and key features. (Outline it's applicability for ABC, focusing upon the supply chain issues such as possible new processes for stock ordering).

(b)   Supply chain definition

Virtual supply chain – definition and major activities for supplier, organisation and customer. Outline the supporting information systems:

- Databases
- Communication links EDI
- Communication links – Internet
- Order tracking

(a)   **Business Process Re-engineering (BPR)** is the fundamental rethinking and radical design of business processes to achieve dramatic improvements in critical contemporary measures of performance, such as cost, quality, service and speed.

In other words, BPR involves significant change in the business rather than minimal or incremental changes to processes. This is essentially different from procedures such as automation where existing processes are simply computerised. Although some improvements in speed may be obtained, the processes are essentially the same. For example, the local warehouse could use EDI to send an order to the supplier, which may be quicker than email. However, the process of sending the order and receiving the goods to the warehouse is the same.

Using BPR, the actual reasons for the business processes being used can be queried, and where necessary replaced with more efficient processes. For example, rather than stock being ordered from the store via the central warehouse, the supplier could monitor stocks in each store using an extranet. When goods reach re-order level, the supplier is aware of this and can send goods directly to the store. Not only does this provide stock replenishment much more quickly, it is also more cost effective for the supplier as the central warehouse effectively becomes redundant.

Key features of BPR involve the willingness of the organisation to accept change and the ability to use new technologies to achieve those changes. In the example, ABC may have to clearly explain the benefits to staff from the new systems, to ensure that they are accepted. ABC may also need to obtain additional skills in terms of IT and ability to implement and use those systems. New hardware and software will also certainly be required. The aim of BPR is to provide radical improvements in efficiency and cost savings of up to 90%. Amending the supply chain as noted above will help to these benefits.

(b)   **A supply chain** is made up of the physical entities linked together to facilitate the supply of goods and services to the final customer. The chain therefore links companies together from the initial extraction of raw materials to the delivery of the final product.

A **virtual supply chain** is a supply chain that is enabled through e-business links, that is the web, extranets or EDI. It is 'virtual' in that 'goods' in the supply chain move electronically rather than physically.

The major activities in a virtual supply chain normally relate to the three main components of supplier, organisation and customer, although there may also be intermediates between each of these three entities. For example, a supplier of software will make the electronic code available for sale by download as well as on CD or DVD. The supplier transfers the code to an organisation (effectively a virtual retailer) on the Internet (eg Amazon or similar company). The retail organisation makes the code available for sale. Customers pay the retailer allowing them to download the program code and use it on their computer.

The virtual supply chain also works with more established product based companies. For example, a manufacturer of 'white goods' that is washing machines, fridges etc will still produce those goods and send them to a retailer. The retailer will still sell those goods to customers. However, transfer of information about the goods is carried out electronically. The customer orders goods on the Internet. If goods are not in stock then orders may be transferred automatically to the manufacturer as a trigger to increase production. Fulfilment still means receiving the physical product, although again various computer systems will be used to facilitate delivery.

Supporting information systems used to develop the virtual supply chain will include:

Databases

Suppliers and retail organisations need to keep track of the raw materials and goods for sale in inventory. A database will maintain stock levels as well as monitor the progress of orders. Within the database, data will be analysed (data mining) in an attempt to identify buying patterns making ordering and production more demand focused.

Communication links – EDI

Good communications will be needed between suppliers and retail organisations to determine stock availability and facilitate re-ordering. Companies may link databases using Electronic Data Interchange or in some cases by allowing access to their own databases using Extranets. Stock replenishment in some supermarkets is carried out in this way by suppliers have access to supermarket inventory systems.

Communication links – Internet

Communications between the retail organisation and the customer will be facilitated by the use of the Internet. This system will be used to display products available for sale, send invoices and receive payment, and in some situations supply the goods purchased. Inherent qualities of the Internet will include security for payments and appropriate bandwidth to actually supply the goods.

Customers will also have access to information systems at the retail organisation in terms of inventory levels and order status. The retailer will need to provide details of order status in real time situations.

Payment systems will include Electronic Funds Transfer, with appropriate encryption technology to maintain security of payment.

Order tracking

Information systems will also be required for order tracking where fulfilment is in terms of physical goods. For example, if the tracking number of a consignment is available, then DHL's website will show the location of that consignment and may be able to estimate delivery time. Information systems required include a real time database of consignment information together with infrastructure to support global tracking of consignments.

Use of global communication systems also allows the virtual supply chain to be available worldwide. Orders can be placed in one country for despatch from others. Similarly, physical goods can be tracked across any country with the use of global networks.

44 Electronic trading room

Marks

(a) (2 marks maximum for each point)
New hardware and software
Need for communication experts
Review prices regularly
Less repeat business
Dependence on one type of communication structure
Lower margins
Change in stocks
Production planning
Other relevant points
Maximum marks awarded part (a)   11

(b) Monitoring of trading room (up to 3 marks)
Access to price lists (up to 3 marks)
Access to external systems (up to 3 marks)
Send bid to trading room (up to 3 marks)
Other similar points (up to 3 marks)
Maximum marks awarded part (b) $\frac{9}{20}$

(a)

> **Top tips.** Use the information provided in the scenario – prior knowledge of electronic trading rooms is not a pre-requisite to answer this question well, as the scenario provides guidance to the type of issues to be discussed.

The electronic trading room is likely to have the following effects upon DLA.

Less repeat business

The trading room will lead to more flexibility in the issuing of contracts, which is likely to mean less repeat business. Customer loyalty is likely to be replaced by decision making based solely on price (at least in the short term – quality problems may cause this policy to be reviewed in the future).

Lower margins

Within the trading room, price is the sole factor in winning a contract. Therefore, DLN may find it has to reduce its margins to win business. To remain profitable, DLN may need to become more efficient, for example by considering Business Process Re-engineering.

Difficulty managing stock levels

Every time a DLN contract comes up for renewal it may be won by a competitor. By the same token DLN may find it wins contracts it did not previously expect to. This increased uncertainty will make stock management more complex. Additional stocks may need to be held in case a large bid is won. This may cause increased stock obsolescence if less contracts than expected are won and then new models are introduced.

More difficult production planning

The increased uncertainty will also impact upon production planning. DLN will require flexibility in staffing levels and working patterns. Production staff and facilities may be under utilised during some periods, and overstretched at other times.

Additional employee skills required

DLN will require employees or contractors/consultants with the skills required to set up, configure and maintain the hardware and software required to use the trading room.

Dependency upon communication infrastructure

To win business in the room will require a reliable communication link. If this link fails at the 'wrong' time, contracts may be lost. A second, back-up link, would be relatively cheap to establish so should be considered.

Set prices on a bid-by-bid basis

DLN may have to consider its prices on a bid-by-bid basis rather than operating using a standard price list and discounting schedule. Pricing decisions are likely to be made on the basis of the size of the contract, current workload (or lack of it), any information regarding possible competitor bid price levels and the long term sustainability of DLN.

(b)

Text reference. Information sources are discussed in Chapter 1 of the text.

Top tips. Place yourself in the position of the manager producing bids; this should make it easier to see what information will be needed and where this could be obtained. Additional detail can then be provided on these two important points.

To ensure that bids are placed into the trading room on an appropriate timescale, managers at DLN will require a range of information from a range of sources.

Information source – the trading room itself

The trading room must be monitored for information relating to bid deadlines. This may be possible to be done electronically (using intelligent agent software), although logging-in to the room to check for information may be sufficient.

Information obtained regarding bid deadlines must be passed on to the manager responsible for making a bid. If an intelligent agent was used it could be programmed to e-mail a direct link to the appropriate page in the trading room to an appropriate manager.

Information source – internal company records

To enable a decision to be made upon a bid price, managers will require access to costing information and historical pricing information in order to help establish a bid price, and to production plans to ensure capacity exists.

The DLN management accounting system should contain the cost and price information. Production planning and stock information may be held in a system such as MRP. This should enable managers to establish which parts are already held in stock, and whether capacity exists for those parts that would need to be produced.

Detailed historical data on previous bids may also be useful. A database containing this information could be queried to show bid price history and bid acceptances/rejections.

Information source – external systems

The trading room is a competitive environment. Success in winning bids depends upon the DLN price and competitors' prices. Information relating to competitor pricing would therefore be extremely useful when placing bids.

Some competitor pricing information is likely to be freely available on external systems, such as competitor websites. However, this will be the 'published price' and could differ greatly from their bid price.

Sales representatives may be able to glean some indication of competitor pricing levels from contacts within the industry. This should be done discretely, but ethically.

45 Question with helping hand: Key indicators

Text reference. CFSs and KPIs are covered in Chapter 2 of the text.

Top tips. The suggestions given here are not the only 'right answers'. If you have suggested other key indicators, and it is likely that you have, test them by re-reading critically your justification for selecting each one.

REPORT

To: The Managing Director, EF Ltd
From: Accountant
Date: 23 November 20X1
Subject: Recommendations for key indicators

In evaluating the effect of the recent changes within EF Ltd the following indicators can be recommended.

(a)   **Added value per employee** is useful as a possible measure of **productivity.** This could, for example, be defined as sales income less bought in services (including finance charges) and material, divided by the number of employees.

The company has proceeded down the route of replacing personnel with capital equipment. The productivity of the remaining workforce should therefore be significantly greater than before.

The **information** for this indicator is readily available from the **usual management accounting sources**. Knowing the cost of capital, the savings in payroll costs, and the budgeted throughput, a target added value per employee can be calculated that represents breakeven on the financial effect of the changes.

A **weakness** with this indicator is that certain elements are susceptible to **changes in economic conditions** as well as to internal changes.

Any business process re-engineering of this nature should bring about significant gains in productivity by **eliminating inefficient and outdated processes** altogether. New procedures should reflect **best practice** in the industry, and, for this reason, some use of **benchmarking against competitors** in the industry is also recommended.

(b)   **Responsiveness** to customers and the marketplace is vital.

The purpose of the changes is not simply to save money, but to enable the company to **react speedily to consumer needs**. The information technology industry is becoming a prime example of 'relationship marketing', wherein the supplier is attempting to become closer to each customer. This is a means of seeking competitive advantage. Thus the organisation will be trying to behave as if it were 'lean and mean' and provide fast response to each customer, not simply manufacturing 'boxes'. Hence the introduction of CAD/CAM.

An **important indicator** therefore, as an example of speed of reaction, is the **speed at which bespoke customer needs are met**. To make this indicator consistent, project times from agreement of customer specification to delivery need to be measured.

A **problem** with this is that the size of the project will affect the speed of delivery. Perhaps project times could be divided by the sales margin for comparability and consistency. The lower the ratio the better. A company target figure should be established as a yardstick.

(c) **Financial** indicators, such as **management accounting ratios** (credit risk, debtor days, WIP turnround etc) should also be used. Although **care** is needed in **interpretation**, because of distortions caused by accounting policies and the need for consistency from period to period, the **traditional measures** of working capital efficiency (summarised perhaps as 'working capital days' being debtor days plus stock days less supplier days) are **as relevant as ever** to modern industry.

The improvement in the **manufacturing systems** will have included measures designed to improve **stock management** and **financial control**, probably one of the variants of JIT and perhaps ABM (activity based management) or other relevant costing/management systems. The effect on cash flow should be dramatic once the new systems are in place.

These cost savings can be set against the capital costs incurred in developing new systems. Standard **investment appraisal** techniques can be used here: current thinking suggests that a balanced measure, incorporating NPV, payback and IRR gives the most rounded view. In addition **project management measures** relating to budget, timetables and quality (availability, response etc) can be used.

(d) **Strategic direction** is extremely difficult to assess as it involves such long-term factors. Major systems change of the type undertaken is certainly part of a strategic process and its success can only be seen by reference to the **overall market position** of the company and its **reputation**. The value of the **brand name** may be measured, but such measures are **subjective**. Better is a **long-term tracking of share price** and **market share**.

Although **strategic planning is long-term**, IT can sit awkwardly with this, as so much **technology is short-term** in nature, with manufacturers reducing product life cycles in their quest for competitive advantage. This means that IT-based decisions may need to be changed within the life of a particular strategy. This problem can to some extent be addressed by a formal **Information Systems Planning** exercise, which creates a framework for development, providing guidelines over a period of time to ensure that activities fit into strategic criteria.

(e) **Critical success factors** can be used. Each CSF will already have been ascribed one or more performance indicators. CSFs are fundamental to the strategic direction of the company. Here, the changes to be evaluated are more than just small improvements to individual parts of the company, they are a fundamental change to the very nature and shape of the organisation.

The ultimate measure of their effectiveness could be said to be in the **bottom line results** of EF Ltd; however, other factors will also be relevant, for example, **reliability indicators**. This might take the form of warranty claims/sales, or claims/number of products supplied, or may be based on customer surveys measuring the elusive characteristic of 'customer satisfaction'.

The reputation of the company, and thus its potential to generate future cash flows – the definition of the value of the enterprise – depends on the quality of its service. It is important to know that the reduction in personnel numbers, and the introduction of automation has not compromised quality.

The above should be read in the light of the assumption that systems development is undertaken in general to meet business needs and fulfil organisational objectives. These might be categorised as:

- Reductions in cost base
- Investment in IT infrastructure

- Responding to, or anticipating, changing market conditions
- Ensuring that IT supports strategic plans

It is only by setting appropriate performance indicators, such as the above, that the success of systems development can be measured.

In conclusion, the measurement of the key components of the strategy of the company are vital to the control and updating of that strategy as it links 'hard' cost/benefit analysis with 'softer' areas which are difficult to quantify and often subjective.

Signed: Accountant

46 Working relationships and communication

Text reference. The impact of IT is discussed in Chapter 9 of the text.

Top tips. The key is to focus upon technology, and how it changes working relationships.

Easy marks. To get the marks, take the opportunity to choose five examples of business information management systems and discuss their implications.

Examiner's comments. This question required candidates to identify and discuss five examples of how the introduction of business information management (BIM) systems can significantly affect working relationships between management and employees within an organisation. The model answer provided examples of eight such systems and the list was not exhaustive. Full credit was given for alternative relevant systems.

Many candidates only wrote about changes to working practices, completely failing to explain, as required by the question, how technology may change working relationships or patterns of communication. Some candidates merely wrote about resistance to change. The overall result was rather disappointing for a relatively straightforward question. The spread of marks awarded for this question was polarised.

Marking scheme

	Marks
Award up to 4 marks per area, to obtain full marks each area should include system/technology. 5 × 4 marks.	<u>20</u>

Five examples of how the introduction of business information management systems can affect working relationships and communication between employees and employers are explained below.

Encourages less adherence to the formal 'chain of command'

The chain of command in an organisation refers to the formal hierarchy or lines of management. There is a set reporting structure and employees and communication flows are expected to follow that structure.

However, the introduction of business information management systems tends to disrupt that system. For example, email allows any employee in an organisation to send a message to any other employee. Any employee can send an e-mail message to the managing director effectively breaking the normal chain of command.

Before email, telephone systems could have been used to break the chain, but secretaries and other administration staff would more readily screen calls or visitors to the MD. E-mail goes direct to the MD's computer.

Efficient channels of communication operating outside of the organisational hierarchy therefore reduce the need to pass communications up and down all of the individual steps in the chain of command.

Wider spans of control and information overload

Electronic information and communication systems have enabled many organisations to develop a flatter management structure, with managers having a wider span of control. The wider span of control and developments in technology have increased the amount of information sent to individuals.

This may lead to employers and employees receiving too much information, potentially missing important facts which are 'hidden' in the glut of information provided. To counter this systems that filter information can be introduced. The use of exception reports in executive information systems is an example of attempting to overcome the information overload problem.

Information overload and the missing of important data has two effects on the employer/employee relationship. Firstly, stress levels increase, making communication more difficult as employees and employers rush to complete jobs. Secondly, the possibility of employers 'blaming' employees for not acting on information sent to them. These problems will make ongoing cordial relationships difficult to maintain.

Changed nature of work

The implementation of many new business information management systems has meant many tasks have been automated, or in some situations changed significantly, as business processes are re-designed using modern technology. This has resulted in the degrading of some skills as well as the requirement for employees to learn new skills.

Some employees manage the transition well, others prefer to move jobs or take early retirement. Others attempt to change but find the situation extremely stressful.

Employers need to recognise the extent of change taking place and provide appropriate training and re-training programs for staff. If appropriate programs are not provided, employee/employer relationships may worsen if employees believe employers are not looking after their interests correctly. Employers emphasising the benefits of change may also make new systems more acceptable to employees.

Telecommuting (working from home) and geographic spread

The development of communication links such s wide area networks, digital telephone lines, broadband and powerful PCs has made it possible for employees to work from home without losing touch with the office.

This brings advantages and disadvantages for both parties. Advantages include cost savings, a larger pool of labour and saved commuting time. Disadvantages include possibly reduced co-ordination, isolation, diluted culture and intrusions. The arrangement requires trust on both sides.

However, increased use of business information management systems, particularly the use of email and shared databases, also means that work can take place in almost any location around the world regardless of where head office is based. Close working relationships can be maintained using email and video-conferencing where necessary. For example, employees can work in call centres in the Far East with employers being located in Europe.

Greater monitoring and control

Employers monitor the work of employees to ensure that they are working efficiently. Historically, monitoring has been relatively informal, with employers observing employees and encouraging employees to ask for assistance with problems encountered.

However, business information management systems provide opportunities to monitor employees constantly. For example, closed circuit TV can be used to observe employees, e-mail can be monitored and specialist software can be used to monitor telephone calls.

While there are laws regarding privacy in many countries, increased monitoring may adversely affect the working relationship between employees and employers. Stress levels may increase for employees, and they may assume that employers trust them less. Decreased staff morale could then also affect customer service, and potentially the sales made by the organisation.

Employers need to be careful to show that monitoring systems are not being used aggressively or to 'catch employees out' if the benefits of these systems are to outweigh these disadvantages.

47 Information age and employee conduct

Text reference. The information age is covered in Chapter 9 of the text.

Top tips. An excellent answer would involve showing awareness of the ethical implications of the new information age and the responsibilities that organisations should identify.

Examiner's comments. This question was not popular. Some candidates looked at the words and 'guessed' the meaning without referring to the information age context. Many candidates completely ignored the second requirement concerning the 'code of practice'.

Marking scheme

	Marks
Award up to 2 marks for each description and 2 marks for each item in the code of practice. Five dimensions @ 4 marks.	<u>20</u>

(a) **Information rights and obligations**

This refers to the rights and responsibilities that individuals and organisations have with respect to the information they hold. Privacy (the right to be free from surveillance or interference) is an important issue in this area. The advent of computerised information systems has increased the dangers of privacy being abused, as so much more information is able to be gathered and stored.

Code of practice

An organisational code of practice should cover the following areas:

- Policies relating to the security and disclosure of corporate information
- Policies relating to the security and disclosure of employee/customer/supplier information
- Clear e-mail use and privacy guidelines
- Regulations governing employee computer and Internet use and the monitoring of this

(b) **Property rights**

Property rights refers to intellectual property created by individuals or organisations which is subject to protection. This could involve trade secrets and material subject to copyright and patents. The growth of information technology has increased the threat to intellectual property. Computer files and other forms of digital media make it easier to copy large volumes of data and information. Computer software and music CDs are two examples.

Code of practice

An organisational code of practice should cover the following areas:

- Statement ensuring the terms of all software copyrights and licences are adhered to
- A policy regarding ownership of software developed by employees
- Back-up and recovery procedures
- File copying and distribution policies

(c)   **Accountability and control**

Accountability and control refers to who the ability to monitor and control activities and ensure individuals and corporations are answerable for their actions. Increased use of technology has made these issues more complex. For example, if a website provides instructions on how to build a bomb, information that is also available at any public library, should those who posted the material held on the site be accountable if somebody acts on this information? Can these people even be traced? What if they're based in another country. Should the organisation hosting the site be responsible? What about the Public Library or the book author? All these questions raise complex issues that are currently unresolved.

Code of practice

An organisational code of practice should cover the following areas:

- Non-disclosure of personal system passwords

- A statement clearly identifying areas of responsibility for all aspects of information systems development

- Responsibilities for system management, maintenance and system audits

- A statement clearly identifying areas of responsibility for all data held on the system

(d)   **System quality**

The concept of quality is subjective and ever-changing. With advances in technology, what was considered a high quality system five years ago may now be considered almost obsolete. Building quality into a system also takes time, and costs money. This brings up the conflict between time, cost and quality. For example, at what point should system developers stop testing and release software even with some minor bugs?

Code of practice

An organisational code of practice should cover the following areas:

- Acceptable general levels of data quality and system error to be tolerated
- Systems development models or methodologies to be used
- Hardware and software performance specifications
- Procedures for documenting system quality including error reports

(e)   **Quality of life**

The increasing role of technology in day-to-day life has the potential to increase the quality of life, but could also adversely impact upon the quality of life of some people. Technological change has seen some jobs become more mundane and repetitive, meaning reduced quality of life for those employed in these roles (eg many accounts clerks now spend most of their time inputting data to computer systems). In other cases technological advances have led to unemployment – a dramatic reduction in quality of life for those concerned (eg Computer Aided Manufacturing plants generally require fewer employees) .

Technology has also created a 24 hour, seven days a week society with people able to use the Internet to pay bills, do their banking, log onto their workplace computer network, make purchases etc at any time of the day or night. Although this allows more flexibility, increasing the quality of life, it also often means less time is set aside for family or other non-work activities.

Code of practice

An organisational code of practice should cover the following areas:

- How technology will be used to help the organisation achieve its goals
- Procedures to ensure systems are used safely eg eye care, ergonomics
- Employee job rotation scheme provisions if particularly mundane jobs are involved
- Training policies to ensure employees are fully equipped to use relevant technology

48 Social and ethical issues

Text reference. Chapter 9 of the text contains material relevant to this question.

Top tips. This question provides a good example of the importance of reading the requirement carefully – some candidates wasted time by describing all three of the methods listed in the question.

Examiner's comments. Part (a) required a description of two of the three methods listed. The information in the scenario provided candidates with ample material to discuss. Generally this part was very well answered.

The second part required candidates to outline the technical infrastructure required to support the new system. This part attracted some excellent responses, as did the final part asking candidates to identify potential social and ethical issues arising from implementing the home-based system. It was pleasing to see that the majority of candidates did relate their answers to the scenario.

Marking scheme

		Marks
(a)	Award up to 3 marks for each.	6
(b)	Award up to 2 marks for each valid point to a maximum of 6 marks.	6
(c)	Award up to 2 marks for each valid point to a maximum of 8 marks.	8
		20

(a) *(Any two of the following)*

An **organisational impact analysis** attempts to explain how a system will affect an organisation in areas such as structure, reporting lines, staff attitudes, decision-making, working methods and information flows. By ensuring all of these issues are considered, the study reduces the risk of system failure.

Ensuring sufficient **user involvement** at all stages of system design and implementation has been shown to greatly reduce the likelihood of the resulting system failing to meet user needs. Involvement in the design process allows user input early in the process, reducing the likelihood of expensive and time consuming reworking later on. User involvement also builds a sense of ownership and acceptance towards the new system.

Focussing on the **sociotechnical design** of a system involves attempting to ensure the technical aspects of the system compliment the social and overall objectives of the system. This is done by producing a social design and a technical design, which are then combined into the overall design.

(b) The system proposed for Teac Household Exteriors would require the following **technical infrastructure**.

A computer network containing the information required by telephone sales personnel

- The necessary **hardware**, **software** and **communication facilities** to enable telephone sales personnel to access this network from home ie a standard personal computer (PC) with the relevant software and a communications link

- The communications link could either be a **dial-up facility** or (preferably) a **broadband** link perhaps through a 'Virtual Private Network (VPN) connection. This link could provide other facilities such as e-mail and conferencing

- **Access/security** controls will have to be implemented eg network user names and access rights, anti-virus software and a firewall

(c)   Implementing the home-based telesales system raises the following issues.

Possible **positive** issues include:

- Some flexibility of working patterns for staff – although this may be limited as potential customers may best be contacted at specific times. If appropriate, staff may contact customers outside what were their 'normal' office working hours

- Staff time saved as they need no longer travel to work in the centre of the city. This should also mean staff are 'brighter' and less stressed

- Fewer distractions and disruptions often encountered in the office environment – although in some cases home distractions may present a problem

- Better quality of life. It is likely that staff will be more able to integrate domestic commitments with work commitments, eg working around children's school times which should make life in general more enjoyable

Possible **negative** issues include:

- Staff feelings of isolation. Some staff working from home may feel cut-off from the organisation and their colleagues. They may miss the social contact. This could also have repercussions in terms of organisational teamwork

- The loss of the traditional barrier between home and work lives may unsettle some people. Maintaining the boundaries between family, work and leisure (eg being able to 'switch off') may be difficult

- Employees working from home may feel less valued by the organisation. Not being involved with the day-to-day activity of the office may be perceived as disadvantageous in terms of recognition and promotion prospects

- Such a change in the working arrangement will have legal and administrative implications such as the need for an amended employment contract and reliance on employee honesty regarding hours worked

49 The moral dimension

Text reference. The five moral dimensions are covered in Chapter 9 of the text.

Top tips. Don't be intimidated if you haven't seen these five moral factors referred to specifically as 'moral dimensions of the information age'. The dimension names indicate the type of issue you should cover in your answer to part (a). Applying a theory such as this is not an exact science – if you quote a reasonable example and explain it sensibly you will score well on part (b). Don't worry if your answer is different to the example answer we provide – a wide range of examples could have been used to answer this question.

Easy marks. As explained above, the names of each dimension provide a guide as to what each dimension covers. Your answer to (c) should follow logically on from your answer to (b).

Examiner's comments. Many candidates were awarded maximum marks for part (a). Therefore it was rather surprising that only a minority of candidates could identify examples of infringements of the principles. This was another example of candidates failing to apply theory to practical situations. Stronger candidates identified excellent examples of infringements and continued to identify the steps that an organisation could take to minimise the risk of the infringements occurring. The overall result was rather disappointing for a relatively straightforward question. An article was previously published in the Student Accountant that discussed all the principles applicable to this topic.

			Marks
(a)		For each dimension, award 1 mark for description (five dimensions)	5
(b)	(i)	Award up to 2 marks for each example	10
	(ii)	Award 1 mark for each step	5
			20

(a) The five moral dimensions of the information society are described below in the context of an organisation.

Information rights and obligations. This refers to the rights of individuals with respect to information held by other individuals and organisations about themselves – and to the obligations of individuals and organisations who hold data to use it responsibly. Individuals/organisations are obliged to collect and process data only for the purposes for which the originator supplied the data.

Property rights. This dimension is concerned with protecting intellectual property rights. For example an organisation may have patented a particular product or production technique, or may be concerned with unauthorised copying of digital property.

Accountability and control. The issue here is whether individuals and organisations who create, produce and sell systems are morally responsible for the consequences of their use. Who can and will be held accountable and liable for harm done?

System quality. This dimension refers to the expected quality of software and hardware expected from suppliers. What standards of data and system quality should an organisation require to protect standards and employees?. What is an acceptable, technologically feasible level of system quality?

Quality of life. What organisational values and practices are supported by the new information technology? Can some tasks be automated? Is working from home possible? Is working from home desirable for employees given that it weakens the traditional boundary between work and family/leisure. Are legal and ethical employment practices followed in relation to VDU workers?

(b) (i) Examples of where an infringement of each principle may have occurred are given below.

Information rights and obligations. An organisation gathers information about customers as part of doing business with them. A breach of this principle would occur if this organisation passed or sold this (eg customer contact details, purchase history, income level) onto another organisation without permission.

Property rights. This principle would be breached if an organisation installs software purchased under a single-user licence on multiple PCs to be used by a number of staff. This not only deprives the software supplier of income, it is also illegal.

Accountability and control. Employees are often provided with Internet access as it is a valuable research/business tool. A breach would occur if an employee used their Internet access at work to view pornographic material – even worse if they then distributed this from their work PC via a web-based e-mail account.

System quality. An example of a breach would be if a software producer rushed the release of a product to beat the imminent release by a competitor of a similar product – but this meant testing was inadequate and as a result the released product contained major bugs.

Quality of life. An issue here could be the blurring of lines between home and work life. For example, after issuing devices such as BlackBerry's to some employees an organisation may expect these people to respond to communication almost 24 hours a day, seven days a week.

(ii) Steps the organisation could have taken to minimise the risk of each infringement identified in b(i) are given below.

Information rights and obligations. An organisation should ensure all employees are aware of the various legal acts relevant to the protection of data and its uses. Policies should be implemented ensuring misuse of data will not occur.

Property rights. Employers should ensure they have the required licences for all software used by their employees. The organisation may develop a policy of only permitting employees to use those software packages required to perform their duties.

Accountability and control. Issue a clear Internet (and related systems) usage policy to all employees. Many organisations also use software that restricts sites available to employees.

System quality. Strict system development standards and procedures should be devised and enforced. Short-cuts to these should not be tolerated. If time is of the essence increased resource should be used to ensure timely release.

Quality of life. An organisation should develop a clear policy outlining when employees should be available. An ethical employer will respect its employees' work/private life balance – and will recognise that to perform well people need to be able to 'switch off'.

Scenario text references. Scenario questions draw material from across the text. References are given to aspects that are directly available in specific chapters.

---

50 TBS – Accounting partnership

(a)

Text reference. Knowledge management in parts (a), (b) and (d) are covered in Chapter 3. Security controls in part (c) are covered in Chapter 1 of the text.

Top tips. To create a framework for your answers, actions to date should be evaluated under appropriate headings. Suggestions as to how things could be improved can then be provided under those same headings.

Timing. The launch announcement 18 months previously seems to have been met with some initial enthusiasm, however what was implemented at the time and soon afterwards failed to live up to the expectations generated. Delaying the announcement until implementation was nearer would have better aligned expectation and reality.

E-mail system. The e-mailing of reports, the first stage of implementation, was a poor way of generating information.

It appears that staff were restricted from receiving information that was potentially useful by being able to subscribe to only one e-mail topic – given the obvious overlaps (eg audit and accounting) this seems to be in direct conflict with the objectives of sharing information of a KM system.

The tax group sending e-mails for the sake of it is likely to add to information overload and provide the impression that the KM system does not create value.

Lack of consultation. Staff do not appear to have been asked about what topics they feel they currently lack knowledge in, or how best that knowledge could be communicated.

Badly aimed communication. The example given was of a tax practitioner making available 'his' loophole. Individuals hearing this may be threatened that they are having to give away their ideas that previously would have resulted in promotion, pay rises or some other form of recognition. The KM system will, for many individuals, have been perceived as one that will take away from them rather than add.

Lack of Internet management. The Internet links appear to be poorly signposted and do not allow people to get quickly to what they might need, rather allowing them to search for themselves. Better labelling of, at least, which sites were accessible as a result of subscriptions paid would be an improvement.

To rectify these problems and to generate buy-in to a KM system I suggest the partner responsible takes the following actions.

Consultation with staff. Staff and managers should be consulted to find out whether there are any particular knowledge gaps. Staff should also be asked to provide references they currently use to access useful information, both within and outside the firm.

Internet/intranet re-design. An intranet should be developed that will categorise knowledge and allow easier access to it. This would include access to external knowledge sources such as the Internet and any subscription services.

Knowledge creation processes. Simple procedures should be designed that will result in knowledge created being made accessible with minimal staff effort.

Marketing the system. After these stages have been completed there should be a re-launch of the system. The re-launch should emphasise what people can get out of the system rather than giving the impression that they are having to put something in.

Providing incentives. The sharing of knowledge should become part of the performance assessment and reward of employees.

(b)

> **Top tips.** Partners in the smaller offices must first be motivated themselves, as they appear to be under the impression that they are being asked to contribute to a system useful at larger offices only.

Partners in smaller offices must first be **motivated** by offering the system to them for free for a trial period, after which they will have an option to continued access for an ongoing fee or by valuing the charges they would incur to obtain that knowledge if they were separate firms outside the partnership.

Once the partners were convinced of the system they might be motivated by using combinations of financial and non-financial incentives.

Financial incentives could be by placing a one-off value on the knowledge entered by an office onto the system or recording and calculating a refund to an originating office based on the number of times a particular piece of knowledge was accessed by other offices.

Non-financial motivations might include clearly stating the office source of particular pieces of knowledge or by publishing a table showing which offices were the highest contributors of knowledge.

(c)

> **Top tips.** When managing staff, consideration needs to be given to the possibility of staff using the information for non-authorised purposes. A partnership like TBS is likely to have controls in this area given the commercially sensitive nature of their work.

There will need to be a number of controls to prevent unauthorised access.

Monitoring of staff. Special consideration needs to be given to the risk of staff trying to remove copies of the KM data when they are leaving TBS's employment. To achieve this, controls would include:

(i)   *E-mail scanning* – any large or compressed outgoing e-mails or series of small e-mails in succession with the same 'to' and 'from' addresses should be scanned for viruses.

(ii)   *Restriction of tape and disk drives* – to prevent copying, user PC's should not have disk or tape drive units (back-ups should be done over the network).

(iii)   *Control over CD-writers* – access to CD-writers should be restricted to staff whose job requires it. They should be asked to keep a register of each CD written stating what source was used to write onto the CD and the staff member who requested it.

Physical security. There should be appropriate security measures to ensure that only staff and authorised visitors have access to TBS's premises. Visitors should be asked to wear visitor badges and staff should be invited to enquire of the identity of anyone they do not recognise (other than those wearing visitor badges).

Password mechanisms. A strong password protection system will be required over the entire network. This will involve the following elements:

(i)   *User identity* – TBS's IT department will allocate each member of staff a user identity, contained within their 'user profile'. This ID must be entered each time that individual starts a computer. (The user profile will detail which elements of the network a user has access to. It may be that some staff will be restricted from accessing the KM system although this seems contrary to the purpose of the KM system.)

(ii)   *Passwords* – each user will be required to provide a password that is imaginative, regularly changed, not displayed on screen when entered and not written down.

(iii)   *Entry restrictions* – upon an invalid user id/password combination being entered three times at the same PC that PC should be locked out of the network until a member of the IT staff investigates.

(iv)   *Automatic log-off* – after a reasonable period of inactivity (15 minutes?) users should be required to re-enter their password before being able to work with that device.

(v)   *Concurrent usage restrictions* – any user will only be able to log on one session at a time for each user ID/password.

Security over inter-office transfers. It is unlikely that there will be sufficient volume of data/voice/fax traffic for offices to make private leased lines economically viable, with transfer coming from standard dial-ups. This should be managed using a callback system where the office with data to send contacts the destination machine with a message that it is in send mode.

The destination device will then dial the source device, check that it does have a message to send and, if so, receive it. The actual data transfer should be managed using encryption and authentication systems to ensure that only authorised users will be able to reassemble the scrambled data.

Security over remote access by individual staff will use the same encryption and authentication mentioned above to manage the actual data transfer. In addition to that there need to be controls ensuring that transfers are only between authorised staff. Since users will be accessing the system from a variety of unpredictable locations (unlike the predictable locations in inter-office transfers) the callback system mentioned above will need to be replaced by a code-generator system.

These systems usually operate by giving staff a small solar powered device that looks similar to a cheap pocket calculator. When accessing the computer remotely the user will be given a (usually 4 or 5-digit) code. That number should be entered into the 'calculator' that will in turn display another code to be entered into the computer. If the remote user returns the expected code they will be given access.

Users in possession of such devices should be required to keep them separate from their laptop computer and to report their theft or loss immediately.

(d)

The idea behind **knowledge management** is that an organisation's knowledge will be documented, in paper and digital form, as a result of business dealings (eg letters to clients/customers, memos to other staff, training courses) and specific KM initiatives.

By extensive referencing of this information, staff are able to access this knowledge and use it appropriately.

KM is now developing to include knowledge within particular processes so, for example, an insolvency practitioner might set up a KM system describing each stage of the process of winding up a company, with the facility to drill down to relevant information for each stage.

A further development, available through companies such as Orbital Software, links knowledge to individuals within the organisation. If someone searches for information not documented on the system the query result would be the names and contact details of people who had contributed information on the most closely related topics and so be the most likely to know.

Its main use is currently within professional partnerships such as accounting (as outlined in the scenario) legal and architectural practices. The application could be used in medical/health services where diagnosis and treatment are documented and shared by other staff on the same network. Engineering design could utilise these principles by documenting the characteristics and behaviour of particular materials providing reference material for any future designs where use of those materials was being considered.

51 ARG International Airlines

(a)

(i)   **Why large companies should have an IT strategy**

IT involves high costs. The scenario does not give specific details, but we know that the system is **large scale**, that it is **state of the art**, that it has **excess capacity** and that an additional fixed capital amount is to be available for **upgrades each year**. This is clearly a major investment that needs care over planning, control and co-ordination.

IT is critical to the success of many organisations. Information access and provision is the **key service** offered by ARG's local offices and the most up-to-date computer and telecommunications technology will allow ARG to **access and provide information more effectively**. It will not be possible to meet the business objectives set for ARG's services unless the appropriate IT infrastructure is in place. Conversely, future developments in IT are likely to lead to **ever more ambitious objectives**. A properly devised strategy is essential to allow the company to **grow in a co-ordinated way**.

IT is seen by the Board of ARG as essential to produce a sustainable **competitive advantage**. ARG needs to be able to make more effective use of information to serve its customers' interests than any of its competitors.

IT involves many **stakeholders**, not just management. **Staff** at ARG, for instance, appear to have welcomed the new system and adapted to it very easily. A less careful approach to development and implementation by the board might have impaired the effectiveness of staff – and therefore the whole business – for months.

Again, the opportunities presented by the new system's excess capacity are leading the company (rightly or wrongly) to diversify away from its main mission, and this impacts upon **shareholders**, who originally chose to invest in an airline, not a computer services company.

The detailed technical issues in IT are important. The Board of ARG recognised that the pace of change in technology meant the system could become obsolete very quickly. Their strategy therefore included easy **upgradability** as a key point. On the other hand the controls proposed over future investment indicate that they intend to ensure that upgrades are not undertaken merely because the technology has become available. The aim is to take advantage of technical developments that bring **real benefits**.

(ii) **Comment on the diversification strategy**

The post-implementation review has found that the full capacity of the system will not actually be needed for another 7 years, and this should have been realised at an earlier stage in the development of the system.

Could other options be considered, such as **renting the excess capacity** to an existing network services provider, and gradually taking back capacity as it becomes needed?

Advantages

The most obvious advantage, and the one that appears to have influenced the Board, is that the proposal will **make use of an idle resource** and give a **positive contribution** to profits.

Given that ARG's core business is **susceptible to events quite beyond its control** (such as wars or terrorist activity) that have in the past led to marked reductions in air traffic, there is **some logic in diversifying** into business **telecommunications**, a growing **competitor to business travel**, thanks to improvements in technologies such as video-conferencing. The new strategy could be seen as a **safety move**, making the future of the business as a whole more secure.

Arguably, ARG's business is **carrying things** from one place to another: being an **information-carrier** could be seen as an extension to being a people-carrier and a freight-carrier. If ARG is perceived as being a market leader in the latter fields, this may inspire potential users' confidence in its ability to deliver information.

ARG's **brand name** can be attached to a device used for communications by other businesses (perhaps even by competitors). Assuming it is successful this will provide valuable publicity.

Disadvantages

ARG has **no experience** at operating the sort of service proposed. The **risks of total failure** are high, and anything less than a service that equals that of ARG's core business will **damage the core business** by association.

If the IT division concentrates on providing this new service it may **lose sight of its responsibilities** regarding the existing business, with the result that the new system **fails to fulfil its original purpose**.

Many other organisations specialise in providing this sort of service. ARG may find it **difficult to establish enough of a presence in the market** to justify the extra investment involved.

Markets may react badly to the new venture. A general business trend is to **outsource** non-core activities, especially those of an IT nature, but ARG is **moving in the opposite direction**. It is likely to be criticised by stakeholders who, like a minority of the Board, see potential conflicts between the strategies.

The company has **already over-invested** in its WAN and the proposed 'fix' for this is to invest even more. **Other possibilities** do not appear to have been considered.

The additional investment is based on what ARG 'expects' users to require. Users may, however, **require considerably more services** and support than ARG envisages. The IT director **does not have a good record** at determining what is required.

Conclusion

On the basis of the information available the disadvantages appear to outweigh the advantages. At the very least, **other options** should be considered. If there is **more work** to be done regarding investigation of the new market and its customers, and detailed costings and revenue forecasts, this should be done before the proposal goes ahead.

(b)

> **Top tips.** Choose the most appropriate qualities of information relevant to the situation at ARG – and explain why these qualities are relevant.

Characteristics of information provided across the WAN

ARG offices use information on flight times and destinations, passenger and freight bookings, and have access to information on aircraft locations, servicing history and personnel details.

The information provided across the WAN should have the following characteristics.

Completeness and timeliness

Full, up-to-date information on **bookings** needs to be available instantaneously, otherwise an office might, say, book a passenger onto a return flight from another country only to discover that the flight is already fully booked.

Similarly, if an aircraft is due for a particular type of **service** when it lands in a country, the office concerned will need timely warning so that they can make advance preparations and ensure that staff and resources are available immediately. **Servicing cannot be put off once it is due**: it is crucial that ARG operates a safe service.

Servicing information needs to be **complete** in the sense that **any** details that servicing staff might need to know about a particular aircraft must be available to them on demand.

Accuracy and clarity

A high degree of accuracy is required: people will miss their flights if they are told the wrong time for checking in and take off. Flight durations and arrival times will also be key issues to customers. Inaccurate servicing information could quite literally be fatal.

Data is to be passed between 200 offices worldwide, so there is clearly **huge potential for errors** in transmission and for data, or parts of it, to get lost in, or corrupted by, the system. Communications **protocols** such as TCP/IP should be adopted. These govern the switching of data, detection and correction of errors and so on.

Relevance to those it is communicated to

It is **not immediately apparent why each office needs salary details** of staff not based in that country: this is sensitive information that should not be available to all. If it is necessary to send these details (for comparative purposes, perhaps, or for planning cost-effective use of cabin staff), it should be **transferred in an encrypted form** to prevent it falling into the hands of those not authorised to see it.

Trustworthiness

Offices will be reluctant to **make promises to customers** if they do not feel they can trust the information provided. Customers will not be amused if, for example, an item of freight needs special handling equipment and they use ARG because a local office claimed that these facilities could be made available at the destination, only to find that this was not true.

As another example, since customers appear to be allowed access to the booking system, **some method of ensuring the integrity of a booking made by a customer is needed**. This might consist of passwords or identification numbers for individual travel agents and requirements to submit details in a prescribed form.

Cost

It should not cost more to provide the information than the value of the benefits derived from the information. ARG's excess capacity indicates that, **at present, it probably does cost too much to provide the information**: hence the decision to diversify, discussed in earlier questions relating to this case study.

(c)

> **Top tips.** We are told in the scenario information that ARG has assumed that its WAN infrastructure – including such items as cabling and communication hardware – will remain unchanged for the next ten years. This assumption is questionable as who knows what developments will occur in that time.

Upgrading the IT infrastructure

The previous ten years have seen phenomenal change in computing and telecommunications fields and there is **no sign that the pace of change is slowing down**, particularly in telecommunications.

ARG may find that it is not in the position to take full advantage of new technologies as they become available, especially as its supplier, AP Ltd, does not always use industry standard systems.

The previous ten years have also seen a huge **change in the business environment** of many industries. A **customer focus** is now held to be essential for success; many organisations now have radically **different structures** and job functions compared with the past; **competition is fierce and global**; and there is a worldwide trend towards **deregulation**.

Again there is no reason to believe that the next ten years will not bring equally dramatic changes that could have a major impact on the way the ARG wants to use IT.

In any case ARG's strategy is aimed at 'sustainable competitive advantage', and if it is successful this will inevitably mean **growth and change, possibly in unpredictable ways**. Competitors may introduce new services that do not form part of ARG's current plans, and ARG will need to match these or better them to maintain its position.

Such growth and change will **not** be sustainable, however, unless core activities are **supported by whatever changes in the IT infrastructure** are needed to keep up with or ahead of competitors.

Upgrades in computer hardware tend to be **led by developments in computer software.** For example, to be used effectively each subsequent version of Windows has required more RAM and hard disk capacity than its predecessor. Many organisations find they need to upgrade their hardware to accommodate the new software.

A **fixed** capital amount for upgrades may not be appropriate: huge developments may occur in year four, say, followed by small changes in years five and six. If applied as rigorously as the scenario suggests, the upgrading strategy **may be too inflexible** to take proper advantage of developments as they occur.

(d)

Top tips. Our part (i) is longer than your answer should have been, to show a wider range of points that could have been made. The Internet continues to be a 'hot topic' that is highly likely to be examined.

(i)   **The dangers and benefits of providing Internet access**

ARG is proposing to offer users of its WAN Internet access to transfer data to customers and receive information back from customers. ARG itself will also be able to use the Internet in this way.

Advantages for ARG and other businesses fall into three categories.

Access to vast amounts of information on computer databases

This includes information that may be highly useful for both **day-to-day management**, such as government department Internet sites, and for **environmental scanning** purposes, such as sites of customers and competitors, and sites devoted to industries and markets.

Ability to send electronic messages to individuals or groups

Internal messaging is, of course, the primary purpose of ARG's WAN, but Internet access means that email messages can be sent (for the cost of a local telephone call) not only to others connected to ARG's WAN, but to **anybody in the world** connected to the Internet. This could save businesses large amounts of time and money that would otherwise be spent on more conventional methods of communication.

Marketing and sales benefits

To date Internet **marketing** activity has mainly been a matter of **providing information about products and services**. The Internet offers a speedy and impersonal way for customers to find out the basics or the details of the products and services that a company has to offer. This saves time both for customers and for the provider, who has less need to employ and train staff to man the phones on an enquiry desk.

In ARG's case many enquiries will be received about flight times and availability, and this information can very easily be made available on an ARG Website. The website of the airline Virgin for instance has an area called 'Flight Plan' that allows potential customers to find out the flight numbers and departure and arrival points and times on any of Virgin's routes, and offers the chance to find out more about Virgin's services such as 'Upper Class'.

The provider of the information can also **collect information about potential customers** who contact their Website. Many sites allow free access to information but require users to fill in a form on screen giving personal information such as income level, address, job title and so on.

Purchasing on the Internet was relatively slow to be embraced initially, but is now expanding at a rapid rate. ARG could provide a **booking service** that allows customers to fill in a form on screen giving all the necessary details, and allows payment by recording a debit or credit card number.

Dangers exist, however, unless proper safeguards are put in place.

The full **legal implications** of doing business on the Net have not been fully worked out, and are highly complex because although it is a worldwide medium it is subject to the different domestic laws of each of the countries in which business is done. ARG or one of its WAN users could easily fall foul of local trading or advertising standards by inadvertently including or leaving out some item of information from their Website services.

People may be able to get access via the Internet into ARG's **internal systems** or those of its WAN users. A mischievous user, for instance, could make **false bookings**, or **delete details** of others' bookings, or launch a **virus** that disrupts internal systems, or obtain confidential information, or alter aircraft servicing information.

Internet browsing tends to be compulsive: it is in the very nature of the medium that users are offered the chance to explore topics related to their original enquiry. A common business fear is that **staff might waste time and money** 'surfing the net' for non-business-related information and entertainment in office hours.

Although access to the Internet is priced at the cost of a local call, finding and downloading data can often be a **painfully slow** process. An innocuous enquiry might turn out to cost the price of an **hour-long** local phone call, which is clearly much less of a bargain than it might have seemed when the enquiry began.

People are reluctant to give credit card details or other sensitive information to a computer and telecommunications link because they fear the information may be **intercepted and used fraudulently**. This is a problem, but it is one that is likely to disappear over time, since it is clearly in legitimate users' interests to make the data transfer process secure. For example, 'secure payment sites' have been developed that encrypt card numbers during transmission. Public confidence in such systems is essential to the growth of e-commerce.

(ii) **Data security**

There are numerous measures that ARG can take to provide the required level of security. A **security policy** should be developed and regularly reviewed, identifying and quantifying risks, identifying, selecting and implementing counter-measures, and formulating **contingency plans** to be operated in the event of a breach of security.

Protocols should be adopted such as the TCP/IP, which includes layers ensuring that individual messages are **switched and routed properly** through the network, that there are **standard formats** for the interpretation of data, and so on.

WAN customers and ARG's airline customers

Users of ARG's WAN must be **prevented from accessing each others' systems** or intercepting data transmission unless they are authorised to do so. Likewise ARG customers should not be able to gain access to all parts of ARG's system. This is likely to entail the use of **'firewalls'**, which allow levels of access to be controlled.

Firewalls **disable** part of the communications technology that normally allows **two-way** communication, so external parties are denied access to parts of the system.

Access can be controlled by various electronic means so that one set of users cannot see information exchanges between members of another set of users.

Access control may be effected by **disabling certain terminals**, so that they are not capable of receiving or copying confidential data, by **user-identification procedures** (different users have different levels of access), and **password procedures**. The normal rules concerning passwords should be applied and monitored: passwords should not be disclosed to others, should be in a prescribed format, and should be changed regularly. **Access control logs** should be maintained, recording unauthorised attempts to gain access.

Encryption of data is a possibility that should be available. This involves scrambling the data at one end of the line, transmitting the scrambled data, and unscrambling it at the receiver's end of the line. **Authentication** is another technique that could be used. This makes sure that a message has come from an authorised sender, by including an extra field in a record derived from the data in the record by applying a previously-agreed algorithm.

Measures should also be taken to **protect data from physical threats** such as a fire that destroys communications equipment or damage to cables, resulting in the loss of data being transmitted.

Computer **viruses** are a real danger: they may be accidentally or deliberately released onto the network by WAN users or ARG customers and do immeasurable damage both to ARG's systems and to those of other users. **Virus control software** should be constantly in use and should be regularly updated.

ARG employees

Care should be taken over the **selection of personnel** to administer the WAN, since these people have large opportunity to impair data security if they choose to do so, or if they are not competent to do their jobs. Obvious measures include taking up references, providing training as necessary, and operating termination procedures restricting access to sensitive data for people about to leave the organisation. Other personnel measures may include **division of responsibilities**.

ARG's employees should be prevented from gaining access to the data or systems of WAN customers, by means such as those described above. Controls must be especially strict if access is necessary for maintenance purposes.

Separate facilities such as servers could be used to operate different parts of the system. If this is a feasible option it is clearly a more secure approach than sharing resources.

52 Orion Insurance

(a)

Text reference. SSM (relevant to part (a)) is covered in Chapter 4 of the text, enterprise and CSF approaches (relevant to part (b)) in Chapter 2 and the Internet (part (c)) in Chapter 7.

Top tips. The examiner provides flexibility when marking answers that include rich pictures – don't worry if your diagram looks different to ours. Your answers to (ii) and (iii) are likely to be similar to ours, but again don't panic if there are differences.

(i)   See next page

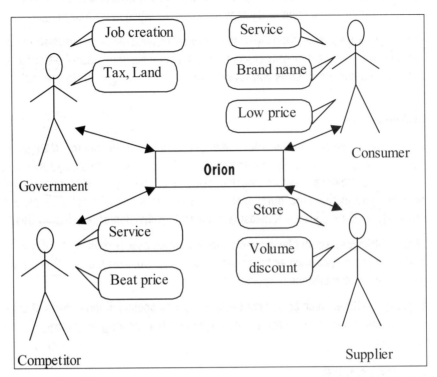

(ii) The CATWOE is defined as:

- **Customers or clients**. Who would be victims/ beneficiaries of the purposeful action?

- **Actors**. Who would do the activities?

- **Transformation** (the benefits or changes which take place in the system). What is the purposeful activity? It is expressed as: Input, Throughput/Transformation and Output.

- **Worldview** (assumptions behind the root definition). What view of the world makes the definition meaningful? It may also be expressed as 'assumptions made about the system'.

- **Owner** (the person who is responsible for the system). Who could stop this activity and/or make or break the system?

- **Environment**. What factors affect the environment?

CATWOE elements in Orion domain.

Clients/customers (C)	Elite/sophisticated computer buyers
Actors (A)	Orion
Transformation (T)	To acquire 30% of the West Midland's consumer market
World view (Weltanschauung) (W)	Superior high-end product & service
Ownership (O)	Orion
Environment (E)	West Midland market

(iii)   The conceptual model of the Orion domain can be shown as:

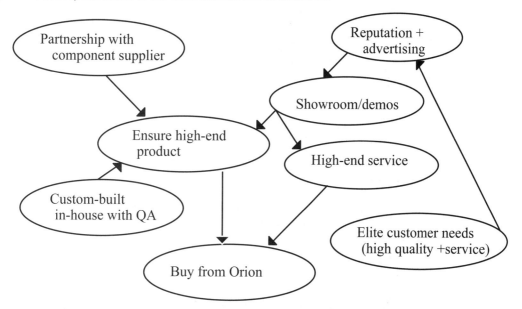

This picture represents some of the activities that may have to be performed in order to reach the goal for providing high-end products and superior service to Orion's 'desired' customers. The major benefit of these concept models is that they can be used to compare the concept with the real world. By doing this it promotes more 'in-depth' thinking about the processes carried out by the business. It also stimulates thinking about how the individual activities can/should be performed, how they can be measured, how efficient they are, etc.

All this promotes better understanding of the proposed system and possible trouble areas.

(b)

Top tips. Both enterprise analysis and CSF approaches attempt to gain a clear understanding of the organisation's long and short-term information requirements. Both also involve the interviewing of managers to help establish information needs.

REPORT

To: CEO
From: Consultant
Date: 21 May 200X
Subject: Approaches for establishing the information requirements at Orion

1   The enterprise analysis approach

Enterprise analysis looks at the entire organisation in terms of organisational units, functions, processes and data elements to identify the key entities and attributes of the organisation's data. The approach takes a sample of managers from each department and asks them:

- How they use information
- Where they get the information
- What the environment is like
- What their objectives are
- How they make decisions
- What their data/information needs are

The results of this survey are combined on a process/data class matrix into sub-units, processes, functions and data matrices. This chart depicts what data classes are required to support particular organisational processes and which processes are the creators and users of data.

2   **The critical success factors (CSF) approach**

The CSF approach determines the information requirements of an organisation from a small number of critical success factor of managers. Managers are asked to look at the environment and consider how their analysis of it shapes their information needs. The method focuses on how information is handled.

Individual CSFs are aggregated to develop CSFs for the entire firm and the system is built to deliver information on all of them.

It differs from the enterprise analysis in that only top managers are interviewed and the questions focus on a small number of CSFs rather than a broad enquiry into what information is used or required.

An example of a critical success factor would be to achieve quoted delivery dates, or to know where a certain customer's order is in the system.

3   **Strengths and weaknesses of both approaches**

Both methods are useful for:

- Aligning IT strategies with business strategies

- Formulating requirements for specific IT systems, or finding ways of using existing systems and data more effectively

- Creating a platform for changing the enterprise

The main strength of enterprise analysis is that it gives a comprehensive view of the organisation and of systems/data uses and gaps. The main weakness is that it produces an enormous amount of data that is expensive to collect and difficult to analyse.

Because this technique helps identify key entities and attributes in the organisation's data, it is both a strength and a weakness. It is a strength in that this information will be required to build the information system, but a weakness because the company is not using a hard systems methodology to develop the system; the individual managers or personnel interviewed will not have been 'thinking' about the entities and attributes involved in the processes.

A unique strength of the CSF approach is that it takes into account the changing environment that the managers are facing and the main weakness is that there is no rigorous way that individual CSFs can be aggregated into a clear company pattern. The individual and organisational CSFs are not necessarily the same. This method is more in line with Checkland's soft systems methodology.

4   **Recommendation**

As this report was requested to provide information only, no recommendation is made. If you would like me to conduct further analysis and make a recommendation, please let me know.

(c)

> **Top tips.** Orion can use the Internet to make product information, ordering and customer support immediately available but there are a few areas where e-commerce may not be appropriate. Your answer should present a realistic, balanced view.

E-commerce, using Internet technologies has many applications for today's business processes. Using the Internet, information can be shared with customers, business partners and suppliers and it can be used to create new channels for **marketing**, **sales** and **customer support**. It allows manual and paper-based procedures to be replaced with electronic alternatives, and by using information flows in new and dynamic ways, electronic commerce can accelerate ordering, delivery, and payment for goods and services while reducing companies' operating and inventory costs.

There are a number of significant advantages to both customer and supplier in conducting transactional business over the Internet.

- The Internet generates **opportunities** for export without local presence and advertising. A website can be seen by a very large number of people – all potential customers – in many countries, because they have access to the Internet.

- The **production costs** associated with disseminating information on the Internet are significantly lower because access and printing costs are borne by the potential customer. It is more likely that only people who are interested in the product/service will access the website and request more information. Therefore there is less waste compared to sending traditional documents randomly to potential customers.

- The **electronic transfer** of business information (EDI) introduces the possibility of 'paperless' trading and promises the end of repetitive form filling, stock orders and other forms of 'paper shifting'. EDI is used predominantly between large business customers and their suppliers eg, General Motors in the automobile industry use EDI as a part of the 'just-in-time' (JIT) organisation of the supply of components and raw materials to their assembly plants.

- When information is maintained on the organisation's website it can be **updated easily**, with the latest version becoming immediately available to all Internet customers. Where traditional media, such as brochures and catalogues, is used for disseminating information, the old document becomes obsolete as soon as the new one is released. However this old document may remain in existence instead of being replaced, leading the customer to act upon incorrect information.

- It gives access to information about products with little or no 'hard sell', leading to higher **customer satisfaction** levels due to improved product knowledge.

When organisations are developing an e-commerce strategy, they should not throw away their traditional business models. Instead, they should look to see where e-commerce provides opportunities to create complementary ways to reach a chosen market.

- **Potential personal customers** for Orion's products who are either without or have very old computers will need to be contacted in traditional ways because only those with a fairly modern computer will be browsing on the Internet.

- The Internet could provide Orion with access to the **business** and **personal market** that would normally be outside their reach; but the market segment has been limited to a specific area – the West Midlands. Because this is a niche market, and all its potential customers are known, then mail-shots, trade advertising, etc, might be the most effective method of reaching the customer. In other markets where there are many potential customers then a website could expand advertising to a worldwide arena.

- It is quite **expensive** to set up and maintain a website and these costs have to be recouped, otherwise the investment is not justified. Also, a website with compelling content that attracts and addresses customers' needs has to be coupled with a solid infrastructure. Users will quickly abandon an e-commerce site if it does not give them exactly what they want – either in terms of service or content – or if it is not open 24 hours a day, every day.

53 Question with helping hand: The SI Organisation

(a)

> **Text references**. Decentralised systems (part (a)) are covered in Chapter 9 of the text, evaluating systems (part (b)) in Chapter 8 and Porter's generic strategies (part (c)) in Chapter 6.
>
> **Top tips.** Apply your book knowledge of decentralised systems to the information provided in the scenario and you will score well. Provide six explained points in (i) and four explained points in (ii).

BPP marking scheme

	Marks
Part (i):	
Strengths of decentralised systems (up to 2 marks per point)	
Weaknesses of decentralised systems (up to 2 marks per point)	
Maximum marks awarded Part (i)	12
Issues with integrating decentralised systems (up to 2 marks per point)	
Maximum marks awarded Part (ii)	8
	20

(i)   **Strengths of SI's decentralised systems**

- **Monitoring customer needs**

    The decentralised systems provide local information efficiently, which enables SI to monitor customer needs within each country. There will be slight differences in user preferences and technical settings between countries. Decentralised systems allow SI to meet customer needs quickly and effectively.

- **Closer relationships with local suppliers**

    The service SI is able to provide will often depend on suppliers meeting agreed quality standards and delivery times. This is more likely to be achievable if SI is able to build up strong relationships with local suppliers – decentralised operations allow this. For example, local offices are able to monitor stock levels and quality more closely and are more likely to be able to obtain urgent deliveries.

- **Reduced impact of internal system failure**

    By operating decentralised systems, SI effectively limits the effect of an internal system failure to a single country. If a centralised system was in place, system failure would impact across all SI markets.

Weaknesses of SI's decentralised systems

- **Lack of shared information**

    Each SI company holds information in its own format. This is likely to prevent organisation-wide information being produced without significant data conversion. This could also mean SI is missing out on being able to establish worldwide customer trends. The lack of shared information also applies to customers, preventing access to a centralised technical database with a wider range of questions and answers.

- ## Loss of economies of scale

  By operating a number of autonomous companies, SI is diluting its purchasing power with suppliers. For example, if SI asked for tenders for the worldwide supply of a particular component, it is likely that suppliers would be prepared to accept lower margins to secure such a large contract.

- ## Duplication of internal systems work/information

  Much of the work performed on internal SI systems within an individual country is likely to be duplicated in other countries, for example similar databases will be maintained in each country and there is likely to be duplicated effort in developing new systems. A centralised IT/systems function would be more efficient.

(ii) **Problems integrating into one worldwide system**

- ## How to combine the 35 separate systems

  Combining 35 separate systems into one is a massive undertaking. The existing systems will use a range of hardware, software and data formats. Deciding upon standard hardware, software and data formats that can accommodate the requirements of all 35 countries will be a complex task.

- ## Maintaining customer service levels during system changeover

  As the integration exercise is so large and complex, it could potentially cause significant disruption to SI customers. A phased, country-by-country changeover plan may limit disruption, but service standards are likely to suffer in the short term.

- ## Staff resistance to the new system

  Staff within each country are likely to be apprehensive of this major change to their way of working. Staff may feel their organisation is being 'swallowed up' by a larger entity they have no affiliation to. Staff motivation may suffer and some resistance towards the new system is likely. To minimise this resistance, SI should ensure local management are 'on-board' and that they stress the benefits of the new system to local staff (such as access to more information making their jobs easier).

- ## Ensuring information is shared

  The centralised system requires information currently held on local systems. Individual countries may be reluctant to co-operate in the information sharing process – they may feel that they would be diluting their power and influence within SI by 'giving up' this information.

(b)

> **Top tips.** The scenario includes an explanation of the R&D department within the SI organisation. This information can be used to discuss how effective the department is, and then to consider the information support system that is required for communication with sales staff.

Marking scheme

Marks

Existing system – strengths (up to 2 marks per point)
Central resource – economies of scale etc
Central control – but allows production of country specific products
Degree of commonality of computers produced
Other relevant points

Existing system – weaknesses (up to 2 marks per point)
Sales department information not available to R&D
One-way communication to individual countries
Other relevant points
New system (up to 2 marks per point)
Requirements for system
Intranet possible – provides for sharing information
Set-up of central database – intranet within each country
Access and use of that database – sales and R&D staff communication   20

This marking guide was produced by BPP.

The strengths and weaknesses of the SI R&D department's information system are outlined in the following paragraphs.

Strengths of the existing R&D unit information system

- **Centralised information resource**

  The centralised pool of information enables SI to obtain economies of scale as R&D information is held in a single, global system – rather than having duplicated systems in the individual countries.

- **Pooled knowledge**

  R&D is a knowledge based activity. It makes sense to conduct an activity such as R&D in a single location to allow the sharing of knowledge and ideas between R&D staff.

- **Allows some flexibility in an individual country**

  Although the R&D function is centralised, the department does not take a 'one size fits all' approach. The department provides country specific specifications for new SI computers to the individual SI companies.

- **Comparison by country**

  By operating a global R&D system that includes specifications for computers in each individual country, SI is able to see how customer preferences differ in different markets. This also enables SI to see what parts or components may be common to all or most countries.

Weaknesses of the existing R&D unit information system

The information system has two main weaknesses.

- **Sales department information is not available to R&D staff**

  Research and Development staff are unable to review information gathered by the Sales department. This is likely to result in the R&D unit becoming out of touch with customer requirements in some or all markets.

- **Communication with individual countries is one way**

  Communication between the R&D unit and individual countries is one-way. Individual countries do not provide information to the R&D unit.

New system to facilitate two-way communication

Two-way communication between R&D staff and sales staff should be encouraged to give the R&D unit a stronger customer focus.

- **Establish an intranet**

  To facilitate two-way communication, an intranet should be established that is able to be accessed and contributed to by the R&D unit and staff within individual countries.

Features of the intranet

- **Familiar features and interface**

  As the intranet will be accessed by users used to a range of information systems, a user-friendly interface is essential. The intranet should use Internet/website features that are now familiar to many users around the world (eg HTML pages, links, sitemap etc).

- **Message board facility**

  The intranet should include a message board facility for informal communication, and specified areas for posting formal reports containing information such as 'common customer requests'.

- **Central database**

  A database should be set up holding information relevant to operations within each country. This information could be searched by people from other countries. A flexible interface that allows easy searching by user defined criteria should be part of the intranet.

Main benefit of the intranet

The intranet would encourage two-way communication and contribute to the growth of the organisation-wide pool of knowledge.

(c)

Top tips. Part (i), which requires you to explain Porter's theories, may be answered from book knowledge alone. Part (ii) is more demanding. The scenario provides an indication of issues relating to strategy, you should have identified and discussed these points.

Marking scheme

		Marks
(i)	Differentiation and cost leadership Explanation of differentiation (2 marks) Explanation of cost leadership (2 marks)	4
(ii)	Current situation – differentiation (2 marks) Issues with centralised system Possible reduction in customer service for small businesses as support not local (2 marks) Corporate customers may like (2 marks) Both customers could be served (2 marks) Cost leadership Does SI use cost leadership? (2 marks) Centralised systems may provide decreased cost (2 marks) However, may also increase costs/not provide necessary product (2 marks) Conclusion with differentiation as long as meets ongoing business strategy (2 marks)	16 20

This marking guide was produced by BPP.

ANSWERS

(i) Porter's concepts of differentiation and cost leadership are explained below:

- **Differentiation**

  Differentiation refers to seeking a competitive advantage by doing something different to competitors. The 'something' could be a different product or service, or a different way of doing business. SI differentiates itself from competitors who also sell computers by allowing the customer greater flexibility in the specification of computer.

- **Cost leadership**

  Cost leadership refers to the strategy of operating at a lower cost level than competitors and therefore being able to offer better value for money to customers. Cost leadership is most appropriate when price or value for money is the most important factor in the buying decision. To achieve cost leadership requires an advantage such as economies of scale or exclusive use of a particular technology.

(ii) SI has historically followed a **differentiation** focus. This differentiation has been achieved by assembling and selling computers to the specific requirements of each customer.

The recent decision of the Chief Executive to provide 24 hour telephone support and access to a centralised database of information worldwide, using a **centralised system**, could have both positive and negative effects on the customer-focus strategy of SI.

Small businesses may find the centralised system leads to a **lower** standard of customer service, as the people dealing with their queries are unfamiliar with their business.

Corporate customers, on the other hand, may find an improvement in **customer service**, as information relating to their operations in several countries will be accessible in one place.

If the centralised system is designed carefully, and all existing information is transferred, the centralised database should ensure no reduction in service level for small, local businesses and improved service for international companies.

The new system need not change SI's current differentiation focus.

Providing a centralised system could be seen as a **cost-leadership** approach, as it should provide economies of scale by requiring only one database to be maintained. However, just because a measure may provide economies of scale does not mean SI is changing focus to cost-leadership.

Some of the changes proposed, such as staffing the 24 hour hotline, will add to existing cost levels. The main changes that customers will notice resulting from the new system are the availability of 24 hour support and access to a larger pool of information.

These factors should provide a superior level of customer service, which is consistent with SI's current differentiation focus. The Chief Executive's decision does not therefore affect the overall strategy of SI.

54 Gravy Train

(a)

Text references. IS strategy (part (a)) and critical success factors (part (b)) are discussed in Chapters 1 and 2 of the text. Using IT to gain a competitive advantage and the Internet (part (c)) are discussed in Chapters 6 and 7 respectively.

Top tips. The IS/IT strategy is a long-term plan for the company's future investment in systems and technology. The business strategy is the means by which the company plans to achieve its overall aims and objectives.

Marking scheme

		Marks
(i)	Award up to 4 marks for each reason and explanation as to why an IS/IT strategy is required up to a maximum of 12	12
(ii)	Award up to 4 marks for each possible problem and explanation up to a maximum of 8	8
		20

This marking guide was produced by BPP.

To be able to use IS/IT to gain a **competitive advantage** and ensure that investments in IS/IT bring the maximum benefits to the organisation, it is essential that the company devises a good IS/IT strategy, which must be based on the business strategy because this will ensure total compatibility between the information systems (IS), the computer hardware and system software (IT) and all future requirements of the organisation as a whole. It also ensures a level of commitment from senior management plus the allocation of resources.

The IS/IT strategy, and the plan that documents it, must be consistent with:

- The **business plan** – the identification of the goals and objectives for Gravy Train has led to the establishment of an overall business strategy. The next stage in the process means that the business strategy feeds down through divisional or business unit strategies, into a number of functional strategies. One of these is the IS strategy, which feeds into a number of sub-strategies eg, the IT strategy and the communications strategy. These, in turn, develop ever more detailed strategy elements.

- The **management view** of the role of IS in the organisation – this system of strategies and its hierarchy is shown in the diagram below.

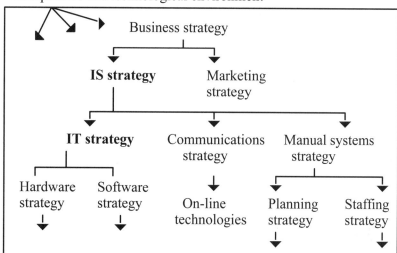

Competitive and technological environment

Information technology needs to be aligned to the business strategy so that the business needs 'pull' the technology, rather than the technology 'pushing' the business in the wrong direction.

- The **stage of maturity** of use and management of IS – the company currently uses technology as a support activity. The new business strategy elevates technology to a strategic activity with future business being critically dependent upon it. Once Gravy Train has made this transition there will be no turning back. Technology will be vital to the future of this business and therefore needs to be managed at a strategic level.

At the moment the money spent on IT is a relatively small amount, as it is used purely as a support activity. To put its new business strategy into operation the company will need to spend a much larger sum of money on technology and view IT as an investment not an expense. The lead-time for implementing technology projects can also be long, and so the short-term operational and tactical decision-making is inappropriate. Management must strategically plan its use of technology.

Problems that are likely to arise without an IS/IT strategy

Without an IS/IT strategy it is unlikely that the business objectives will be met, and technology will become an inhibitor rather than an enabler. Customer service may decline rather than improve, and the company may suffer a competition disadvantage. As the future of Gravy Train depends upon technology, the ultimate consequence of not having an IS/IT strategy is that its long-term survival will be at risk.

Costs are likely to rise as hardware and software may be purchased that are inappropriate to the long-term direction of the business. Decision-making concerning the technology is likely to become difficult, as without standards and purchasing policies, incompatible hardware and software may be purchased resulting in 'islands' of information.

Project management will also become difficult with problems in allocating resources and keeping within time scales. With no long-term goals, planning is likely to become ad-hoc with projects being postponed and improperly implemented.

The effect upon the staff at the Gravy Train may be detrimental. They may feel that the company has lost direction and lose confidence in the technology. Staff morale may fall, motivation diminish, and resistance to change set in.

(b)

Top tips. The philosophy behind the CSF approach is that managers should focus on a small number of critical objectives, and information systems should focus on providing information to enable managers to monitor these objectives. Factors critical to the success of the quality of service include quality of materials, delivery and support. The determination of key performance indicators related to the CSFs is not necessarily straightforward. Some measures might use factual, objectively verifiable, data, while others might make use of 'softer' concepts, such as opinions, perceptions and hunches.

Marking scheme

		Marks
(i)	Award up to 2 marks for each valid point up to a maximum of 12	12
(ii)	Award up to 2 marks for each valid point up to a maximum of 8	8
		20

This marking guide was produced by BPP.

(i) **Critical success factors** are a small number of key operational goals vital to the success of an organisation. They are used to establish organisational information requirements.

Two separate types of critical success factor can be identified. A **monitoring CSF** is used to keep abreast of existing activities and operations. A **building CSF** helps to measure the progress of new initiatives and is more likely to be relevant at senior executive level.

Monitoring CSFs are important for maintaining business. Building CSFs are important for expanding business.

One approach to determining the factors that are critical to success in performing a function or making a decision is as follows.

- List the organisation's corporate objectives and goals.
- Determine which factors are critical for accomplishing the objectives.
- Determine a small number of key performance indicators for each factor.

Rockart claims that there are four sources for CSFs:

- The industry that the business is in – each has CSF's that are relevant to any company within it.

- The company itself and its situation within the industry – eg, its competitive strategy and its geographic location. CSFs could be to develop new products, create new markets or to support the field sales force.

- The environment eg, the economy, the political factors and consumer trends in the country or countries that the organisation operates in.

- Temporal organisational factors – these are areas of company activity that are unusually causing concern because they are unacceptable and need attention.

CSFs provide a way of achieving a clear definition of the information that is needed, limiting the costly collection of more data than is necessary. For example, Jo may have a business strategy where the CSF is to minimise the length of time a study guide is kept in stock. One of the key decisions related to that CSF might be to decide what quantities must be ordered. The information requirements may be the demand for guides.

Meeting the CSF ensures that the investment in stock is kept low and that guides are distributed quickly. IS can support this strategy eg, a key report would compare study guide purchasing with demand patterns to help Jo anticipate demand without overstocking, whilst at the same time helping to avoid shortages.

More specifically, possible internal and external data sources for CSFs include the following.

- The existing system. The existing system can be used to generate reports showing failures to meet CSFs.

- Customer service department. This department will maintain details of complaints received, refunds handled, customer enquiries etc. These should be reviewed to ensure all failure types have been identified.

- Customers. A survey of customers, provided that it is properly designed and introduced, would reveal (or confirm) those areas where satisfaction is high or low.

- Competitors. Competitors' operations, pricing structures and publicity should be closely monitored.

- Accounting system. The profitability of various aspects of the operation is probably a key factor in any review of CSFs.

- Consultants. A specialist consultancy might be able to perform a detailed review of the system in order to identify ways of satisfying CSFs.

(ii) One of the objectives identified by Gravy Train is improved quality of service. Jo Stafford is hoping that students will opt for Gravy Train rather than a rival if the on-line support is adding sufficient value, enhancing the quality of service, and ultimately leading to an improved chance of a pass in each of the examinations. Similarly, with those students studying purely on-line at a distance with no class contact, Jo knows that they will return to local training companies if they do not feel that they are getting a quality service.

Performance indicators to measure quality of service could be at a number of levels. The percentage pass rate in each of the examinations is quite a high level indicator. This can be compared to national averages produced by the professional bodies, to other competing organisation if they are made public, and also to previous years' pass rates when there was no on-line service. While this is a good indicator, it should also be realised that part of a student's performance in exams is down to their own ability. One-off calculations of this indicator are misleading – trends are more important.

Lower level performance indicators to measure the quality of support and delivery could include:

- Average time taken to respond to student queries.
- Average time taken to mark and return work.
- Average student rating of lecturers' learning materials.
- Percentage time that on-line service is not available due to technical problems, maintenance etc.

The company will be able to provide subject content for its students on its website. Instead of being dependent upon commercial publishers who only update study manuals twice a year, Gravy Train will be able to amend its site as required. Immediately the pages are updated all the Gravy Train students will see the new version, as the technology provides a single point of update with no distribution problems. Therefore Gravy Train students will get the most up-to-date information, instead of being dependent upon the latest manuals.

(c)

> **Top tips.** Gravy Train can use a number of on-line technologies to offer a different service to both the student and the student's employer. Remember that competitive advantage relies on out-performing competitors in one or more areas (eg service levels, cost).

Marking scheme

	Marks
Award up to 2 marks for each valid point and explanation up to a maximum of	<u>20</u>

This marking guide was produced by BPP.

The Internet site will provide students with a much more **interactive** learning experience than simply reading manuals; on screen text can be supported by images, sound, and short video clips. This **multimedia** environment should lead to students finding that studying with Gravy Train is more interesting than with Gravy Train's competitors, and that motivation to study is high. Active learning can be encouraged by providing study activities that students must do on-line before they continue.

Some of these learning activities may take the form of objective tests that are completed by the students on-line, which are then marked immediately – this could be done **automatically**, giving the students their results plus helpful feedback advising where the student made mistakes and importantly what the student should do next. Regular testing in this way will provide the students with a sense of progress, and also ensure that they keep to their studies. For those students attending traditional classes, some of the activities can be used in preparation for the following class. This would lead to face-to-face tuition being more interactive and reduce the amount of lecturing to students.

Where students' employers have paid their study fees, they could have access to parts of Gravy Train site to check up on their students' results and progress for themselves. Offering this service to employers may bring considerable **competitive advantage** to the Gravy Train, as employers are more likely to pay for the type of service where they can monitor progress and make more informed decisions about financially supporting students or not.

The Gravy Train website can also include a **bulletin board** system and **on-line conferencing** facilities. The bulletin board will allow tutors to post a message that can be read by all students and the on-line conferencing takes this concept one stage further, so that on-line discussions take place between the tutor and the students. These discussions can be continuous, showing the group who has replied to whom, and a full dialogue can take place about a range of topics.

Those students **learning at a distance** should feel less isolated and find the contact with other students valuable. Providing there are no language problems, students from anywhere in the world can use the technology.

Whilst considerable learning can take place in these on-line conferences, students experiencing private problems with their study will be able to **e-mail** their tutor. Both the conferences and e-mails benefit from being asynchronous technologies. With a phone call a tutor has to be there to answer the call. With an e-mail or conference, the message can be left whenever the student is studying and the tutor can reply when next on-line.

In summary, considerable **competitive advantage** could be achieved, leading to a greater market share. However, it should be mentioned that the company will be totally dependent upon the technology, and should there be problems with this, then competitive disadvantage may result.

Also, there may be a number of factors that may limit the success of the on-line technology at the Gravy Train including: the steep **learning curve** for Gravy Train staff and the **acceptance** of the need for change, **time** taken to develop the on-line resources, time taken to participate in the on-line conferences and answer e-mails, and also very importantly, whether or not students accept this new way of studying.

55 Patterson's Electrical Suppliers

(a)

> **Text references**. Material from Chapters 1, 2, 3, 4, 7 and 8 is relevant to this question.
>
> **Top tips**. If you have used the Internet to buy something, think what attracted you to a specific organisation's website. In part (ii) our answer, and the suggested outline from the ACCA, explains methods of sharing information electronically. For part (iii), think about the information that would prove useful if shared. This will help provide some of the business applications for the Intranet.

Marking scheme

			Marks
(i)	Award up to 2 marks for description of user requirements	2	
	Award up to 1 mark for each valid point on retaining the customer up to a maximum of 8 marks	8	
			10
(ii)	Award up to 2 marks for description	2	
	Award up to 1 mark for each valid point up to a maximum of 6 marks	6	
			8
(iii)	Award up to 2 marks for description of provision of e-mail and discussion forms	2	
	Award up to 1 mark for each valid point on remote sharing of information up to a maximum of 5 marks	5	
			7
			25

(i)   The **Internet** provides businesses with access to a rapidly expanding market of customers as the number of computers connected to the Internet increases. Many businesses are establishing their own websites in an attempt to take advantage of this growth. A business that does not provide some form of web purchasing option, or at least viewing of products on-line, may be in danger of losing customers to competitors who do provide these options.

User requirements

Potential customers need to know some basic information when visiting a store or a website. Key data that must be available includes product price, availability, features of the product and any additional charges such as delivery or insurance contracts to guard against product failure. The website must provide this information in an easy-to-use format.

Pattersons could establish a website providing this information (the site can be linked to the integrated stock system). However, the concept of cash-and-carry would be lost as all purchases would have to be delivered to the customer, unless a 'pick up from store' option was made available. Also, Pattersons would not be able to offer the services of their trained sales representatives, as the Internet simply displays text and pictures, and not interactive customer service. An alternative would be to provide a telephone call back system (similar to Dell computers) where customers can click on a web-link and receive a call from a Patterson sales representative to discuss their purchase.

Retaining the customer

Customers are likely to visit a number of websites to compare prices and product details. Providing some form of personalisation of the website for repeat visits, such as welcoming the customer by name or displaying a list of products already reviewed, would help make the site more customer-friendly. Software is available to provide this type of service on the Internet.

Again Pattersons could establish a website to provide these features. Any other features that will add value to the site, such as offering a list of related products or spare parts for the product being purchased could also help to make the site more attractive to customers.

Incentives to use the website

Using the Internet for purchasing does provide a risk that sales will fall in the individual shops maintained by Pattersons. However, new customers may also be reached, especially those who are not located within travelling distance of a Pattersons store, or who do not like shopping for large electrical items. In this situation, providing some incentive to use the web site such as coupons or a loyalty points scheme may help to attract additional purchasers.

Other value-added activities

When a purchase is made on a website, customer information will be stored by the supplier's computer system. This information can be used to help provide repeat business for the organisation.

For example, if a vacuum cleaner is purchased from Pattersons, then an e-mail can be sent to that customer in a few weeks with information about replacement bags for that cleaner. Similarly, data can be mined to identify relationships in purchases for example, Pattersons may find that customers purchasing a washing machine often purchase a tumble dryer a few months later. Offers can be sent via e-mail direct to the customer including coupons for tumble dryer purchase.

(ii)   An **extranet** is an extension of an internal intranet. The intranet provides information about an organisation such as stock levels, customer details, product information etc to employees within that organisation. An extranet means making this information available to specific third parties. For example, the Dell database of technical information about computers is made available to some customers to help diagnose faults with those computers.

Pattersons may be able to use direct electronic links with customers and suppliers to provide business benefits, particularly in managing the supply chain.

Stock levels. Suppliers can be given access to stock levels at Pattersons. Where stocks fall below a re-order level, either at head office or a store, the supplier will automatically send replacement stocks. This will benefit Pattersons because less employee time is spent reviewing stock levels and replacement stocks will be sent immediately they are required.

Supplier communications. E-mail can be used to inform suppliers about new stock requirements or changes to trading conditions. This communication method provides significant time and cost savings over other forms of communication. For example, Pattersons can inform suppliers about upcoming promotions on specific products so that more of those items can be produced ready for re-sale.

Stock purchasing. Information concerning stock deliveries and receipts can be sent by Electronic Data Interchange. This will again provide time and cost savings in terms of staff as well as providing up-to-date information on stock movements. Pattersons already has an integrated order system, so linking this to an external EDI system is possible.

Payment. Payments can be made electronically using Electronic Funds Transfer. This will speed up the payment process, if Pattersons want to do this. Similarly, payments can be made automatically based on the receipt of goods. For example, Pattersons may want to reward quicker delivery of goods by paying those suppliers in a few days rather than a few weeks.

Other Intranet applications, such as financial management of funds are available, although these may have limited use for Pattersons at the moment.

(iii)   An **intranet** is an internal Internet-like network for use within an organisation. The Intranet uses the same technology as the Internet, namely a web-browser to view web ages. However, those pages are only available to employees in the organisation and so they will normally contain information specific for use by those employees.

An intranet may be able to assist staff at Pattersons in various ways.

Provision of internal e-mail and discussion forums

E-mail can be used as a basic communication tool within the company. However, discussion forums can be set up to provide a forum on various matters such as product queries. A sales representative in one store may not know the answer to a question concerning a product. This query can be placed on a discussion database, and a representative in a different store may be able to provide the answer. This system will help to improve the knowledge of different products being sold.

Remote sharing of information

Intranets allow information on central databases to be viewed from any location. In this situation, stock levels at head office and all stores could be viewed enabling sales representatives to confirm stock availability across all stores, and hopefully increase overall sales. This system will provide a significant advantage over the current system of centralising information at head office only.

Sharing of reference material

Any reference material, such as detailed information about products or even the organisation's telephone list, can be placed on the intranet. As well as making it more accessible to all members of staff, this also allows for efficient and timely update. The information can be updated frequently in one location rather than having out-of-date paper-based copies of the information in each store. Having better information on products will also help provide enhanced customer service.

Other information such as competitor prices and promotional activities can also be shared via the intranet, making all staff more aware of the competitive environment.

(b)

> **Top tips**. Think about the integration of IT/IS and business strategy, and how one supports the other, then important areas such as information provision and the benefits of IT may start to become apparent. This provides an outline of an answer to part (i).
>
> In part (ii), structure your answer around the three key points mentioned in the question. If you explain these and show how Pattersons has implemented these processes, then you should have an appropriate answer.

Marking scheme

			Marks
(i)	Award 1 mark for each valid point up to a maximum of 10 marks		10
(ii)	Award up to 2 marks for description of automation plus 1 mark for an example	3	
	Award up to 2 marks for description of rationalisation plus 1 mark for an example	3	
	Award up to 3 marks for description of re-engineering plus 1 mark for an example	4	
			10
			20

(i)   Business strategy and IS/IT strategy are normally developed together in an organisation, because the IS/IT provides essential support to the overall business strategy. For example, information systems will be required to provide appropriate information for each level of management to enable the business to be run efficiently.

The information that can be provided by the IS/IT systems is outlined below.

Strategic level information. This is for the use of senior managers and will relate to long term planning. For example, in Pattersons, information may be provided to assist in decisions regarding the location of new stores.

Management level information. Information to support the activities of monitoring, controlling and decision making carried out by middle managers. In the case of Pattersons, information may be provided on total sales by product line and current stock levels to help in planning promotions or special offers within certain stores.

Knowledge level information. This is information to support the knowledge workers in an organisation. Pattersons may provide customer databases for workers to try and identify trends in customer data in order to improve advertising and overall sales.

Operational level information. Within Pattersons, as in any retail organisation, this will relate to current stock levels, re-order details, information about individual sales invoices etc. The information will be summarised and input to the MIS for additional analysis.

Almost any organisation can provide these information systems for their managers and workers. To remain competitive, Pattersons will need to ensure that the appropriate systems are in place to provide the necessary management information.

If the business and IS/IT strategies are not congruent with each other, then there is a danger that either appropriate information will not be provided, or that the IT infrastructure will be built up without reference to the information requirements of the organisation. Careful planning is therefore needed, with control from the Board level, to ensure that these errors do not occur.

Appropriate IS/IT strategy planning will be facilitated by the appointment of a Chief Information Officer to the Board of directors. This individual will be responsible for:

Developing the information systems in-house to meet business needs. For example, there may be the opportunity to re-structure the whole ordering and sales processes within Pattersons by using Internet related technology. However, any change must be carried out in accordance with the business aims of Pattersons.

Looking for opportunities to use IT to create business advantage. Within Pattersons, this will involve the use of the proposed Internet site.

Ensuring that the IT systems support the overall business strategy. The proposed Internet site must fit in with the overall strategy at Pattersons. Establishing the site without appropriate planning may cause significant problems, such as rejection of the site by store managers because they feel that their store income is threatened.

Ensuring that sufficient IT resources are available to maintain and develop systems. For example, the directors may require additional information about actions of competitors including Internet links to their sites and information services such as Reuters. The CIO will need to ensure that appropriate IT infrastructure is available to support this business requirement.

The important point is to ensure that the IT/IS strategy is congruent with the business strategy. Pattersons appears to have achieved this, although changes in the future will need to be planned and monitored closely to ensure that this remains the case.

(ii) **Automation** (or 'automate') refers to the computerisation of existing tasks and procedures. IT is used to make those existing tasks more efficient and effective, rather than to amend or change the tasks to provide additional benefits.

This use of IT is a fairly low risk strategy, as the business processes are essentially unchanged. Within Pattersons, automation will have occurred in the sales systems, probably by installing electronic point of sale equipment and in stock control and monitoring by maintaining the stock balances on a database. However, the underlying process of the customer paying for goods at a checkout, and stock balances being available from some form of stock recording system, are essentially unchanged.

Rationalisation (or 'infomate') involves some changes to the business, normally to make existing processes more effective or efficient in some way by linking them together.

The need for rationalisation can occur from two main areas:

Business reviews indicate that existing IT systems would be more efficient if they were linked. For example, stock control information is available on a computer system, and details of stock items sold are also recorded electronically. However, the stock database is only updated with sales information at the end of each working day. Linking these two systems on-line will provide the benefit of sales being recorded immediately in the stock system. Real-time stock information is now available.

The process of automation may start to cause inefficiencies in other areas. For example, when a sale is made, customer details are entered into a computer system. However, those details are printed out to provide a list of goods to obtain from a warehouse, with the list being sent in the post to arrive at the warehouse next day for delivery in, say, one week. Previously, when customer details were recorded manually, there was no expectation that goods would be available within say 48 hours, but now that information is captured electronically, a seven-day delivery seems a very long time. Automation is also needed to link the sales systems with warehouse stocks to provide quicker response times.

The Pattersons business appears to have rationalised the IT systems already as an integrated accounting system and 48 hour delivery of goods from a warehouse are already available.

Re-engineering (or 'transformate') involves the re-design of business processes to try and maximise the benefits from IT. Savings are normally obtained in terms of reduced cost, elimination of duplicated activities, or improved speed of response from the processes.

The process of re-engineering will involve a review of the entire business processes, with the expectation that IT will provide different, and significantly more efficient work methods. Change in this respect will be much more significant than either automation or rationalisation. Because change is significant, re-engineering is a high-risk strategy for any organisation.

Before re-engineering can take place, the organisation will need to consider what the objective of each business process is, and how IT can best support that process. This means re-designing the process, rather than simply making it more efficient by automation. In the context of Pattersons, setting up the Internet site is a form of re-engineering because this is a different method of carrying out business compared to cash and carry; the latter could not be adapted to provide Internet trading so new processes are required.

(c)

Top tips. Remember to use the scenario information about the shift work project – there is not a lot of detail but by making a few tentative assumptions, some of the reasons for failure can be identified.

Marking scheme

	Marks
Award up to 2 marks for each valid point up to a maximum of 15	<u>15</u>

Answer plan

Refer to the four main reasons for systems failure during implementation.

(i)   **Lack of user involvement**

(ii)   **Level of management support**

(iii)   **Level of complexity and risk**

- Large project is more likely to fail at implementation than a small project
- The type of project structure
- The experience available in respect of the technology being used

(iv)   **Management of the implementation process**

- Poor estimation of the time to complete the project
- Not allocating sufficient resources to the project
- Poor communication between members of the project team

There are four main reasons for systems failure during implementation.

(i)   **Lack of user involvement**

One of the key success criteria for system implementation is to have user input with effective communication between the users and designers of the system. User involvement means that:

- Users have opportunities to ensure that the new system meets their requirements.

- Users are more likely to feel that they own the finished product, and so are more likely to use the final system.

- It will be more difficult to reject the final system.

In Pattersons, it is unclear how much involvement users have actually had in system development or implementation. The fact that users see the system as a failure indicates that user involvement was severely limited. Any lack of involvement, or breakdown of communication will increase the risk of system failure.

(ii) **Level of management support**

Management support is normally essential to ensure the success of any project. Managers will normally be involved with a project to:

- Show commitment to that project.
- Understand the issues and problems involved so these can be addressed quickly.
- Ensure all other interested parties are also involved with the project.

The fact that management also views the shift system as a failure indicates lack of management support for the project. The change in work practices also appears to be cumbersome, which may be one of the reasons for lack of support and potential rejection of the project now. If management were not involved, then this is another reason why users will also not been involved with implementation.

(iii) **Level of complexity and risk**

There are three factors, which affect the level of complexity and risk in a project.

Firstly, a large project is more likely to fail at implementation than a small project. Size can be stated in terms of expenditure, duration of the project, number of staff involved and number of business units affected.

In Pattersons, the shift project appeared to affect the whole organisation; this gave a high risk because many business units were affected and many staff. The duration and expenditure are unclear, but given the size of the project, it is likely to have been expensive and lasted a reasonable amount of time. The risk of failure based simply on project size, is high.

Secondly, the type of project structure also affects the risk of failure. Well-structured projects are less likely to fail at implementation than poorly-structured projects. Structure provides a framework for the project, decreasing the risk of failure.

In Pattersons, it is not clear how structured the project actually was. However, the high level of user intervention now indicates that the initial analysis was not carried out very effectively. Similarly, the resistance to the system indicates lack of involvement and appropriate user sign-off of the different project stages. It is therefore likely that the project suffered from poor planning and structure and this has increased the risk of failure.

Thirdly, the experience available in respect of the technology being used. The user of newer technology and relative inexperience of IT staff will also increase the risk of failure. Newer technology may not be fully understood, while lack of experience will increase risks, as staff may not understand how the software works.

In Pattersons, it is not clear why the IT system requires manual amendments. This situation may have arisen because the technology is new and it has not been implemented correctly, so this has increased the risk of failure.

ANSWERS

(iv) **Management of the implementation process**

Poor management of the implementation process in the following areas will increase the risk of project failure.

- Poor estimation of the time to complete the project
- Not allocating sufficient resources to the project, and
- Poor communication between members of the project team

In the case of Pattersons, it is not clear how far these factors actually affected the project. However, not meeting user requirements does indicate poor management, possibly in terms of communication, which may have contributed to the failure of the project.

56 Ancient World

(a)

Text reference. Chapters 1, 2, 5, 6, and 7 contain information relevant to this question.

Top tips. In part (ii), don't just list the strengths, weaknesses, opportunities and threats in terms of management perceptions, the idea is to undertake a more structured analysis so as to yield findings, which can contribute to the formulation of strategy.

Examiner's comments. The examiner commented that in general candidates did very well in answering the first part of the question. The second part of the question enabled candidates to select and expand on elements chosen from the SWOT analysis that had particular relevance to the development of e-commerce. Weaker candidates merely expanded on all of the elements from part (i) giving little evidence of being able to select and apply the results to the development of an IS strategy.

Marking scheme

		Marks
(i)	Award up to 2 marks for each element, 4 elements, maximum of 8 marks.	8
(ii)	A wide range of answers will be given depending on the answer to 1(a). Answers should point to the opportunities of exploiting technology in the development of an e-commerce based strategy. Award up to 3 marks for each element chosen, maximum of 12 marks.	12 / 20

(i) **Strengths**

- Near to delivery infrastructure
- Established customer base
- Good reputation among the specialist customers
- Good domain name
- Web software allowing use of 'cookies'
- Efficient order handling service
- Newly appointed Technology manager and IT director

220 BPP LEARNING MEDIA

Weaknesses

- Fewer website visitors than would be liked
- Stock-outs fairly common – causes failure to meet delivery targets
- No urban centre within easy reach
- Customer base does not appear to be increasing
- IT staff recruitment and retention problems
- Web-based ordering system not integrated with inventory management system

Opportunities

- Existing customer base/mailing list could be source of increased sales
- Web-based technologies, such as cookies, should enable the customer base to grow
- Develop a business and information systems strategy to exploit new purchasing trends
- Use new technologies to develop another source of customers

Threats

- Exposed to customers switching to on-line specialists
- On-line retailers able to undercut prices
- New technology allows customers to purchase from a wider range of suppliers
- These new trends in purchasing may lead to lost business

(ii) Some elements from the SWOT analysis will impact upon the development of an information systems strategy more than others. The early introduction of e-commerce is a significant element of AW's IS strategy. The following elements of the SWOT analysis are particularly relevant in this context.

- **Web-based ordering system not integrated with inventory management system**

  As AW incorporates web-based technologies into its operation it is essential that these activities are integrated into the day to day activities and systems – rather than being treated as a technical add-on. A coherent IS strategy must therefore provide for integration of web-based systems with back-office systems.

- **Use new technologies to develop another source of customers**

  A likely aim of the IS strategy will be to exploit the opportunities offered by the introduction of the website. Currently the site is attracting fewer hits than is desirable. AW has an opportunity to develop the site using the latest technologies and techniques, although overly complicated features should be avoided as these delay data transmission. Failure to exploit these new technologies is likely to lead to some customers defecting to competitors.

- **Develop a business and information systems strategy to exploit the new purchasing trends**

  It is essential that the IS strategy developed by AW compliments the overall business strategy. Therefore, the IS strategy can not be developed until a coherent business strategy has been decided upon. The overall aim of the IS strategy should be to help achieve general business objectives. For example, if AW decides to take on web-based retailers such as Amazon, this will impact significantly on the IS strategy.

- **IT staff recruitment and retention**

  The company's failure to retain permanent IT staff is a major obstacle to the implementation of a consistent on-going IS strategy. The new IT Director and new IT Manager should take steps to improve this situation, introducing suitable measures to recruit and retain staff. Other options, such as a stable outsourcing partner, could also be considered within the IS strategy.

(b)

> **Top tips.** The discussion for part (ii) could include: a consideration of the point of view of the Board of Directors in developing a range of IS systems; whether the current IT staff situation should undertake the development in-house or should it be outsourced? Can software packages be purchased? Is bespoke software required?
>
> **Examiner's comments**. The first part of this question was answered very well with only a small proportion of candidates failing to suggest an appropriate information system.
>
> The second part of this question caused problems for some candidates. The question required a discussion on the impact of the need to develop a range of new IS systems to support e-commerce in the four support activities. Many candidates did not respond to this requirement and merely answered this part of the question in an identical manner to the first part.

Marking scheme

		Marks
(i)	Award up to 2 marks for each activity, 5 activities, maximum of 10 marks	10
(ii)	Award up to 5 marks for discussion of the impact plus up to 2 marks for each example, maximum of 10 marks	10

A wide range of answers is expected; this allocation should be used as a guideline. Some students may just discuss the impact whilst others will give examples. Allocate marks accordingly.

$$\underline{\underline{20}}$$

(i) Inbound logistics

Inbound logistics is concerned with inbound activities to receive, store and internally distribute materials arriving at AW sites. Activities will include goods received, material handling, inventory control, warehousing and contacts with suppliers. An appropriate information system at AW would be an Inventory Control module linked to an integrated accounting package. Such a system would include the use of bar-code readers to facilitate the quick and accurate recording of arriving goods.

Operations

Operations refers to the general day to day activities involved in selling books at AW. An appropriate Sales Order Processing system, that provides an automated link between orders being received and the dispatch of the goods, would be an appropriate information system. Such a system should include web-links – incorporating orders placed via AW's website.

Outbound logistics

Outbound logistics describes activities associated with the distribution of goods or services. For AW, this would involve the distribution of books to customers. An order tracking system, including access via the Internet, would be a relevant information system.

Marketing and sales

Marketing and sales activities involve making customers and potential customers aware of the product, and the product qualities, and also with ensuring customers have easy access to a means by which they can purchase the product. Relevant activities include advertising, personal selling, pricing policies, merchandising and sales promotions. Customer Relationship Management (CRM) software would provide AW with the required functionality to monitor and control these activities.

Service

Service activities are those activities that involve direct contact with the customer, for example customer service telephone lines or those staff responding to electronic queries via the Internet. A customer query tracking system, that records the details and status (eg pending, resolved) of customer service queries, is one appropriate system that could be used at AW.

(ii) AW will need to develop a wide range of information systems to support e-commerce. The discussion below focuses on the systems required in relation to the four support activities in Porter's Value Chain.

Infrastructure

The move into e-commerce will require new systems to support the organisations infrastructure. New, web-based systems will need to be integrated into the existing infrastructure to ensure activities are controlled and monitored. The impact will be felt in all areas of AW, for example management reports will have to be amended to incorporate the new activities.

Human resource management

The move into e-commerce will require increased human resource with relevant IT knowledge. This will impact on all activities involved in the recruiting, training, development and remuneration of staff. New or amended personnel and payroll systems may be required by AW to reflect the changing nature of the workforce.

Technology development

The move into e-commerce will require significant technological expertise in areas such as website design and system security. New supplementary systems may also be required, for example online help systems. The expertise required to develop and implement these systems may not be available within AW. It is likely therefore that an outsourcing partner will be used.

Procurement

Procurement refers to activities involved in the purchase of goods to be used in production or simply sold on. In AW, the website could also be used to facilitate an extranet link with important customers and suppliers. The extranet would change the way resources are procured by AW, encouraging closer relationships with suppliers which could be used as a source of competitive advantage.

(c)

Top tips. Read the requirement carefully – your discussion must relate to the points specified. The knowledge required (the relationship between business strategy and information systems strategy) should be second nature to you by the time you come to sit your exam. Remember though to apply your knowledge to the scenario.

Examiner's comments. Candidates who engaged in a discussion generally produced some excellent answers and were rewarded accordingly. The majority of answers clearly demonstrated a strong relationship is required between the two strategies and many candidates referred to the scenario to emphasise their points. Candidates who obtained marks in the higher range did include components of an information strategy as requested.

In the second part of this question, the 'Going To Get There' stage, candidates generally provided good answers. The majority of candidates identified the two main reasons for change, changes in the business environment and new developments in technology. Some candidates clearly spent more time and effort on this part of the question even though the majority of the marks were allocated to the first part of the question.

Marking scheme

		Marks

(i) Guidelines for mark allocation

0-7 marks. Answers that only briefly describe a link between the strategies. Answers towards the top of this range may discuss the link, but with little depth of understanding evident.

8-15 marks. Answers that demonstrate an understanding of why such links are imperative. Better answers, towards the top of the range must make relevant links to Ancient World. **15**

(ii) Award up to 3 marks each for discussion of flexibility and co-ordination, overall maximum 5 marks.

5
———
20

(i) As the impact of **information technology** has grown in organisations of all types and sizes, it has become more important than ever to ensure that an organisation's business strategy and information systems strategy are treated as closely linked. The information systems strategy should facilitate the achievement of business strategy objectives.

However, this does not mean that the business strategy could be developed first, and an information systems strategy then be developed to support this. In many situations information systems technology can **drive** or **strongly influence** the business plan. For example, a website can open up new markets, and web technologies can lead to virtual companies.

Developing and implementing a new information system involves many people from different areas of an organisation. A new or amended information system may lead to involves changes in work, management and the social fabric of the organisation. It is important therefore that development is **planned** and **controlled**, and that development is driven by business goals rather than a simple desire to introduce new technology.

The information systems strategy will include what the information systems should achieve, and should specify the likely systems that will achieve these aims. This strategy should be incorporated into the **overall strategic plans** of the organisation.

These strategic plans may be broken down into a **lower level** information systems plan that contains a statement of corporate goals and specifies how information systems supports the attainment of those goals. The plan indicates how general goals will be achieved by specific systems projects, and includes specific dates and milestones. Actual progress is then able to be judged against this plan.

The relationship between business strategy and information systems strategy in the formation of a business plan is summarised below, with reference to AW.

1. **Business alignment**

   The first step in to ensure investment in information technology is consistent with AW's business vision and strategic business goals.

2. **Competitive advantage**

   AW may be able to exploit information technology for competitive advantage.

3. **Resource management**

   Plans must be developed for the efficient and effective management of AW's information systems resources, including staff, software and hardware.

4. **Technology architecture**

The overall IS/IT infrastructure, including all information systems, should be designed and developed to enable business goals to be achieved. The action required to achieve this should form the Information Systems plan.

(ii) During the 'Going to Get There' stage of combining business and information systems strategy the two strategies are implemented. As the **business environment** is subject to change, it is likely that business and information systems strategies will also require change. Both strategies must therefore be flexible.

Strategic business plans often cover around **five years**, during which time many changes could occur. For example, AW could be subject to increased competition from publishers deciding to distribute their own products via the web.

Technological change could also require a re-think of business and information systems strategies. For example, the technology surrounding electronic books (e-books) could develop and gain acceptance requiring AW to consider this format.

Organisations must monitor their environment to ensure they are aware of factors that may require **amendments** to their **current strategies**. This should enable significant changes in political, economic, social and technological factors to be identified and responded to.

When changes are made to one or both strategies, it is important to always ensure that the two remain **complimentary**. For example, a change in AW's business strategy (eg focus on mail order only) would require significant amendment of the information systems strategy.

57 Moonshine Corporation

(a)

Text reference. Sourcing arrangements in part (b) are covered in Chapter 6 of the text, and three leg analysis in part (c) can be found in Chapter 2.

Top tips. Ensure your SWOT analysis relates to the CRR system – refer to the scenario as much as possible in your answer.

Examiner's comments. Candidates did very well in answering the first part of the question. The second part of the question enabled candidates to apply the findings of Part (i) and draw upon them to highlight the essential links between formulating an IS strategy in conjunction with a business strategy. An apparent weakness in many of the answers was the balance between the requirements.

Marking scheme

		Marks
(i)	Award up to 2 marks for each element, 4 elements, max of 8 marks.	8
(ii)	Award up to 6 marks for the use of SWOT analysis plus up to 6 marks for reference to the scenario.	12
		20

(i) **Strengths**

- Good, innovative products
- Strong customer base
- Well-established company
- Robust mainframe system

Weaknesses

- Insufficient IT staff and expertise to keep the CIS project in-house
- Databases are currently product rather than customer focused
- Mixture of local and central systems and data redundancy
- Other major projects are competing for resources

Opportunities

- Customer focussed information systems should result in competitive advantage
- The technology is available to develop an innovative customer oriented system
- The market is fairly flexible providing an opportunity to increase market share
- Organisational structure is being redesigned around customer/market needs

Threats

- The system won't deliver the expected benefits
- The change could result in the loss of market share
- Strong competition in the market increases the risk of other offers appealing more
- Competitors may develop similar systems

(ii) The format and structure provided by a **SWOT analysis** ensures a wide range of factors are considered when developing an IS strategy. It also ensures that both internal (strengths and weaknesses) and external (opportunities and threats) factors are considered. The assessments of opportunities and threats ensures factors in the environment are considered, while the assessment of strengths and weaknesses focuses on the capabilities of the organisation.

The format also encourages the effect on all **major stakeholders** (eg customers, suppliers, competitors, managers, employees etc) are considered in relation to the new system.

A SWOT analysis encourages a balanced approach by ensuring potential **rewards** and **risks** are considered. In almost all situations, the analysis will reveal both positives (strengths and opportunities) and negatives (weaknesses and threats). Making the right decision therefore is still likely to come down to the skill and knowledge of management – the SWOT analysis helps in the process by encouraging relevant factors to be considered in an orderly manner.

In relation to the CRR study, there appears to be a strong **business case** for developing the Common Interfacing System (CIS) at Moonshine. The system is viewed as innovative and customer focussed, and is expected to enable Moonshine to better meet customer needs.

Competitors also appear to be considering providing a similar service, which gives rise to the threat of lost market share if Moonshine can not match or exceed competitor service provision standards. A SWOT analysis would also highlight the risks of reorganising and restructuring the organisation and business processes around the new system.

In the case of the CIS project opportunities are present but there are as many weaknesses as strengths to consider. The system architecture and the existing applications have all been developed to meet different **business strategies**. The organisation is certainly facing threats from its competitors and maybe it should take steps to protect itself, that is develop systems that will allow the business to compete in a competitive market place at least on equal terms. Currently Moonshine may be in a position to lead the market with this latest innovation.

(b)

Marking scheme

	Marks
Award up to 3 marks for a suitable general overview.	3
For each alternative award up to 2 marks for a description of the sourcing method and up to 3 marks for reference to scenario; 3 alternatives = 15 marks.	15
Award up to 2 marks for recommendation.	2
	20

REPORT

To:	IT Manager
From:	Deputy IT Manager
Date:	2 December 20X2
Subject:	**Common Interfacing System (CIS)**

Overview

This report covers the options available to source the Common Interfacing System (CIS).

The proposed CIS system is of strategic importance to Moonshine's future as a financial services provider. As our internal IT division cannot support such a development and due to the unique requirements of the system, we are limited to three general approaches. These three options are total outsourcing, multiple/selective sourcing, and insourcing.

Total outsourcing

Total outsourcing usually means responsibility for Information Technology (IT) and Information Systems (IS) is passed to an external vendor. This would mean that responsibility for all hardware, software and telecommunications infrastructure (ie complete control of all IT/IS activities) would be handed to an outside supplier.

In the context of the development of the CIS system, total outsourcing of that development would not necessarily require the complete outsourcing of the whole IT/IS function. All aspects of developing the CIS system could be totally outsourced, and then when complete the system could be incorporated into the existing infrastructure. The outsourcing exercise could then be seen to be at an end with maintenance and management of the CIS system performed in-house.

However, this approach may not be viable. Historically all development at Moonshine has been completed in-house. Only Moonshine employees know in detail how these existing systems (which the CIS will interface with) are set up. It is unlikely therefore that the project can be separated from other existing systems and outsourced to a single supplier (which would be a complete departure from the existing strategy).

Multiple/selective sourcing

Multiple/selective sourcing describes the situation where a range of suppliers are used to provide aspects of IS/IT services. Some organisations outsource some parts of their IT operations to one or several suppliers. This frees up the in-house IT team to focus on high priority, value-added activities. Depending upon the actual services outsourced, this type of outsourcing often carries less risk, as routine processing operations should be able to be performed by an outside supplier with little difficulty and little business risk.

In the context of Moonshine and the development of the CIS, some other IT operations could be outsourced to free-up Moonshine staff to work on the CIS. For example, we currently operate a range of legacy systems on mainframes – these systems could be outsourced. Other areas to consider include 'standard' systems such as payroll. Offering aspects of IT operations to a range of external vendors would create supplier competition and allow internal staff to focus on core systems.

However, in practice it is unlikely we would be able to find a supplier with sufficient understanding to support our legacy systems – particularly the older ones developed in older software languages. While other 'standard' systems could successfully be outsourced, this alone would not release sufficient IT staff time to enable them to develop the CIS.

Insourcing

Insourcing refers to an arrangement whereby a third party provides technology and/or skilled staff to perform work on the client's site under the day-to-day direction of the organisation's own business managers. Insourcing is usually successful when IT is seen as being an integral part of the business and there is an existing high level of in-house IT expertise.

This option would appear to be the most suitable for us at Moonshine. IT/IS is now viewed as a core activity at Moonshine as we have recognised the need for a close relationship between our business strategy and our IS strategy. The internal IT department could remain and IT contractors brought in to provide greater capacity to enable the CIS to be developed. So, the CIS system would be worked on by existing in-house IT staff, IT contractors with additional expertise, and Moonshine business managers to provide guidance relating to how we operate.

Recommendation

My recommendation is to insource. This option has the lowest risk factor and the highest likelihood of producing a high quality CIS (as long as sufficient contractors with the required skills can be found and hired on flexible contracts). An additional factor in support of this option is that other organisations within the financial sector have used it successfully.

(c)

Top tips. Use your textbook knowledge of Earl's three legs to answer part (i). Then, apply this knowledge to the scenario in parts (ii) and (iii).

Examiner's comments. Many candidates provided good descriptions of the three generic approaches. The answers to the second part of the question, which required candidates to identify where each of the approaches had been used within the scenario appeared to cause problems. Many candidates provided good responses to part (a) but then apparently could not apply their knowledge to the scenario.

The final part of this question required candidates to discuss a statement concerning the three approaches with reference to Moonshine Corporation. A minority of candidates did not attempt this part. Note that a range of answers could have scored well in this question – the model answers are not the only possible answers.

		Marks
(i)	Award up to 2 marks for each description.	6
(ii)	Award up to 3 marks for each application.	9
(iii)	Award up to 1 mark for each valid point. Maximum 5 marks. To obtain 4 or 5 marks candidates are required to make reference to the scenario.	5
		20

(i) The three legs of IS strategy development (as described by Earl) are described below.

Business led. The overall objectives of an organisation are identified and then IS/IT systems are implemented to enable these objectives to be met. This approach relies on the ability to break down the organisation and its objectives to a series of business objectives and processes and to be able to identify the information needs of these. This is an analytical approach. The people usually involved are senior management and specialist teams.

Infrastructure led. Computer based transaction systems are critical to business operations. The organisation focuses on systems that facilitate transactions and other basic operations. This is an evaluative approach. The people usually involved are system users and specialists.

Mixed. The organisation encourages ideas that will exploit existing IT and IS resources. Innovations may come from entrepreneurial managers or individuals outside the formal planning process. This is an innovative/creative approach. The people involved are entrepreneurs and/or visionaries.

(ii) **Business led – top down**

At Moonshine, one example of a business led approach to IS strategy is the planned development of the Common Interfacing System (CIS). This system is driven by the business requirement that operations must be client focused rather than product focused. The decision to develop the CIS is a strategic business decision and was based upon the Customer Review Requirement (CRR) study. The people involved are senior management and a review team and the approach adopted is analytical. The development of this system is a massive commitment as Moonshine has several million clients residing in several product-orientated databases.

Infrastructure led – bottom up

An infrastructure led – bottom up approach can be seen in Moonshine's intention to equip the self-employed sales force with laptop computers. This involved the use of IT to facilitate the updating of business information systems as quickly as possible, which will be achieved by updating the relevant databases on a daily basis. Technology is being utilised to enable the efficient transfer of information throughout the business. It is most likely that this approach was led by the sales force and supported by specialist staff.

Mixed – inside out

An example of the mixed – inside out approach at Moonshine was the introduction of PCs into the user environment and the following expansion of the tasks undertaken using PCs. This occurred largely as a result of departments becoming responsible for their own budgets and competing over output, turnover and bonus rates. This example shows how staff realised they could utilise the technology they had to meet business objectives which resulted in the growth of a number of independent systems outside corporate policies concerning hardware and software. The trend was towards decentralised IS, which conflicted with the corporate centralised strategy. The drivers behind this inside-out, creative approach were the departmental managers.

(iii) The **three legs** or **IS strategy planning approaches** are not mutually exclusive – over time an organisation is likely to use all three. IS strategy should be driven by a combination of business needs, technological opportunities and organisational capability. If the organisation followed one approach only, key aspects would be ignored (eg the bottom up approach neglects business plans and the top down approach undervalues customer needs).

So, different legs will be **dominant** at different times depending upon the situation. In fact, the three approaches compliment each other. In large organisations such as Moonshine Corporation, it could be argued that innovation requires a supporting infrastructure, while on the other hand an infrastructure for the sake of it stifles innovation and creativity. Therefore, often a balanced approach is best.

Customer service is a key **competitive element** for Moonshine and its competitors. Today, efficient fast customer service invariably depends upon efficient and effective IS/IT systems. To achieve this requires the use of all three legs – no one approach to developing an IS strategy is adequate when used alone.

58 TEAC

(a)

Text reference. IS strategy (part (a)) covers material in Chapters 1 and 2 of the text. The 3Cs (part (b)) are covered in Chapter 8. Gap analysis (part (c)) is discussed in Chapter 7.

Top tips. The first part of this question requires you to discuss the importance of formulating an information systems strategy that aligns with a business strategy. This topic is a core area of the syllabus. No particular theory or framework is specified, which gives you the chance to include one or more relevant theories. The second part of the question requires you to discuss how effective TEAC has been in the alignment of their business and information systems strategies. There is evidence to suggest that TEAC has not always been successful in maintaining a close alignment of the strategies.

Easy marks. The relationship between information systems strategy and information systems strategy is an important area – and one that you should be familiar with.

Examiner's comments. In part (i), many candidates provided good answers by applying one of more different theories to the question requirement. Some used frameworks such as Earl's reasons for having an IS strategy, his 'three leg' analysis or other theories.

Better answers to part (ii) applied theory to the case study. Weaker answers tended to simply restate the stages in IT development in TEAC without showing how this development related to business strategy.

Marking scheme

		Marks
(i)	Award up to 2 marks for each valid point up to a max of 10 marks.	10
(ii)	Award up to 2 marks for each valid example. Max 10 marks.	10
		20

(i)   **Overview**

In general terms, the information systems strategy of an organisation needs to align with the business strategy to ensure that both are successful. In situations where the business strategy is not supported by the information required to meet that strategy, or where information systems are attempting to 'take over' the business without regard for the strategy, the two strategies will be in conflict and the business overall will suffer.

Other, more specific reasons, for aligning the strategies include:

Cost

Provision of appropriate IS remains a high cost activity for any business. Appropriate budgets and control are therefore required to ensure that expenditure on IS actually meets the business requirements. Without control, IS expenditure could be on inappropriate systems which do not support the business. This may lead to expensive mistakes in information provision, meaning that the organisation cannot afford to implement other necessary IT systems.

Competitive advantage

In many organisations, information is a source of competitive advantage. Organisations therefore develop information strategies to provide the information necessary to provide that advantage. However, to obtain competitive advantage information, provision must be focused on the business strategy to ensure appropriate competitive advantage is obtained.

Success of the business

Provision of appropriate information is critical to the success of the organisation. Information systems are required in many different roles to provide the necessary information to enable the business to run effectively. For example, support and operational systems are required to capture basic transaction data and strategic systems are required to obtain competitive advantage. The IS strategy must be set to provide this information to ensure that the business operates successfully.

Stakeholders

Alignment of business and IS strategy is essential to provide stakeholders with confidence in the organisation. If strategies are seen to be at odds with each other, this will decrease confidence in the company, adversely affecting share price and the ability of the company to raise capital. Also, customers may not be attracted to the organisation simply because they are not provided with the information they need to make purchases (eg lack of appropriate product information). The ability of the company to make sales will therefore be limited.

(ii)   TEAC has managed to align its business and IS strategies as follows:

Historical development

TEAC appears to have been one of the first companies to implement various new IS developments such as computerised warehousing, management information systems and EPOS terminals. Presumably these additions to the IS systems assisted TEAC by decreasing costs and providing good customer service. These features would be of use in the retail trade where customers are price conscious but also expect to be able to pay for goods and leave a shop quickly after choosing their purchases.

Current provision of company information

As a company with many retail outlets and subsidiaries, TEAC needs to collate information from each location on a regular basis in order to provide company wide reports. This objective is facilitated by provision of EPOS terminals to collect sales information on a timely basis and a Wide Area Network to transfer sales data to head office for amalgamation into group reports.

Project development

TEAC has a large in-house IS department to provide the applications that TEAC needs. This means that systems development can be focused on the precise requirements of TEAC rather than having to purchase 'off the shelf' which may mean software does not have the specific functionality needed. Project development is therefore focused on business needs and systems can be amended in line with changes in those needs.

Different systems

One of TEAC's business objectives has been to acquire subsidiaries and retails outlets as required. However, each acquisition resulted in different IS systems being introduced into the company. The IS strategy has been to amend those systems to conform to the standard systems already run by TEAC. IS strategy supports the business strategy by continuing to provide the appropriate information to run the company efficiently.

Business requirements not met

There are some indications that IS strategy does not always meet the business requirements in TEAC. Specific examples of this include the lack of user involvement in some projects and cancellation of a project following cost overruns. This implies that at least one project was not specified correctly, possibly because the exact business need for that project had not been determined.

(b)

Top tips. These topics are standard textbook knowledge and were supplemented by an article in the March 2003 issue of *Student accountant*. Refer to the ACCA website for copies of past articles relevant to this paper.

Easy marks. Define the concepts and then relate them to the case study.

Examiner's comments. Most answers explained the three concepts of commitment, coordination and control in an appropriate amount of detail. The main weakness of most answers related to lack of provision of examples from the scenario. Most answers were therefore too short to obtain a pass standard.

Marking scheme

	Marks
Award up to 3 marks for each description of Commitment, Coordination and Communication.	
Award up to 3 marks for identifying an example of each of the Cs within TEAC.	
Award up to 2 marks for extra examples.	<u>20</u>

Commitment

Commitment to any change must be universal including all parties involved in the system development.

Senior management show commitment by allocating appropriate resources to system development. In this case, resources are identified in terms of people, money and time.

In TEAC, it appears that senior management are committed to systems development because they have enabled the introduction of new IT systems such as the EPOS terminals. There is some indication that commitment may be slightly less now, given that the IT manager considers that management need to take more responsibility for the IT infrastructure. However, the IT department does have a large budget and apparently sufficient staff, indicating ongoing commitment of senior management in these areas.

Other groups in the firm appear also be committed to change. The IT manager may have expressed doubts about current system development, but she still wants appropriate system development to take place. Similarly, the IT Committee expects development to take place where required. The comment 'if it's not broke then don't fix it' may be interpreted to limiting development to essential areas.

There may also be a need to obtain more commitment from individual divisional managers. Making the managers jointly responsible for the success or failure of projects in their departments will help to improve their commitment.

Coordination

To implement any new systems successfully requires coordination. This involves ensuring those involved in the process work in an efficient and effective way toward an agreed common goal. This objective requires appropriate planning and control to help ensure that the right people are using the right resources at the right time to facilitate completion of the project on time.

Coordination will need to start at the beginning of a project. Lack of coordination will result in the project taking longer and costing more than budgeted. It is not clear in TEAC whether the large budget and failure of one systems project was actually a result of lack of coordination due to some other cause. Large budgets can result from a lack of ability to coordinate projects, leading to higher budgetary demands. Similarly, project failure may result from lack of coordination, resulting in project time overruns making the project too late to be effective. It is not clear from the scenario whether appropriate project management tools such as Gantt charts and network diagrams had been used to control projects. Lack of these tools will mean less overall control of projects, leading to risk of overruns. However, there does appear to be scope for better project coordination within TEAC indicating deficiencies in this area.

Control of projects within TEAC is currently assigned to the IT department. While this department should have the appropriate project management skills, additional involvement may be useful to ensure appropriate coordination. Providing some input from managers of user departments may be helpful as they will have a vested interest in projects being completed on time. External assistance may also help the IT department focus on the bigger picture of completing projects rather than being task orientated and missing the need for overall coordination.

Communication

Implementation of new systems is unlikely to be achieved without good communication. The right people must communicate the right things at the right time and in the right way. Specifically, good communication early in any project will help to ensure that team members are aware of what the project is to achieve, enabling them to work towards that objective.

Communication during the project will also aid coordination and help maintain momentum in the project. Finally, on completion, communication is likely to focus on ensuring that there is no revision to previous behaviour, with a review of the project ensuring that lessons learnt are recorded for future reference.

Within TEAC, there appears to be good communication in some areas:

- The steering committee communicates with the Board to authorise new projects, so the latter are aware of projects being undertaken.

- Board requirements requiring implementation of new technology have been met resulting in TEAC becoming one of the leaders in this area.

However, communication is limited in some areas:

- Insufficient user input is obtained. A new system may be rejected either because it does not meet user requirements, or because users do not take 'ownership'.

- The implementation of Internet sales within a single retail group does not appear to have been well communicated. Other groups were surprised to learn of this system.

- The recent gap analysis showing considerable investment required in information systems is also indicative of poor communication. This suggests requirements have not been monitored.

In summary, better communication is needed to try and ensure success of all projects.

(c)

Top tips. The question provided candidates with clear guidelines with regard to the contents of the report. Your report should '… briefly explain and critique the use of structured methodologies'.

Easy marks. Both gap analysis and the applications portfolio are standard textbook knowledge. Explaining these should gain some easy marks – but you must apply them to the circumstances described in the scenario to do well.

Examiner's comments. In part (i), the main weakness in many answers was the lack of any comment on the applications portfolio. This severely limited the marks that could be awarded. However, severe time pressure may have been one of the reasons for this apparent omission.

Answers to part (ii) were of a mixed standard. There were a few very good answers although a significant number of poorer answers. Weaker answers tended to focus on describing TEAC's systems or soft system methodology rather than the weaknesses of hard system design. Only a few answers used the scenario information to show the weaknesses in structured methodologies, to meet the question requirement.

Marking scheme

		Marks
(i)	Award up to 5 marks for a description of gap analysis.	5
	Award up to 5 marks for a suitable grid and a discussion of applications portfolio.	5
(ii)	Award up to 2 marks for each valid point up to a max 10 marks.	10
		20

(i) **Gap analysis**

Gap analysis is used to show the **difference between the desired (or planned) position with the actual or predicted progress.**

A graph is developed by ascertaining the information requirements of the organisation and use of information analysis to show where those needs are being met. The different between the desired information requirements and the actual information provision becomes a gap. Having identified the gap, information systems can be developed in an attempt to close the information gap.

Two types of gap are recognised:

- A **simple gap** where the current position does not meet the current expectation level.
- A **continuous gap** where the predicted position does not meet the predicted expectation level.

Information strategy is concerned with closing the continuous gap, that is a gap identified in the future. A range of options can be developed which will attempt to close the gap, including in-house and off-the-shelf purchases. The option which best closes the gap will be chosen and implemented.

Applications portfolio

Peppard developed the strategic grid (also called the applications portfolio) to analyse the strategic impact of individual applications within an organisation. The Portfolio was described in a table as shown below.

Strategic importance of individual applications in the current competitive environment

		Low	High
Strategic importance of applications in the predicted future competitive environment	Low	Support	Key Operational
	High	High potential	Strategic

Applications are placed onto the table in accordance with their strategic importance in the competitive environment now and in the predicted future.

- **Support** applications are of low strategic importance now or in the future. They include accounting systems and legally required systems

- **Key operational** applications are important now but may not be in the future, as they may be replaced by newer systems

- **Strategic** applications are important now and in the future and are therefore vital to the success of the organisation

- **High potential** applications are of low importance now but may be more important in the future. They are innovative and therefore provide significant benefit to the organisation

The scenario indicates that there is a continuous gap in TEAC which needs to be filled by new information systems. Using the grid, the IT manager can determine which application will provide the most benefit in the future and focus resources on developing those systems. They are likely to be high potential systems. Resources will also be focused on maintaining the strategic systems as they are currently providing the most benefit to TEAC.

(ii) **Report**

To: IS Steering committee
From: IT Director
Subject: Use of structured methodologies
Date: June 200X

The use of structured methodologies may be one reason for the backlog of information systems development within TEAC. These traditional methodologies tend to inhibit development of systems as outlined below.

Analysis of existing systems

A great deal of time is spent analysing existing systems to determine what processes they use and their weaknesses. This process was useful in TEAC where existing systems were being automated, as happened with large systems projects in the past. It may be more effective to start with a clean sheet of paper and decide what processes are actually needed, rather than analysing what is currently available.

Data driven

Structured methodologies tend to focus on the data within the system enabling the production of multiple standard documentation such as Data Flow Diagrams. While useful for system analysis, the documentation again assumes that similar data will be needed in old and new systems. However, data requirements are likely to change with TEAC as the main data processing systems are already in place. Focusing on the processes required, as noted above, may provide a more effective method of system development.

Defined structure

Structured methodologies follow a defined and fairly rigorous structure, with each stage in the design process having to be complete prior to the start of the next stage. This has been of benefit to TEAC where systems development was structured and the focus was on amending and upgrading existing systems. As systems requirements become less clear, a defined structure is of limited use. We need the ability to amend specifications quickly without having to revisit previous design stages. Alternative methodologies provide this flexibility.

User perspective

Users are correctly involved in the design of systems using structured methodologies. However, actual examples of screen layouts and user input requirements are only provided a significant way into the design processing, leaving little room for amendment. Within TEAC, many applications such as Management Information Systems need to be clearly designed around user input.

System amendments

Amendments to systems using structured methodologies are possible, but they make take significant time to implement. Given that transaction processing systems tend not to change much anyway, few amendments were necessary. However, the strategic systems that TEAC now requires are likely to change more frequently as managers' and directors' information requirements change. A more flexible design and amendment process may allow this to happen.

In conclusion, the current methodologies are constraining development work and alternatives need to be considered.

59 CAET Co

(a)

Text reference. The SWOT analysis in part (a) is discussed in text Chapter 6. Business case justification in part (b) is covered in Chapter 5.

Top tips. You must be able to produce a SWOT analysis based on a particular information system. Refer to Chapter 6 of your BPP Text if this question caused you problems. In this question, you must apply your knowledge to the situation described in the scenario. Ensure your answers to (ii) and (iii) refer to the four possible strategies given to you in the question.

Easy marks. The grid in part (ii) is relatively self-explanatory even if you are unfamiliar with *McLaughlin's* grid – an opportunity to pick up six easy marks.

Examiner's comments. Part (i) was normally answered very well with many candidates obtaining maximum marks. Part (ii) was also answered well. Part (iii) was the weakest of the three sections due to some lack of application of the theory to the situation outlined in the scenario. Many answers tended to repeat information from part (ii) rather than showing how the theory applied to Caet.

		Marks
(i)	Award up to 2 marks for each element, 4 elements. Max 8 marks.	8
(ii)	Award 1 mark per quadrant description and up to 2 marks for an understanding of the grid. Max 6 marks.	6
(iii)	Award 1 mark for each valid point about each strategy up to a max of 4 marks.	4
	Up to 2 marks for explaining which strategy applies best to Caet. Max 6 marks	6
		20

(i)

Strengths	Weaknesses
• Already has website and experience with web technology • Resources available for POP development • Strong customer base • Recent experience in installing IT systems (Intranet and extranet)	• Current website basic – no online purchases • Unclear how much additional sales or profit new system will generate • Change in business strategy – can Caet support? • Query whether existing bespoke systems acceptable for e-commerce
Opportunities	**Threats**
• Enhance website • Provide another channel to market • Enhance customer database – more effective marketing • Extend customer base – don't need to shop in-store • Update image of company – more modern	• Market share falling last three years • Competitive market place • Competitors have better online presence • Must ensure can establish appropriate security on Internet site • Pricing issue – may be competing against own stores • Caet's customers may not like/be unable to shop online

(ii) This grid was devised by *McLaughlin*. The four broad SWOT responses it identifies are explained below.

Attack – 'go for it'

This approach is appropriate where the organisation has a strong IS capability and a suitable opportunity to exploit. The organisation can attack competitors using IS. If an organisation has strong IT and can see an appropriate opportunity, then this strategy can be used.

Explore – 'if we have time'

Appropriate where an organisation has strong IS capability and is facing a possible threat. The organisation needs to explore ways of using IS to maintain its strong competitive position.

Beware – 'don't do it'

This strategy is appropriate where an organisation has poor IS capability but is considering an IS opportunity. The opportunity should be investigated, but care is needed as a lack of appropriate IS capability may mean the opportunity is wasted. Additional IS skills may be required.

Protect – 'watch yourself'

The strategy is appropriate when an organisation has a poor IS capability and is facing threats from its competitors. The organisation needs to take steps to protect itself from its competitors, which almost certainly will mean upgrading its IS capability.

(iii) At present, Caet has a good IS capability as indicated by the in-house development of projects and the experimental use of newer IT such as Internet. The company also have good IT infrastructure and a large IT department indicating it should be able to take on board new IT projects without too much problem.

The external environment indicates that Caet is under threat from newer Internet based companies. Its website is a showcase only, and does not support e-commerce. This is an area that Caet needs to improve, assuming it has the time and will benefit from the strategy. The online shopping system (POPS) therefore fits into the **explore** section of the McLaughlin grid.

However, it could be argued that other sections of the grid may also apply.

The online shopping system could fit into the **beware** category if the current IS capability was seen to be weak. A lack of e-commerce experience within the IT department would be indicative of this area.

The system could fit into the **protect** category if online shopping was seen to be replacing store shopping. Caet does not have any online presence, and store profits are falling.

It is unlikely that online shopping fits into the **attack** section of the grid because there does not appear to be any competitive advantage to be gained by Caet in this area. Other companies are already trading on the Internet and Caet appears to be more in a catch up phase rather than obtaining competitive advantage over rivals.

(b)

Top tips. You should be familiar with the typical elements included in an IS business case report (eg terms of reference, summary of the present position, what the system will provide, how this links to the IS and overall objectives of the organisation, evaluation of the different options considered, conclusions and recommendation).

Easy marks. If you follow the guidance given in our answer plan below, your answer will be well structured and the marks should flow relatively easily. List the headings, then flesh out the content.

Examiner's comments. In part (i), high marks were obtained where candidates mentioned the different sections of a business case report along with explanation of each section and some application to the situation in Caet. Answers obtained fewer marks where the report headings only were provided with little or no discussion within each section.

Part (ii). A significant number of answers presented a discussion of tangible benefits, which did not meet the question requirement. However, other candidates did discuss different approaches to valuing intangible benefits to obtain a good pass standard.

Marking scheme

		Marks
(i)	Award up to 3 marks for each element with appropriate suggestions up to a max 15 marks.	15
(ii)	Award up to 2 marks for each approach. Max 5 marks.	5
		20

Answer plan

An answer plan is provided to part (b) as a guide to producing a business case report.

(i) *Explanation of structure of report*

Based on the definition: 'reasoned discussion to show why a particular project should be undertaken'.

Explanation of cost benefit analysis

Outline suggestions for contents of report (apply each to CAET circumstances)

Key areas of a business case report:

- Introduction and terms of reference
- Outline of the current position
- Relevant objectives
- Gap analysis
- Different options explored
- Summary cost benefit analysis
- Conclusion and recommendation

Outline of possible technical solution

In store information on stock availability.

(ii) Methods of appraising system projects taking into account intangible benefits:

- Estimating the value of intangibles
- Ignore the 'too intangible' benefits
- Adopt a qualitative approach

(i) **Explanation of report aims and structure**

A business case report presents a reasoned discussion to show why a particular project should be undertaken. It summarises the current situation and explains where the organisation would like to be (a gap analysis). The report considers different methods of closing the gap and finally recommends a course of action.

One of the key areas of the report is a **cost benefit analysis**. This presents all relevant costs and benefits relating to the proposed course of action. Costs are relatively easy to determine as these relate mainly to the tangible elements of the system such as new hardware, software, training requirements and data conversion. Benefits may be difficult to identify and quantify as they are normally intangible eg improved staff morale, better customer service and retention, improved decision making. However, to complete the CBA, the value of benefits should be estimated.

Suggested **outline contents** of a business case report is provided below.

1 Introduction and terms of reference

This section explains why the report is being written, referring to the Board minutes or similar evidence authorising the report. In Caet, the report will refer to the need to enhance customer services by access to the store stock recording system.

2 Outline of the current position highlighting problem areas

This section provides detail on why there is currently a problem and the reasons for it. In Caet this would include the problem of customers paying for goods and then queuing for items only to find that they are out of stock. These customers are likely to then leave the store without purchasing alternatives. One of the key issues that need to be addressed is that the whole ordering process has to be repeated, which customers find unacceptable due to the time involved.

3 Relevant objectives from the organisation's information system strategy

These objectives will be stated to show that the system will bring benefits related to the IS strategy and contribute to the achievement of organisational goals. Caet wants to enhance customer satisfaction – the proposed PIPS system will help achieve this by allowing earlier checking of stock balances.

4 Gap analysis

The gap analysis will show the gap between the information provided by current systems and the information required. In this situation, the gap does not appear to be excessive. Information on stock balances is already available – the main issue is how to allow users access to this information.

5 Different options explored and a summary cost benefit analysis

This section will outline possible different methods of meeting the needs identified. Various options will be considered and a cost benefit analysis produced for the most popular suggestion.

6 Conclusion and recommended course of action

A conclusion will be drawn for which system to implement along with the proposed method for implementing that solution.

Outline of one possible technical solution for the proposal

Caet already hold the information on stock balances on the organisation's intranet. This information needs to be made accessible from within each store. Terminals that allow access to the intranet should be installed that provide this access to stock information to customers (restricted, 'read only' access to this information only). Customers should input the part number to determine stock availability, which will be displayed on screen. The 'available items' figure should be reduced upon payment to ensure records of available items are accurate.

(ii)   Alternative methods of appraising system projects taking into account intangible benefits include:

Estimating the value of intangibles. While this is possible, realistically it is little more than guesswork and so is normally discounted. The method may assist the PIPS application by identifying some of the benefits such as customer satisfaction and retention. However, the Board may well reject the results due to the estimation involved.

Ignore the 'too intangible' benefits. Values can be placed on some intangibles, but the 'very' intangible ones are ignored. While this approach is possible, it will still underestimate the value of intangible costs and benefits. As benefits are likely to be more difficult to quantify than costs, the overall benefit of a project will still be understated. Again this will not help the PIPS application as many of the benefits are intangible and need to be included in the analysis in some way to justify the project.

Adopt a qualitative approach. In other words find a reasonable method of measuring the intangibles. For example, customer satisfaction ratings can be used to determine quality of customer service, or increase in market share as an indication of increased competitive advantage. Unfortunately this approach also has weaknesses as much of the information will only be available after implementation and appropriate measures may be hard to determine. An alternative will be to use changes in customer satisfaction ratings from previous projects such as the initial implementation of the Internet site within Caet to try to provide a realistic valuation of benefits.

(c)

> **Top tips.** The three key factors provided in the example answer are project size, project structure, and the technology involved – but credit would be given for alternative viable suggestions.
>
> **Easy marks.** In part (ii), use the factors highlighted in part (i) and apply them to the case study.
>
> **Examiner's comments.** In part (i), various alternatives were given for the different factors affecting project risk apart from the textbook size, structure and experience with technology.
>
> In part (ii), many answers tended to discuss risk in general terms with little or no application to the case study. High marks were obtained where the three risk factors were applied to the case and clear recommendations given regarding the risk inherent in the project.

Marking scheme

		Marks
(i)	Award up to 4 marks for each factor. Max 12 marks.	12
(ii)	Award up to 2 marks per factor plus 2 marks for overall assessment. Max 8 marks.	8
		20

(i)   **Factors affecting project risk**

Project structure

In general terms, the more structure the project has, the lower the risk of project failure.

In terms of a project, a high degree of structure indicates that the project sponsor is clear on the deliverables required from the project. This means that a precise project plan can be drawn up and progress of the project monitored against the plan as the project progresses. There is a high probability that implementation will be successful because users have also agreed to the deliverables.

Projects with unclear deliverables are more likely to fail, simply because it is not clear what the project has to deliver. Where the outcomes keep changing it is very difficult to amend the project specification, while cost and time overruns will almost certainly develop. The project will 'fail' not only on meeting deliverables, but also by being over time and over budget.

The technology involved

In general terms, the more a project uses new technology, the greater the risk of project failure.

In a project, limited use of technology indicates a low risk of failure either because the technology is understood, or because there is a lower reliance on technology to provide the deliverables. Where technology is understood, it can be implemented without risk because IT staff will already have experience with that technology.

However, where technology is new or untested, risk is increased as IT staff may not have experience with that technology. Risk can be minimised by providing ongoing training of IT staff. However, as technology is continually changing, there will still be situations where technology has not been used before. As the actual outcomes in an operational environment are unclear, risk of failure is increased.

Project size

In general terms, the larger the project, the higher the risk of project failure.

The size of a project can be defined in terms of cost, number of staff involved and the duration of the project. As the size increases, it will become more difficult to monitor expenditure, control and coordinate the staff and retain focus on project deadlines and deliverables, thus increasing the risk of failure.

Small projects are easier to control in terms of the budget, staff and focus on the final deliverables. Small projects are less complex, so there is less chance of the project manager missing a critical issue and literally fewer activities that may fail.

Summary

Projects that are small, have limited use of technology and have a high degree of structure have less risk than projects which are large, use newer technology and have a low degree of structure.

Project risk is minimised by assessing the importance of these three items at the beginning of the project and then assigning appropriate control procedures to limit each risk. For example, large projects are controlled by using network analysis and similar project management tools. Choice of the correct tools, which appear to be outside the scope of this answer, will help to ensure project success.

(ii) **PIPS – risk assessment**

Project structure

The project sponsor has a clear idea of the deliverable, ie allowing customers access to the stock database prior to ordering goods. This objective will be accomplished by placing terminals allowing access to Caet's intranet within each store.

As the deliverable and the method of achieving that deliverable are clear, there will be a high degree of project structure. Risk analysis for this category is 'low'.

Project size

The project appears to be of a large size as all of Caet's 150 stores will need terminals to enable customers to access the intranet. Also, hardware will need to be purchased, software written and tested and terminals installed to meet the project objective. Project duration in terms of installing terminals in all stores and cost in terms of hardware will be high. In this sense the project size is large.

However, activities in the project will be duplicated across each of the stores, so successful implementation in one pilot store should mean successful implementation in the other 149 stores. Overall project risk is therefore limited provided the first implementation is satisfactory. Risk analysis for this category is 'medium'.

Technology

Caet already have the necessary information on stock balances on their databases, with an intranet being used to access that information. Provision of additional terminals and access to the database for the PIPS system is therefore duplicating existing systems to a large extent. The only new area is ensuring that terminals are dedicated to accessing only the stock system. IT staff are therefore familiar with the use of the technology. Overall risk assessment for this category is 'low'.

Conclusion

Overall risk evaluation for the project is 'low'. Although the project is large, there is little use of new technology and a high degree of project structure which limits the overall risk involved.

60 Seemore Co

(a)

Marking scheme

		Marks
(i)	Award up to 2 marks for each element, 4 elements, max of 8 marks.	8
(ii)	Award up to 2 marks for introduction. Award up to 2 marks for each valid point in the body of the report, max 8 marks. Award up to 2 marks for conclusion.	12 20

(i) **PEST analysis** is used to examine the various influences on an organisation.

Political

The proposed use of the Internet site for ordering will require an analysis of current legislation concerning data protection, EU directive on SPAM e-mail etc. The development of the new system may affect internal politics within Seemore. Will disputes about growth strategy affect the company's trading ability?

Economic

Is Internet trading a viable option. More information will be required on potential sales, competitors etc. Will Internet trading compete with, enhance or replace the existing supply of videos and DVDs?

Funding will be required for either expansion in the number of outlets or Internet trading and cashflow, interest rate etc information will be required.

Social

What is the market for Internet provision? The decline in the monthly rental system may be due to social changes and trends which may impact on other areas of the business.

There may be changes in the job structure within Seemore and possible redundancies which need to be planned for.

Technological

Previous technology developments have been successful in Seemore but do they have the appropriate skills for development of the Internet site? Can the new system be integrated with the existing system? Do sufficient customers have the required technology to use the Internet ordering service?

(ii) **REPORT**

To: Irvine Seymour
From: IT Specialist
Subject: Implementation of Video ordering system
Date: 20th June 200X

As requested, I have prepared a brief report on the possible development and implementation of an Internet based video ordering system in Seemore.

Introduction – rationale for system

Seemore provides a video/DVD rental service, currently using shops and a limited postal system. The Internet is seen as a way of expanding the customer base while maintaining focus on video/DVD rental.

Factors to consider

It is hoped that using the Internet will expand Seemore's customer base, particularly in rural areas. The Internet can also be used to provide information and improve service for existing customers, either providing details of DVD's currently available, or checking stocks on-line in shops to ensure titles are available prior to visiting the store. Online reservation may be provided for shop customers.

Changes to technology will be required in two areas. Firstly, implementing and maintaining the Internet site, and secondly linking the site with the existing stock systems. Given that Seemore has successfully implemented IT systems in the past, it can be expected that the Internet site can also be established successfully. The current systems will need to be enhanced and adapted.

Development of the Internet site could take place in-house, as long as the existing IT staff have the appropriate skills. If not, Seemore does have a good history of working with external consultants to develop new IT systems, and this option can be used again. Where third party assistance is required, care must be taken to ensure Seemore retains ownership of the code for the Internet site, or appropriate escrow agreements are established.

As Seemore is unlikely to be the first company to offer video rentals on the Internet (the initial boom in Internet companies was three or four years ago), then significant advertising will be necessary to promote knowledge of the new service. Appropriate budgets will have to be agreed.

Obtaining customer details via the Internet is unlikely to be a problem as Seemore already maintain customer databases. Some work will be required linking the Internet data with the existing systems. Computer security may need to be enhanced given that online update of customer details will now be necessary.

Other options

Other options that are also being considered are:

- Opening new stores
- Closing the existing mail order systems

Any review of the company must also consider these options in more detail.

Conclusion

Given that Seemore needs to expand its customer base, the Internet option is attractive because it is not limited by the physical location of stores. Seemore also has the appropriate skills and the development appears to fit the overall business strategy. The next stage of development will be for a full Board discussion and presentation of a cost benefit analysis.

(b)

Marking scheme

		Marks
(i)	Award up to 2 marks for each valid point, max 8 marks.	8
(ii)	Award 1 mark for each CSF in the correct level of management. 3 × 2 marks.	6
(iii)	Award 1 mark for each PI and 1 mark for information required. 3 × 2 marks.	6
		20

(i) **Critical Success Factors (CSF)** are the limited number of areas in which results, if they are satisfactory, will ensure successful competitive performance. They are the few key areas where things must go right for a business to flourish.

CSF analysis was developed by Rockhart. CSFs help to determine the information requirements of an organisation by identifying the key areas that the organisation must pay attention to. Initially, the organisation will set its business strategy and objectives. CSFs are then developed to check whether the strategic objectives are being met. For example, an organisation may have the objective of expansion and so a CSF will be to increase the market share. To determine whether or not market share is actually increasing, information will be required; in this case, the total market size and the sales of the organisation to compute market share. Setting the strategic objectives and CSF's will lead directly into determining the information requirements of the organisation.

Rockhart identified **four general sources for CSFs**:

- The industry that the business is in

- The company itself and its situation within the industry

- The environment, eg customer trends, the economy and political factors in the country the organisation is based in

- Temporal organisational factors, that is short term objectives relating to areas where the organisation's performance is currently unacceptable

All of these areas will generate information requirements. The organisation will need to ensure that appropriate information systems are in place to enable the CSFs to be adequately monitored and reported on.

Each CSF will be monitored by establishing appropriate Performance Indicators, as shown in part (b) and (c) of this answer.

(ii)&(iii)

CSF	Performance Indicator
Strategic	
Increase in market share, specifically by attracting new online customers	Obtain a 5% market share in the Internet market within next 12 months
Maintain a high level of customer satisfaction	
Tactical	
Ensure sufficient stock is available to meet customer demand	Stockouts limited to 1% of videos/DVDs offered for rental each month
Ensure prices charged on the Internet are competitive	
Operational	
Orders fulfilled within the stated timescale	99% of orders despatched to customers within 24 hours of the order being received
Customer video/DVD hire monitored and late returns identified and investigated	

Additional comment for part (ii)

Each CSF can be measured by establishing Performance Indicators (PIs). The PI will be SMART, that is Specific, Measurable, Attainable, Relevant and Timely. The PI must relate to the CSF and be capable of being checked by including specific and measurable objectives. The PIs next to each CSF meet these criteria.

The PI also identifies the information requirement to check whether or not that PI and therefore the related CSF has been attained. Information systems will need to be established to provide this information.

(c)

Top tips. When discussing the characteristics of an effectively designed website, don't provide overly technical information. For example, you will earn a mark for saying download/communication speed is important so overly complex graphics and animation may not be appropriate – but there is no need to go into the technical details relating to this.

Easy marks. Ensure in part (ii) that you answer from the perspective of the customer. You should provide two or three advantages and two or three disadvantages – see the marking scheme below.

Examiner's comments. Part (i) was well answered. The mark earning ability of some answers was limited where reference was not made to the situation in Seemore.

Part (ii) again provided some good answers. The main weakness in some answers was answering the question from the point-of-view of Seemore rather than the customer.

Marking scheme

		Marks
(i)	Award up to 1 mark for each valid characteristic. Max 5 marks. Award up to 5 for relating them to the scenario.	10
(ii)	Award up to 2 marks for each advantage and disadvantage. Up to a max of 5 marks in each category. Max 10 marks.	10
		20

(i) **Website characteristics**

Response time

The website must load onto the customer's PC quickly, otherwise they may abort the download and select another site. Seemore must ensure that a balance is achieved by providing the necessary information for customers to identify the purpose of the site, without downloading full product listing until requested by the customer.

Response quality

The website must 'look good'. It must be legible, present appropriate graphics and be easy to navigate. Again, if the site appears cluttered, or customers cannot quickly find the options and information they require, they will move on to another video/DVD renting site.

Security/Trust

As Seemore will be taking video/DVD bookings over the Internet, together with personal information for each customer including credit/debit card details, the website must have an appropriate degree of security. Use of Secure Socket Layer (SSL), with the 'padlock' symbol displayed on the Internet page will provide re-assurance to the customer. Similarly, Seemore can have the website assured by a third party such as Verisign to confirm that transactions are secure.

Fulfilment

Seemore's customers must believe that after an order for videos/DVDs has been placed, the film will actually arrive within the specified time frame. Similarly, re-assurance must be provided on the web site to explain that if films do not arrive, Seemore will take appropriate action. The website must contain clear links to Seemore's delivery and complaints procedures so customers can see the service levels provided.

Up-to-date

Seemore will be offering videos/DVDs for hire, with the customer determining availability by seeing stock on the website. The site must therefore be linked to the back-office stock systems in Seemore to ensure that videos/DVDs are not offered for rental that are out of stock.

Availability

The Internet site should be available 24 hours per day, 7 days per week. This will help to maximise Seemore's sales and provide service when required by the customer.

(ii) **Advantages of Internet video ordering**

The customer can order videos at any time, they are not constrained by the opening hours of Seemore shops.

Videos can be ordered from the comfort of the customers home, they do not have to go out to the shop to order or collect the video. Travelling time and costs will be saved.

Videos provide a relatively safe form of sale media. Customers have a good idea of the product they are buying and are less likely to return a video as being unsuitable (as compared to clothes, for example).

Additional information can be provided with each video such as the actors, type of film, brief summary etc making the renting experience more interesting, as well as helping the customer to choose a video to match their requirements quickly and easily.

Customers can compare prices across a range of companies quickly and easily. Given the price sensitivity of videos, Seemore will need to set its pricing strategy very carefully to ensure sales are maximised. Customers can easily move to other video hiring companies if a cheaper alternative is found.

Disadvantages of Internet video ordering

The customer may lose some social interaction gained from going out of their house and meeting people at the shops etc. Society as a whole starts to become more insular.

Not all potential customers will have access to the Internet, limiting potential sales to some extent.

Many customers are uncertain about the security of purchasing goods from the Internet. Seemore must provide re-assurance on the website or provide details of telephone ordering if this is considered appropriate.

Lack of personal contact with Seemore shop staff may have an adverse impact on perception of service offered by Seemore.

Fulfilment relies on the postal system. This is effectively out of Seemore's control unless more expensive delivery options such as timed delivery are chosen.

61 Question with helping hand: ACET Co

(a)

Text reference. The framework in part (a) is covered in Chapter 5 of the text. SWOT analysis (part (b)) in Chapter 6 and ethics (part (c)) in Chapter 9.

Top tips. Refer back to this material if you struggled with this question. As there are four stages to cover for these two factors, that's eight separate areas to cover in your answer.

Easy marks. Ensure your answer relates to the case study and covers both business strategy in general and also the GMPP system.

Examiner's comments. A pass standard answer needed to include both an explanation of each stage and application of information in the scenario to that stage. The ACCA marking scheme notes that maximum marks can only be obtained by mentioning the case study. Unfortunately, there is no split to show marks available for pure theory and then application to the case.

Marking scheme

	Marks
Up to five marks for each stage. To obtain max marks for each stage candidates must make reference to the case study.	<u>20</u>

Where we were

Where we were refers to a review of the past. It includes a review of the development of both business and information strategies. The main reason for this stage of planning is to review the historical context of the current systems so that reasons for failure can be understood and avoided in the future.

Within ACET, it appears that information systems have been developed to support the overall business strategy. The decentralised structure has meant that individual divisions have developed their own systems. While this may lead to issues such as lack of compatibility, there has been some central control with major developments having to be authorised by head office. Setting of hardware and software standards will also have helped to limit any compatibility issues. It is not clear how successful the different projects have been and additional information may be needed to complete this section of the planning project within ACET.

Where we are

This stage of planning establishes what the current position is within ACET. The main aim of the stage is to understand why any new information system is being proposed. Activities carried out will include documenting the current information systems and using tools such as SWOT analysis to understand the situation of the current information systems. On completion, there will be a clear picture of where ACET is at present.

Within ACET, there is a decline in sales which is causing some concern for management. The decline appears to be being caused by additional competition in the marketplace and some weaknesses in the information technology systems in ACET. There has been a decline in the number of hits on the company website (down to 10,000 from 35,000) and information held within the individual divisions may not be being used effectively. Finally, there may also be high supply costs as each division obtains suppliers independently, minimising the possibility of gaining any purchasing economies.

Where we want to be

This stage involves devising a statement of where the organisation would like to be (also called the desired position) along with some justification in terms of cost benefit analysis, showing why that position is desirable. The stage may provide a detailed list of benefits so they can be reviewed on completion to ensure those benefits have been obtained. Both business and IS benefits will be considered.

ACET has the objective of being a leading fashion retailer. However, the organisation is currently not able to reach this objective for various reasons including:

- Lack of investment in its website
- High costs caused by purchasing inefficiencies
- Internal communication problems, with ideas in one division taking months to reach head office

There is also some uncertainty on the board regarding the feasibility and success of investing more money in new IT projects.

ACET therefore needs to state clearly its business strategy. Information systems can then be developed to meet that strategy. Investment in external and internal information systems will then have a clear justification.

Going to get there

This stage focuses on the actual work that needs to be done to move from *where we are* to *where we want to be*. A plan will be developed using techniques such as network analysis to show exactly what is involved in the project. The plan will use information from the *where we were* stage to ensure that actions in the past that resulted in failure are not repeated in this project.

Within ACET, implementing the new Global Marketing and Purchasing Project (GMPP) will be a large project. The total project may need to be broken down into a number of stages. The decentralised structure of ACET may assist here, with implementation being trialled in a limited number of divisions before world wide rollout. Alternatively, only certain parts of the system may be implemented worldwide. Taking some staged approach will also enable IT budgets to be managed effectively, as well as spreading the financial cost over a number of years.

(b)

Top tips. In part (ii), *McLaughlin*'s four possible strategies resulting from a SWOT provide an excellent framework for your answer.

Easy marks. Now you're near the end of this Kit, you should be confident producing a SWOT analysis.

Examiner's comments. Part (i) of this question was normally answered very well, with many candidates obtaining maximum marks. Answers to part (ii) varied considerably, although the McLaughlin alternative presented in this answer was recognised as a valid approach by the examiner and has the benefit of focusing clearly on the NEWS system.

		Marks
(i)	Award up to 2 marks for each element, 4 elements, max of 8 marks.	8
(ii)	Award up to 2 marks for each valid point, max 12 marks.	12
		20

(i)

Strengths	Weaknesses
Good brand name	Decentralised structure
Worldwide network in place	Divisions completing for supplies – no economies of scale
Workers have innovative ideas	Lack of IS integration
Useful IT/IS infrastructure	Website hits falling
Good customer base	Sales also falling
Experience in internet trading	
Opportunities	**Threats**
Interest in the fashion market (people always need clothes)	Competition increasing in marketplace
Can improve internal communications	Economic recession
Develop organisational learning (using NEWS)	Ability of ACET to keep up with fashion changes in the clothing industry
Above may lead to improved staff morale	
Results of the regional business process re-engineering exercise	

(ii)   **SWOT analysis** can be used as part of business case development to help provide an analysis of the current situation of the organisation. McLaughlin produced a grid based on SWOT analysis to assist in this analysis. *McLaughlin* suggests viewing the organisation in two ways:

- The situation IT currently faces in terms of providing opportunities or threats
- An evaluation of IS capability in terms of strength or weakness

Depending on the inter-relationship between these factors, different IS strategies can be determined, as noted below.

Attack – go for it

Where an organisation has strength and an opportunity to use that strength, then an appropriate response is to *attack* or use that strength. The organisation will be in a position to attack competitors using IT.

In the case of the NEWS system, ACET has strength in that employees have good ideas, but information concerning those ideas takes a long time to be disseminated throughout ACET. There is the opportunity to use that strength by setting up NEWS, allowing information to be sent around ACET quickly. Additional benefits include 24/7 system availability and third parties being able to access specific parts of NEWS to obtain information on ACET.

Explore – if we have time

In this situation, an organisation has strength in a particular area and is facing a possible threat in that area. An organisation therefore needs to *explore* ways of maintaining the position of strength. If the threat is not significant, then the amount of investigation may be limited, as indicated by the rider *if we have time* in the title to this section.

Regarding the NEWS system, it has already been noted that there is a strength regarding information that is being created by employees. There is also a potential threat that ACET is losing market share, possibly because information and good ideas are not being shared around the company. The implementation of NEWS will help to minimise that threat, and the benefit of this should be recognised in the cost benefit analysis for this new system.

Beware – don't do it

This situation arises where an organisation has a poor IS capability and is considering an IS related opportunity. However, the organisation needs to *beware* of pursuing that opportunity because of the poor IS knowledge. The general advice is not to take on the opportunity in case the opportunity is mismanaged with potential poor publicity.

Within ACET, there is an issue or weakness of a lack of overall IS integration in the organisation. ACET is decentralised, and while there are hardware and software standards being enforced, this may not guarantee compatible systems worldwide. The opportunity of NEWS relates to providing a worldwide information system. ACET will need to ensure that the IS weakness is addressed during the planning of NEWS to ensure that NEWS does work effectively.

Protect – watch yourself

This strategy is appropriate where an organisation has a weakness regarding IS capability and is facing threats from competitors. The organisation needs to take steps to *protect* itself from those threats.

The relevant in this situation is the ability of ACET to keep up-to-date with changes in the fashion industry. The weakness, as noted above, is the potential for lack of integration within the organisation resulting from decentralisation. However, if NEWS is successfully implemented, and employees can share information more effectively, then ACET has an effective method of minimising this threat.

(c)

Top tips. Follow the five-stage approach in conducting an ethical analysis suggested below.

(i)   Identify and separate facts from judgements
(ii)   Define the conflict or dilemma and identify the issues requiring judgement
(iii)   Identify all the stakeholders
(iv)   Identify the options that are available
(v)   Evaluate the consequences of the options identified

Easy marks. Use the above five-stage approach to structure your answer.

Examiner's comments. Part (i). Candidates tended to either provide a good discussion of the ethical issues, or simply list the five morale dimensions without any discussion.

Part (ii) was answered fairly well – as the subject area had been flagged in *Student accountant* (refer to the ACCA website for copies of past articles).

Marking scheme

		Marks
(i)	Award up to 1 mark for each valid point. Max 5 marks.	5
(ii)	Award up to 3 marks per stage. 5 stages @ 3 marks = 15 marks.	15
		20

(i) The introduction of information systems can raise various ethical questions for individuals and organisations. For example:

Accessibility/privacy

Information systems allow the collection and storage of large amounts of information. Much of that information will relate to individuals. The ethical question for an organisation is how much access to allow to that information while retaining the right of the individual for privacy. The Data Protection Act provides appropriate guidelines in this area, although determined hackers may still be able to break into a system and steal information. The issue then becomes how much money should the organisation spend on security.

Use of information

Individuals expect personal information to be kept securely, and only used for specific purposes. An ethical issue may then be whether an insurance company should use information on family history or the individual's own medical testing to set insurance premiums? The individual will want the information to remain private, although organisational ethics *may* be broken by using it.

Summary

There are many ethical issues regarding information systems. Information systems can affect individuals, as shown above, and those systems are growing quickly. There is therefore a case for addressing ethical issues and implementing appropriate legislation to ensure that information systems are used correctly.

(ii) **Ethical analysis**

Step 1 Separate facts from judgements

There is a need to ensure the analysis focuses on facts to remove any type of prejudice from the analysis. Facts of the dilemma include:

- The accountant has developed this system
- The system provides the accountant with some advantage over her colleagues
- The system is not being shared
- Colleagues feel disadvantaged by lack of access to the system
- The system does access company data

Step 2 Identify the ethical issues requiring judgement

The accountant has developed the system herself out of the office – should she be paid?

The company may not have been aware that the system was being developed – should development of non-standard company systems be made illegal?

Colleagues believe that information systems should be shared – are they correct?

Step 3 Identify the key stakeholders and their vested interests

- The accountant
- The company
- Colleagues in the accounts department
- ACET management
- ACET employees

Step 4 Identify the options available

- Enforce sharing of system within the accounts department
- Allow the accountant to keep using the system, but not enforce sharing
- Stop everyone, including the accountant, using the system
- Ask the IS department to provide similar functionality within ACET's systems

Step 5 Evaluate these options and their consequences, including the wider ethical consequences.

Sharing the system will make the accounting colleagues happy, although the accountant may be disappointed she has not been paid. The IS department may be concerned that systems development work will be unsupervised so a restriction on any further 'unauthorised' work will be necessary.

Letting the accountant continue to use the system will please her, but not her colleagues. There is the same issue regarding system development work already noted above.

Stopping the use of the system altogether will not please the accountant or her colleagues because their job will retain some inefficiency.

Step 6 Is a compromise required/available?

Allowing sharing of the software, but at the same time requiring any future system development work to be authorised by the IS department appears to be an acceptable compromise.

Step 7 Decide, communicate and implement the most appropriate course of action.

Whatever is decided, management must carry out this step.

62 Mercord Co

(a)

Text reference. PEST analysis (part (a)) is covered in Chapter 2 of the text. IS strategy is covered in Chapter 1. Legacy systems (part (b)) are mentioned in Chapter 9. Outsourcing (part (c)) is covered in Chapter 4.

Top tips. Ensure you are comfortable answering questions like the one in part (ii). The importance of information systems strategy aligning with business strategy is examined regularly. Ensure your answer relates to the situation described in the scenario.

Easy marks. Reproducing theory will earn some easy marks, but to score really well you must apply theory to the scenario information.

Examiner's comments. Candidates answered the first part of the question very well, with many candidates gaining maximum marks. Strong candidates in part (ii) took the opportunity to apply the theory to the case study and provided some excellent answers.

Marking scheme

		Marks
(i)	Award up to 1 mark per factor for each Sociological and Technical category. Max 4 per category. 2 × 4 marks.	8
(ii)	Award up to 2 marks per valid point, max 12 marks.	12
		20

(i) Sociological and technological factors are normally considered part of PEST analysis – which can be used as part of the strategic planning process for information systems.

Sociological factors

Job security. The number of staff required in all departments post merger. The case study suggests that already there have been staff reductions in several departments. This may affect all existing staff fearing they may be next.

Possible **power struggle** or **conflict**. There may be some duplication of management roles and confusion over responsibilities in the new structure.

Resistance to new ways of working. The new organisation will require different working practices. Change such s this often generates resistance – particularly if the change process is not managed correctly.

Bias towards own system. There appears to be some conflict on the Board of Mercord regarding the integration of systems of Mercord and Rendi. As the purchasing company, directors in Mercord may believe that their business information systems are 'better' than Rendi, and be less willing to accept Rendi's systems. On the other hand, the Rendi IS manager believes that Mercord systems are 'legacy systems or dinosaurs from a bygone age'. This bias will not help in obtaining assistance to integrate the two systems.

Technological factors

Database architecture. Databases in Mercord are based on hierarchical design while those in Rendi are relational. These are two completely different designs which will make integration difficult. It is likely that Mercord's databases will have to be re-written to remove duplication and transfer them into relational format.

Systems development. Systems design and development in Mercord has been mainly in-house while Rendi has relied on outsourcing. Managers in Mercord must decide whether to train Mercord staff in Rendi systems or take the potentially more expensive option of using outsourcers to amalgamate the systems.

Links to suppliers. Mercord design and build in-house while Rendi assemble plant and equipment from bought in parts. Rendi's IT systems will therefore have close links with suppliers to allow Just-in-time delivery and assembly – links which will be lacking in Mercord systems. Given that the Board want to continue production the Mercord way, the status of Rendi's possibly superior IT systems is unclear.

System integration. There also appears to be some denial about the difficulty of integrating systems. Hardware and software platforms are incompatible. Although Mercord has IT staff available, these don't have knowledge of Rendi systems.

(ii)   An organisation's information system should support the overall business strategy for the following reasons.

Competitive advantage. IS/IT may provide a possible source of competitive advantage. Competitive advantage in this sense could result from use of new technology or existing technology in a different way.

For example, both Mercord and Rendi developed websites. However, Rendi's website was successful because it not only allowed purchase of goods over the Internet, but also customers could amend products to their own specifications. This feature provided competitive advantage leading to greater market share.

Provision of information that shapes business strategy. Information is used to formulate business strategy. Information systems that provide high quality information from internal and external sources should result in a more appropriate business strategy.

Morcord has developed systems to support business strategy. However, most of those systems appear to focus on supporting production systems (CAD/CAM) rather than information. In Rendi, systems also appear to have been developed to support production activities, eg the electronic supply chain. However, Rendi's relational databases are more likely to provide management information in a more usable format eg sales per customer. Analysing this information will help Rendi identify purchasing trends and amend business strategy accordingly.

Channels for distribution and collection of information. Developments in IT may provide companies with new ways of distribution and collecting information. One of the main examples of this in recent years has been the Internet.

Both Mercord and Rendi have developed Internet sites. However, Mercord's site was not successful in attracting new customers and collecting additional customer information. Rendi's site was better in this regard eg self-selection of product features provided Rendi with a new stream of information about customer preferences.

Supporting JIT and lean practices. Rendi have used **electronic supply chains** effectively to support their business objectives of supplying goods to customer order (lean manufacturing). Good supply chain links are essential in obtaining inputs when needed so that production can continue without undue delay.

Worthwhile IS development. Development of information systems should be aligned with the overall business strategy of the organisation. Systems must provide benefits that help achieve organisational goals – they should not be developed simply because new technology is available.

Appropriate approach to IS systems. Business strategy will impact upon the approach taken to information systems development and management.

Consistent with a lean approach to business, Rendi outsourced development of information systems. Mercord's strategy has been to manufacture whole products in-house and not rely on assembled parts from suppliers. In this sense the IS strategy again follows the business strategy because systems are developed in-house.

(b)

Top tips. Use clear headings for your evaluation and discussion to give a defined structure to your answers.

Easy marks. In part (i) you will be awarded up to 2 marks for each relevant point that you make. Choose a relevant framework that you are most comfortable with (eg PEST) and apply that.

Examiner's comments. No framework was suggested for Part (i), giving candidates the opportunity to use a framework of their choice. All approaches were given full credit when used appropriately. In general, candidates answered this part very well. The majority of candidates were awarded high marks for part (ii). Strong candidates applied the theory to the case study using a structured approach to the discussion. Weaker candidates listed points and did not engage in a discussion.

Marking scheme

		Marks
(i)	Award up to 2 marks for each valid point, max 8 marks.	8
(ii)	Award up to 2 marks for each valid point, max 12 marks.	12
		20

(i)   The acquisition of Rendi and its accompanying information systems infrastructure and strategy, coupled with the existing need within Mercord to replace legacy systems, means the **current situation** regarding information systems in untenable.

Currently the company has two very different information systems strategies. One that has developed **historically** within Mercord, the other that was **inherited** with the acquisition of Rendi. Within Mercord, IT resources have been spent maintaining and modifying legacy systems. Rendi on the other hand appear to have consistently updated their infrastructures to maintain and encompass new technological innovations.

'**Doing nothing**' would require all existing information systems and information technology used to be supported. The on-going cost and resource implications are too high – and this approach would not support the organisation's business strategy.

The proposed **Total Integration Project** (TIP) would aim to integrate all existing Mercord and Rendi systems as a basis for developing a company wide information systems strategy. This would allow the development of integrated systems appropriate to the new integrated organisation.

Integration has the distinct benefits that company wide information systems will be available. The task will be difficult given the different hardware, software and database structures used in the two companies – but it is one that must be tackled.

A clear **terms of reference** document is required for the Total Integration Project, followed closely by analysis of existing systems leading to a feasibility study for integration. Only then can an informed choice be made regarding the future strategic direction of information systems in the two companies.

(ii)   A **legacy system** is a computer system or application program which continues to be used even though the technology it uses is outdated. These systems often use older hardware and software making it difficult to communicate or interact with more modern systems.

Organisations are often reluctant to replace these systems due to either the cost involved or because it would be a large project and the legacy system, although perhaps not ideal, does a decent job.

Problems of migrating legacy systems to new systems include the following.

- Replacing legacy systems in Mercord is likely to be **expensive**. New hardware and software will be required. Other factors explained below will add to the expense.

- The **skills** required may be hard to find. Older systems in Mercord will have been written in older computer languages. Many developers will have moved onto more interesting projects and learnt newer languages. Finding developers who understand the old code may be difficult and expensive as their knowledge will be in short supply.

- As the systems are old, it is also possible that **documentation** is **missing** or incomplete. Many older systems were not produced with full documentation. There may be a need to attempt to document the system to gain a full understanding of how it operates and how data is stored – this is time consuming and costly.

- **Data formats** between the Mercord and Rendi systems will be different. Data translation programmes will be required to transfer Mercord data into the Rendi system. Again this will be time consuming and expensive (in Mercord data is currently maintained in a hierarchical database, but Rendi maintain relational databases).

- There may be a general **reluctance to change** from systems that have been in use for so long. Education of all staff from the Board down will be required to show the problems with the Mercord systems and to justify replacement of those systems.

- Any changeover is also likely to be **disruptive** because there will have to be extensive testing of data migration and any new systems, and staff in Mercord will have to learn how to use a new system.

(c)

Marking scheme

		Marks
(i)	Award 1 mark per valid point, max 6 marks.	6
(ii)	Award 1 mark per valid point, max 6 marks.	6
(iii)	Award up to 4 marks for each type, to obtain full marks reference must be made to Mercord. 2 × 4 marks.	8
		20

(i)   To: Finance Director
         Subject: Outsourcing – briefing notes

Benefits of outsourcing information system development at Mercord

- **IT department knowledge**. Mercord staff may not have the knowledge or experience to cope with a large systems changeover. The outsourcing company may provide this knowledge.

- **Cost**. System changeover can be expensive. Use of an outsourcing company with a fixed price contract will limit the risk of escalating costs.

- **Core business focus**. Outsourcing IS development allows organisations to concentrate on their core business functions rather than on developing information systems.

- **Flexibility**. An outsourcer should be able to add or remove resource allocated to Mercord relatively quickly (compared to employing new in-house staff).

- **Economies of scale**. The outsourcing company may be able to obtain new hardware and software more cheaply than Mercord due to purchasing economies of scale.

- **Quality**. By outsourcing IS functions to experts, it may be possible to improve service provided to internal and external customers. This is shown by the superior quality of Rendi's systems (outsourced) compared to Mercord's (in-house).

(ii)　To:　　　IT Manager

Subject:　Outsourcing – briefing notes

Problems of outsourcing information system development at Mercord

- **Importance of IT**. IT services may be too important to contract out. It may be seen as essential that Mercord maintain knowledge and control of its information systems.

- **Risk**. Outsourcing provides some risk of third parties being given access to confidential information. Mercord's databases will include details of customers as well as manufacturing details of products.

- **Competitive advantage**. Outsourcing is likely to reduce the need for internal management to actually understand the systems being used. There is a danger that the outsourcing company, lacking industry specific expertise, will miss an opportunity to establish competitive advantage.

- **Lock in**. There is also a risk that Mercord will be unable to reverse the decision to outsource. Mercord may find it difficult to take control of its systems again should the need or will arise.

- **Redundancies**. Changing to an outsourcing solution will almost certain mean redundancies in the IT department in Mercord. This may lead to poor staff morale and a lack of willingness to work effectively with an outsourcing company.

- **Cost**. Given the problems inherent in the TIP project (that is the change to more modern databases) there is a danger of lack of cost control. Care must be taken that any reasons that would justify an increase in contract price are clearly stated in the contract.

(iii)　Two types of outsourcing that Mercord may consider are explained below.

Multiple/Selective sourcing involves breaking up the overall information function into different areas and outsourcing each area to different vendors. Care must be taken to ensure areas of responsibility are clearly defined.

Some organisations divide their functions into categories such as: hardware, software, communications and applications development. It may be possible under this approach to keep some key in-house staff (eg involved in strategic application development) and outsourcing non-critical information systems functions. If in-house expertise is available then this option is a good, low risk approach to outsourcing.

In Mercord the lack of in-house staff with the required skills for the TIP project mean this option is not viable. It does not currently employ staff with the required skills or knowledge to migrate its critical business systems to the target system.

However, Mercord could outsource the TIP project and also second to the project some of its existing staff to provide business knowledge and to learn about the new system.

During this period, IS support functions could be outsourced to a different vendor.

Total outsourcing involves a third party providing the vast majority of an organisation's IS/IT services. The outsourcing company is responsible for the IT equipment, software and staff.

The appeal of this option to Mercord is it would provide a total solution for the company's IT systems; there would be no need to maintain an IS/IT department.

However, it would leave Mercord completely dependent on the outsourcing company. If the company ceases to trade then Mercord will have no IS/IT support.

The existing Mercord systems were predominantly developed in-house and the overall strategy is to integrate these with the Rendi systems that were developed by outsourcers. It is unlikely that a new third party could take the TIP project on without considerable input from both Mercord staff and those involved developing Rendi's systems.

63 Gervil Investment Co

(a)

Text reference. Porter's value chain (part (a)) is covered in Chapter 6 of the text. Knowledge management (part (b)) is in Chapter 3. Gap analysis (part (c)) is covered in Chapter 5.

Top tips. In part (ii), use a separate heading for each of the five primary activities – then provide sufficient evaluation to earn two marks for that heading. Your evaluation should include a brief explanation of the current situation and a brief suggestion for improvement. Be careful not to spend more time on each of the five items than is justified by the two marks for each activity available.

Easy marks. Reproducing general theory in part (i) will earn some marks. Be careful not to just explain the value chain – your explanation should focus on how the value chain model can assist the development of an effective information systems strategy.

Examiner's comments. Strong candidates answered the first part of the question very well and were awarded high marks. Weaker candidates did not identify the elements of Porter's value chain. A minority of candidates described either Porter's five forces model or a general structured approach to developing information systems. Strong candidates answered part (ii) well, applying the theory to the case study and identifying where new information systems could improve the current situation. Weaker candidates made no attempt to apply Porter's value chain to the case study, some candidates stating that the model could not be applied to a financial company. These responses were surprising and disappointing as a recent article published in the Student Accountant provided a discussion of Porter's value chain model and included a section describing how the value chain model can be applied to financial companies.

Marking scheme

		Marks
(i)	Award up to 2 marks for each valid point	10
(ii)	Award up to 2 marks per activity (5 activities)	10
		20

(i)   The value chain model, developed by Michael Porter, provides a framework for analysing the **internal activities or processes** carried out by an organisation.

       The model divides an organisation's activities into **nine generic activities**; five primary (Infrastructure, Human Resource Management, Technology development and Procurement) and four support (Inbound logistics, Operations, Outbound logistics and Sales and marketing).

       Each activity has both a **physical** and an **information-processing** component. The physical component includes all the tasks required to perform the activity. The information-processing component encompasses the steps required to capture, manipulate and channel the data necessary to perform the activity.

       An important aspect of value chain analysis is the identification of **information needs and flows** within an organisation. If an organisation uses the model to analyse its current position, this should identify areas where competitive strategies could best be applied. This information can be used to develop **effective information systems strategies**.

       When looked at in this way, the value chain may be used as a **framework** to stimulate thinking in relation to the use of information systems and the development of an **overall information systems strategy**. This approach should help ensure systems are developed with a clear vision of their overall role and how they will add value.

To gain competitive advantage, an organisation must either perform some or all of the generic activities at a lower cost than competitors, or perform them in such a way that provides differentiation (eg an information system may facilitate better customer service levels).

(ii)   The five primary activities from Porter's value chain are identified below, with an evaluation of the current position within Gervil.

Inbound logistics

This activity involves the inputs into the system. In the case of Gervil the major inputs are enquiries and requests for products and services. These currently come via telesales activity, advertising campaigns, the website or branch visits.

Use of the website and the related database should be encouraged as this is a relatively cheap way of gathering details of prospective clients.

Operations

Gervil's major activity is that of turning a request for a particular product or service into a delivered product service received by the client.

Currently, this process relies on administrative staff who maintain details of clients and their products locally. These details are routinely checked to ensure appropriate action has been taken.

The recently implemented intranet could facilitate a more centralised approach and provide a link between all departments, but as yet the intranet is not being utilised to its full potential.

Outbound logistics

This activity supports the distribution of products or services. For companies such as Gervil, this involves the distribution of policies, bond certificates, etc which would out of necessity probably be paper-based.

There may be potential to involve systems such as e-mail in this process in the future, for example e-mailing a standard contract out to a customer to be printed out and then signed and allowing 'simple' policies such s Home Insurance to be downloaded from the website. Electronic payment systems could play a part in the settlement process.

Marketing and sales

This category covers the activities associated with how buyers are encouraged to purchase and the purchase process itself (eg advertising, selling, pricing and promotion).

Gervil is currently making limited use of information held in the customer database (eg cross-selling). The database could be used to target market segments with suitable direct marketing material (paper based and over the Internet). Better use of website registration and cookies could help this process.

Service

This activity covers all aspects of customer service including the provision of after sales service. Gervil is doing reasonably well in this area. It has a customer service department providing knowledge and expert specialist advice on its products.

The company could consider the development of a complementary service eg providing a 'frequently asked questions' section, possibly subdivided by product, on the website. This material would be based upon the most common themes of calls to the customer service centre. Other questions could be e-mailed to customer service representatives.

(b)

Marking scheme

		Marks
(i)	Award up to 2 marks for each valid point	8
(ii)	Award up to 3 marks per function (four functions)	12
		20

REPORT (*draft*)

To: The Board
From: Frank Maloney (this draft prepared by Business analyst)
Date: 5 December 20X5
Subject: The need for a knowledge management strategy

The following information could be used in the final report.

(i)   Four reasons why we need a knowledge management strategy are outlined below.

To help achieve business objectives

Knowledge management describes the process of creating, collecting, storing and using the knowledge held within an organisation. An appropriate knowledge management strategy should encourage knowledge held is used to help achieve business objectives and to ensure investment in information systems produces real benefits.

To make use of what we already know (including tacit knowledge)

Studies have suggested that a significant proportion of company resources are wasted because organisations are not aware of what knowledge they already possess. This is particularly true of informal internal knowledge/experience often referred to as tacit knowledge. A knowledge management strategy aims to ensure we capture this knowledge and make it available where it can be of use.

To enable us to extend our knowledge

A knowledge management strategy should enable an organisation to build on what is already known and extend it further. The strategy should encourage an organisation to consciously and comprehensively gather, organise, share and analyse its knowledge and to utilise its existing information systems or develop new information systems to support the knowledge management strategy..

To achieve competitive advantage

Knowledge has become a key asset, and is commonly viewed as a sustainable source of competitive advantage. The production of services that are superior to the competition, or lower in cost, is based upon superior knowledge.

(ii) An assessment of the four functions normally associated with knowledge management with reference to the existing information systems within our company follows.

Create knowledge

The creation of new information and knowledge is essential (for example to better serve customer needs and to allow the creation of new products/services) in a competitive market such as that faced by Gervil.

Information systems that facilitate the creation and integration of this new knowledge are referred to as Knowledge Work Systems (KWS). These often have access to external knowledge bases. People involved in this work are often referred to as knowledge workers

Within Gervil, financial analysts would benefit from access to a specialist financial investment workstation. This could be used to control knowledge and information from brokers, traders and portfolio managers. These workstations could streamline the investment process.

Distribute knowledge

Effective distribution of knowledge (communication) is essential if knowledge is to be utilised. Office Automation Systems (OAS) (this term includes applications such as word processing, spreadsheets, database, e-mail, voicemail and electronic schedulers) are most often used to distribute knowledge.

Within Gervil, these systems could be utilised to ensure head office staff and branch staff are aware of each others' actions. Currently, e-mail is used extensively but greater use could be made of other OAS. Distributing information electronically provides a permanent record and should mean fewer misunderstandings.

Share knowledge

The sharing of knowledge held within an organisation is a key element of knowledge management.

Two systems that support the sharing of knowledge are an intranet and the use of groupware. Together, these allow collaborative working. Intranets provide a common interface using Internet based technology. Gervil successfully implemented an intranet several years ago, but there is a need to evaluate how this is used and could be improved.

Gervil should consider using groupware software such as Lotus Notes or Microsoft Exchange. This would enable people in different parts of the organisation to work on or refer to the same documents, to schedule meetings, use electronic forms, access shared folders and develop shared databases.

Capture and codify knowledge

'Capturing' knowledge means ensuring it is entered/held in an appropriate information system. 'Codifying' involves defining the rules relating to how knowledge is held and referred to.

A good example of a system that captures and codifies knowledge is an expert system. This is a program that captures human expertise and allows it to be applied within a given situation.

The automated investment advisory system (AIA) at Gervil follows the expert system approach. Other possible areas could include a system that held financial economic indicators and historical data and used this to forecast economic/financial developments.

Conclusion

Gervil has the majority of the necessary information systems currently in place to support a knowledge management strategy. However, a formal strategy is required to ensure a coordinated approach is taken that allows maximum benefit to be obtained from current and future systems.

(c)

Top tips. This question is structured in a similar way to Question 2 – with 8 marks available in part (i) for explaining relevant theory and 12 marks in part (ii) for applying this theory. This demonstrates the importance of being able to apply knowledge. Question practice is the key to this.

Easy marks. Some easier marks are available in part (i) for demonstrating your knowledge of gap analysis. However, your discussion should provide more than this – it must related gap analysis to the development of an information systems strategy that aligns with a business strategy.

Examiner's comments. The first part of this question was generally answered well. Full credit was given to candidates who chose the generic W's framework as an alternative to the standard graphical representation of gap analysis. In part (ii) strong candidates applied gap analysis theory to the development of the AIA system. The case study clearly described the presence of a gap between the business strategy and the supporting information system before the introduction of the AIA system. Weaker candidates answered this part without reference to the AIA system, merely repeating the part (i) answer. A minority of candidates did not attempt to answer part (ii), thus limiting the total marks available to eight for this question.

Marking scheme

		Marks
(i)	Award up to 2 marks for each valid point, max 8 marks	8
(ii)	Award up to 2 marks per valid point, max 12 marks	12
		20

(i) The increasing importance of information and information technology in business has led to the need for a close link between business strategy and information systems strategy. Gap analysis can be applied to help develop and maintain this relationship – as explained below.

Step 1 Devise business strategy. This strategy will determine what information is required and enable possible information systems to be investigated.

Step 2 Establish organisational current and predicted information and information system needs.

Step 3 Use gap analysis to identify whether the organisation's information systems meet the current and/or predicted organisational information requirements. The use of gap analysis can be shown in a graph-style diagram such as the one on the next page.

Gap analysis: Information systems strategy

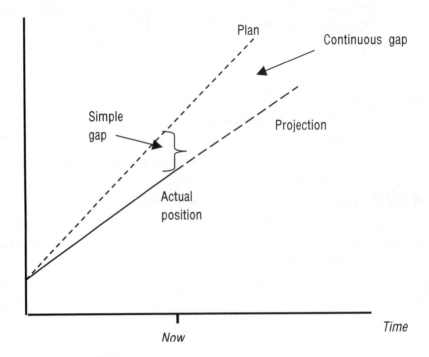

Gap analysis would involve:

- The actual position could be established by way of a current situation analysis.

- The projection would be obtained by taking the current position and projecting forward to account for imminent projects.

- The plan line (sometimes referred to as the expectation line) would be obtained from the information needed to support the organisation's overall business strategy.

Step 4 As the plan line is based on what is required to support business strategy, devising an information systems strategy that focuses on closing the continuous gap will ensure the IS strategy aligns with business strategy.

(ii) Before the development of the AIS system, the original company had adopted a business strategy of purchasing independent financial companies and an information systems strategy that encouraged decentralised and/or distributed systems.

The case study suggests main branches were permitted to develop their information systems independently, a decentralised information systems strategy. This arrangement had benefits, allowing advisors to make decisions quickly, face-to-face, using local client knowledge. Problems with this approach included customers being given different advice from branch to branch – there was a general lack of consistency across the organisation.

When the CEO decided to centralise the investment decision-making process, a large gap existed between this centralised business strategy and the decentralised information systems strategy.

The automated investment advisory system (AIA) was developed based on expert systems technology using the knowledge of best advisors as the main source. The AIA was developed centrally and rolled out to the branches, who accessed the system over a network.

This represented a change to a centralised information systems strategy. Therefore, the development of the AIA system represented a move to a centralised information systems strategy aligned with the centralised investment decision-making process decided under business strategy.

The AIA development was a departure from the decentralised approach. The CEO decided that Gervil should change its information systems infrastructure to accommodate the implementation of the AIA on a network technology – even though this option was the most expensive. This demonstrates that business needs should drive technological change.

The change in the technical infrastructure will enable Gervil to adopt a centralised approach to other developments if required. For example, new products may now be more easily launched and controlled centrally, which could lead to competitive advantage.

The AIA system development is an excellent example of how an organisation should align business strategy with its information systems strategy and of how if 'gaps' appear between required information provision and actual provision they should be closed.

64 KGDB Co

Text reference. SWOT analysis is covered in the text Chapter 6. In particular, the application of the SWOT in Part (b) is explained in section 1.2 of that chapter.

Top tips. Part (a) should not pose you many problems as there is plenty of good information in the scenario for you to generate a SWOT. The examiner will expect you to show a good understanding of the business and its environment, so be sure to list a broad range of issues rather than take a narrow focus.

Part (b) (i) requires you to approach SWOT from a slightly different angle and follows the approach of McLaughlin (and others). Do not be put off by this, and remember that 'assess' means to put forward arguments for and against a particular issue – in this case, does each quadrant apply to the situation KGDB finds itself in regarding the website?

The four mark Part (b) (ii) requires you to state which of the personnel match each of the four quadrants. Although it is tempting, you should avoid explaining your opinion in too much detail. Provide the name and a sentence or two why you have chosen them.

Easy marks. The SWOT analysis in this question provides you with a ready-made template for structuring your answer and the marking scheme makes it clear how many points you should cover in your answers – for example Part (a) is worth eight marks, there are four quadrants, therefore you need two good points per quadrant.

There are no easy marks in this question as you need to search the scenario for the required information, but when you have the information you need, it is easy to structure your answer to maximise your marks.

Examiner's comments. In general, candidates did very well in answering the first part of the question and many candidates obtained maximum marks. Strong candidates answered part (b)(i) by assessing the relevance of each quadrant to the current position of KGDB. Weaker candidates either concentrated only on one quadrant, or simply provided a marketing analysis. Many candidates were awarded maximum marks for part (b)(ii). Weaker candidates did not match the named members of senior management with a strategy from within the grid. Some answers provided a description of management roles without reference to the grid. Overall this question was answered well.

Marks

In many questions suggested model answers were given to open-ended questions. Credit will be given for any valid alternative responses within the limits of the marking scheme.

(a)	Award up to 2 marks for each element, 4 elements.			8
(b)	(i)	Award up to 2 marks per quadrant.	$4 \times 2 =$	8
	(ii)	Award 1 mark per explanation.	$4 \times 1 =$	4
Total marks				20

(a) **Strengths:**

- **Supported by managers** (due to customer requests)
- **Information systems already in place** to support the website
- **Strong brand** and **reputation** should make the website successful
- The business is of **sufficient size** to exploit the benefits that a website would bring

Weaknesses:

- **No in-house IT team** to develop the website
- **Lack of web experience** within company
- **Poor track record** of completing IS projects
- **Current systems are cumbersome** and may need updating in order to effectively support the website

Opportunities:

- **Additional revenue** stream for the business through e-commerce
- **Recording** and **storing customer information** would support future **marketing campaigns**
- **Allows expansion of customer base** as the products will be available to customers globally
- **Internet sales have a lower cost base** as they are automated

Threats:

- The business has been built on **customer service**; a website could erode this identity
- **Customers** may be **unwilling to buy** such expensive, high quality goods through a website
- A website may cause **resentment** within the employees if it is in direct competition with their stores
- The project is likely to be **costly with no guarantee of success**

(b) (i) The grid shows how **SWOT analysis** can be used to develop strategies based on internal factors (strengths and weaknesses) and external factors (opportunities and threats).

The top left box describes a situation where the business has an **internal strength** which can be used to exploit an **external opportunity**. This is the most advantageous situation for a business to be in. It is **unlikely that this box is relevant to KGDB** as there are question marks over the IT resources in terms of internal expertise and the quality of existing systems, therefore the business does not have IS/IT as a major strength.

Where the **opportunity exists** for exploiting IS/IT, but the organisation has an **internal weakness** in this area, the suggested strategy is **to beware** or not **to proceed**. This is usually because there is a **high risk** that the project will fail, costing the organisation time, money and other resources. It could be said that this strategy applies to KGDB; however there is an **additional risk** of it falling behind its competitors if it does not follow the strategy. Many organisations view a website as **crucial** to presenting a modern, credible business – the risks associated with not developing a website are likely to outweigh any risks of developing one.

The bottom left box is associated with organisations who have **strong IS/IT resources** and find themselves under **a position of threat**. The strategy given to businesses in this situation is to **explore** the possibility if time or other resources allow. Whilst it could be said that a threat may exist from competitors who have already developed websites, it cannot be said that KGDB has strong IS/IT resources. Therefore this quadrant does not apply to the business as exploring the option is not realistic.

The final quadrant describes a strategy of **protection**. It applies to organisations who find themselves **under threat** from competitors and who have **weak IS/IT resources**. Protection usually involves developing strategies to guard against the weakness. Although this quadrant describes the situation KGDB finds itself in fairly accurately, the strategy it suggests is not an option as it is difficult to protect against a weak IS/IT capability.

KGDB does not fit into any one of the four quadrants precisely, although it does demonstrate elements of them. Its **weakness** is the IS/IT resource and this appears to be holding the company back from following a particular strategy. The company should **consider its position** and other IS/IT options before making any further decisions.

(ii) David, Anne, Katherine and Alexandra each have exhibited behaviour that supports one quadrant in the grid.

Attack

David Boswell is described as a keen supporter of **exploiting technology** to enhance business opportunities and has already asked Michael to **present a business case** for the website. He clearly wants to attack the opportunity that is presented.

Beware

Anne Brown has formally complained about the service provided by the IT consultancy company. Her concerns result from the new accounting system which was only **moderately successful** and she believes the consultancy firm is only interested in **quick fixes** – therefore the business should beware before using the current IS/IT resources to develop the website.

Explore

Katherine Goodison only sees the website providing advantages from an **advertising perspective** and it should not become a **major strategy** for sales. From her point of view, the company should only explore the possibility of a website at this stage as she does not want to upset the existing clientele.

Protect

Alexandra Smith and other store managers are concerned that the website may affect their **sales**. She would prefer the company to **watch out for developments** and to protect itself at this stage rather than commit to a website strategy.

Text reference. Business case reports are covered in Chapter 5 of the text.

Top tips. You must be aware of the contents of a business case report to be able to answer this question. If you do not remember them, make sure you revise this area thoroughly. As there are up to four marks available for each element of the report, you should make sure each element is sufficiently covered.

Easy marks. Knowledge of the headings in a business case report would earn you marks in each element of the report. Ensure you learn the layout. A good gap analysis and sensible evaluation and conclusion should earn enough other marks to pass the question.

Examiner's comments. Generally the answers to this question were disappointing. Only a minority of candidates constructed a business case report using an acceptable format. The recommended textbooks suggest the following contents for a business case report: introduction and terms of reference; aims, approach and scope; resources; summary of present position; summary of relent IS objectives; gap analysis; evaluation of the different options considered; cost-benefit analysis; conclusions and recommendations. The W's framework was an acceptable alternative. The majority of candidates did not demonstrate an understanding of a business case report. Many of the answers were generic, merely describing features of both a 'view only' website and a website with online purchasing facilities, with no specific references to the case study. There was little evidence of any formal structure for the business case report. Answers tended to be very brief, comprising a couple of paragraphs. This was not adequate because 20 marks were available.

Marking scheme

Marks

In many questions suggested model answers were given to open-ended questions. Credit will be given for any valid alternative responses within the limits of the marking scheme.

Award up to 2 marks per valid point up to a maximum 4 marks per element.	$5 \times 4 =$	20
Total marks		20

(c)   **Business Case Report**
        To: KGDB Senior Management
        Prepared by: A N Accountant
        Date: 5/6/x6

(i)   **Terms of reference:**

        Aims:

        To develop a KGDB website that promotes the organisation and to enhance the customer experience.

        Approach:

        To analyse two possible options for website development.

        Scope:

        Option one is the provision of a general company website to provide customers with information about the company such as store locations, products and company philosophy. This option does not change the scope of company activities.

        Option two enhances option one by the addition of online purchasing facilities. This would provide an opportunity for the business to expand but would require additional investment in back-office technology to handle the fulfilment of online orders.

Resources:

KGDB currently uses an external IT consultancy firm for IT projects on an ad hoc basis. There are no internal IT resources. No indication of finance availability has been supplied.

(ii) **Current position:**

The business currently has no website. Its IT infrastructure is functional without being effective. IT is a weakness in the organisation as several previous projects have previously failed.

Customers can currently only purchase goods that are available in store and this limits the business to customers who are prepared to travel to them. Many have complained about the lack of a website. Therefore customer expectations have created a demand for KGDB to create an online presence.

(iii) **Company objectives for its IS strategy:**

An objective of KGDB is to take advantage of IT developments to enhance the customer experience of the company whilst maintaining or improving the high standards of customer service it has set for itself. It is also an objective to ensure the business keeps pace with its competitors regarding the use of IT. Customers may take their custom elsewhere if it fails to do so as the business would lose credibility.

(iv) **Gap analysis:**

There is currently a large gap between what the current systems provide and what is required.

Where we are (W2R):

Currently the business is only able to provide products to customers who are able and willing to visit its stores. It is likely that there are many potential customers who would be only too willing to purchase from the brand if only they knew it existed.

Where we want to be (W32B):

There are two options that provide a vision of where the company wants to position itself:

Option 1:

This option is the provision of a website to promote the brand products, and provide general information to customers.

Option 2:

This provides the facility for customers to purchase products online in addition to the information in option 1. It would allow a much greater customer base as customers would no longer have to visit a store.

Going to get there (GT2):

Option 1:

This option could be provided and maintained by a third party website design service at a relatively low cost. No further input would be required by KGDB other than a design specification so no further investment into IT would be required. The website would become an addition to the systems portfolio.

Option 2:

This option requires extensive integration of back-office systems such as stock control and order fulfilment. It is likely that IT professionals would be required on site most of the time to ensure the systems are maintained and functioning correctly. The required investment in people and systems makes this a major undertaking.

(v)   **Evaluation of the options:**

Option 1:

KGDB can either develop a website or do nothing. By developing the website, the company will address consumer demand for a website and reduce customer complaints for its current absence. It will provide additional sources of promotion for the business and an expanded customer base for its stores. However, it will not create an additional revenue stream or act as a catalyst to improve the other IT system the company has.

By not developing a website, the business is likely to fall behind its competitors and may lose customers as a result.

Option 2:

This option represents a major change in the use of IT within the business and would require substantial commitment from senior management. A large investment would be required in terms of technology, finance, time, and employees. This would mark a significant change in the strategic direction of the business in terms of how the business operates and how IT is used. However, a question mark remains – would customers be willing to spend significant sums of money on goods that they can only see a picture of? Customers may prefer and even expect a more personal shopping experience when spending large amounts of money.

A cost-benefit analysis would normally be performed at this stage. This analysis involves comparing the costs and benefits of the project over a specific period of time. Costs would include investments and other one-off costs, expenses and other reoccurring items as well as intangible costs. Benefits include revenue streams that result directly from the project as well as intangible benefits (such as increased brand awareness).

The main purpose of the comparison is to discover whether the project will make a profit, how long it would take to repay the initial outlay (payback period), and to calculate the overall return to the business using methods such as net present value or return on investment.

(vi)   **Conclusion**:

It is clear that pressure from competitors and customers have made it of vital importance that KGDB develops some kind of internet presence. There is support for a website within the senior management and store managers, however there are differences of opinion of how far any development should be taken.

It is the recommendation of this report that option one is implemented. This option has the most overall support within the organisation and will meet the requirements of customers and competition. A further decision regarding option two could be taken at a later stage once it is known how effective the basic website has been. There is currently not enough support for option two and the risk of wasting precious resources on another project that may not be effective is too high.

Text reference. Chapter 8 of the text contains a description of Boehm's Spiral Model.

Top tips. In Part (d) we have taken a different approach to the format of the answer than the examiner. We recommend the use of headed paragraphs for each point that you wish to make rather than one large paragraph as this makes it easier for markers to spot points and give you marks.

The description of Boehm's spiral model in Part (e) should not have presented many problems – make sure you learn as many academic models as you can as the examiner often tests them in this way. This model was the subject of an examiner's article in April 2006 and this is another good reason to stay up to date with articles in the student magazine.

BPP

LEARNING MEDIA

Top tips. (cont'd) Your higher-level skills of application are tested in Part (f). Unless you understand how the model works and situations that its use is appropriate, you would struggle with this question. When learning any academic model, ask yourself how the model would work in real-life as it prepares you well for questions such as this. **Easy marks.** You should easily be able to pick three or four deficiencies of the current IS provision from the scenario. The benefits of an in-house IT team over outsourcing are assumed Paper 2.1 knowledge.

Examiner's comments. Part (d) was answered very well and many candidates were awarded maximum marks. Strong candidates provided a good description of Boehm's spiral model in part (e) and continued, in part (f), by evaluating its appropriateness for the development of the website with online facilities. A minority of candidates had little or no knowledge of Boehm's spiral model and thus could not answer parts (e) or (f) satisfactorily. An article in Student Accountant published earlier this year focused on development methodologies including the spiral model. Boehm's spiral model is also discussed in all the recommended textbooks. Overall this question was answered well.

Marking scheme

		Marks

In many questions suggested model answers were given to open-ended questions. Credit will be given for any valid alternative responses within the limits of the marking scheme.

(d)	Award up to 2 marks per valid point.	6
(e)	Award up to 2 marks per valid point.	6
(f)	Award up to 2 marks per valid point.	_8_
Total marks		_20_

(d) This briefing note outlines the current problems of IS provision at KGDB and the benefits of employing internal IT professionals.

Current problems of IS provision at KGDB

KGDB currently employs external consultants to provide all of its IS requirements and there is general unhappiness with the level of service and the functionality of the systems provided by them. Such problems include:

Unsatisfactory integration of accounting and back office systems

The accounting system was recently integrated with other back office systems, however there are concerns that this integration was not as successful as it should have been.

Ineffective stock ordering system

The system provided allows orders to be submitted in different media (email, fax, telephone), there is a risk that they may become lost. For example, a telephone order could be accidentally thrown away, faxes may not reach the destination and emails may be deleted in error.

Lack of relevant statistical data

From a management point of view, it would be useful to record and monitor orders and sales from the various stores. The current system does not allow analysis of stock ordering data and analysis of sales trends, often data is out of date when the reports are run.

No alignment of IS strategy to business strategy

Systems development has been of an ad hoc nature, where a system is required the consultants have developed a solution. However, there has been no attempt to provide systems that meet the needs of business strategy or the changing business environment. Such a policy should be adopted to ensure any future investment meets the needs of the business, and is used effectively.

Benefits of employing IT professionals:

There are many benefits to KGDB of employing its own in-house team of IT professionals.

Employees are more likely to understand the business

Staff who work for an organisation are more likely to understand the needs of the business and will build up significant knowledge and expertise that can benefit the company in other ways. This should mean systems would meet the needs of the business more effectively. Staff from external consultants may not have worked on projects for the client before and so would not have sufficient experience of the business to do as thorough job.

An in-house team may be cheaper to employ than consultants

It is likely that a group of in-house professionals would be cheaper to employ than if the same group came from an external consultancy as the consultancy is in business to make a profit.

Improved control of systems development

IT staff would report directly to an IT director and therefore the board would have more control over systems development. Should the website development go ahead, a small internal IT team could manage the project and insource expert personnel as required. This provides better control than allowing consultants to manage the project themselves.

(e)   **Boehm's spiral model for systems development** is a new approach for developing systems. It is applied in situations where the **requirements** of the system are **hard to specify**, or where sequential development models such as the **systems development lifecycle** (SDLC) are **not suitable**. Such systems require one set of items being completed before the next can be started.

The spiral model is based on **four quadrants**; each cycle of development takes one swing through each quadrant. The process starts at the centre of the spiral and moves outwards.

The four quadrants are:

- Top-left: **Objectives are determined**. Alternatives and constraints are identified.
- Top-right: **Alternatives are evaluated**. Risks are identified and resolved.
- Bottom-right: **The system is developed**.
- Bottom-left: **The next stage of the project's development is planned**.

The first revolution through the spiral is concerned with **project specification**. Further circuits result in prototypes being developed and adjustments being made. With each revolution the project becomes **increasingly** more **sophisticated** and closer to the final version.

The advantage of this **evolutionary approach** is that developers and users are encouraged to **communicate** and **react** to development at **each stage**. Developers will become increasingly familiar with the needs of the user and users will have **frequent input** into the project as their ideas and views are incorporated at each stage. At the end of each cycle, users are presented with a current version of the system and the next stage is planned with the developer.

(f)   The spiral model would be **highly appropriate** for the development of the enhanced website for the following reasons.

Project complexity and scale

The **gradual stage process** and development by iteration that the spiral model provides is very well **suited to large complex projects** as development by way of **easy to handle steps**. The website project will be vastly more complex than the business has managed before and the main problem area is likely to be the integration of web sales into the back office systems. These systems are all interrelated and involve many different staff, all of whose input is required to make the project a success. Therefore the required user input at each stage of development in the spiral model will ensure this communication takes place.

Risk management

The website will be a flagship project for the company and its success or failure will be of great importance to it. The **risks and costs of failure are high**, so it is of vital importance that risk is handled correctly. The **spiral model address risk at each stage** and involves user participation to ensure problems are addressed. The nature of the project means it could be developed in stages, creating the website and then integrating it into the other systems one at a time. This process **minimises** the **risk** of a **complete systems failure** if an error in one system has a knock on effect on the others. Here only the system under development is at risk of failure, the others should be sheltered from any problems.

Enhance existing systems

The **evolutionary approach** of the model means existing **back office systems** could be **developed at the same time as the website** is integrated into them. This would be an iterative process driven by user participation and would ensure that the development process takes into account existing systems and the inherent risks involved when changing them.

Suitable for external consultants or internal professionals

There is current uncertainty of whether the **external consultants** should continue to develop systems (including the website), or whether the company should **employ** a team of IT professionals to manage the project. The spiral model is just as **effective** for **external consultants** as for **employees** and it is recommended that whoever develops the project adopts it. In the situation where an external consult is used, the company will have an input at each stage and therefore more control of how the project develops.

Mock Exams

ACCA

Paper 3.4

Business Information Management

Mock Examination 1

Question Paper		
Time allowed		**3 hours**
This paper is divided into two sections		
Section A	**THREE compulsory questions to be attempted**	
Section B	**TWO questions ONLY to be attempted**	

DO NOT OPEN THIS PAPER UNTIL YOU ARE READY TO START UNDER EXAMINATION CONDITIONS

SECTION A – ALL THREE questions are compulsory and MUST be attempted

The following information should be used when answering questions 1, 2 and 3

Seven-Eleven

Seven-Eleven was set up in 1973 as a convenience-store operator. By the mid-1980s it had already replaced old-fashioned cash registers with point-of-sale (POS) systems that monitored customer purchases. By 1992, it had overhauled its information technology systems four times. But the biggest overhaul of all took place in 1997. The new system that Seven-Eleven installed was based on proprietary technology – albeit state-of-the-art – rather than on the still barely tested open structure of the Internet, because it would have been hard to build on the back of the Internet alone a system that satisfied all Seven-Eleven's complex demands.

It wanted an easy-to-use multimedia system with pictures and sound, since most workers are part-timers with scant computer skills. It also wanted a system that could quickly repair itself if something went wrong. Then the chain needed a network to speed up the transmission of orders, ideas and feedback. It wanted all the companies in its supply chain to use one common system, and it wanted a system that could be easily updated to take advantage of technological advances. Then it wanted the system to run for at least 15 years.

Such connectedness – hooking up suppliers, stores, staff and even banks – is the sort of thing that most retailers can still only dream of, even with the Internet around to reduce the cost and the complexity. What made Seven-Eleven's task more daunting was that the system had to serve some 6,000 stores (the figure is now more than 8,500 and growing) scattered across Japan. These stores operate round the clock and are manned by a dozen or so workers, some of whom never see each other.

It built the system itself, creating the hardware with NEC, a consumer-electronics company. Coming up with the right software was harder, and it eventually asked Microsoft, America's software giant, to help it build a tailor-made Windows-based system.

By 1998 the software was being installed in some 61,000 computers at Seven-Eleven's stores, head office and vendor firms. By 2000, the overhaul was complete. A pipeline to Microsoft's offices in Seattle provided instant support. The software backup constantly monitored and automatically rebooted the system when it crashed, and alerted local maintenance firms if such errors occurred more than twice.

All Seven-Eleven stores now have a satellite dish. Cheaper than using ground cables, this is often the only option for shops in rural areas. And in earthquake-prone Japan, the satellite dish provides an extra layer of safety on top of two sets of telephone lines, and separate mainframes in Tokyo and Osaka.

Seven-Eleven is already using the Internet to lower its annual overhead costs. It plans to install an e-commerce software package offered by the Japanese arm of Ariba, an American e-procurement company, to bulk-buy goods and services such as office equipment and insurance policies for its employees.

The big question is whether Seven-Eleven can integrate the Internet into its other operations. In the past, it has been clever at finding new ways to use its technology. Back in 1989, after installing bar-code recognition systems, Seven-Eleven turned its stores into payment points for utility bills. Almost 15 years later, the move (which required only a small incremental investment in software) has given Seven-Eleven 3% of a massive market that includes big rivals such as banks and post offices.

Now the company has increased its customer traffic by turning shops into payment and pick-up points for Internet shoppers. This was a clever move in a country in which people are still wary of using credit cards over the Internet, preferring instead to pay cash at a store.

Question 1

Using the value chain model, describe the activities at Seven-Eleven where competitive strategies can be best applied. **(20 marks)**

Question 2

Because of the volume of data available to the management at Seven-Eleven, they are planning to incorporate a data warehouse into their head office system.

(a) Explain the components and workings of a data warehouse. **(13 marks)**

(b) How would the managers at Seven-Eleven benefit from this acquisition? **(7 marks)**

(Total = 20 marks)

Question 3

Although Seven-Eleven expect the system to last for fifteen years, there will be a constant need to maintain and improve it and to keep up-to-date with technological advances and changing user requirements.

Explain the methods the company could use to evaluate the success of the new system. **(20 marks)**

SECTION B – TWO questions ONLY to be attempted

Question 4

The JB Company provides specialist information services to organisations which do not have either the staff expertise or financial resources to maintain an information services department. Information provided ranges from weather forecasts (both regional and national) to railways and airlines, stock market information to stockbrokers and general news bulletins to major TV and radio stations.

Information is collected by the JB Company through a variety of systems including Internet monitoring, reports from employees from any of the 129 offices worldwide, on-line links to stock markets, reviews of newspapers from around the world and monitoring of news reports on TV and radio. Most information is reviewed and summarised by a team of specialist information analysts, so only the appropriate highlights are sent to clients.

Mr A is one of the senior account managers in the JB Company. It is his responsibility to ensure that his clients receive appropriate information, and that he is up-to-date with information supplied to those clients should queries arise. Mr A therefore receives information through a variety of sources including:

- E-mail messages from staff and clients. Between 30 and 40 e-mails are received on a typical day.

- Telephone calls from information analysts and clients. Information analysts require strategic decisions regarding the information to provide to clients, while clients may request clarification of information received.

- Detailed information from the company's databases and Intranet connections.

- Detailed information from Internet sites which Mr A reviews every hour or so during the day.

- Verbal reports from staff who prefer to see Mr A face-to-face.

Mr A believes that he is suffering from information overload.

Required

(a)   Explain what is meant by information overload, and how this could affect the working efficiency of Mr A.

(10 marks)

(b)   Describe the IT and manual procedures that could be used to reduce the information overload on Mr A.

(10 marks)

(Total = 20 marks)

Question 5

Senior management in SGI need to make certain strategic decisions in respect of information technology in the organisation.

They particularly want to know whether the information technology function should be centralised or decentralised. Their main concern regarding decentralisation is that they might lose control over the group's diverse operations.

Required

(a)   Discuss the general arguments for and against centralisation/decentralisation.   **(12 marks)**

(b)   Explain how an open system can help a distributed information system.   **(8 marks)**

(Total = 20 marks)

Question 6

Required

(a)   Define and briefly explain gap analysis.   **(5 marks)**

(b)   Consider how gap analysis might be applied to an information systems strategy. Include reference to the Peppard/McFarlan strategic grid (Application portfolio) and Earl's systems audit grid in your answer.

(15 marks)

(Total = 20 marks)

Answers

DO NOT TURN THIS PAGE UNTIL YOU HAVE
COMPLETED MOCK EXAM 1

A PLAN OF ATTACK

Tackling scenario questions

Section A of the examination for Paper 3.4 comprises a written scenario with three compulsory questions from across the syllabus **linked** to the narrative scenario. The information provided usually includes some discussion of the organisation's current situation, and there is often one or more central characters charged with the task of resolving the problem, or exploiting the opportunity.

The function of this type of question is to test a candidate's ability to tackle unstructured problems, and to **apply** what they know to 'real' situations. There **may be several feasible solutions** and candidates should not necessarily expect there to be a single definitive answer. The solution will involve the use of techniques which have been learned, but usually also requires the exercise of judgement. Preparation to scenario-based questions cannot rely on reading alone, but must be supplemented **by question practice under examination conditions**.

The **ability to structure a coherent answer** which leads logically to its conclusion is essential. Recommendations are often required. Acceptable recommendations may vary, but must be sensible and justified.

Key points to remember when tackling scenario questions:

- Answer the question asked – tailor what you know to fit the scenario
- Prepare a rough plan – this will help clarify your thoughts
- Structure longer answers eg introduction, body of answer, conclusion
- Justify any recommendations

Mock exam 1

Start by spending 5 minutes looking through the paper, gaining an understanding of the scenario, and considering how it relates to the requirements.

We will now provide some specific advice regarding this exam. We'll consider two options.

Option 1 (if you're thinking 'Help!')

If after reading the scenario and requirements for Questions 1 to 3 you are not confident of scoring well, you may find it helpful to start with the question from Section B that you feel most confident about. (But remember – you will still have to come back and answer Questions 1 to 3!)

For example, if you feel confident about your ability to discuss information overload, you may wish to start with **Question 4**.

Starting with a question you find 'easier' should help you 'get into' the exam and **build your confidence**. At the start of the exam you will be fresh – you should be in a frame of mind that enables you to recall and apply your knowledge, getting off to a good start before attempting the questions you expect to find more difficult.

Attempting a question you find difficult at the start of an exam could result in a **loss of confidence**. The danger is that as a consequence, you may go on to perform poorly in later questions even if you know the area well.

Option 2 (if you are thinking 'No problem!')

Try not to be overconfident, but if you are feeling fairly comfortable with the content of the paper, then choose the optional questions you wish to answer, then tackle questions in the order they appear – starting with Question 1.

Question 1

After reading and re-reading the scenario take a calm look at Question 1. Ensure you read the requirement correctly, and that your answer meets this requirement. Question 1 tests your ability to apply the value chain model.

Question 2

This question takes a different approach and tests another area of the syllabus. Even if you cannot remember technical details of data warehouses, you should be able to explain them and generate some benefits to the managers of Severn-Eleven.

Question 3

A very open ended requirement and you will be awarded credit for sensible answers. Remember you are only required to explain evaluation methods.

Section B requires you to answer any two questions from a choice of three. Some Section B questions are also based on scenarios, although the individual scenarios are shorter than the one contained in Part A. The principles of answering scenario-based questions (as explained in the front pages of this book) can also be applied to apply to those Section B questions that are based upon short scenarios.

To reiterate, the key points are:

- **Answer the question asked** – not the question you hoped would be asked
- **Apply your knowledge to the scenario**

Question 4

Information overload is an easy topic area to miss during revision, but you should be prepared for anything to be examined at this level. However, your own work experiences might help you answer the question if you have not revised the subject in detail.

Question 5

This question uses some brought forward knowledge from Paper 2.1 regarding centralised and decentralised systems, but you must take a deeper, more strategic approach when answering. A 2.1 level answer would not earn good marks here.

Question 6

Three theories and models are tested here. Gap analysis and the two grids are key subjects in the syllabus and it is important for you to demonstrate a good understanding of them and how they are related. Always draw diagrams when asked to explain a theory to earn quick marks.

Time allocation...

Allocate your time according to the marks for the question in total (36 mins for each 20 mark question) and then according to the parts of the question. **Always follow the question requirements exactly**.

If you have allocated your time properly then you shouldn't have time on your hands before the full three hours is up. But if you do find yourself with a spare ten minutes, check that you have answered all questions **fully**.

Finally...

After sitting the 'real' exam, do not worry if you found the paper difficult. Chances are, others will have too. Forget about that exam and prepare for the next one!

Question 1

BPP marking scheme

	Marks
Award 1 mark for each valid point	20

The **value chain model** divides an organisation's activities into nine generic activities; five primary activities and four support activities. Every value activity has both a physical and an information-processing component. The physical component includes all the tasks required to perform the activity. The information-processing component encompasses the steps required to capture, manipulate and channel the data necessary to perform the activity.

The following illustration shows the activities of the value chain with various examples of systems for the primary and support activities that would add a margin of value to Seven-Eleven's products and services.

Firm infrastructure	Electronic scheduling		Minimum HQ involvement		
Human resource management	Work force planning systems		Interactive management training and development		
Technology dev.	CAD for store layout		Electronic market research		
Procurement	On-line ordering systems	Finding suitable sites	Comparison of promotions		
	Automated warehouse	Flexible store layout	Hand-held scanners for faster checkout	Ordering systems	Remote servicing of equip.
	Inbound logistics	Operations	Outbound logistics	Marketing and sales	Service

Support activities — Primary activities

The **role of IT** at the business level is to help the firm reduce costs, differentiate products, and serve new markets. Here are some more examples of how Seven-Eleven can use IT to lower costs, differentiate, and change the scope of competition.

In the **primary activities** of inbound and outbound logistics, IT can be used to advantage. Materials planning systems eg, (MRP II) can help capacity and production scheduling. Warehousing can benefit from bar codes to identify information about stock held. Automated forklift trucks could be used for picking and stocking in the warehouses.

Security in the **operations activities** can be aided by radio controlled tags used on higher value goods to control pilfering.

Marketing and **services activities** can be made more effective by databases such as mailing lists or the information provided by EPOS systems.

In the **support activities**, IT can be used in procurement activities with electronic data interchange (EDI) to link purchasing with sales order systems. It can also be used to monitor supplier prices automatically and recommend which supplier should be used. It can be used similarly in marketing with a system to monitor the prices of all the main competitors so that Seven-Eleven can maintain their market position on pricing.

Question 2

Text reference. Data warehousing is covered in Chapter 3 of the text

Top tips. A well implemented data warehouse should enable the production of high quality information that improves managers understanding of the business. Effective business analysis is possible through a warehouse's ability to contain multiple years of data and permit a high level of query activity.

Easy marks. Describing a data warehouse in part (a) would earn a few easy marks.

BPP marking scheme

		Marks
(a)	Award 1 mark for each valid point	13
(b)	Award 1 mark for each valid point	7
		20

(a) A **data warehouse** supports information processing by providing a solid platform of integrated, historical data. It is a database, data extraction tool and decision support system that extracts data from the organisation's production database, reformats it and loads it into a database designed for querying with an on-line analytical processing systems (OLAP). OLAP allows users to extract significant summary information.

The conventional data warehouse model is a system in which a **large centralised store** of consolidated **business data** is maintained by constant updates from the operational systems (branches/stores). This centralised store is usually a relational database, but often it can be a proprietary multi-dimensional data store, optimised for OLAP queries.

A data warehouse extracts **current** and **historical data** from operating systems inside the organisation. The data is combined with data from **external sources** and reorganised into a central database designed for management reporting and analysis. The information directory provides users with the information about the data available in the warehouse. The components of a data warehouse are shown in the following diagram:

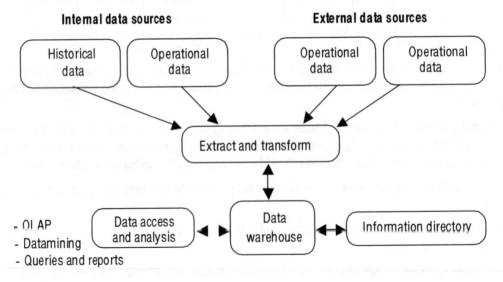

BPP
LEARNING MEDIA

(b)   A **data warehouse** has the ability (through its flexibility) to allow analysis that provides answers to questions or reveal patterns that would remain undetected in a traditional system. Not only does this empower management to analyse such information as past products' sales to determine success or failure attributes, it also allows them to manipulate the data by providing an interactive table so that they can drill down and obtain more details from the data.

It differs from an **operational system** in that it can provide historical information as opposed to a snapshot view of the business and it gives immediate information delivery, enabling the managers to exploit opportunities that they would otherwise miss. For example, it may be possible to track all interactions a company has with a particular customer – from that customer's first purchase, through the take up of special offers and extra services. This makes it possible for managers to have answers to questions like, 'is there a correlation between the amount of money spent in a store with increases or decreases in promotional spend or training of managers?'

Question 3

Text references. Evaluating systems is covered in Chapter 8 of the text.

Top tips. How can the managers at Seven-Eleven tell whether the new system is successful? It is important that the system should have been designed with clear, specified objectives that allow justification in terms of a cost-benefit review and other performance criteria.

Easy marks. Remember efficiency and effectiveness as methods of evaluating a system – use them to generate performance measures for easy marks.

BPP marking scheme

	Marks
Award 1 mark for each valid point	20

The following measures of system success could be used at Seven-Eleven.

- **User information satisfaction** can be ascertained by questionnaire or interview, asking their opinions on the accuracy, timeliness, and relevance of information and on the quality of service and the schedule of operations. Especially critical are managers' attitudes on how well their information needs were satisfied and users' opinions about how well the system enhanced their job performance.

- Levels of **system use** can be measured by polling users, employing questionnaires, or monitoring parameters such as the volume of on-line transactions.

- **Metrics** enables **system quality** to be measured eg, system response time, number of transactions that can be processed, number of system crashes per week and number of calls to help desk per month.

- The **adequacy of system documentation** can be measured in terms of how often manuals and on-line help systems are actually used and found to be effective, and the number of errors found or amendments made.

- The **growth** rates in file sizes and the number of transactions processed by the system. Trends should be analysed and projected to assess whether there are likely to be problems with lengthy processing time or an inefficient file structure due to the volume of processing.

- The clerical **manpower** needs for the system, and deciding whether they are more or less than estimated.

- The identification of any **delays** in processing and an assessment of the consequences of any such delays.

- An assessment of the efficiency of **security** procedures, in terms of number of breaches, number of viruses encountered.

- A check of the **error rates** for input data. High error rates may indicate inefficient preparation of input documents, an inappropriate method of data capture or poor design of input media.

- An examination of whether **output** from the computer is being used to good purpose. (Is it used? Is it timely? Does it go to the right people?)

In any evaluation of a system, two terms recur – efficiency and effectiveness of the organisation.

Efficiency – can be measured by considering the resource inputs into and the outputs from a process or an activity. If the same activity can be performed using fewer resources eg, fewer staff or less money, or if it can be completed more quickly, then the efficiency of the activity is improved. This represents an improvement in productivity.

Effectiveness – is not so easy to measure. It focuses on the relationship of the organisation with its environment. The new system might have been pursued to increase the market share of Seven-Eleven or to satisfy customer needs. Market share can be measured but there are many different factors that can be reflected in these figures and customer satisfaction is measured indirectly through the market share – if the customers are satisfied they will keep returning.

Question 4

> **Text reference**. Information overload is discussed in Chapter 9 of the text.
>
> **Top tips.** Information overload reduces efficiency as it is necessary to sift through too much information to find what is relevant. There is so much information that something vital may be missed.
>
> **Easy marks**. To maximise your marks in part (b), split Mr A's work down into a few categories and generate solutions for each.

BPP marking scheme

		Marks
(a)	Description of information overload	2
	Affect on Mr A (one mark for each valid point)	8
(b)	Manual procedures	5
	IT procedures (one mark for each valid point)	5
		20

(a) **Information overload**

Information overload occurs when a person receives more information than they can efficiently process. There are two main causes of information overload. An individual may simply receive too much information, or the number of information sources may be too numerous.

Mr A at JB Company suffers from both of these causes. He receives so much information from a variety of sources (e-mail, telephone, face-to-face, reports) that he is swamped.

The efficiency of Mr A

Too much of Mr A's time is spent gathering and deciphering information. Between 30 and 40 e-mails are received from staff and clients each day. Some of these may contain vital information requiring urgent action, others could be classified as low priority and others could be 'junk' mail. Widely circulated messages from both within and outside the organisation may be of little interest or value to Mr A, but identifying these messages is time consuming.

Mr A will also receive telephone queries from information analysts and clients. In many cases, queries will have to be answered at once, and therefore he should be in a position to give quick and accurate replies. He also receives information from Internet sites every hour or so. Dealing with queries and digesting further information is time-consuming. It also seems that Mr A will have very few periods of uninterrupted work, which is likely to lead to inefficient work practices.

Mr A needs to delegate query handling to a suitably able colleague, as the potentially large number of clients are taking up too much of his time. (His workload needs to be reduced, as discussed in part (b) of this answer).

(b) To tackle the problem of information overload affecting Mr A the following areas need to be considered:

- Mr A's role and responsibilities
- The information he needs to fulfil his role and responsibilities
- The possible use of IT and other measures to manage information

Manual procedures

The number of clients that Mr A is responsible for will be a driver of the amount of information he needs to do his job. If Mr A is able to delegate client queries his workload and the amount of information flowing to him would reduce.

Mr A seems to be involved in many operational tasks. A personal assistant could be appointed to him, who would have the responsibility of handling incoming telephone calls and e-mail. There is a risk here that, unless this assistant is suitably qualified in this respect, there may be times when information required by Mr A does not get through to him.

Depending on the number of clients Mr A deals with, it may not be realistic to receive so many telephone calls, requiring him to retain the information mentally, as is also the case where face-to-face discussions are held. It would seem that he simply has too many queries to deal with, hence the need to re-organise his responsibilities, so that he deals only with those decisions that it is necessary for him to make.

IT procedures

Mr A reviews Internet sites every hour or so. This alone could be more than enough work for one person, depending on the number of sites visited. This may already be being done by the analysts. Alternately, an Internet-monitoring agent could do this job and automatically advise Mr A when particular events occur, such as information being updated.

The JB intranet could enable information to be retrieved and searched on using client name or client code. This would make information retrieval more efficient.

E-mail messages could be prioritised so that Mr A is aware primarily of only the urgent ones. Defining 'urgent', however, could be a problem; if left to the sender, there is the danger that all messages could be classed as urgent, and hence the effectiveness of the system would be compromised.

Clients could also be given access to the intranet where they could access the information or also be re-directed to other sites containing additional information. There may also be areas where support systems such as Expert Systems (ES) or Executive Information System (EIS) may be employed.

The EIS could present Mr A with summarised high-level information so he does not have to sift through low-level data. If Mr A required lower-level detail he could 'drill down' to view it.

Question 5

Text reference. This question uses some brought forward knowledge and some elements from Chapter 9 of the text.

Top tips. The distribution of computer processing throughout SGI raises a number of issues, most of which centre on the *degree of centralisation* which the group wishes to employ.

Easy marks. Your brought forward 2.1 knowledge will give you a solid base to build on for your answer.

		Marks
(a)	Award 1 mark for each valid point	12
(b)	Award 1 mark for each valid point	8
		20

(a) As the directors have identified, distributed computer systems, either in the form of minicomputers or networked PC-based systems, imply that the organisation is willing to tolerate a **high degree of departmental or individual autonomy** in systems utilisation.

Not only are the systems widely dispersed but the data/information held by the systems is similarly widely dispersed and used. In terms of organisational control this indicates a high level of trust and belief that the individuals will use the information effectively and responsibly.

(i) **Centralised** systems are typically employed for one of two reasons: there are often significant **cost savings** in using a single mainframe computer to provide the information service; and secondly, there are often concerns about the **security** of the information which make centralised processing necessary.

A further justification for centralised computer services follows from the **higher degree of control** which may then be exerted over the use of these services.

Centralised systems also mean that **specialised IT personnel** are in a **single location** and unit. This will reduce the risk of lack of necessary expertise at individual units.

(ii) In a **decentralised** system each department may decide its own computing investment and usage. This tends to weaken the control which might otherwise be imposed. However, the major drawback to centralised control is a tendency to **over-control** activities so that economically **justified actions are overruled** on technical grounds or the organisation **lags behind new developments**. Decentralisation promotes faster response to local problems.

The distribution of information processing throughout SGI is dependent upon a number of factors.

(i) At the simplest level only **economic considerations** are involved: is it cheaper to use PCs or minicomputers than a mainframe?

(ii) At a more sophisticated level, consideration of **data control** and **systems development** are important: are distributed systems less secure and/or less controllable than are centralised systems?

(iii) At the most intangible level, **organisational and internal political considerations** become significant: does the distribution of systems, information or the control of expenditure on them to individuals or departments reflect movements of power or influence within the organisation?

Distribution certainly gives **greater flexibility** to units and offers **greater operational efficiency**; the risk of **loss of control** or **excessive expense** must be balanced against this.

(b)   **Open** systems and **distributed** information systems

At one time computer systems were developed on a **proprietary basis**, which meant that software was developed for use on specified hardware. In large organisations where a wide variety of computer applications were used, this led to inefficient generation and use of information.

An **open system** is a system that ensures that all of its constituent parts, hardware and software, are **compatible** and therefore can **operate together**.

The enormous increase in IT usage over recent years, in particular the development of PC technology, has resulted in demands from computer users for open systems. The compatibility allowed by open systems means that different applications can **'talk' to each other**.

The processing and exchanging of data and information has become more efficient, allowing information to be analysed and presented without duplication of work or other inefficiencies.

Over a similar period of time, **distributed processing systems** have also been developed and have become extremely popular. Using **networks** and local computers they allow a more flexible and efficient approach to information generation than do the more centralised options. In addition they are generally cheaper to purchase and operate and have allowed much smaller organisations to introduce sophisticated computer technology for the first time.

Open systems have made distributed processing and information systems more viable. Open systems technology means that distributed systems can now be developed using different types of hardware, allowing customers to choose on the basis of price and performance; in addition, customers can now develop information systems that match their needs rather than having to compromise because of compatibility issues.

Question 6

Text reference. The theories and models contained in this answer feature in Chapter 5 of the text.

Top tips. This question provides an example of how the examiner expects you to be able to apply general business models to the specific area of information and information systems. In the context of information systems strategy, gap analysis could be used to identify whether the organisation's information systems meet the current and/or predicted organisational information requirements.

Easy marks. Drawing the models in part (a) will earn you easy marks

BPP marking scheme

		Marks
(a)	Award 1 mark for each valid point	5
(b)	Award 1 mark for each valid point (6 marks available for Earl's grid and Peppard's/McFarlan's grid, 3 marks for application)	15
		20

(a)   **Gap analysis** is a technique that analyses the difference or 'gap' between a desired outcome of a process or entity and its extrapolated existing performance, and investigates the ways in which the gap might be closed.

The two broad stages in gap analysis are:

(i)   To assess the size of the gap between the organisation's targets for achievement compared with a projection of what the organisation will actually achieve based on extrapolating its existing activities and performance.

(ii)   Considering strategies to close the gap, so that a strategic plan can be devised for achieving the organisation's targets.

A variety of gaps can be analysed. These include a profit gap, a performance-risk gap, a sales revenue gap, a manpower gap, an Earnings Per Share gap, and in the case of information and information systems, an information gap.

(b)   **Earl's grid** could be used as part of the gap analysis process, to establish and classify the value of existing information systems. The grid analyses an organisation's current use of information systems by plotting them on the following grid.

		Low	High
Business Value	High	Renew	Maintain, enhance
	Low	Divest	Reassess

Technical Quality

The grid suggests the following:

- Systems of poor quality and little value should be disposed of (divest)

- A system of high business value and low technical quality should be renewed (invested in)

- A system of high quality but low business value should be reassessed

- High quality systems with a high business value should be maintained to preserve the high quality, and if possible enhanced in the quest for competitive advantage

The range of options open to an organisation to close an information gap can be considered as a portfolio of potential applications. **Peppard's** strategic grid or **application portfolio** (based upon McFarlan's grid) goes a step further than Earl's grid in that it attempts to allow for expected future developments.

Peppard's grid may be used to prioritise potential new systems. It shows the strategic importance of individual applications in the predicted future competitive environment against the strategic importance of individual applications in the current competitive environment.

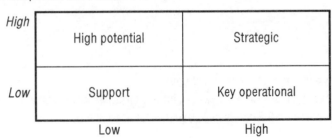

Strategic importance of individual applications in the predicted **future** competitive environment	High	High potential	Strategic
	Low	Support	Key operational
		Low	High

Strategic importance of individual applications in the **current** competitive environment

- **Support applications** are not critical to business success, for example, in some circumstances an accounting system

- **Key operational applications** support established core business activities, for example a production planning system, and should be allocated a high priority

- **Strategic applications** are vital to the organisation's future success and are also likely to be high priority

- **High potential applications** are likely to have a significant impact in the future environment

Analysis of an information gap should therefore help in the identification and evaluation of possible information strategies.

ACCA

Paper 3.4

Business Information Management

Mock Examination 2

Question Paper	
Time allowed	**3 hours**
This paper is divided into two sections	
Section A	THREE compulsory questions to be attempted
Section B	TWO questions ONLY to be attempted

DO NOT OPEN THIS PAPER UNTIL YOU ARE READY TO START UNDER EXAMINATION CONDITIONS

SECTION A – ALL THREE questions are compulsory and MUST be attempted

The following information should be used when answering questions 1, 2 and 3

CAET Ltd

CAET Ltd is a large importer of homecare products; CAET has its head office situated in the centre of the capital city. This head office supports its area branches; a branch consists of an area office and a warehouse. The branches are spread geographically throughout the country; a total of seven area branches are supported. Each of the area offices is run fairly autonomously, each office having its own management team including, in the larger areas, IT support personnel. CAET sells its entire range of products through third party dealers. Each area office can support up to fifty dealers. Each dealer is rated individually, based on their turnover, the amount of floor space devoted to CAET's products and the length of their association with CAET. Most dealers are local and have multiple outlets.

The rating awarded to a dealer determines which categories of products they are able to sell, although few dealers sell all of the products for which they are authorised. Head office sets the dealer rating, but leaves the daily interaction with dealers to area management. Each area office works within a price range determined by head office for each product. There is a preset upper and lower limit per item. The price ranges are reviewed quarterly and any changes in prices are faxed or e-mailed to the branches following the review. This allows for local price bargaining and price setting. The overriding focus is based on annual profit as a percentage of turnover; individual targets are set annually for each area. Salaries and bonuses depend on meeting and beating these targets.

Currently each CAET area office and warehouse supports and supplies its 'own' dealers with the required products. When stocks become low they place a required stock form (RSF) with head office. On receipt of the RSF, head office despatch the goods from their central warehouse to the appropriate area office. When the central warehouse becomes low on any particular item(s) CAET will raise purchase orders and send them to one of their many international suppliers. Typically, each area office has its own stock recording system, running on locally networked computer systems (PCs). RSFs are e-mailed to head office.

Data concerning dealer information is currently held both locally and centrally on independent systems. If a change to the basic information is required, the appropriate office invokes the change and informs the other. Thus each change requires two updates. Each office maintains a simple database. Basic dealer information contains the dealer's name and address, contact details and their credit rating. Full details of which products this dealer is entitled to sell are available and, for each product sold, the quantity sold this month and to-date this year. Basic product information will include: the trade and retail prices of each product, number in stock, reorder level, etc. For each area office, the database provides: the name of the area manager, a full list of all the dealers (or branches) dealt with, and the name of the local dealer contact.

During the last two years, three of the branches have developed independent websites in an attempt to increase their market share. One benefit that has arisen from this enterprising strategy is that orders are now being received from around the world. A new trend in purchasing patterns is emerging: some dealers are purchasing products from more than one area outlet, depending on the price of each product.

In addition, summaries of total business volumes for the current month and the current year to-date are required for each area office. These latter figures are transferred to head office on a monthly basis via e-mail or fax.

CAET was created in 1985, initially dealing from the head office only. Branches were added on a periodic basis. Average expansion has been approximately one new area branch every two years. No new area branches have been opened for the past three years, and there are no immediate plans for opening a new branch. The original business strategy of cloning the head office in the creation of area branches was successful in the early days of expansion, but has proved to be rather cumbersome in terms of management and inventory control during the last few years. The Procurement Director has often been quoted as stating that CAET has eight stock control systems which individually all work well, but when combined, require huge resources, both in terms of human and technological requirements. As a result the accuracy is now becoming questionable.

The information systems strategy has developed under the same regime; basically the stock control system was a bought in packaged system which has been modified to meet the individual requirements of CAET head office. The package is based on an Oracle database and housed on a mini computer. A small team of information technologists based in the head office, and managed by the Information Technology Director, then further developed interface systems to meet the area office's particular requirement, and shipped versions out to the areas for local implementation. These interfaces were developed in Microsoft Access with user interfaces written in Visual Basic. These were then implemented onto local area networks within the local offices and warehouses. Some of the area offices that employ IT personnel have further modified the basic system to meet local needs. Although not formally planned, all the area offices use compatible hardware platforms.

CAET's overall profits and market share of products have gradually been falling during the past four or five years. The original founder, and Chief Executive Officer (CEO), of CAET retired recently and the board of directors appointed a new CEO. For this appointment they broke with tradition and selected an external candidate. The general consensus of the directors was the need to introduce 'new' blood into the management team, someone young with a successful record in business innovation, someone who could revitalise the once very successful business.

During his first few months in the post, the new CEO produced an outline vision and strategy document. The document covered a whole range of areas and topics; several references were made to the information systems/information technology sections, including the following:

The company must rethink and rationalise its information systems strategy and bring it in line with modern business strategy. It was foolhardy to permit the area offices to develop independent systems. Some of the successful developments should be implemented company wide. A good example is the independent development by three branches of a website; the negative side to this development is the company now has three different websites representing it on the world market. A company wide e-commerce strategy must be a priority for the central IT department, as the business as a whole will be moving into the world marketplace: 'Think globally, not locally!' is the CEO's motto. Communication generally is poor between the eight sites – this will be addressed in the near future. The current situation, where the company supports up to eight different IS systems is deemed appalling by the CEO. Integration of IS systems and the development of a single IS strategy is, he believes, the most important feature for the survival and future growth prospects of the company.

The CEO questions whether there is a business requirement for seven cloned branches. The CEO believes the company should investigate the possibility of implementing modern technology, especially e-commerce, to overcome some of the business problems inherent in the current structure. Expanding the market does not require expanding the physical presence of the company, as has previously been the case.

The central focus of the development centred on the notion of developing a business strategy and an information systems strategy in unison. The combination would enable CAET to develop and expand in the future.

Question 1

Internal communications between the eight sites has been identified as a weakness within the current structure. The establishment of an intranet may help to solve this problem.

(a)   Describe the major characteristics and benefits of an intranet.   **(5 marks)**

(b)   Assess the impact of implementing an intranet across the head office and branches. Assume that CAET is going to maintain its current physical structure (ie central office and seven branches).   **(15 marks)**

(Total = 20 marks)

Question 2

The CEO's views include:

'Think globally, not locally'

The CEO questions whether there is a business requirement for seven cloned branches. The CEO believes the company should investigate the possibility of implementing modern technology, especially e-commerce, to overcome some of the business problems inherent in the current structure. 'Expanding the market does not require expanding the physical presence of the company, as has previously been the case.'

(a)   Briefly describe the technology that enables companies to think in terms of global markets.   **(4 marks)**

(b)   Assess the impact of Technological, Sociological, Economic and Political factors on CAET's proposed adoption of e-commerce in a move to global markets.   **(16 marks)**

(Total = 20 marks)

Question 3

(a)   Explain Nolan's Six-Stage Growth model.   **(6 marks)**

(b)   Apply Nolan's Six-Stage Growth model to the CAET scenario.   **(8 marks)**

(c)   Describe a major weakness in the Nolan's Six-Stage Growth model that an analysis of the CAET environment might highlight, within the context of organisations with multi-generation system platforms and applications. Your answer should include the relationship between the model and an IS strategy.   **(6 marks)**

(Total = 20 marks)

SECTION B – TWO questions ONLY to be attempted

Question 4

Consultants have recently been employed by ACCA to analyse the requirements for a revised education programme. The consultants used Checkland's Soft System Methodology in their initial investigation and proposed the following root definition.

Root definition:

'An ACCA owned system which is operated by ACCA staff and students, employers and sponsors; to transform a collection of differently rated professional modules into a highly rated professional programme which offers increased student choice and provides greater practical relevance and cogency within each named module, with students, employers and sponsors having a major say in its structure, content and style of delivery.'

Required

(a) List an appropriate set of CATWOE criteria for the Root Definition.   **(6 marks)**
(b) Draw a conceptual model based on the Root Definition and the CATWOE criteria.   **(10 marks)**
(c) Explain the role that conceptual models play in Checkland's Soft Systems Methodology.   **(4 marks)**

(Total = 20 marks)

Question 5

Required

(a) Giving examples where appropriate, discuss the problem of user resistance to new information systems (IS).   **(6 marks)**

(b) Suggest strategies that may overcome user resistance to new information systems (IS).   **(6 marks)**

(c) Discuss measures of success that can be used to identify how successful a system implementation has been.   **(8 marks)**

(Total = 20 marks)

Question 6

The general environment that an organisation operates within is subject to Political, Economic, Social and Technological (PEST) factors.

Required

For each PEST factor, identify and discuss the issues you believe to be most relevant to the role and use of information systems within organisations and in society as a whole.   **(20 marks)**

BPP)))
LEARNING MEDIA

Answers

DO NOT TURN THIS PAGE UNTIL YOU HAVE
COMPLETED MOCK EXAM 2

A PLAN OF ATTACK

Tackling scenario questions

Section A of the examination for Paper 3.4 comprises a written scenario with three compulsory questions from across the syllabus **linked** to the narrative scenario. The information provided usually includes some discussion of the organisation's current situation, and there is often one or more central characters charged with the task of resolving the problem, or exploiting the opportunity.

The function of this type of question is to test a candidate's ability to tackle unstructured problems, and to **apply** what they know to 'real' situations. There **may be several feasible solutions** and candidates should not necessarily expect there to be a single definitive answer. The solution will involve the use of techniques which have been learned, but usually also requires the exercise of judgement. Preparation to scenario-based questions cannot rely on reading alone, but must be supplemented **by question practice under examination conditions**.

The **ability to structure a coherent answer** which leads logically to its conclusion is essential. Recommendations are often required. Acceptable recommendations may vary, but must be sensible and justified.

Key points to remember when tackling scenario questions:

- Answer the question asked – tailor what you know to fit the scenario
- Prepare a rough plan – this will help clarify your thoughts
- Structure longer answers eg introduction, body of answer, conclusion
- Justify any recommendations

Mock exam 2

Start by spending 5 minutes looking through the paper, gaining an understanding of the scenario and considering how it relates to the requirements.

We will now provide some specific advice regarding this exam. We'll consider two options.

Option 1 (if you're thinking 'Help!')

If after reading the scenario and requirements for Questions 1 to 3 you are not confident of scoring well, you may find it helpful to start with the question from Section B that you feel most confident about. (But remember – you will still have to come back and answer Questions 1 to 3!)

For example, if you feel confident about your ability to apply your knowledge of soft systems methodology, you may wish to start with **Question 4**.

Starting with a question you find 'easier' should help you 'get into' the exam and **build your confidence**. At the start of the exam you will be fresh – you should be in a frame of mind that enables you to recall and apply your knowledge, getting off to a good start before attempting the questions you expect to find more difficult.

Attempting a question you find difficult at the start of an exam could result in a **loss of confidence**. The danger is that as a consequence, you may go on to perform poorly in later questions even if you know the area well.

Option 2 (if you are thinking 'No problem!')

Try not to be overconfident, but if you are feeling fairly comfortable with the content of the paper, then choose the optional questions you wish to answer, then tackle questions in the order they appear – starting with Question 1.

Question 1

There is a considerable amount of scenario information to digest, but do not panic. You are required to describe intranets and think about how CAET will be affected by implementing one

Question 2

The Internet, e-commerce and globalisation are related subjects in Paper 3.4. This question requires to you to asses their impact in a number of areas.

Question 3

Nolan's six-stage growth model is examined in this question – make sure you know all the stages. Most of the marks are available for applying the model so look for clues in the scenario for items that can slot into the six headings.

Section B requires you to answer any two questions from a choice of three. Some Section B questions are also based on scenarios (eg Question 4 in this exam), although the individual scenarios are shorter than the one contained in Part A. The principles of answering scenario-based questions (as explained in the front pages of this book) can also be applied to apply to those Section B questions that are based upon short scenarios.

To reiterate, the key points are:

* **Answer the question asked** – not the question you hoped would be asked
* **Apply your knowledge to the scenario**

Question 4

This question, on soft systems methodology, is one that you are likely to do either very well on (if you have revised this material and practised similar questions) or very poorly on (if you haven't). If you haven't revised this material, don't attempt this question – select the other two questions in section B!

Question 5

This is a fairly theoretical question that tests your understanding of some of the implications surrounding the implementation of new information technology systems. If you are comfortable with this, and have a solid knowledge theories in of this area you should score well.

Question 6

The examiner has often set whole questions on a specific theory or model. These give you a ready made structure for your answer so take advantage. PEST is a useful tool and providing you make reasonable points you should score well.

Time allocation...

Allocate your time according to the marks for the question in total (36 mins for each 20 mark question) and then according to the parts of the question. **Always follow the question requirements exactly**.

If you have allocated your time properly then you shouldn't have time on your hands before the full three hours is up. But if you do find yourself with a spare ten minutes, check that you have answered all questions **fully**.

Finally...

After sitting the 'real' exam, do not worry if you found the paper difficult. Chances are, others will have too. Forget about that exam and prepare for the next one!

Question 1

Text references. Intranets are discussed in Chapter 3 of the text.

Top tips. The wording of part (b) provides a clue that the relationship between the structure of the organisation and of the information system is relevant here.

Easy marks. Setting out the major characteristics of an intranet should earn you easy marks.

Examiner's comments. Candidates did very well on the first part of the question with many obtaining maximum marks.

The second part of the question enabled candidates to apply their knowledge of intranet technology to the scenario. Many candidates identified both positive and negative aspects of introducing an intranet within the company. Candidates who obtained high marks related their answer specifically to the scenario. Overall, this question was answered very well.

Marking scheme

		Marks
(a)	Award up to 2 marks for each valid, explained point – to a maximum of 3 marks for characteristics and 2 for benefits.	5
(b)	A wide range of answers will be given. Award up to 2 marks for each valid explained point up to a maximum of 15.	15
		20

(a) An **intranet** is in effect an 'internal website' used to provide information to individuals within an. The user interface on an intranet is based upon the same technology as used in websites and web browsers (eg hyperlinks using Hyper Text Mark-up Language or HTML).

The content available on an Intranet will differ greatly depending upon the nature and preferences of the organisation involved. Some common features include **staff directories** and **organisational policies** and **procedures**.

Benefits of intranets include the following:

- Relatively low start-up costs
- User-friendly/easy to use as uses familiar interface
- Provides wide availability of information within an organisation
- Flexibility –intranets can be developed to suit the size of the organisation

(b) Implementing an intranet at CAET would have a significant impact in a number of ways.

A **computerised inventory (stock) system** could be implemented on the intranet, replacing the manual system including the Required Stock Forms. Having stock information available on the intranet would allow branches that required a specific item to see whether other branches had excess stock of this item – and to request a stock transfer. Currently, a new order may be placed by head office for goods required by some branches but overstocked in others.

The intranet could also be used to **distribute company policies** and to **dissemination best practice** throughout the organisation. This should improve organisation efficiency, and consistent working methods should allow for relatively easy transfer of staff between branches – providing greater flexibility.

The intranet could provide a platform for the development of a centralised integrated database system. This would provide quick and easy access to and updating of information, a significant improvement on the current system of faxes and e-mails being sent to head office.

Introducing an intranet that held copies of company manuals, catalogues and handbooks should bring savings from reduced printing costs (both internal and external). Staff should be encouraged to view information on-screen rather than automatically printing a hard-copy.

The dissemination of operational and management information would be made easier by the implementation of an intranet. For example, an area on the intranet could be set aside for the quarterly price setting figures and an area could be set aside for information such as 'Monthly sales to date'.

The intranet could be utilised to produce a forum for the exchange of ideas for staff with similar areas of responsibility or shared interests. For example, several area offices have their own IT personnel working independently on similar projects – the intranet would allow ideas and work performed to be shared, avoiding duplicated effort and ensuring a consistent approach.

The introduction of a company wide intranet may be opposed by some area offices, who may see it as a tool that reduces their autonomy. Therefore, the new management team need to stress the benefits of a more centralised organisational structure, enabling the company to become more efficient, but still retaining some branch autonomy where appropriate.

As intranets use a user-friendly interface, very similar to an Internet browser, establishing an intranet should allow more staff to become confident in the use of computers. This should result in employees being more likely to accept the introduction of other new systems in the future.

Question 2

Text reference. Globalisation is covered in text Chapter 7, PEST analysis in Chapter 2.

Top tips. Part (a) provides an opportunity to pick up easy marks for reproducing book knowledge. Be concise though – this part is only worth four marks. Part (b) requires you to apply your PEST analysis skills to the situation at CAET.

Easy marks. PEST analysis in part (b) is always a good opportunity to earn marks as a wide rage of answers will be given credit.

Examiner's comments. Part (a) required a brief description of the Internet and related technologies. Many candidates scored very high marks.

The second part of the question required an assessment in the form of technological, sociological, economic and political factors. Marks were awarded for both internal and external factors. Many candidates produced excellent answers that were related to the scenario, identifying specifically in terms of political and sociological factors, the possible changes that could occur, ie the change in relationships within the company between branches and dealers, the requirement to maintain seven branches etc. Weaker candidates supplied answers that were generic in nature and not always applicable to CAET Ltd.

Marks

(a)   Award up to 2 marks for each valid, explained point to a maximum of
4 marks.   4

(b)   A wide range of answers will be given. Award up to 2 marks for each
valid explained point up to a maximum of 4 for each PEST factor –
overall max 16. $\frac{16}{\overline{20}}$

(a)   The Internet, the World Wide Web and related communications technologies enable organisations to think
and act globally.

The Internet describes the way computers all over the world are able to communicate with each other in a
global international network. The Internet connects governments, businesses, universities and household
computer users all over the world.

The World Wide Web allows organisations of all sizes to establish a website accessible from all over the
world – encouraging a global perspective. Individuals and organisations are now able to communicate and
conduct business efficiently with other organisations and individuals all over the world.

(b)   CAET's proposed adoption of e-commerce in a move to global markets will be affected by Political,
Economic, Sociological and Technological (PEST) factors, as explained below.

Political factors

In relation to the internal politics of CAET, the adoption of e-commerce will have a significant impact upon
the overall strategy of the organisation, with resulting changes in authority and power for some individuals
and departments.

A move to e-commerce is likely to result in a single centralised operation, rather than the current
decentralised operation with eight separate points of business. The management structure would need to be
revised to compliment the new organisation structure. Branches and branch managers will have less power
and autonomy.

Wider political considerations include the need to consider different legal considerations across
international boundaries (eg different data protection requirements). The political stability of new export
markets should also be considered.

Economic factors

Internally, the economic impact will depend to a large extent on whether e-commerce will add to current
methods of doing business or replace them. A move to e-commerce only could facilitate the removal of
retailers from the supply chain, resulting in improved margins for CAET.

Global distribution may be possible from a single central office and warehouse, or may require setting up
sites overseas. If so, the financing of these new sites must be considered.

The economic climate and spending patterns of consumers in overseas markets will also be an important
factor in the economic viability of e-commerce.

Sociological factors

One of the main social implications is likely to be due to the different skills required by the organisation if e-commerce is introduced. Some existing staff are likely to lose their jobs, others may have to retrain and some new staff with different skills will be recruited.

Redundancy payments, changes in status, and the break-up of established social groups will all impact upon operations. Some degree of resistance to this change is likely and should be planned for. Ultimately, the move to e-commerce will require a significant change in the internal culture.

Technological factors

Establishing a website with e-commerce capability will require significant software development including integrating the site into back office systems such as stock control. Integrating this new technology with existing legacy systems may not be possible, requiring other new systems to be implemented.

The site may be hosted on CAET hardware, which may need to be purchased, or could be hosted by an external party who charge a lease fee.

Existing CAET systems staff may not possess the skills required to set up and maintain the site, so new staff or the use of contactors or consultants should be considered.

Question 3

Text reference. Nolan is covered in Chapter 6 of the text.

Top tips. The initial part of the question requires an explanation of Nolan's six-stage growth model: initiation, contagion, control, integration, data administration and maturity. The second part requires an application of the model to the scenario, and the final part seeks a discussion of the weaknesses inherent in the model when applied to organisations with multi-generation system platforms and applications such as CAET Ltd.

Easy marks. Stating Nolan's six stages will earn you easy marks.

Examiner's comments. The examiner commented that it was apparent that a significant number of candidates, albeit a minority, were not familiar with Nolan's model. This was rather surprising as it is covered in depth in all of the recommended study texts. Better prepared candidates obtained maximum marks for the first part by listing and giving a brief description of each stage. Generally, high marks were obtained for the application of the model to the scenario with many candidates identifying the various stages of the model with systems/applications within the company. Reasonable marks were awarded for the final part, where candidates recognised a relationship between Nolan's model and CAET's information systems strategy.

Marking scheme

		Marks
(a)	Award up to 1 mark for identifying each stage	6
(b)	Award up to 2 marks for each valid, explained point applying the model to the case study – to a maximum of 8	8
(c)	Award up to 2 marks for each valid, explained point to a maximum of 6	6
		20

(a) Nolan's six stage growth model explains how the use of IS/IT within an organisation develops over time. The model lists six stages:

Stage 1 Initiation. This involves the automation of clerical operations such as payroll and letter writing.

Stage 2 Contagion. Rapid growth occurs in the use of IS/IT as users become familiar with technology and realise the benefits technology can provide.

Stage 3 Control. Management realises that IS/IT is an important part of operations, so formal planning and methodologies are introduced in an attempt to control developments.

Stage 4 Integration. This stage involves the integration of previously separate systems/applications within the organisation. The need for, and value of, involving users in systems development is understood.

Stage 5 Data administration. The emphasis moves towards information provision and requirements rather than on transaction and data processing. The need for management of how data id held and administered is recognised.

Stage 6 Maturity. In this stage IS/IT strategy is considered alongside business strategy. IS/IT is seen as inherent to operations, not separate.

(b)

Examiner's note – the following answer is only one example, a variety of answers would have been appropriate.

We will now apply Nolan's model to CAET.

Stage 1 Initiation. The automation of the stock recording system by head office.

Stage 2 Contagion. The spreading of the automated stock recording system to branches, and three branches setting up their own websites could be seen as examples of the contagion stage.

Stage 3 Control. Some branches took control of the system, modifying it to meet their own requirements. Senior management will control any move to e-commerce.

Stage 4 Integration. CAET hasn't really achieved this stage, as although all branches are running similar systems they aren't really integrated. If e-commerce is introduced, integration between front and back office systems will be essential.

Stage 5 Data administration. Some data administration has taken place, within the stock recording system. All branches appear to use the same data structure.

Stage 6 Maturity. The e-commerce proposal has forced senior management to consider the need to align IS/IT strategy with business strategy. Increased control, integration and data administration will also be required.

(c) One weakness of Nolan's model is that it implies that organisations move from a **low awareness** and use of IS/IT through to **maturity** in one sequential process. In reality this is seldom the case.

As new technologies emerge almost **constantly**, an organisation well versed in IS/IT may suddenly find that a new technology emerges that results in the organisation finding itself back in an earlier stage of Nolan's model.

For example, in the past CAET experienced **contagion** with the expansion of the automated stock control system – and has recently experienced contagion again with some branches setting up websites.

This concept is also demonstrated by the relatively recent emergence of **mobile** and **global IS**. This has resulted in many 'IS/IT mature' organisations having to educate themselves about the new technology. Introducing this new technology sometimes also requires **changes** to **established systems** – to enable integration with new systems. Older generation systems were devised before the demands of later technologies were known, which is why **significant changes** may be required to enable what were previously considered state of the art systems to interact with new technology.

The regular emergence of **new technologies** has also shown the need for flexibility in an organisation's IS strategy. Although Nolan's model is sequential, and therefore relatively inflexible, it does encourage a planned and coordinated approach.

Although Nolan's model may be considered of **limited value** if viewed in the context of one model per organisation, the model may best be utilised by producing a different model for each relevant system or technology. This will allow for **different ages** of different technologies to be taken into account. Then, these multiple models may be looked at and considered when revising or considering overall IS strategy.

Question 4

Text reference. Soft system methodology is discussed in Chapter 4 of the text.

Top tips. The information in the question provides almost all of the answer to part (a), allowing some easy marks to be obtained. Part (b) is more difficult, although again most of the events are provided within the question. For part (c), some basic comments about SSM are required – there are only four marks available in this section – don't waffle but make four concise points.

Easy marks. There are few easy marks unless you are comfortable with SSM. If you are, setting out the CATWOE criteria in part (a) is a good opportunity to gain easy credit.

Marking scheme

		Marks
(a)	Award 1 mark for each criteria or suitable equivalent (max 6 marks)	6
(b)	Award 1 mark for each correctly defined (or equivalent) activity up to a maximum of 8 marks	8
	Award 1 mark for each boundary correctly identified (maximum 2 marks)	2
(c)	Award 1 mark for each valid point (up to a maximum of 4 marks)	4
		20

(a) The CATWOE criteria for the root definition can be listed as follows.

Client or customer	Future ACCA students
Actor	ACCA staff, Students, Employers and Sponsors
Transformation	A highly rated professional programme offering increased practical relevance and cogency
Weltanschauung	Students, Employers and Sponsors should have a major say in the structure, style and delivery of the programme
Owner	ACCA
Environment	Professional business and commerce

(b)

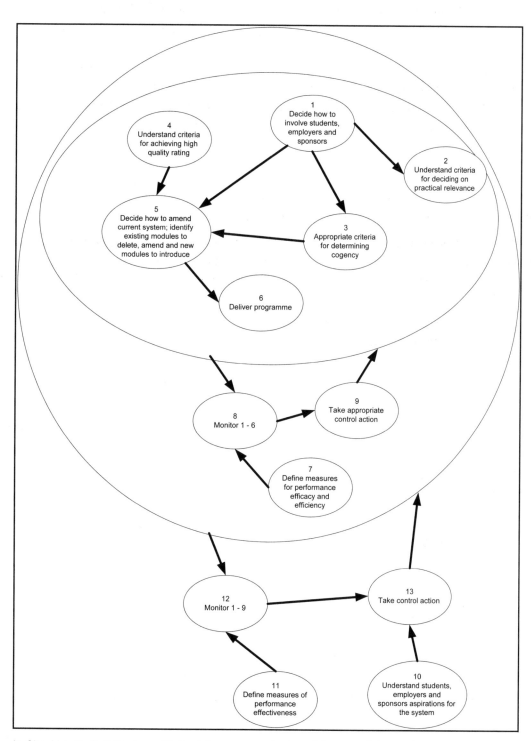

(c) In Checkland's Soft Systems Methodology, conceptual models are activity models focusing on what needs to be done in a system. The model therefore shows key activities such as 'deliver program' or 'take control action' rather than explaining how these activities will take place.

The model provides the actions necessary to satisfy the root definition, based on the worldview in the CATWOE criteria. How the activities will actually be carried out in the 'real world' is unclear, and discussion will be needed to clarify the situation. The model does provide a basis for this discussion by ordering the activities or events that must take place and noting some of the feedback that is required within the system.

Question 5

Text reference. User resistance is discussed in Chapter 8 of the text.

Top tips. The logical thing to do here is to relate your answer to part (b) to the points you made in part (a).

Easy marks. As the question requires, give examples where appropriate as this will boost your answer and earn quick marks.

Examiner's comments. Parts (a) and (b) provided some very good answers. The mark earning ability of some answers in part (b) was limited where candidates did not provide sufficient breadth of comment.

Part (c) was again answered very well with the examiner noting that many candidates obtained full marks. A minority of answers provided discussion on financial aspects only, limiting the marks that could be awarded.

Marking scheme

		Marks
(a)	Award up to 1 mark for each valid point. Max 6 marks.	6
(b)	Award up to 2 marks for each strategy. Max 6 marks.	6
(c)	Award up to 2 marks per measure. Max 8 marks.	8
		20

(a) **User resistance**

User resistance to new information systems can be discussed under three areas:

(i) **People-orientated theory**

User resistance is caused by factors internal to users as individuals or as a group. Users may be generally fearful of change and do not want to or are unwilling to accept new working practices. They may see new systems as disrupting their current work or social groups.

For example, offices workers may be unwilling to accept a new office automation system because it amends the way their work is carried out. Users may find themselves in different groups or be unwilling to work different hours or work at home where required.

(ii) **System orientated theory**

User resistance is caused by factors inherent in the new system design relating to ease of use and functionality. For example, the user interface may be poorly designed generating user resistance.

System orientated theory is particularly relevant where users are not involved in the design process. The user interface may be incorrectly designed so it does not reflect the work method of the user. For example, fields may become active, but not in the order that follows the users' work-method.

(iii) **Interaction theory**

User resistance is caused by the interaction of people and the system. For example, the computer system may be well designed, but its implementation will cause organisational changes that users resist. The system may inhibit bonus payments, cause redundancies or be the source of monotonous work.

For example, a computer may replace a human in a production process such as car assembly. Expert systems also cause user resistance because the importance and decision making ability of the human is reduced.

(b)   **Methods of overcoming user resistance**

(i)   **People orientated theory**

User resistance can be overcome by:

- User training to explain the purpose of the system and how to use it
- User involvement in system development
- Persuasion
- Coercion

The last two methods may work, but should be used only as a last resort as they may result in resistance and resentment against management and/or the system.

(ii)   **System orientated theory**

User resistance can be overcome by:

- User training and education
- Improving the user-interface to make it more user friendly
- Ensuring user contribute to the system design process
- Making sure that the system 'fits in' with the way work is carried out in the organisation.

It is also important to design the work area around the computer correctly. The ergonomics in terms of chairs, tables, height of keyboard etc, must also be correct to help users accept the system.

(iii)   **Interaction theory**

User resistance can be overcome by:

- Re-organising the organisation prior to implementing the computer to ensure that the computer 'fits in' with the company systems

- Redesign any affected reward or incentive schemes to ensure that they can be used with the computer system

- Promote user participation and encourage teamwork to reduce the organisational impact

- Emphasising the benefit of the new system

- Use of socio-technical design to ensure that the technical design of the system and the social requirements for system use are matched as far as possible

(c)   **Measures of system success**

(i)   **Usage levels**

If users actually use the new system then this is indicative that the system is meeting their requirements and is an overall success. System use can be monitored by checking network traffic, or recording keystrokes made for example. Lack of use of any old system is also indicative that the new system is successful.

(ii)   **Help desk use**

Calls to the help desk can be monitored in terms of overall frequency and content. Success may be determined by overall fall in help desk calls and focus on more technical aspects of system use. Many calls on basic system features, repeated frequently from the same people will be indicative of lack of success as users cannot be bothered to learn how to use the system correctly.

(iii)   **Pre– and post implementation questionnaires**

These can be used to determine whether or not users like the system and therefore whether it is successful. Increase in user satisfaction determined from the two questionnaires will be indicative of system success.

(iv)   **System objectives met**

The post implementation review will check whether the initial system objectives have been met. If they have, then this again is indicative of success.

(v)   **User acceptance of IT**

IT departments in many companies are not always well thought of. If the IT department and IT support staff are viewed favourably then this indicates that users are happy with the IT system and the support provided.

(vi)   **Cost**

IT systems may not be implemented to achieve cost savings. However, where the system allows work to be carried out more efficiently, or allows transfer of electronic documents rather than paper, then cost and efficiency savings will be generated. If these meet targets for savings then the system will be successful.

(vii) **System availability**

A system will be successful if it is available for use when required. Monitoring system downtime will show how successful the system is; downtime should be limited to a few minutes at the most per day.

Question 6

Text reference. PEST analysis is covered in Chapter 2 of the text.

Top tips. Organisations and the information systems they use exist within the general environment. Within this environment are many factors that could potentially impact upon the organisation. Issues relevant to the role and use of information systems within organisations and in society in general are examined regularly – ensure you are familiar with these issues.

Easy marks. Wider reading will benefit you in questions such as this and provide you a source of good points to make and easy marks.

BPP marking scheme

		Marks
Award 1 mark per valid point for each factor up to a maximum of five per factor	5 × 4	20

Political issues

Personal privacy

Advances in data storage techniques and reduced storage media costs have led to a dramatic increase in the amount of information organisations are able to hold about individuals. The need to balance an individual's right to privacy against the convenience and other advantages of allowing information to be collected and stored has led many governments to update data protection legislation. Further changes in response to new developments are highly likely.

Protecting intellectual property

Intellectual property is intangible property created by individuals or organisations that is subject to protections under trade secret, copyright and patent law. Information technology has made it difficult to protect intellectual property because computerised information can be so easily copied or distributed on networks.

Economic issues

The economy and economic growth

New systems and technology are often expensive. Organisations are less likely to be prepared to invest in these technologies in times of economic uncertainty.

Greater dependency on business partners

The closer business relationships that result from increased technological links with business partners mean that organisations are increasingly dependant on their key suppliers and customers.

The need for organisational flexibility and an acceptance of change

Organisations now operate in an environment where the pace of technological change is fast. Organisations must therefore be flexible enough to adapt quickly and must plan for change and innovation.

Social issues

Inequality

Governments may feel a responsibility to ensure technological know how does not result in an increased gap between the 'haves and have-nots'. Initiatives allowing access to technology to lower socio-economic groups may be required to prevent the growth of a 'digital divide'.

Globalisation

Global information systems such as the Internet help facilitate the growth of global organisations and encourage a global outlook. This may have social effects that some consider undesirable – such as the loss of local businesses, and the dilution of local culture.

Ethics and the moral dimensions of the information society

Ethics refers to the principles of right and wrong that can be used to guide behaviour. Information systems raise ethical questions for both individuals and societies because they create opportunities for intense social change and threaten existing distributions of power, money, rights and obligations.

The five moral dimensions of the information society, listed below, raise a number of ethical issues.

(a)   Information rights and obligations – what information rights do individuals and organisations possess with respect to information about themselves? What can they protect?

(b)   Property rights – how can traditional intellectual property rights be protected in a digital society in which reproduction of intellectual property is so easy?

(c)   Accountability and control – who can and will be held accountable and liable for the harm done to individual and collective information and property rights?

(d)   System quality – what standards of data and system quality should we demand to protect individual rights and the safety of society?

(e)   Quality of life – what values should be preserved in an information and knowledge– based society? What institutions should we protect from violation? What cultural values and practices are supported by the new information technology?

Technological issues

The need for improved system reliability and quality

The use of information systems in many organisations' core production processes has resulted in an increased dependence on systems to conduct day to day operations. It is essential therefore that these systems are free from major errors, and are fairly robust.

Infrastructure development

Information systems require an infrastructure that allows them to operate effectively eg communications links must be of sufficient standard. The responsibility for infrastructure development may not always be clear, or may require joint-ventures between unlikely partners eg government agencies and private sector organisations.

Cost-benefit justification

In the past some organisations and individuals have been willing to upgrade simply because a new system is available. There now appears to be a trend towards sticking with current systems if they appear adequate. Some organisations aren't fully utilising existing systems, so see little point adding more features.

ACCA

Paper 3.4

Business Information Management

Mock Examination 3

December 2006

Question Paper	
Time allowed	**3 hours**
This paper is divided into two sections	
Section A	**THREE compulsory questions to be attempted**
Section B	**TWO questions ONLY to be attempted**

DO NOT OPEN THIS PAPER UNTIL YOU ARE READY TO START UNDER EXAMINATION CONDITIONS

SECTION A – ALL THREE questions are compulsory and MUST be attempted

The following information should be used when answering questions 1, 2 and 3

Vinylattac Co

Introduction

In 1992 Mark Smith set up a company Vinylattac Co that supplied rare vinyl records to individuals within his local area. Mark had a large collection of records and was an avid collector of all types of music. He originally began his business as a way of supplementing his income. However Mark was soon turning his passion and hobby into a business venture. He had just completed a computer science degree at a local university and he was keen to exploit technology he had learned about. He successfully used the recently developed internet to advertise his business. During the following two years, as Mark's business began to grow, he was surprised at the number of new clients who were contacting him for requests and information. Mark had numerous contacts in the record industry and personally knew many of the record suppliers and record shop owners who specialised in this business area. In 1995 he quit his job as a computer programmer/analyst in order to pursue his business interests full time. He expanded his services and began to supply audiotapes and compact discs (CDs) through the website.

Business Expansion

In 1997 Mark purchased a commercial outlet, which consisted of a retail shop, small warehouse and office space. He employed eight people to help with the business expansion. Mark continued to invest in technology, setting up electronic links with suppliers and maintaining a comprehensive customer database and stock recording system. Four years ago, when Vinylattac was seeking further expansion, Mark required extra financial support and actively sought financial backing. Eventually Gregory Coster, a former university colleague, provided the financial support. Gregory is a successful business entrepreneur with an interest in music. He does not share Mark's enthusiasm with the music business but has proved to be an able and willing business partner.

Current Position

Vinylattac is in a highly competitive market. There are threats from many other companies who also provide online purchasing facilities and the mass illegal copying/pirating that is becoming common practice in the music industry. Vinylattac is currently supplying CDs, DVDs, audiotapes and vinyl records throughout the country. The company has recently moved to larger premises and now employs fifteen staff. Even in the new larger premises space is at a premium. There are two full time members of the technical team. This team maintains and modifies the website and organises the product, supplier and customer databases. There are over two million titles on the product database, in the region of one hundred thousand customers and over thirty suppliers.

Vinylattac receive supplies from many of the major music distributors, but due to the size of its operation it cannot achieve the economies of scale of large retailers such as supermarkets and national music suppliers. Gregory has suggested that they form a consortium with local independent retailers with whom they currently conduct business, to purchase the latest recordings and thus benefit from bulk purchasing. Furthermore, Mark's wife Gloria, who manages the three purchasing clerks, encourages the clerks to continually scan the supplier's databases and websites to ensure that Vinylattac is purchasing its products at the lowest prices available. Vinylattac has developed some excellent working relationships with a small number of suppliers and receives very competitive prices for certain purchases. Orders with a limited number of suppliers are handled completely electronically, with deliveries being staggered to meet customer requirements. In some cases Vinylattac has negotiated a sale or return agreement with its major suppliers.

Online purchasing

The online ordering system permits customers to place an order and make payment via credit card on secure lines. When an order is received it is normally despatched within twenty four hours. However, older selections and particularly rare vinyl recordings can take up to four weeks before being despatched. Despatch times are communicated to customers upon receipt of order. Mark is aware that Vinylattac does not use its customer information to promote sales and analyse customer purchasing habits. This is a major weakness in Vinylattac's information systems strategy and as a result of this Vinylattac's expansion has slowed down in the last two years. Additionally, during this period, there has been increased competition in this market.

Vinylattac offers a unique search service to individuals and small record shop retailers. Customers requesting particularly rare recordings often do not know the title or artist. In such cases customers often supply clues such as 'it was recorded in the seventies and has three men on the sleeve, and I think one of them is sitting on a sofa', 'it was on a pink label and it had an amazing reworking of something or other by Bach which went on for a whole side of the LP', etc. To fulfil such queries is both time consuming and requires expert knowledge. There is little financial payback from this service but it does provide a unique selling point. Queries of this nature have been increasing during the last few years. Gregory Coster has suggested that they should employ teleworkers to deal with this side of the business. He is aware that Mark has several personal contacts worldwide with expert knowledge, who would welcome the idea of earning extra money while working from home. Due to the expansion of the business and the lack of space in Vinylattac's premises Gregory also believes that other functions of the business could be adequately served by teleworkers. Mark is a little apprehensive about employing teleworkers. He has always managed the business in a personal manner, often employing friends and people with a genuine interest in the music business. Mark believes that the workers at Vinylattac are colleagues and friends rather than just employees. The majority of the employees share Mark's enthusiasm and commitment to the business and they often voluntarily extend their working hours to complete tasks.

Computing facilities

The computing facilities within Vinylattac are advanced for such a small sized company. Mark has not lost his enthusiasm for technology. Each department is equipped with the latest personal computers (PCs) and they are supported by a modern client server based technology. The software includes the latest versions of standard office systems and a relational database management system. The systems provide access to company information as and when required. Mark controls user access rights.

Mark is continually developing the Vinylattac website and wishes to pursue this as a business strategy. He is currently planning to introduce a monthly magazine that will be posted on the site. The magazine will provide customers with the latest news and previews of forthcoming releases. The electronic magazine will also include a section for customers to publish news items and comments.

Over ninety per cent of Vinylattac's current business is conducted in the home country. Overseas clients normally make specific requests for recordings that are no longer available in their home countries. The cost of postage and packaging for overseas clients is often more than the purchase price of the order. Gregory has suggested they should contemplate entering the global market place. In a recent meeting with Mark he stated, 'Our business should take advantage of the global marketplace. We should expand and rise to the challenge, I am sure we can provide a global service and reap the benefits.' Mark responded, 'It's not that easy to expand and provide our services in the global market. To make such a change may involve a complete rethink of our business strategy.' Gregory replied, 'I thought the business strategy was to exploit technology and make as much profit as possible'.

Question 1

An analysis of Porter's five competitive forces can help organisations identify opportunities for information systems to provide a strategic advantage.

Required

(a) Briefly describe each of Porter's five competitive forces and explain how an understanding of each can help an organisation to develop an information systems strategy. **(10 marks)**

(b) Produce a five forces analysis of Vinylattac, showing how IT/IS has been used to manage the threats so far.

(10 marks)

(Total = 20 marks)

Question 2

(a) Discuss why the relationship between business strategies and information systems strategies has changed during the last few decades. **(10 marks)**

(b) Evaluate how effective Vinylattac has been in aligning its business and information systems strategies.

(6 marks)

(c) With reference to the conversation between Mark and Gregory (in the last paragraph of the case study) concerning globalisation, identify technical and economic factors that may influence the decision.

(4 marks)

(Total = 20 marks)

Question 3

(a) Briefly describe in general terms the technical facilities that are required to support teleworkers. **(4 marks)**

(b) With reference to Vinylattac, identify the advantages and disadvantages of employing teleworkers from the employer's perspective. **(8 marks)**

(c) With reference to Vinylattac, identify the advantages and disadvantages of employing teleworkers from the employee's perspective. **(8 marks)**

(Total = 20 marks)

SECTION B – TWO questions ONLY to be attempted

Question 4

(a)   Discuss ethical issues and political/legal issues in the context of business information management.

(10 marks)

(b)   DRGB is a market research company. The company employs market research consultants to gather information from the public concerning their purchasing habits, personal details, financial circumstances, etc. These consultants are paid bonuses based on the number of questionnaires completed by respondents. This information is gathered in public areas such as shopping centres. The normal procedure is to approach people and offer them entry into a prize draw if they cooperate in the completion of a questionnaire. The interviewees are casually informed at the end of the interview, although apparently this does not happen in all cases, that the data gathered might be used by companies that may contact them in the future.

DRGB inputs all the information into a central database that has data mining facilities. DRGB's main business is selling this information to clients that require lists of people who meet specific criteria for their products or services. These companies then promote their products/services by contacting the targeted people in a variety of ways, such as telesales, mail shots and visits to the individual's homes. Some of these companies use hard sales tactics, preying on the vulnerability of some of its potential customers. Others use standard sales techniques of merely informing potential customers of their products/services. Recently the CEO of DRGB has received numerous complaints concerning the use of data/information collected by his company. Apparently many customers have suffered stress and financial loss. Many of DRGB's respectable clients are concerned by the complaints, as some have been made very public and have received extensive press coverage.

Required

Produce an ethical analysis for the dilemma referred to in the case study.   **(10 marks)**

(Total = 20 marks)

Question 5

(a)   Describe the role of Critical Success Factors (CSFs) and Performance Indicators (PIs) in the determination of an organisation's information requirements.   **(12 marks)**

(b)   During the last twelve months Moveit, a national haulage company, has received an increasing number of complaints from its clients regarding the late delivery of goods. Moveit contracts its services to major retail companies. It maintains long running contracts to pick up goods from distribution centres and deliver them to the client's retail outlets within the terms of their contracts. The CEO is concerned about the increasing number of complaints. Following an internal investigation, the CEO has found that most complaints are related to late deliveries, competitive pricing and a delay in responding to client queries. The CEO has recently circulated an updated company mission statement that states the company will provide the best possible service to its clients.

Required:

In your role as the sales manager with responsibility for responding to client enquiries, orders and complaints, identify two specific critical success factors, their associated performance indicators (PIs) and a source of information that may be used to quantify the PI in an effort to improve the current situation.   **(8 marks)**

(Total = 20 marks)

BPP
LEARNING MEDIA

Question 6

(a)   The output from a portfolio analysis that categorises information systems can be illustrated in the following grid.

Portfolio analysis grid

		Low	High
	High	Identify and develop	Examine carefully
Potential Benefits			
	Low	Routine projects	Avoid

Low   . High

Project Risk

Required

Explain how the portfolio analysis grid shown above can help a company to prioritise its information systems developments.   **(8 marks)**

(b)   A medium sized light engineering manufacturing company that provides its products to local larger businesses and, to a lesser extent, to private customers, has recently conducted a gap analysis. The company currently runs its business on a low technology strategy with few information systems. In terms of Parsons' generic strategies it would be situated between 'scarce resource' and 'necessary evil'. In an attempt to modernise its approach and to develop an information systems strategy that would enable it to exploit technology, a list of possible proposals for information systems has been compiled for consideration by the CEO. These include: a computer aided design (CAD) system, a data warehouse system and an extranet system.

Required

In the context of the business described above, briefly describe each of the proposed information systems, a CAD system, a data warehouse system and an extranet system, and explain where each of the proposed information systems may map onto the portfolio analysis grid presented in (a).   **(12 marks)**

(Total = 20 marks)

Answers

**DO NOT TURN THIS PAGE UNTIL YOU HAVE
COMPLETED MOCK EXAM 3**

A PLAN OF ATTACK

Tackling scenario questions

Section A of the examination for Paper 3.4 comprises a written scenario with three compulsory questions from across the syllabus **linked** to the narrative scenario. The information provided usually includes some discussion of the organisation's current situation, and there is often one or more central characters charged with the task of resolving the problem, or exploiting the opportunity.

The function of this type of question is to test a candidate's ability to tackle unstructured problems, and to **apply** what they know to 'real' situations. There **may be several feasible solutions** and candidates should not necessarily expect there to be a single definitive answer. The solution will involve the use of techniques which have been learned, but usually also requires the exercise of judgement. Preparation to scenario-based questions cannot rely on reading alone, but must be supplemented **by question practice under examination conditions**.

The **ability to structure a coherent answer** which leads logically to its conclusion is essential. Recommendations are often required. Acceptable recommendations may vary, but must be sensible and justified.

Key points to remember when tackling scenario questions:

- Answer the question asked – tailor what you know to fit the scenario
- Prepare a rough plan – this will help clarify your thoughts
- Structure longer answers eg introduction, body of answer, conclusion
- Justify any recommendations

Mock exam 3

Start by spending 5 minutes looking through the paper, gaining an understanding of the scenario and considering how it relates to the requirements.

We will now provide some specific advice regarding this exam. We'll consider two options.

Option 1 (if you're thinking 'Help!')

If after reading the scenario and requirements for Questions 1 to 3 you are not confident of scoring well, you may find it helpful to start with the question from Section B that you feel most confident about. (But remember – you will still have to come back and answer Questions 1 to 3!)

For example, if you feel confident about your ability to apply your knowledge of critical success factors, you may wish to start with **Question 5**.

Starting with a question you find 'easier' should help you 'get into' the exam and **build your confidence**. At the start of the exam you will be fresh – you should be in a frame of mind that enables you to recall and apply your knowledge, getting off to a good start before attempting the questions you expect to find more difficult.

Attempting a question you find difficult at the start of an exam could result in a **loss of confidence**. The danger is that as a consequence, you may go on to perform poorly in later questions even if you know the area well.

Option 2 (if you are thinking 'No problem!')

Try not to be overconfident, but if you are feeling fairly comfortable with the content of the paper, then choose the optional questions you wish to answer, then tackle questions in the order they appear – starting with Question 1.

Question 1

After reading and re-reading the scenario take a calm look at Question 1. Ensure you read the requirement correctly, and that your answer meets this requirement. Question 1 tests your knowledge and application of Porter's five forces.

Question 2

This question is a good theoretical test of strategy that requires you to demonstrate evidence of your understanding of the relationship between business and information systems strategy.

Question 3

A straightforward question tackling the subject of teleworking from and employer's and employees' perspective.

Section B requires you to answer any two questions from a choice of three. Some Section B questions are also based on scenarios (eg Question 4 in this exam), although the individual scenarios are shorter than the one contained in Part A. The principles of answering scenario-based questions (as explained in the front pages of this book) can also be applied to apply to those Section B questions that are based upon short scenarios.

To reiterate, the key points are:

- **Answer the question asked** – not the question you hoped would be asked
- **Apply your knowledge to the scenario**

Question 4

Ethics are likely to be examined regularly in this paper. This question requires you to demonstrate a knowledge of issues and a framework to tackle ethical dilemmas.

Question 5

This question requires a demonstration of your knowledge of critical success factors (CSFs) and performance indicators (PIs) in part (a), and application of the knowledge in part (b). Ensure your answer clearly distinguishes between CSFs and PIs.

Question 6

This is the third of the optional question that requires a demonstration of knowledge in part (a) and application in part (b) – in this case the theory is portfolio analysis. You must consider the nature of the industry to score well in part (b).

Time allocation...

Allocate your time according to the marks for the question in total (36 mins for each 20 mark question) and then according to the parts of the question. **Always follow the question requirements exactly**.

If you have allocated your time properly then you shouldn't have time on your hands before the full three hours is up. But if you do find yourself with a spare ten minutes, check that you have answered all questions fully.

Finally...

After sitting the 'real' exam, do not worry if you found the paper difficult. Chances are, others will have too. Forget about that exam and prepare for the next one!

Question 1

BPP marking scheme

		Marks
(a)	Award up to 2 marks per force. 1 mark for description and 1 mark for explanation. 2×5 forces	10
(b)	Award up to 2 marks per force. 2×5 forces	10
		20

(a)   Porter's five forces:

Threat of new entrants

This threat is particularly relevant in markets that are traditionally highly profitable or new. Rapidly expanding markets are likely to attract businesses who wish to take a share of the profit or grow their business.

An information systems strategy may aim to use IS/IT in a defensive manner.

IS/IT can be used by existing businesses to defend their position (by increasing their economies of scale or tying in suppliers in the supply chain). An understanding of this force can also help an organisation develop an offensive information systems strategy. For example, a new entrant may use IS/IT to leap over the barriers to entry to take a piece of the market.

Bargaining power of suppliers

An organisation's suppliers become powerful when there is no option but to use them. This may be due to the quality of the goods the supplier provides or the delivery time that they meet.

An effective information systems strategy may erode this power by allowing the administrative integration of the supplier into the business, by allowing the business to share in the design of the products supplied, or by increasing competition between suppliers by allowing quick and easy comparison of products and prices.

Bargaining power of customers

Customers gain power when it is easy for them to switch between suppliers and the goods they want are homogeneous.

One possible strategy would be to use technology to improve customer analysis, enabling the tailoring of products to best meet the needs of the consumer. Another would be to 'lock-in' customers – for example by providing a convenient distribution channel for their products. Both methods will reduce the power of customers.

Threat of substitute goods

Substitute goods are those that consumers could purchase to fulfil the same purpose or need instead of the products offered by the business. A common example is rice and pasta.

To reduce the threat of such goods, IS/IT may be used to provide new supplementary activities or products that did not exist before, or to add value to the existing product that enables the business to compete for effectively on price or service.

Existing competitive rivalry in the industry

Established markets will contain a number of competing businesses who are all seeking to improve their market share and profitability.

An information strategy may aim to use IS/IT to create a competitive advantage. For example, to link up with suppliers down the value chain to reduce cost and improve the quality of the goods provided, to enable it to provide a slicker service to its customers or to completely revolutionise the industry to gain market share.

(b) **Threat of new entrants**

Vinylattac has used IS/IT to create a number of barriers to entry that should protect it from new entrants for a reasonable amount of time. It has developed electronic links with a number of suppliers. Mark, supported by Gregory's finance, has also invested both money and time into developing the website – any new entrants would need to go through this before it would be a threat. The comprehensive customer database and the stock recording system should also provide some protection.

Bargaining power of suppliers

The business is doing all it can to reduce the power of its suppliers. It has already struck good deals with its suppliers, is electronically linked with many and analyses supplier databases and websites to source the cheapest supplies. By developing the consortium that Gregory suggests, supplier power will be eroded further.

Bargaining power of customers

The expert advice and personal service is a unique selling point for Vinylattac. IS/IT could be utilised to exploit this further, for example a Customer Relationship Management (CRM) System. The business needs to exploit its customer database to improve its marketing activities. Customers could receive suggested purchases through email or fed directly to them when they visit the website through the use of cookies. IS/IT will also play a part in the imminent monthly electronic magazine, which should also help attract and 'tie' customers to Vinylattac.

Threat of substitute goods

Vinylattac is an online CD, DVD, audio tape and vinyl record retailer. Downloadable MP3 and other audio files are one substitute that Vinylattac needs to address. Traditional high street retailers, and other leisure/entertainment activities are other possible substitutes for disposable income spent with Vinylattac The business must endeavour to maintain the lowest price it can and the level of customer service it provides to counter these threats. The website should be kept up to date and easy to use to enhance the purchase experience. It could also be used to reinforce the commonly held view that vinyl has much more character than its electronic rivals (to counter the MP3 threat).

Existing competitive rivalry in the industry

Customers use Vinylattac rather than its rivals because of the customer service, the efficient user interface and the value added features such as the one-on-one expert assistance to track down recordings. It has already started to use IS/IT to communicate with its customers through the electronic magazine, and has utilised IS/IT to establish links with suppliers. 'Major players' are active in the downloadable audio market (eg iTunes) – these are likely to impact Vinylattac significantly.

Question 2

BPP marking scheme

		Marks
(a)	Award up to 2 marks per valid point	10
(b)	Award up to 2 marks per valid point.	6
(c)	Award up to 2 marks for Economic and Technical factors. 2 × 2	4
		10

(a) There are a number of reasons why the relationship between **business** and **information systems strategies** has developed in the last few decades.

The main change in the relationship has been the realisation that an **effective information systems** strategy is now an important strategic tool in the modern business environment.

This has been brought about by a number of underlying factors.

Firstly, in the last few decades, technology has taken massive leaps forward; the **size** of computers has shrunk and their **power** has increased. This led to growth in the number of applications and processes that can be computerised.

Secondly, communications technology has developed equally as fast. The development of the **internet**, **broadband** and fast **network** connections have enabled machines across the globe to be linked together and information can now be developed, shared, transformed and used quickly and easily.

As a result, **IS/IT is no longer seen as a mere support activity**. The pace of change has meant that technology is a source of **competitive advantage** and as the source of new products and services. The **cost** of information systems and the reliance that organisations place on them has increased the importance of the IS/IT strategy within organisations.

Therefore it is now vital that **business strategies are aligned with information strategies** to **maximise** the **benefits** and **opportunities** that IS/IT brings. The business strategy is dependent on the information strategy and vice versa – one cannot succeed without the other.

(b) Vinylattac has grown from humble beginnings to the large organisation it is today. Mark has embraced technology from the very start and used it to form the **backbone** of his expansion plans.

The dot.com boom of the late 1990s onwards saw the development of e-commerce as a legitimate method of doing business. Vinylattac entered this market at an **early stage**, clearly a risk for Mark, as many commentators doubted the potential of the internet to succeed. However, he stuck to his strategy to drive the business forward using the technology.

As the business grew larger, Mark saw the importance of managing **suppliers** and **customers** to achieve the maximum benefit from them. He set up **electronic links** with suppliers and uses a database to monitor prices to ensure he gets the best deal possible. A **customer database** was established to help the business get to know its consumers and is now well placed to exploit it for marketing purposes.

Mark has a clearly wants his business to grow and develop by exploiting new technologies as they become available. Significant investment has been made to set-up **online purchasing facilities** and **the hi-spec computer systems** (both in terms of hardware and software) that the business is run on.

The business has been **very successful** at aligning its IS/IT strategy to its business strategy and will reap future success if it continues to do so.

(c) **Technical factors**

Vinylattac is well placed to expand globally. Its website, e-commerce facilities and the internet has the potential to exponentially increase the number of its overseas customers. However, as the product would need to be supplied through the post, the business would be at a delivery disadvantage when compared to a customer's local supplier.

To overcome this, the business would need to invest in technology to supply the product as a download (without delivery costs), so the customer would receive it almost instantly, enabling Vinylattac to compete with local shops. This would require significant additional investment in more technology.

Economic

Sending its products by post to worldwide destinations puts Vinylattac at a cost disadvantage to local overseas suppliers. This is because it costs more to post items overseas. There is nothing the business can do about this unless it goes down the download route mentioned above.

Question 3

Text reference. The issues surrounding teleworking are covered in Chapter 9 of the Text.

Top tips. This type of question has the potential to be a goldmine for marks. Maximise them with an answer plan.

In Part (a) list four facilities that would be required – think about what you would need to be able to work from home if it helps.

In Parts (b) and (c) you should list down two advantages and disadvantages for employers and employees. It may help to think about the pros and cons for you and your employer, but don't forget that your answer should relate to the situation in the scenario.

Once you've listed your points in the plan, write a short paragraph on each in your answer.

Easy marks. You should be able to score almost 50% on the question by stating the technical facilities and sufficient advantages and disadvantages.

		Marks
(a)	Award 1 mark per valid point.	4
(b)	Award up to 2 marks per advantage and up to 2 marks per disadvantage with a maximum of 4 marks for each category. To obtain the 2 marks reference to case study is required.	8
(c)	Award up to 2 marks per advantage and up to 2 marks per disadvantage with a maximum of 4 marks for each category. To obtain the 2 marks reference to case study is required.	8
		20

(a)   Facilities required for teleworking:

A **personal computer** (PC); to operate the software required to perform the role.

A **communications link**; to connect the PC to the main computer system at the organisation and to allow the transfer of data between the two. The main options are a dial-up connection or 'always on'. Either way, broadband would be required for effective working.

Email facilities; to allow the teleworker to communicate with their colleagues and management.

User access; the teleworker requires access permissions, passwords and usernames to access the main network of the organisation. A VPN (virtual private network) could also be provided.

(b)   **Employer's perspective**

Advantages

Cost

Employees who work from home do not use up office space, unlike those who are employed on-site. This could save Vinylattac cost of purchasing more office space to house additional staff.

Flexibility

Teleworkers can be employed on a freelance basis and can therefore be used as and when the business requires them. This means Vinylattac can ensure it maintains optimum staffing levels at all times, even when demand rises and falls. This means the business does not pay for staff that it does not need and can maintain good customer service during peak periods.

Disadvantages

Co-ordination

Having staff geographically dispersed may make it difficult for management to co-ordinate and organise them. These problems would be magnified for Vinylattac as the contacts are dispersed worldwide. Therefore it would need to manage staff located in a range of time zones who may speak a number of different languages.

Training/culture

Due to the distance the employees would live from the business it is unlikely that they visit the organisation or meet each other due to the expense of travel. This makes training them and developing a culture that fosters staff loyalty very difficult to achieve. However, some investment in IT – for example video conferencing facilities may go some way to redress this.

(c)   **Employee's perspective**

Advantages

Better use of time

Teleworkers can organise their working hours around their family commitments – for example those with children can arrange to work while they are at school. This helps maintain their motivation and enjoyment of their work. As Vinylattac's teleworkers are personal contacts of Mark it should be easy for them to negotiate suitable working arrangements that meet their needs.

Cost savings

As Mark's contacts are spread worldwide, Vinylattac would need to provide technology that allows its teleworkers to work from any location they choose. By working from home, teleworkers would save the cost of commuting to work and the time lost during travel.

Disadvantages

Isolation

By employing teleworkers that are spread across the globe and far from Vinylattac's headquarters, the employees would not enjoy the social contact and support of their fellow workers. Email and telephone are no real substitute for such contact and therefore, staff may not feel as if they are part of a team and may stop enjoying their work.

Domestic intrusion

To co-ordinate working hours worldwide, staff may be required to work hours that clash with their domestic arrangements. Teleworkers may find it difficult to work with children or partners being around them. Some may shut themselves away from their family to concentrate on work, causing problems in their home-life in the long-run.

Question 4

Text reference. Ethics are covered in Chapter 9 of the Text.

Top tips. Do not panic when confronted by ethical questions such as this. In Part (a) you should assume that equal marks are available for ethical and political/legal issues. If you did not know the method of producing an ethical analysis in Part (b) then you would have been wise to avoid this question as you would have struggled to earn many marks.

Easy marks. Setting out the five stages in Part (b) – if you knew them!

BPP marking scheme

			Marks
(a)	Award up to 4 marks for discussion of ethical issues.	4	
	Award up to 4 marks for discussion of political issues.	4	
	Award up to 2 marks for demonstrating an understanding of the difference	2	
			10
(b)	Award up to 2 marks per stage. 5 stages × 2		10
			20

(a) **Ethics**

Ethics are concerned about what is morally **right** or **wrong**. They reflect the views of members of **society** as a whole and these views tend to evolve over time.

Advances in technology and the impact it has on individuals raises questions that need to be answered. For example, **information** about individuals can now be stored electronically, ethics considers whether or not this invasion of **privacy** should be permitted.

As products are increasingly provided in an easily **distributable** electronic form, questions are asked about whether or not individuals should still **pay** for them, or just take **copies**.

The role of technology in **monitoring employee activity** also raises ethical issues (eg should employees be monitored without their knowledge?)

Political/Legal

Political and legal issues are in regard to the laws of the land and how individuals are **governed**. From an IS/IT perspective, there are many laws that have been developed to deal with problems that have been created by technology.

The **Computer Misuse Act** has created new criminal acts when individuals hack into systems or spread viruses. The **Data Protection Act** has laid down rules that those who hold information about individuals must follow to protect the interests of the data subjects. These rules aim to ensure the individual is **aware** that information is being collected, that **no more** information is collected than necessary; the data is **accurate** and is **held** no longer than needed.

New rules that cross international boundaries have been created to protect the interests of those who own **intellectual property** and many governments work closely to reduce the incidence of illegal copying and distribution of such material.

The key difference between ethics and political/legal rules is that the latter can be viewed as the **minimum level** of behaviour that society will tolerate and therefore it must be laid down in legislation to ensure all members of society are aware and adhere to it. Ethical values are held by **individuals** and their **communities**, but agreement is seldom reached by all members of society. Individual's who meet high ethical standards are often viewed as exceeding the behavioural standards laid down by society.

(b) Ethical analysis

Separate facts from judgement

Data is collected by DRGB about individuals
DRGB sells data collected to third parties
Information about individuals is used by third parties who may contact them
Individuals may face 'hard sell' by the third parties
DRGB has received complaints concerning data misuse

Identify ethical issues requiring judgement

Should DRGB be held responsible for the actions of the third parties?
Are the tactics used by the third parties really unfair, the individuals can always say no
Not all the third parties have been complained against
What can DRGB do to prevent unscrupulous third parties?

Identify key stakeholders and their interests

DRGB – to make a profit from selling the data
The market research consultants – to earn money from DRGB
The third parties – to sell their products to as many customers as possible

The customers – have a right to be made aware of products and sales tactics and not to have their data misused

Identify options available

Do nothing
Ensure researchers inform the public of all the consequences of filling in a questionnaire
Do not sell data to unethical third parties

Evaluate the options and their consequences

Doing nothing will mean DRGB continues to receive complaints from the public and may also be subject to adverse media attention, it may lose some clients as a result.

Ensuring researchers fully inform the public would mean that they enter into the research with their eyes open and cannot complain if they receive unethical treatment. This may mean fewer questionnaires are completed, reducing DRGB's sales and their researchers' bonuses. There is no reason for researchers to follow the correct procedure whilst they earn bonuses. Their pay structure would need to be changed.

DRGB can stop selling data to companies who it has received complaints about, but it will find it difficult to vet future clients. It may need to ensure new clients sign up to an agreement limiting how they can use the data – this may reduce the number of clients it can sell to, but should also reduce the number of complaints.

Question 5

Text reference. Critical success factors are covered in Chapter 2 of the Text.

Top tips. The marking scheme allows up to three marks to be awarded for four points in Part (a) and although this is not made clear in the requirement, the wording in the question should have lead you to produce a deeper answer than two marks per point. Students who wrote shorter answers would have limited the maximum marks they could achieve. Watch out for this in other questions and try to identify questions that require a deeper explanation.

Easy marks. Stating the CFs and PIs in Part (b) – the short scenario gives you plenty to go on.

BPP marking scheme

		Marks
(a)	Award up to 3 marks for discussion of CSF, PI and information requirements	3
	Award up to 3 marks for discussion of overall process. 3 × 4	12
(b)	For each CSF award 1 mark for CSF, up to 2 marks for PI and 1 mark for information	8
		20

(a) **Critical success factors** (CSFs) are determined by starting with the organisation's mission and drilling that down into smaller business goals. They are used to help identify the information requirements of an organisation as they form a link between the **business strategy** and the **information strategy**.

Different **management levels** have different CSFs, senior management have CSFs that have a wide general scope and lower level managers will have CSFs that focus on their narrow area of responsibility. For example a sales director may have a CSF to increase the volume of sales for the company, but an area sales manager would have a CSF to increase sales within their geographical area.

The type of CSF will be determined by the business strategy. Where the aim is to maintain business, a **monitoring CSF** would be used to ensure existing operations perform as expected. Where the goal is expansion, a **building CSF** would be used to measure the progress of new projects.

The success of CSFs is measured using **performance indicators** (PIs). These consist of **quantitative data** rather than qualitative goals. A PI for the area sales manager mentioned above could be to achieve a certain percentage increase in the number of customers or the value of their orders.

The structure of the CSFs and PIs provides a **blueprint** for the information requirements of an organisation. The information system should provide reports enabling the CSFs and associated PIs to be monitored in a **timely** and **efficient** manner. The system should enable management to drill down through the layers of the **hierarchy** and determine the areas of the business that they should focus their attention on.

The main objective is to **provide information** about performance to help achieve long-term **corporate goals** rather than data that has no purpose or context. CSF's and PIs are used in the top-down method of strategy development, where senior management actively set goals and objectives for an organisation that feed down through all its layers.

(b)   **Critical success factor 1:**
       To improve the quality of service to customers

       Performance indicator 1:
       Provide an on-time delivery on x% of deliveries

       Source of information 1:
       Driver's delivery logs/customer feedback

       Critical success factor 2:
       To retain existing customers

       Performance indicator 2:
       To ensure x% of existing customers renew their contracts

       Source of information 2:
       Renewal records

Question 6

Text reference. Portfolio analysis is covered in Chapter 5 of the Text, the systems in Part (b) in Chapter 3.

Top tips. Students who 'knowledge dump' all they know about portfolio analysis in Part (a) are unlikely to earn high marks – you must use it to explain how a company can prioritise its IS/IT developments. Make use of the distinction it creates between risk and benefit.

You must use the grid again in Part (b) – this is where well prepared students have an advantage over those who merely rote learned the theory.

Easy marks. Describing the systems in Part (b) should not present you with any problems.

BPP marking scheme

		Marks
(a)	Award 1 mark per valid point for explanation up to 4 marks. Award 1 mark per quadrant description = 4 marks	8
(b)	For each system award up to 2 marks for description. Award up to 2 marks for fitting into quadrant. 3 systems × 4	12
		20

(a)   Portfolio analysis is used to assist with the **selection** between potential systems when making an investment decision. A range of options are presented and after the strategic direction of each is identified, the portfolio analysis begins.

Each potential system is analysed in terms of **risk** and **benefits**, and is graded as **high** or **low** in each category. The system is then located on the grid depending on its benefit and risk gradings. The grid gives a suggested course of action based on this result.

Benefits can be **financial**, such as increased profit, or **intangible**, such as improved goods and services. **Risks** include, the impact that **'bugs'** would have on the business, that will **costs** rise during development or will the system be delivered on **time**.

The grid **recommends** the following courses of action when systems fall into the follow categories.

High risk, high benefit – the organisation should cautiously examine the system as although the benefits are high, so is the risk of failure.

Low risk, high benefit – the organisation should identify and develop such systems, this is the best possible result.

High risk, low benefit – the organisation should avoid such systems, the risk of failure is high with little benefit to show. This is the worst possible result.

Low risk, low benefit – these are usually routine systems that should be implemented, they have little risk but little benefit either.

(b)   **CAD systems**

CAD systems are used to **design** and **develop** new products for the business to produce. Tools are provided to draw, model and even test designs without the need to spend resources producing a **physical** version. Once a design is made, it can be easily refined, amended and improved. Previous versions can be saved so if a certain alteration is not successful, the designers do not have to begin again from scratch. This means **money** is saved and the prototype that is finally produced is likely to be successful.

In certain industries, such as engineering, CAD is the **standard tool** that is used by almost all businesses. Therefore, it has great benefit for the organisation in the scenario, and as such systems are often brought 'off-the-shelf' they are low risk. Putting them into the **identify and develop** category.

Datawarehouse systems

Datawarehouses consist of a **database** containing data from the organisation's **operational systems** and certain **external sources** with search and query tools. The data is updated regularly and is broken down into individual transactions that users querying the data can drill down into. The main uses of datawarehouses are for management decision making and analysis.

BPP
LEARNING MEDIA

Such systems are usually only of use to **large organisations** that have considerable existing systems that produce **large quantities** of data to be stored and analysed. The company in the scenario does not match this description, making it of low benefit to it. The high cost involved when developing a datawarehouse makes it highly risky, therefore putting it into the **avoid** category.

Extranet systems

Extranets are similar in nature to intranets – **internal information**, such as contact details, designs or databases are available for users to view. Users are able to browse the information using a **browser** in a similar way that they would surf the internet. However, where intranets are accessible by individuals within an organisation, extranets are available to **external users** such as customers and suppliers providing they have been given a username and password. External users usually have access restricted to areas relevant to them. They are a popular means for business partners to **exchange information**.

The benefits they bring to engineering organisations can be great. Especially where **close links** are forged and **collaboration** on designs and specifications are required. Providing the correct **security** procedures are in place, they are a low risk system – putting them into the **identify and develop category**.

ACCA
Examiner's answers

Part 3 Examination – Paper 3.4
Business Information Management.

June 2006 Answers

1 (a) Strengths:

Strong IT/IS infrastructure
Successful company
Steady increase in market share
Good name and reputation in the existing market
Much experience in the market
Senior management keen to exploit technology

Weaknesses:

Management information often out of date
No in-house IT expertise
No web experience
Current information systems are cumbersome
Not sure how effective the new system will be in generating new sales
Previous IS projects have been abandoned
Not all management support the idea
KGDB may need to support two competing strategies

Opportunities:

E-trading can provide a new sales channel and revenue stream
Identification and recording of details of customers as a business resource
Enhancement of customer relationships
The majority of store managers support the development
Extension of customer base
Global market potential
Cut costs in many areas
Creation of a vision of a modern company

Threats:

Customer resistance to on-line shopping
Loss of unique identity; may become just another website trader
May cause a change in the overall business strategy
Internal competition
Resistance within the company
Effects on existing personnel
Costs of developing system may outweigh benefits
Security issues

(b) (i) The grid illustrates four types of strategy created by the combinations of external and internal factors and can give an indication of the type of response that might be most appropriate to deal with each strategy. Attack: 'go for it', Beware: 'don't do it', Explore: 'if we have time', Protect: 'watch yourself'. The ability to balance and judge the options available is often subject to individual perspectives and interests.

KGDB's current situation with regard to the proposed development of website facilities may fit into more than one of the suggested quadrants. The 'Attack' quadrant normally implies that both opportunities and strengths are present. In this case opportunities are present but there is a question mark over the strength of the IS capability. Several IS projects have failed in the past. Where there are value adding opportunities for IS accompanied by weak IS capabilities, companies normally adopt a 'Beware' strategy. This quadrant may apply to KGDB but there is a demand for developing a website facility: failure to do so may result in the company falling behind its competitors. Many companies would consider the development of a website as a crucial and inevitable asset. With respect to the 'Explore' quadrant, normally associated with strong IS resources alongside threatening situations, KGDB finds itself with threats from competitors and not a strong IS capability. 'Explore' may not be a viable option. The final quadrant 'Protect', where a company finds itself under threat and having weak IS capabilities, normally indicates that a strategy should be developed that will protect itself from its vulnerability. In the case of KGDB, it is difficult to develop a strategy to protect itself. Doing nothing is probably not an option.

KGDB is in a difficult position and does not fit neatly into any of the quadrants. Its major problem is the weakness in its IS capability. The case study suggests that the current IS systems are fairly robust but inefficient, eg out of date sales statistics. Before making any decisions with regard to developing a strategy the company should consider its position and its options in the provision of IS capability.

(ii) David Boswell (Attack): is keen to exploit technology to enhance business opportunities. In addition to supporting the initial proposal to develop a website he also instructed Michael to include the fully enhanced version of the website in his business case report.

Anne Brown (Beware): has previously complained about the provision of IS services to the company. She is unhappy with recent developments conducted by the external contractors and cited the contractors' inability to meet company requirements.

Katherine Goodison (Explore): believes that the development of a website may be useful as an additional form of advertising. She does not feel that the company should develop an online purchasing facility. She is more involved with the business strategy than exploiting technology.

Alexandra Smith (Protect): may support this strategy. She and other managers are apprehensive about any website development. They fear such a development may negatively affect the current levels of business in their stores.

2   Suitable headings...........

Business case report.

Option one: to develop a website that will enable customers to view goods online and provide details of the company.
Option two: to develop a website that fully integrates with the company's back office information systems that would permit customers to view and purchase goods online.

Introduction and Terms of Reference:

The terms of reference include:

Aims: To enhance customers' experience of shopping with KGDB and promote the exploitation of technology within the company.

Approach: In this case it is a problem solving approach, as a problem has been identified.

Scope: The option one system will not really affect the range of organisational activities. It will enhance existing systems, providing the customer with the opportunity to view goods and learn about the company online.
The option two system will change the organisational activities. This option will permit customers to view and purchase goods online, thus creating an alternative method for the company to expand its business activities.

Resources: Not yet determined. Personnel: IT services and support staff. Constraints eg deadlines, deliverables.

Summary of the present position, including problems and issues:
Currently customers have only one choice when shopping at KGDB. They must visit a store in order to see what goods are for sale. It has been reported by several store managers that customers have enquired about the location of a company website. This suggests there is a customer requirement for the development of the system. The company has received numerous complaints from customers who have been disappointed with the current facilities.

Summary of the relevant IS objectives of the organisation:
An IS objective of the organisation is to exploit technology to enhance customer service and meet their expectations. Both of the options fit into the overall IS objective and business objectives of the organisation. Many of the company's major competitors provide similar services. It is important for the company to maintain the highest quality of service to its customers.

Gap analysis:
In this case there is a huge gap between the current systems and the required one. Where We Are (W^2R): The company is currently only able to show customers the product range available inside a store. Where We Want To Be (W^32B): The company wants to enable customers to explore the products from home (option one), and possibly permit customers to purchase products online (option two). Going To Get There (GT^2): Option one is appropriate if the company chooses to develop a website limited to advertising goods. The process should be relatively straightforward. There are many website developers who could be employed to develop a suitable website. The use of websites is becoming almost universally accepted as a must for businesses of all sizes.

The proposed system would purely be an addition to the current systems portfolio.

Option two would require a massive change/enhancement to the existing back office systems. These systems would have to be modified to integrate with the web services being offered. This would be a major undertaking.

Evaluation of the different options considered:
There are few choices available with regard to the development of option one. The company must decide whether to develop a website or not. The option of not developing a website will mean falling behind competitors and an increase in customer complaints. If the company decides to develop the website it will provide itself with an opportunity to develop further website facilities in the future.

Acceptance of option two would require a radical development project. It would involve a high degree of commitment in terms of technical, financial and human resources. Option two could change the future direction of the company's business strategy and information systems strategy. Will option two be compatible with clients expectations, ie will clients actually buy the goods without trying them on?

This section would normally include a cost-benefit analysis, where the investment criteria set by the organisation must be satisfied. An analysis comparing the costs of developing the system with its likely benefits is required, as is an evaluation of whether the solution is practical from the point of view of the technological requirements and from an economic point of view. This is calculated by identifying all the costs involved, one-off costs, recurring costs and intangible costs. Then the benefits must be identified - tangible and intangible benefits. The costs and benefits are then compared to identify when and if the outlay will be recovered and possibly what savings/profits would amount to at the end of a predefined period. Methods used to complete this task may include; 'payback period', 'net present value', 'return on investment' or 'internal rate of return', etc.

Conclusions and recommendations:
There is a customer expectation for the provision of website facilities. There is clear support from both head office and the majority of store managers to develop a website. The problem is what level of facilities can the company realistically provide? Option one is a safe approach to developing a culture of e-business. It would be relatively inexpensive to develop and meet the current business requirements. Option two is a radical change in terms of both business strategy and information systems strategy. The report recommends that option one is accepted and implemented. The success or otherwise of the implementation can be evaluated in the future when a decision can be made as to enhancing the system to provide the extra facilities proposed in option two.

3 (a) The current situation: The company relies on external consultants for the provision of its IT/IS systems. There have been several complaints lodged concerning enhancements to the current systems. There were integration problems with the accounting and back office systems that were not satisfactory. The processing of out of stock items from the stores is cumbersome and requires major enhancements. There is difficulty with providing statistical management information, eg monthly sales figures. Apart from one general systems review conducted a couple of years ago, there has been no attempt to align systems strategy with a changing business environment. A comprehensive review of current systems and business objectives is urgently required. With the latest proposal to implement a website facility, it may be an appropriate time to rethink the company's strategy for the provision of IT/IS.

The company has suffered from all the disadvantages of outsourcing: they have become completely dependent on a supplier. It is difficult to determine the terms of any contract. The company has no internal expertise or control over development.

Information systems are becoming a core feature in the future of the company.

There are definite advantages of employing internal IT professionals. The staff will quickly become familiar with the business operations and the requirements of the users. They will integrate into the business and generate responsibility and loyalty to the company. The company has reached a watershed and now has the opportunity to reappraise the future role of IS provision. If the proposal to develop the advanced website system is accepted it would provide a good opportunity for new permanent staff to develop the system and concurrently evaluate and enhance the current information systems. Initially it may be possible to employ a minimal number of permanent staff. These staff could manage the project and insource other expert personnel as and when required.

(b) The spiral model adopts an evolutionary approach towards the development of information systems. It is an appropriate technique when developing information systems where requirements are not clear and a sequential systems life cycle approach would be inappropriate, eg a new development where users and IT professionals are lacking in experience. The spiral model provides an iterative approach to development. Activities are often repeated in order to clarify issues or provide a complete definition of user requirements. The development process begins at the centre of the spiral. Normally at this stage the requirements are not fully defined. System requirements are refined with each rotation around the spiral.

The model is divided into four quadrants.
Top-left. Identify and determine objectives, alternatives and constraints.
Top-right. Evaluate alternatives, identify and resolve risks.
Bottom-right. Develop system and verify next level.
Bottom-left. Plan next iteration.

As the project progresses the development team moves around the spiral. The first circuits result in the development of a product specification. Subsequent passes around the spiral might be used to develop a prototype and then progressively more sophisticated versions of the software. Each pass through the planning region results in adjustments to the project plan. The key to the model is that software evolves as the process progresses; the developer and the customer better understand and react to risks at each evolutionary level. Prototyping is used as a risk reduction mechanism and enables the developer to apply the prototyping approach at any stage in the evolution of the product. The spiral model sets a framework for user/developer communication.

During the standard requirements analysis stage, eg in the Waterfall approach, if the users are asked to describe their ideal system they probably would not be able to supply a comprehensive answer. Alternatively if the users are periodically shown a working model and asked how a few things can be added to make the system better, the users will be able to decide and respond accordingly. Based on this premise, the spiral model can be used to bring out the user requirements a few at a time.

A major advantage of the spiral model is the inclusion of objective setting, risk management and planning throughout the development process. A benefit is that the user can be given limited functionality of the system prior to its overall completion.

(c)   The proposed project is a major undertaking. The project would be required to integrate with many of the existing information systems thus making the development very complex. Undoubtedly the existing information systems will require major enhancements to accommodate the requirements of the online purchasing system. The company has not previously undertaken a project of this size or complexity. The staged approach adopted by the spiral model would be appropriate for such a major development. The spiral approach would involve user participation - an essential ingredient in a project of this nature. Previous user involvement in the development of information systems has been minimal. As the project will involve users from several departments and use different information systems, it will provide an ideal opportunity for them to share their views and requirements.

The project involves a fairly high-risk element and the spiral model builds into its cycle stages for evaluating and minimising risk. Due to the nature of this project it may be possible to implement the system in stages, ie develop the basic website, then implement integration into the existing systems, a system at a time. KGDB have previously mismanaged the development of several IS projects. Some projects have been abandoned due to poor requirements definition. The spiral approach tends to alleviate such problems by the process of iteration.

The case study suggests that many of the existing information systems are rather cumbersome, eg the process of replenishing stock in each of the stores. If the new project is developed using the spiral approach there will be an opportunity to enhance the existing systems in line with the development of the new system. An evolutionary approach may be the best method to ensure that the development strategy includes all the existing requirements and takes into account the risks involved in developing such a large and complex system.

Previous developments have been abandoned due to lack of understanding between users and developers and presumably through a lack of risk management procedures. The development team should adopt the spiral model approach, whether they are external consultants or in-house developers. The approach appears to meet the criteria of the development process in this case.

4   (a)   Business automation is generally associated with using technology to enhance existing tasks or processes that are currently being performed manually. The existing tasks/processes are assumed to be the best way of conducting business. The role of technology is to increase the efficiency of the existing tasks. Automation was and still is very successfully implemented in manufacturing processes. The use of robotics in the automobile industry is an excellent example. In the period when business automation was prominent many processes were merely automated, such as the creation of computer based stock systems or the introduction of stand-alone word processors etc.

Early automation in retail businesses such as supermarkets required the automation of the sales process. This normally involved cashiers inputting codes of items, later replaced with bar code reading. Cash registers then calculated the total purchase price and supplied the purchaser with an itemised receipt. This automation of processes led to the development of point of sales systems (POS). Basic electronic stock recording and purchasing systems were introduced as a result. In many outlets staff members had to alert the stock controllers when items reached a reorder level, this process then created a further process whereby purchasing were informed of the need to order more stock.

(b)   Business rationalisation is the next step in exploiting technology. Rationalisation involves the questioning of processes. It may involve analysing a business in terms what it does rather than in terms of how it does it. Rationalisation of procedures is the streamlining of standard operating procedures, eliminating obvious bottlenecks so that automation can make the operating procedures more efficient. Rationalisation was/is associated with integration. The integration of departments/systems can be accomplished using technology, eg integrating the stock recording system with the order processing system. Currently many organisations are still using rationalisation as their major underpinning strategy for developing information systems.

Rationalisation tends to be the next stage after automation. Rationalisation can be adopted to eliminate bottlenecks within and between processes. In the context of supermarkets a good example of rationalisation involved the integration of the existing systems, thus integrating several business functions. The advances in technology permitted supermarkets to develop fully integrated inventory systems. Point of sales systems were developed that could not only perform the recording of the purchasing function but could also update the stock recording system, which in turn automatically requested the purchasing function to replenish stocks. In a regional company warehouse, a common function, supplying individual supermarkets, the warehouse is informed of the shortage and deliveries are made. The introduction of electronic data interchange (EDI) between supermarkets and suppliers can be viewed as the rationalisation of processes. Many supermarket chains are currently at this stage of development.

(c)   Business process re-engineering involves the fundamental rethinking and radical redesign of business processes to achieve dramatic improvements, such as cost, quality, speed and service. The majority of strategic changes involve changing existing processes and procedures. Business process re-engineering normally refers to the process of reconfiguring activities to create improvement in performance. BPR combines a strategy of promoting business innovation with a strategy of making major improvements to business processes thus permitting a company to become stronger and more competitive in the marketplace.

Information technology is being used to restructure work by transforming business processes. A business process is any set of activities designed to produce a specified output for a customer or market. BPR focuses on the how and why of business processes: major changes can be made in how work is accomplished.

Re-engineering often involves complete changes to a company's structure to enable this radical redesign to take place. This is a very high-risk strategy, which goes much further than rationalisation of processes, revolution as opposed to evolution of business strategy.

In the context of supermarkets, business process re-engineering can be viewed as changing existing processes to enhance the business operation, as opposed to changing the nature of the business. Supermarkets' core business remains fundamentally in the notion of 'cash and carry'. Additionally many large national supermarkets are actively involved in selling commodities and services not traditionally viewed as in their domain, eg supplying credit cards, insurance, and other financial services.

An example of using business process re-engineering is the development of virtual supply chains (VSC), where the traditional processes of ordering goods from suppliers has changed dramatically. Walmart is often cited as a pioneer in the development of VSC. Walmart has developed a system that co-ordinates the supply chain. The system permits suppliers to view Walmart's inventory system; only when stocks require replenishment do the suppliers supply the goods. Thus the onus is on the suppliers to provide adequate stocks when and where required, not on the purchasers to inform them that supplies are required.

Many supermarkets now permit customers to order online. Customers place orders and arrange for home delivery or a convenient time to visit the store and pick up their goods. This is accomplished using internet technology. This type of process is moving away from the cash and carry function.

Technology and changes in business practices have allowed supermarkets to provide cash back facilities to their customers, thereby reducing cash management and insurance costs.

The analysis of goods purchased by customers has enabled supermarkets to display their goods in non-traditional areas. If knowledge of associated selling items is available then these items are displayed in close proximity, thus encouraging customers to purchase additional items. Data warehousing and data mining have been invaluable in this functional change.

5 **(a)** Lewin suggested a model for change that incorporated three stages: unfreeze, change and refreeze.

Unfreeze: This stage involves getting an organisation receptive to change. This may be accomplished by identifying bad practice, listening to and noting staff complaints, convincing staff there are better and alternative methods of performing tasks, generally creating a positive attitude towards change.

Change: The second stage is proposing a solution to a problem/process that may have been identified in stage one. The change must then be implemented. This stage may involve change in working practice, learning new skills, change in methods of communication, establishing new attitudes, culture and patterns of behaviour.

Refreeze: Following the successful implementation of change, the final stage is to refreeze or stabilise. This implies that the change is positively reinforced. The new practices implemented in stage two become the norm and are accepted by the participants.

The strength of the unfreeze, change, refreeze model is in its simplicity. It can be argued that it gives very clear guidelines for implementing change. The model suggests all three stages must be accomplished. Some stages may be very quick, e.g. the unfreeze stage could be tackled by the notion of 'if you don't change your current way of performing your task, you won't have a job'. This type of reason for changing is fairly common in different guises. This is a very heavy-handed method and not always practicable. Lewin's model presupposes that it is possible to unfreeze a situation. The change stage within the model, in common with the first stage, assumes that change can always be successfully implemented. There are many theories and models that suggest the implementation of systems is far from straightforward. The final stage in Lewin's model involves developing a belief that the changed system is better than the old system and everyone will settle down and use the new system. Within a short period of time this system will be adopted.

It could be argued that Lewin's model is based on scientific reasoning. Indeed his famous analogy was that of changing the shape of a block of ice. The weakness in the model is that it takes no account of the changing nature of business. The model assumes that change occurs as a discrete process periodically. This may have been true historically but in modern business change is constant. Developing business strategies and information systems is a dynamic process. The inherent failure to recognise the vibrant nature of the modern business environment limits the model's usefulness.

(b) Two of the main reasons why there are differences between the initial system requirements and the implemented version are:

There are rapid and constant changes occurring in the business environment which may affect the requirements of a long term project. Business strategies, and consequently goals, are changing constantly. The life of the proposed information system may be measured in years and sometimes the benefits to be reaped may take longer. During the period between system inception and system implementation, the business requirements will probably change. The changes in business plans may be due to a variety of reasons including: changes in legislation, changes in security requirements, changes within the organisational structure and changes in working practices (home working).

Technology changes on a daily basis. Therefore organisations must attempt to align information systems development in order to exploit new technologies. This may require changes to the original specification. The development of new input and/or output devices may require change to the system e.g. mobile technologies have recently changed the manner in which communication can take place.

Nonetheless many organisations have a need to develop large, time consuming, complex, technically demanding and expensive information systems. Good practice suggests that organisations are required to develop both business and information strategies that are flexible and coordinated within the project lifecycle.

To combat the technical changes, an organisation should adopt a strategy of flexible and logical design. An organisation should identify the future changes in business, logical requirements, continually track the emerging technologies and exploit new products to achieve information systems objectives as and when they become available and proven.

6   (a)   E-trading has enabled consumers to trade in places and with companies they would never have considered or even known about. Consumers now have the ability to search for items or services via the internet in minutes. Previously, similar searches may have taken days or weeks. Rather than visit shops or businesses, the consumer can now sit at home and make enquiries. This may also have an impact on traffic congestion and over-crowded shopping centres. Rather than being confined to business hours the consumer can shop twenty-four hours a day, seven days of the week. This may free up time to pursue other activities. E-trading normally means that there is less face-to-face interaction with people. This may affect people in both positive and negative ways. If human contact is valued it will have a negative effect, while on the other hand it may remove possible conflict.

The range of choices has dramatically increased and product information is easily accessible. Comparisons of prices and quality can be obtained from a variety of independent sources. The purchase of goods or services can be instantaneous. Many consumers still like to touch and feel certain products, eg clothes, fresh food and personal items. Security remains an issue. Consumers are still very concerned about divulging personal and financial information via the internet. A social drawback of the expansion of e-trading is that not everyone has the facilities to participate in e-trading and some consumers could be disadvantaged.

    (b)   E-trading has extended the potential market place. This may impact on advertising and selling as products/services may have social or legal restrictions in certain countries. Organisations will have to develop new methods for advertising and promoting their goods. There is now a relatively level playing field for all companies regardless of size. Small companies are now competing with the established large international companies in many sectors. E-trading and its related technologies has permitted the development of virtual companies. There is no longer a requirement to have a physical presence in the market place. The development of markets in a global environment requires an advanced supply chain with suppliers and customers worldwide.

The supply and delivery of goods and services must now be extended to meet demand. Competition for the supply of goods and services has increased dramatically. As the number of providers increases then so does the competition. New entrants into any sector pose a threat to the established companies in the sector. Established traders must now compete in two different markets ie high street and the internet. It is becoming the norm for all traders to trade on the internet. The market place is constantly changing and traders must keep up with all the latest developments in both goods and technology. Security has become a major concern of the consumer. To overcome security issues requires additional expense to maintain and update systems. The mix of employee skills is changing e.g. there will be less need for staff with people skills and more need for staff with technical skills.

Part 3 Examination – Paper 3.4
Business Information Management

December 2006 Answers

1 (a) (i) Potential entrants (barriers to entry): If a business or industry is financially attractive, other organisations often seek to enter the market. Information systems can provide two strategic roles. (i) Defensive. In this role information systems can be used to create barriers that new entrants must overcome if they wish to enter the market. (ii) Offensive. In this role the company uses information systems to break down the barriers of entry to permit entry into a market. For example, to create a new distribution channel, say through ebay.

(ii) Competitive rivalry (rivalry among existing competitors): Rivalry between competitors is usually greater in mature or declining industries. Important factors may include industry growth, fixed assets/value-added, intermittent over-capacity, etc. Competitive rivalry normally comes from businesses or organisations making/supplying similar products/services to the same market. There are several approaches to this situation that can be adopted and supported by IS. Just in time (JIT) systems can be used to reduce costs or by reducing the number of administrative personnel required to deliver the same service. Cost reduction implies that the product is perceived as a commodity and purchasers buy on the basis of price and service.

(iii) Threats from substitutes: Substitute products or services are those that are within the industry, but are differentiated in some way. If suppliers alienate their customers they increase the readiness of those customers to use an alternative product whenever it becomes available. If the price/performance balance of product shifts dramatically then this will increase the threat of a substitute being used. A classic example is the replacement of typewriters with the introduction of word processors. In this context e-commerce can be viewed as a substitute for high street shopping. IS may offer a substitute product or approach.

(iv) Buyers' bargaining power: Buyers (customers) can exert power over any business by choosing to purchase the product or service from another provider. Many businesses attempt to deter customers from transferring their business to alternative companies by the introduction of switching costs. Switching costs may be financial or may require the customer to learn new systems. Customer Relationship Management (CRM) systems can be developed using analysis techniques and sophisticated software tools to exploit information kept in databases of customer details and activity. CRM can be used to develop customer profiles; such information permits businesses to target certain customers in terms of direct marketing and incentives such as loyalty schemes.

(v) Suppliers' bargaining power: Suppliers provide the necessary inputs of raw materials, components or information for the organisations' ability to supply their goods or services. These suppliers can exert their bargaining power on an organisation by pushing up their prices or taking their supplies elsewhere to a competitor business in the same or similar industry. Information systems can be used to provide a spread purchases database that enables easy scanning of prices from a number of suppliers. The implementation of electronic data interchange (EDI) systems is another way of establishing good relations with suppliers that benefit both parties. The benefits include: reduced delivery times, reduced paperwork and associated labour costs and increased accuracy of information. EDI can also be an important component of a just in time (JIT) strategy.

(b) (i) Potential entrants: Vinylattac is relatively well placed to protect itself from new entrants. It has experienced the high cost of technology required to set up the business. This will help in its defence from new entrants. Vinylattac is a relatively well-established company and has built up expensive technological links with its suppliers and customers. They have experienced staff with a wide range of knowledge of the products. They should be able to exploit new channels to raise barriers to entry even further.

(ii) Competitive rivalry: Vinylattac should seek to use IS to reduce costs and provide a better service. Currently Vinylattac offers a good service to its customers. It has good delivery times and all transactions are supported by its electronic interface. Vinylattac provides the service of acquiring specialist recordings for customers and friendly retailers by providing customers with additional search facilities when they are not sure of the product they require. The staff at Vinylattac provide this unique service by maintaining contact with customers on a one-to-one basis until the customer places an order. This is supported by electronic communication links with its customers eg email, and the experts using advanced internet searches based on their knowledge to find the required products.

(iii) Threats from substitutes: The music business is in competition with other forms of business in the low cost leisure entertainment sector; for example going to the cinema, hiring videos or playing electronic games. Vinylattac has historically maintained its position by supplying the latest products starting with vinyl records and progressing through audiotapes, CDs and DVDs. Vinylattac must continue to deliver a high quality service at the same time as maintaining a competitive pricing strategy. Vinylattac must be aware that it needs to make internet shopping more attractive to its customers than retail shopping.

(iv) Buyers' bargaining power: The case study suggests that Mark is aware that Vinylattac maintains a large customer database and does not exploit the information to improve buyer relationships. Vinylattac could develop a CRM system that would enable it to collate and analyse customer information and this information about customers could be used to target customer needs directly. The company could develop loyalty schemes or discount schemes that would encourage customers to use Vinylattac. Intelligent agents could be used to help customers navigate through the website based on previous purchase history.

(v) Suppliers' bargaining power: Vinylattac is currently in a strong position with regard to suppliers' bargaining power. The purchasing department is constantly scanning suppliers' websites and databases to obtain the best available deals.

Vinylattac has direct electronic links with its major suppliers and has negotiated good contracts. Gregory is also considering forming a consortium with other retailers that will increase Vinylattac's purchasing power through economies of scale.

2 (a) Developing business strategies and information systems strategies that complement and support each other is becoming one of the key factors in determining the success of many businesses in the twenty-first century. If business management is to adopt a strategic approach then it follows that a strategic perspective must also be taken for information systems. During the 1970s and 1980s information systems were viewed as a support function. The standard approach was to develop information systems that would support business strategies. This approach is referred to as business-led and demand-oriented.

Beginning in the 1990s, due to the rapid developments in information technology both hardware and software and particularly communications technology, the internet and related technologies, information systems adopted a role that was far more significant than merely a supporting one. Business strategies are becoming more dependent on the exploitation of information technology. Globalisation and e-business are examples of technologies often used in support of the formulation of business strategies.

Businesses and organisations are evolving their information systems strategies from a support type role into a proactive use of technology innovation, where developments in technology can lead to or initiate changes in business strategies. There is a trend towards developing business strategies and information systems strategies in unison. The interdependence between the two strategies is now firmly accepted. Without this interdependence either or both strategies are doomed to failure. Strategic planning for information systems arises from the need to align business and information systems plans.

Exploiting technology to gain business advantage is a high expenditure activity. Businesses are aware of the increasing amount of investment required to maintain and develop information systems. The continuing development of new technology determines that businesses must continue investing if they are to maintain their current position in competitive markets.

(b) During the initial period of Vinylattac's business Mark Smith used his technological expertise to develop information systems that would enable Vinylattac to compete in the music sector. In the early 1990s the use of the internet would have been pioneering especially for a very small business. The success of aligning his business strategy with his information systems strategy was a key factor in the rapid growth of Vinylattac. As Vinylattac's business grew Mark continued to align the information systems strategy with the business strategy. He moved to business premises, expanding his products and expanding the use of information technology. In the late 1990s Vinylattac had set up electronic links with suppliers and developed a comprehensive database system to support the business expansion.

Vinylattac is currently thriving in a very competitive market. Further expansion of the business has been supported by additional information systems. The company has developed an online purchasing system and is continually developing its website. The growth in business activity has been accompanied by investment in the information technology. Vinylattac has the latest versions of hardware, software and communication systems. In summary to date Vinylattac has aligned its business strategy with its information systems strategy. The successful outcome of this alignment has enabled Vinylattac to continually expand its business.

(c) Economic: The music business is a universal business with existing worldwide suppliers. Unless Vinylattac can offer a unique cost effective service it would be difficult to compete against local providers. The case study suggests that in the case of overseas orders the cost of postage and packaging is often more expensive than the cost of the product(s).

Technological: Vinylattac is in a strong position from a technological perspective. Vinylattac successfully trades using e-commerce. The case study suggests that Vinylattac has a strong website, yet only a small percentage of its trade is conducted overseas. If there were a demand from overseas customers for Vinylattac's services and products the company would be receiving orders. The latest trend amongst major suppliers in music business is to provide the product online. Customers can purchase music and instantaneously download it from the supplier. If Vinylattac chose to compete in this market it would need to invest in expensive new technology, however this would reduce/remove the post and packaging costs.

3 (a) A personal computer (PC) with the relevant software will be required. The PC will require a communications link; this could either be permanent or dial-up facility. This link may also provide other facilities such as email and conferencing. Periodically relevant information can be downloaded and/or uploaded. Access/security controls will have to be implemented; access rights can be managed in the same way as internal access rights are maintained. Access rights would ensure that all teleworkers could use the company databases and information systems in the same way as internal staff. Using the internet related technologies the setting up of facilities required to support teleworkers are similar to the facilities required for implementing an intranet.

The suggested answers are not exhaustive. Viable alternative answers will be given full credit.

(b) Employer advantages:

There are considerable savings in the cost of office space. The case study suggests that currently office space is a problem in Vinylattac. Furthermore Vinylattac is planning to expand its services and this would not be possible in the current environment.

Vinylattac will be able to employ individuals with the required skills and expertise who might not be available otherwise. Many of Vinylattac's enquiries need prolonged interaction with customer and specialised expertise.

Vinylattac can extend its working day. After normal working hours enquiries can be handled by teleworkers who can be contracted to work at different times than the office staff, perhaps in different time zones.

The teleworkers will face fewer interruptions from colleagues in the office and can therefore be more productive. Many of the tasks performed by Vinylattac can be performed outside the office environment.

Employer disadvantages:

Mark runs the business with a very personal approach; this approach may be difficult to maintain with home workers.

It could prove difficult to monitor the performance of home workers. Vinylattac will have to develop methods for assessing the performance of its teleworkers. Mark could introduce a payment scheme that would reward workers for the number of queries handled or the number of orders taken.

The cost of providing and maintaining the required hardware, software and communication links may be prohibitive and outweigh some of the perceived cost savings. Can Vinylattac, a relatively small company, economically provide the backup service to support teleworking?

Providing adequate security within the system could be a problem and incur additional cost for Vinylattac.

It may prove to be difficult to maintain the company image.

(c) Employee advantages:

Employees spend less time and expense incurred in travelling to work. The case study suggests that Mark has several contacts that would be prepared to use their skills and expert knowledge on a part-time basis. Working from home would facilitate this requirement.

Employees can work more flexible hours; they have the ability to plan their schedules and work around other commitments. Providing Vinylattac can ensure that there are staff always available to answer urgent enquiries and accept orders, this flexibility should not affect its business activities.

Employees are no longer required to live in the commutable area of the business or even in the same country. Experts from anywhere can work for Vinylattac. The case study suggests that Mark has contacts worldwide.

Employee disadvantages:

Some employees may feel they are isolated from Vinylattac and their colleagues. Social contact may be an important element in their lives. Many theorists believe that workers enjoy and thrive in the social context of work. This will affect staff from Vinylattac and as they currently work in a friendly and social environment, many of them share a common interest in their work and will undoubtedly miss the social contact and shared experience.

Perceived isolation of the individual has repercussions in terms of organisational goals and teamwork. Much of the work conducted by Vinylattac is founded on the premise of providing a personal service.

Maintaining boundaries between family, work and leisure. The danger that ubiquitous computing and the 'do anything anywhere' computing environment is that it might actually happen. If so, the traditional boundaries that separate work from family life and leisure will be weakened. The case study suggests that many of Vinylattac's employees share Mark's enthusiasm for the music business. With the ability to work from home some of the employees may be tempted to spend more time conducting work activities and less time with their families and leisure activities.

4 **(a)** Ethics refers to the principles of right and wrong, individuals acting as free moral agents to make choices to guide their behaviour. Society can be viewed as an integrated system of balances between individuals, social systems (including businesses) and political systems. Changes in any part of the system may well affect all or some of the interlinked parts. The individuals and the institutions within the given society often define what is ethical over a period of time. The laws and regulations of most societies are a reflection of the society's ethical qualities. This statement can equally apply to individual businesses. Ethical standards in all institutions should be supported by etiquettes, expectations, quality standards and examples of leadership (management).

The advances in information technology have enabled businesses to change their methods of working, manufacturing and marketing. They have increased competitive advantage and dramatically changed the way businesses and individuals can obtain, store and analyse information concerning private citizens. Information systems/technology can be used positively to enhance individuals' welfare eg advances in the medical sector or the use of robotics (performing tasks that previously endangered humans) are often cited to support this perspective. The opposite perspective is that information systems and communications have permitted businesses and organisations to collect, store and share information pertaining to individuals at a level previously unattainable. It is estimated that the average adult may have personal data listed on more than two hundred computer files, any of which may contain errors.

In the context of management information systems many countries have legislation to protect individuals and groups with regard to information rights. These laws require certain standards to be maintained. Examples of these laws are: the UK Data Protection Act, European Data Protection legislation and the US Freedom of Information Act. These laws have their basis in the principles of fair information practices, which include:

– There should be no personal record system whose existence is secret.
– Individuals have the rights of access, inspection, review and amendment to systems that contain information about them.
– There must be no use of personal information for purposes other than those for which it was gathered without prior consent.
– Managers of systems are responsible and can be held accountable and liable for the damage done by systems.

There are also many international laws with regards to property rights including trade secrets, copyright and patents.

There is a grey area between ethical and legal issues. Ethics can be defined as the principles of right and wrong that can be referenced by individuals in making a personal decision or judgement. Often these references are made from a combination of sources. Companies, cultures and countries have different views on specific ethical issues. Information systems have the ability to instantaneously affect individuals, companies, cultures and countries. This heightens the need to take into account ethical issues.

There are several professional bodies that publish codes of conduct or guidelines for its members with reference to the use of information technology. A general consensus among professional bodies is that when groups of people claim to be professionals, they enter into a special, even more constraining, relationship with employers, customers and society given their special claims to knowledge, wisdom and respect. A generic set of guidelines would contain the following: avoid harm to others, be honest and trustworthy, contribute to society and human well-being, honour property rights including copyrights and patents, access computing resources only when authorised and respect the privacy of others. The majority of professional bodies add to the generic list and propose specific guidelines relating to the appropriate profession.

Many theorists believe that if organisations do not create and adhere to ethical codes of practice then new legislation will be designed to counteract unethical behaviour. This is particularly relevant in the context of business information management where developments in new technology often outpace the legislative process that is required to guard against misuse of information and the protection of individuals and society.

(b) **(i)** **Identify and separate facts from judgements:**
DRGB collects the data legally.
The interviewees are informed that other companies will have access to the data.
Some companies use the data in an unprofessional manner.
Complaints have been received from numerous customers.
Some clients are concerned about the apparent misuse of data.

(ii) **Define the conflict or dilemma and identify the issues requiring judgement:**
Is DRGB responsible for the conduct of its customers?
People believe that some companies are using unscrupulous tactics to target vulnerable sections of the public.
Some companies use the data supplied by DRGB correctly.
How can DRGB identify unethical companies?

(iii) **Identify all the stakeholders:**
DRGB.
Research consultants.
DRGB's clients.
The public.

(iv) **Identify the options that are available:**
Continue as present.
Vet clients prior to selling them the data.
Ensure that market research consultants emphasise the possible uses of the data to the interviewees.
Change the payment/reward system for market research consultants as it could be argued that the current payment system encourages unethical behaviour.

(v) **Evaluate the consequences of the options identified:**
If they continue as present DRGB may lose some of its long standing respectable clients. The company image will suffer.

Vet clients before selling them data: this may be a difficult option, how can this be achieved? If DRGB receive complaints about certain clients DRGB could refuse to do business with the relevant clients.

Ensure that market research consultants fully explain the possible uses of the data being collected: this would be difficult to establish. The consultants are paid bonuses based on the number of completed questionnaires.

Change the payment system for the market research consultants: This may result in fewer questionnaires being completed. Currently the market research consultants are paid on a commission basis. Without this incentive DRGB may require more consultants.

5 **(a)** Critical success factors (CSFs) and performance indicators (PIs) play a central role in defining organisations' information system requirements. They are used to facilitate the identification of requirements for information that provides support for decision-making. The identification of CSFs is an idea that leads to strategic alignment by highlighting the way better information might help an organisation achieve its business goals. The first step is to identify the organisation's overall mission and the objectives that define satisfactory overall performance. The mission statement of an organisation is often phrased in general terms, such as to produce the highest quality products or to provide the highest level of customer satisfaction.

Critical success factors are then obtained for management at all levels. These CSFs state what the organisation has to do correctly to meet the overall mission objectives. As a consequence the requirements of individual managers are aligned with organisational objectives. CSFs defined by senior management may have several lower level CSFs that are required to contribute to its achievement. For example to improve customer service at one level may involve lower level managers defining a CSF that states all enquiries will be dealt within N hours. Following the identification of all the relevant management CSFs, a hierarchy of CSFs may result from this process. Often the CSFs can be organised within specific areas of an organisation ie sales, finance, etc.

To check whether or not the CSFs of an organisation have been achieved, performance indicators will be set. Performance indicators identify a measurable aspect of organisational performance and will be associated with each CSF. The achievement of a CSF can be gauged from the combined achievement of its associated performance indicators. A major factor with regard to performance indicators is that PIs are quantifiable and show specific targets that the organisation is trying to achieve. Performance indicators may include: N% increase in market share, decrease number of complaints by N% and N% reduction in the number of late deliveries.

The resultant CSF/PI hierarchy provides specific input into the definition of an organisation's information requirement. The successive levels of CSFs and their associated PIs can be used to define the overall structure for information reporting. The information systems strategy can be defined to show what information is needed to check each PI. Information requirements may include: information on orders not processed within 24 hours of receipt, information pertaining to customer's payment history and increased profit against increased cost of system.

This is a top-down approach to information requirements identification and specification. CSF is an active approach to the design of management information systems, rather than the passive acceptance of reported information based on tradition and collected historical data. The CSF approach is therefore genuinely information rather than data-led. Its chief importance is the recognition that the purpose of providing information is to serve corporate goals.

(b) Only two required

CSF: Provide a quality service.
PI: Reduce number of complaints by 'N%'.
Information: Previous number of complaints, current number of complaints.

CSF: Maintain competitive pricing.
PI: Ensure Moveit's prices are 'N%' less than its competitors.
Information: Moveit's prices, prices from competitors.

CSF: Create loyal clients.
PI: % of clients who renew annual contract.
Information: Client renewal details.

CSF: Improve client-ordering service.
PI: Ensure that all client orders are acknowledged within 'N' hours of receipt.
Information: Client sales record.

CSF: Maintain customer satisfaction.
PI: Ensure client enquiries are dealt with within 'N' hours of receipt.
Information: Record of client enquiry, date time etc.
Record of the response to the client enquiry, date, time etc.

6 **(a)** The portfolio analysis grid is constructed during an investigation into future information systems development. The output from portfolio analysis may consist of suggestions to develop several information systems/applications in order to close a perceived gap. The grid is used to determine which information systems should be developed, assuming there are no legal requirements in determining the priority of system development. Having identified several information systems each system is assessed in terms of benefits and risks. These benefits may include: financial benefits, increased revenue, cost reductions in products or services, increased customer satisfaction and a range of other intangible benefits. The risks will include: complexity of the system, cost exceeding the planned budget, staff rejecting the system, system not meeting the specification, technical restrictions. The assessed benefits and risks are then placed in the appropriate areas and thus the information system is allocated a quadrant on the grid.

If a system falls in the high benefit – low risk quadrant this indicates that the system should have preference over other systems that do not fall into this category. The outcome is normally to develop such systems.

If a system falls into the high benefit – high risk quadrant this may indicate that further investigation is necessary and that low risk systems should take precedence.

If a system falls into the low benefit – low risk quadrant these types of applications can be easily implemented. This category often refers to routine systems that are standard with little risk involved.

If a system falls into the low benefit – high risk quadrant then these systems should be avoided. It would be dangerous to embark on such systems, as the benefits are small compared to the identified risks.

Like many generic grids of this nature, many of the variables identified are based on subjectivity or experience. Nonetheless they can be used to prioritise systems development. The major advantage of using the grid is that in its construction management have been encouraged to identify and quantify both expected benefits and risks involved in developing individual information systems.

(b) This section may attract a whole range of answers. The quadrant chosen should be justified. The answers below are for guidelines only; the process of fitting information systems into appropriate quadrants is a subjective process. All responses will be marked on merit. In general terms the question requires the candidate to apply the theory to a specific information system and seek justification in practical terms of their choice of quadrant.

Computer aided design (CAD) is used to automate the creation and revision of drawings and designs. Products can be designed and amended using the computer software with a physical item being produced only at the end of the design process. This approach saves the time and money normally spent in producing and refining many different physical designs. CAD systems are widely used throughout industry for the design of products ranging from ornaments to motor vehicles. CAD systems are almost standard in engineering design and manufacturing companies. This type of system would fit into the 'identify and develop' quadrant. The potential benefits are very high and the risk due to the proven technology is fairly low.

A data warehouse is similar to a large database that collects and stores current and historical data from various internal processing systems. It also has the facility to integrate data collected from a variety of external sources. The data is consolidated to provide management reports and analysis using specific reporting and query tools. These types of information systems are normally incorporated into large organisations that are technologically advanced. The company described in the case study is small and does not currently use advanced technology. A data warehouse requires a high level of cost in terms of development, support and resources. Data warehousing would fit into the 'avoid quadrant' as it has a high project risk and the benefits are potentially minimal. This type of system may not be suitable or beneficial to the company.

An extranet is similar to an intranet but permits access to authorised outsiders. Only outsiders that have the required authorisation can gain access to the company's system. Extranets are becoming a very popular means for business partners to exchange information. The engineering company described in the case study may benefit from having this type of system as it supplies many large companies with its products. If specifications/designs must be agreed between the company and its clients an extranet system would facilitate this process. This type of system is common within the engineering sector and has the potential to enhance the company's relationship with its clients. The extranet application fits into the 'examine carefully' quadrant as it has high potential benefits and for this specific company that does not generally use technology extensively it may have a high project risk. If the company is competent with technology the extranet may fit into the 'identify and develop' quadrant.

Review Form & Free Prize Draw – Paper 3.4 Business Information Management (1/07)

All original review forms from the entire BPP range, completed with genuine comments, will be entered into one of two draws on 31 July 2007 and 31 January 2008. The names on the first four forms picked out on each occasion will be sent a cheque for £50.

Name: _____   Address: _____
_____
_____

How have you used this Kit?
(Tick one box only)

☐ Home study (book only)
☐ On a course: college _____
☐ With 'correspondence' package
☐ Other _____

Why did you decide to purchase this Kit?
(Tick one box only)

☐ Have used the complementary Study text
☐ Have used other BPP products in the past
☐ Recommendation by friend/colleague
☐ Recommendation by a lecturer at college
☐ Saw advertising
☐ Other _____

During the past six months do you recall seeing/receiving any of the following?
(Tick as many boxes as are relevant)

☐ Our advertisement in *Student Accountant*
☐ Our advertisement in *Pass*
☐ Our advertisement in *PQ*
☐ Our brochure with a letter through the post
☐ Our website www.bpp.com

Which (if any) aspects of our advertising do you find useful?
(Tick as many boxes as are relevant)

☐ Prices and publication dates of new editions
☐ Information on product content
☐ Facility to order books off-the-page
☐ None of the above

Which BPP products have you used?

Text	☐	Success CD	☐	Learn Online	☐
Kit	☑	i-Learn	☐	Home Study Package	☐
Passcard	☐	i-Pass	☐	Home Study PLUS	☐

Your ratings, comments and suggestions would be appreciated on the following areas.

	Very useful	Useful	Not useful
Passing ACCA exams	☐	☐	☐
Passing 3.4	☐	☐	☐
Planning your question practice	☐	☐	☐
Questions	☐	☐	☐
Top Tips etc in answers	☐	☐	☐
Content and structure of answers	☐	☐	☐
'Plan of attack' in mock exams	☐	☐	☐
Mock exam answers			

Overall opinion of this Kit   Excellent ☐   Good ☐   Adequate ☐   Poor ☐

Do you intend to continue using BPP products?   Yes ☐   No ☐

The BPP author of this edition can be e-mailed at: stephenosborne@bpp.com

Please return this form to: Nick Weller, ACCA Publishing Manager, BPP Learning Media Ltd, FREEPOST, London, W12 8BR

Review Form & Free Prize Draw (continued)

TELL US WHAT YOU THINK

Please note any further comments and suggestions/errors below.

Free Prize Draw Rules

1   Closing date for 31 July 2007 draw is 30 June 2007. Closing date for 31 January 2008 draw is 31 December 2007.

2   Restricted to entries with UK and Eire addresses only. BPP employees, their families and business associates are excluded.

3   No purchase necessary. Entry forms are available upon request from BPP Learning Media Ltd. No more than one entry per title, per person. Draw restricted to persons aged 16 and over.

4   Winners will be notified by post and receive their cheques not later than 6 weeks after the relevant draw date.

5   The decision of the promoter in all matters is final and binding. No correspondence will be entered into.